Essays on Being

Essays on Being

Charles H. Kahn

OXFORD
UNIVERSITY PRESS

OXFORD
UNIVERSITY PRESS

Great Clarendon Street, Oxford, OX2 6DP,
United Kingdom

Oxford University Press is a department of the University of Oxford.
It furthers the University's objective of excellence in research, scholarship,
and education by publishing worldwide. Oxford is a registered trade mark of
Oxford University Press in the UK and in certain other countries

First Edition published in 2009
First published in paperback 2012

Published in the United States of America by Oxford University Press
198 Madison Avenue, New York, NY 10016, United States of America

British Library Cataloguing in Publication Data
Data available

Library of Congress Cataloging in Publication Data
Data available

ISBN 978-0-19-965435-2

Acknowledgments

These essays were previously published as follows:

Essay 1 in *Foundations of Language*, 2 (1966), 245–65;

Essay 2 in S. M. Stern, A. Houvani, and V. Brown (eds.), *Islamic Philosophy and the Classical Tradition: Essays presented . . . to Richard Walzer* (Oxford: Cassirer, 1972), 141–58;

Essay 3 in *Archiv für Geschichte der Philosophie*, 58 (1976), 323–34;

Essay 4 in *Phronesis*, 26 (1981), 105–34;

Essay 5 in *Ancient Philosophy*, 24 (2004), 381–405;

Essay 6 in *The Review of Metaphysics*, 22 (1969), 700–24;

Essay 7 in *La Parole del Passato*, 43 (1988), 237–61;

Essay 8 in *Presocratic Philosophy: Essays in Honour of Alexander Mourelatos* (Aldershot: Ashgate, 2002), 81–93.

I gratefully acknowledge permission for republication from Springer Verlag, University of South Carolina Press, Walter de Gruyter & Co., Koninklijke Brill NV, *Ancient Philosophy*, *Review of Metaphysics*, for Essays 1–6 respectively and Ashgate Publishing Company for Essay 8.

The variations in presentation of Greek here reflect the different editorial policies of the original publications. For the convenience of readers, the pagination of the original papers is indicated in double square brackets, thus ⟦245⟧.

Contents

Introduction

The papers reprinted here, published over a stretch of forty years, reflect my continuing concern with two distinct but intimately related problems, one linguistic and one historical and philosophical. The linguistic problem concerns the theory of the Greek verb *to be*: how to replace the conventional but misleading distinction between copula and existential verb with a more adequate theoretical account. The philosophical problem is in principle quite distinct: to understand how the concept of Being became the central topic in Greek philosophy from Parmenides to Aristotle. But these two problems converge on what I have called the veridical use of *einai*. In my earlier papers I took that connection between the verb and the concept of truth to be the key to the central role of Being in Greek philosophy. I think that clue pointed in the right direction, but I would now interpret the veridical in terms of a more general function of the verb that I call 'semantic', which comprises the notions of existence and instantiation as well as truth. More on that below.

The veridical use was not a new discovery on my part. It had long been recognized by Hellenists that *esti* could mean 'is true' or 'is the case'.[1] However, the philosophical importance of this connection between the verb and the notion of truth seems to have been generally neglected. I think this neglect was due to the traditional assumption that uses of the verb could be assigned either to the copula or to the verb of existence. In terms of this distinction, the veridical use is an

---

[1] Liddell–Scott–Jones illustrates the meaning 'be the fact or the case' in section A. III of its entry on εἰμί, with examples from Herodotus and Thucydides. For a rare instance of scholarly attention to the role played by this use of the verb in Platonic texts see Burnet's commentary on *Phaedo* 65c3, 66a3, c2.

anomaly, since the syntax of the verb is absolute (without predicates) but the meaning is not 'to exist'. I decided that, in order to understand the fundamental role played by the verb (and its nominal derivatives such as *ousia*) in the formulation of Greek philosophy, it was necessary to replace the copula–existence dichotomy with a more adequate account of the verb. Thus my linguistic study of *to be* was motivated by the desire to comprehend the philosophical concept of Being, and above all to understand why the introduction of this concept by Parmenides had such a profound and lasting impact on Greek philosophy.

It was for philosophical reasons, then, because of the connection with truth, that the veridical use was at the center of my attention in these earlier publications. On the other hand, from a linguistic point of view the predicative function of the verb as copula had to be recognized as more fundamental. In the memorable phrase of G. E. L. Owen, *to be* in Greek is *to be something or other*. The copula use is not only the most frequent; it is also the natural basis for any unified account of the diverse system of uses of the verb. That was my conclusion from the description of these uses in my 1973 book. But at the time I did not see how best to formulate this conclusion. I could not claim chronological priority for the copula use, since there is absolutely no evidence that this use is *older* than the others. (The existential use occurs in the Rig-veda for the cognate verb; and the words for truth in Sanskrit and Scandinavian demonstrate that the veridical use is also prehistoric.) I was able to give a precise transformational statement for the priority of the copula only much later, when I had the opportunity to reformulate my account of the verb in the introduction to the reprinted book in 2003. (That account appears here as Chapter 5: 'A Return to the Theory of the Verb *Be* and the Concept of Being'.) The outcome is a strictly syntactical analysis, which takes the copula construction as the basic, first-order use of the verb, but construes existential and veridical uses as second-order, semantic transforms from the copula construction. In addition, I now recognize a third semantic transformation, corresponding to an instantiation of the predicate concept (to be described below). Hence I propose now to replace the copula–existence dichotomy with a distinction between the syntactic role of the verb as copula and the semantic (extralinguistic) function of the verb as an expression of existence, instantiation, and truth. I will have more to say on this in Essay 5.

My syntactical analysis is presented as a linguistic theory of the verb, not as a philosophical account of the concept of Being. On the other hand, this linguistic picture is designed to clarify, and also to be confirmed by, the role of the verb in philosophy. Thus the fundamental nature of the predicative function is neatly illustrated in Aristotle's theory of the ten categories, which is a device for showing 'how Being is said in many ways': the syntax of the verb is copulative in every category. (What is it? How large is it? Of what quality is it? What is it related to? Where is it? and so forth.) From an entirely different point of view, the basic importance of the predicative function appears again in Plotinus' doctrine that Being (*ousia*) does not belong to his fundamental principle of the One. The One does not have Being because it cannot have predicative structure. Subject–predicate structure would pluralize it, but the One admits no plurality. Note that in this argument *einai* itself is construed as the predicate, not simply as the copula. But the *einai* denied for the One cannot mean 'to exist'. For Plotinus, if the One did not exist, nothing else could exist. In both cases what the philosopher has to say about Being—for Aristotle, that Being is said in as many ways as there are categories, and for Plotinus that Being does not belong to the One—is immediately clear if Being is understood as a verb of predication rather than as an expression of existence. For purposes of reference, then, the concept of Being can be identified as the nominal term corresponding to *einai* as copula or verb of predication. For the philosophic analysis of predication, of course, other notions must come into play—not only existence but also instantiation and truth. These concepts are essentially interconnected. We recall that the notion of predication introduced by Aristotle's term *katêgoreisthai* is not merely syntactical: *katêgoreitai* means 'is *truly* predicated'.

Concerning predication, then, the linguistic and philosophical accounts will be distinct, but they are not independent of one another. The syntactic analysis that I have proposed, with existence and truth construed as transforms of the predicative verb, suggests a parallel philosophical interpretation. On this view the predicative function will be fundamental; both existence and truth will be conceptualized in terms of the role they play in predication. Asserting existence will mean positing a subject for predication, something to talk about; truth will be interpreted as the correct ascription (or denial) of an attribute. (And instantiation means positing this attribute itself.) The interconnection between this trinity of concepts—predication, existence, and truth—is at the heart of Greek ontology from Parmenides to Aristotle. We have a succinct formulation of this linkage in Plato's account of true and false discourse in the *Sophist*: a true statement says 'things that are (*ta onta*) as they are (*or* that they are, *hôs estin*)' concerning a definite subject, in this case 'concerning (the mathematician) Theaetetus' (263b). Both predicative function and veridical confirmation are explicit here in the use of *onta* and *estin*. The existential notion is also implied in the emphatic reference to the subject (things that are 'about you', *peri sou*), although in this case the existence of the subject is *not* expressed by the verb. Such a passage illustrates my claim that the topic of existence is not thematized in Greek discussions of Being—even though, in other contexts, the verb may of course be used to express existence.

Are there any philosophical advantages to this relative neglect of the concept of existence in the Greek discussion of Being? I am tempted to reverse J. S. Mill's complaint (see p. 18 below) and suggest that it is not the confusion between copula and existence that is dangerous in metaphysics but rather the isolation of the notion of existence from a context of predication. The unexpressed Greek assumption that *to be* is *to be something or other* (expressed concretely as the view that *to be* is *to be somewhere*) protects us against an abstract notion of being which is not to be anything definite at all. To ask whether centaurs exist is to ask whether such things can be found in nature, in the world of time and space. But what does it mean to ask whether the world exists, or whether the past exists? This is a notion of existence that the Greeks seem not to have explored. One might conclude that they were better off without it.

My role as a historian is not to express a preference either for the ancient view of Being or the modern concept of existence. I have attempted simply to clarify the differences between them. However, when an ancient view is different in this fundamental way, historical understanding of the ancient view can provide a perspective for critical reflection on modern assumptions of which we are otherwise unaware.

To the extent that we succeed in understanding an alternative view, the contrast can bring to light deeper elements of our own conception that have escaped notice. To take a minor but significant example, it is only the contrast with the ancient data for *einai*, *huparchein*, and *exsistere* that reveals the importance for the modern view of a verb *to exist* that does not take predicates. Let this example stand as an emblem for the larger project undertaken in these essays: attempting to grasp the unfamiliar dimensions of the Greek concept of Being.

There follows a brief review of the essays reprinted here.

Essay 1. 'The Greek Verb "To Be" and the Concept of Being' (1966) was my first attack on the copula–existence dichotomy and my first attempt to redirect attention to the veridical meaning of the verb: 'to be true' or 'to be the case'. In order to compensate for the relative rarity of this usage in Attic literature, I emphasized the prehistoric, Indo-European roots of this sense of *einai*, roots that are represented in Indian and Scandinavian cognate words for 'truth' and in archaic English 'sooth'. For Greek philosophers from Parmenides to Aristotle, I claimed, the concept of Being is the concept of 'what is or ˙can be truly known and truly said' (p. 35).[2]

This early paper also makes a point that I will return to in the discussion of Parmenides; namely, that the Greek usage of *on* and *onta* makes no type distinction between the existence of things or objects, on the one hand, and the being-so of fact or events, on the other. This is part of what it means to claim that Greek philosophers do not have (or do not attend to) *our* notion of existence. (Of course they have their own notion: they can easily deny or affirm the existence of gods, centaurs, and the void.) I think more attention to the absence of this type distinction between *einai* for things and for facts would show that the debate between veridical and existential readings of *einai* is often misleading. Attention to this overlap may also help to explain some puzzling texts. A noteworthy example is the contrast between *ti*

---

[2] This claim is limited to the classical period. The conception of Being changes in Hellenistic philosophy and most radically in Stoic theory, where the category of Being or *to on* is restricted to bodies; *lekta* or 'things said' belong to the broader category of *ti* or 'something'.

esti and *ei estin* in *Posterior Analytics* 2. 1–2, where the question *ei estin* seems sometimes to mean 'does X exist?' but also 'does XY take place?'.

Essay 2. 'On the Terminology for *Copula* and *Existence*' (1972) is a philological study of the emergence of the two terms for the copula–existence dichotomy. The evidence for *copula* is straightforward. The interpretation of the verb *is* as copula or syntactic link in a sentence of the form *S is P* is clearly prepared in Aristotle's discussion, and elaborated by the Greek commentators. However, no fixed term for this notion appears in Greek, nor (it seems) in Latin before Abelard. Abelard can be held responsible not only for the term but for a fuller conception of the copula function, involving finite verbs in general and not only the verb *is*. (Abelard's discussion seems to be independent of an earlier, parallel development of a term for copula in Arabic.)

Unfortunately, things are much less clear for the development of the modern concept of existence. When I wrote this essay I did not realize the extent to which the fundamental novelty of the modern notion depends on the availability in modern languages of a verb *to exist* that does not take predicates. Only if we have a nonpredicative verb *to exist* do we get a sharp contrast between existence and predication. Both the Latin verb *exsistere* and its Greek equivalents (*huparchein* and *hupostênai*) can all be construed with predicate nouns, adjectives, or locatives. Hence in ancient philosophy there is no tendency towards a radical contrast between *to exist* (as expressed by these verbs) and *to be* (*something or other*), as in the modern existence–copula dichotomy. As far as I can see, the history of the concept of existence remains to be written.[3]

Essay 3. 'Why Existence Does Not Emerge as a Distinct Concept in Greek Philosophy' (1976) is a defense of my claim that the concept of existence is not thematized in Greek philosophy, but that it is the notions of truth and predication that dominate in the classical concept of Being from Parmenides to Aristotle. The philosophers go in search of knowledge, and that implies a search for truth. Being becomes

---

[3] Some beginnings are to be found in J. Brunschwig, 'La théorie stoïcienne du genre suprême et l'ontologie platonicienne', in J. Barnes and M. Mignucci (eds.), *Matter and Metaphysics* (Naples: Bibliopolis, 1988), and in papers by J. Glucker and others in F. Romano and D. P. Taormina (eds.), *HYPARXIS e HYPOSTASIS nel Neoplatonismo* (Florence: 1994).

a fundamental concept in philosophy because it provides the notion of reality that is needed for the object of knowledge and the criterion of truth. Thus the veridical connotation points to the central role of the verb in philosophy. (As noted above, I would now add that the veridical performs this role as the most prominent of the three semantic transforms, identified below in Essay 5.) However, the concept of Being is introduced by, but not structured by, its connection with truth. When the notion of truth gets articulated, in thought or in speech, it appears as predication. As a rule, existence will also be presupposed for the subject of true predication. But it is a feature of the Greek use of *einai*—and hence of the philosophical analysis—that the existence of the subject is rarely distinguished from the holding or being-the-case of the predication as a whole. As I have mentioned, in the philosophical use of *on* and *onta* for 'what is', no distinction is normally drawn between the existence of things and the being-so of states of affairs.

Essay 4. In 'Some Philosophical Uses of "To Be" in Plato' (1981) I discuss two sets of passages, the first of which illustrates the use of the verb and its nominal forms to express Plato's metaphysical theory of Forms in the *Symposium*, *Phaedo*, and *Republic*. I show that in expressing the being of the Forms the verb normally appears in copula syntax, reflecting the answer to an underlying request for definition: 'What is X?'. The notion of truth is implicit in such a request: 'What is *really* X?' or 'What is X *essentially*?'. Hence many key passages are overdetermined, with both predication and truth expressed in a single occurrence of the verb, and other nuances often implied. Thus what I call the copula of definitional equivalence—the verb as it appears in technical expressions of the form *to ho esti X*, 'the what-is-X' or 'what-X-is'—often entails the contrast of being versus becoming (the stative nuance) as well as being versus seeming (one aspect of the veridical).

The grammar of the *ho estin X* formula is discussed in detail in the appendix to Essay 4. It often turns out that the term *X* can be construed either as subject or as predicate of *estin*, as in a statement of identity. The earlier uses of this phrase in the *Meno* and *Phaedo* are idiomatic, after a verb of knowing ('to know what X is'). But in later texts from *Republic* 10 and *Timaeus* the *to ho estin X* phrase has become a frozen formula, sealed off from the surrounding syntax. Although the grammar of the verb is copulative in all these texts, existential and veridical nuances are often implied by the heavily charged epistemic context.

In my second set of passages (one from the *Parmenides* and two from the *Theaetetus*) the theory of Forms is not in view; but the connection between *einai* and truth remains fundamental. The *Parmenides* text is one of a series of paradoxical arguments deriving contradictory conclusions from a premise about the One, in this case from the hypothesis *that the One is not*. Plato here slyly anticipates the insight later formulated by Aristotle, that being is said in many ways. In this case the apparent contradiction depends upon the fact that, on the one hand, the negative *is not* of the hypothesis (*The One is not*) is left grammatically absolute, suggesting that the One does not exist or is not real, while, on the other hand, an affirmative *is* as copula is shown to be necessary if that hypothesis is to be true. For if, by hypothesis, this One is not, it must nevertheless *be* a thing-that-is–not (*einai mê on*); that is, it must share in Not-being, with the copula *einai* interpreted here as participation (*mê ousias metechein*). The apparent contradiction exploits this ambiguity between the negation of an *einai* with absolute syntax ('to exist') and the affirmation of an *einai* as the veridical copula ('to be truly X'). Plato has anticipated the later conception of the copula by insisting here on the need for *einai* as a veridical link (*desmos*) connecting the subject (the One) with its attribute, even if this attribute is not-being (162a4).

The first of the two passages from the *Theaetetus* is the famous Man-the-Measure doctrine of Protagoras, the ancestor for the formula for truth in Plato and Aristotle ('saying of what-is *that it is*, and of what-is-not *that it is not*'). Since 'Truth' was apparently the title of Protagoras' work, the relevance here of the veridical notion does not need to be emphasized. I argue that it is arbitrary to construe *einai* in this formula as a copula ('to say of what is X *that it is X*'), although that construal is also implied. Even to call the verb here an 'incomplete copula' can be misleading. The most natural reading for *einai* in these formulae is simply 'what is so' or 'what is the case', with a sentential subject.

More subtle, but not different in meaning, is the role of *einai* and *ousia* in the second *Theaetetus* text, the concluding argument against Theaetetus' attempt to define knowledge in terms of perception. The argument is too complex for summary here, but the crucial point in this final refutation of sense perception is the conception of Being as the propositional structure required for a truth claim. So conceived, Being includes both existence for a subject and predication for an attribute. The argument implies that both of these notions are required for an elementary judgment or assertion, which must *say something about something*. Thus Being, as the universal property applying to everything, is first introduced with absolute syntax (*hoti eston* at 185a9) suggesting an existence claim, but soon afterwards repeated in the copula construction with predicate adjectives (185b10); in between these two occurrences there are half a dozen predications with *einai* understood. Later the noun form *ousia* also serves to suggest the notion of nature or whatness, reflecting the 'What is X?' question (186a10, b6–7). The notion of Being is thus presented, on the one hand, as general enough to include both existence and predication as elements in propositional structure, while at the same time alluding to questions of essence and truth. The final argument against sense perception rests, then, on the claim that propositional structure—saying something about something—is required for any judgment that can aspire to truth, and hence for any candidate for knowledge.

Note that this is a weak and general condition for knowledge, designed to appeal to a wide philosophical audience. It is typical of arguments in Plato's later dialogues to avoid any reliance on Plato's distinctive metaphysical commitments, after his own attack on such commitments in the *Parmenides*. At the same time we have the hint of a stronger, more strictly Platonic requirement for a knowledge claim: saying *what a thing is*, with *ousia* understood as the answer to a question of whatness.

The hope, expressed in 1981, that this would be my last word on *to be*, turned out to be premature. Twenty years later the following *retractatio* appeared.

Essay 5. In 'A Return to the Theory of the Verb *Be* and the Concept of Being' (2004) I offer not only one more attack on the copula–existence dichotomy but also my formal account of how both existential and veridical uses of *einai* can be derived as second-order transforms from the copula use of the verb in elementary sentences. Here, finally, in terms of syntactic transformations, is a theoretical justification for the claim of logical priority for the predicative function of the verb. This claim was presented in the 1973 book as my 'Copernican Revolution'—putting predication rather than existence at the center of the system of *to be*. But it did not there find an adequate formulation.

Both veridical and existential uses are now construed as second-order, semantic transforms of an elementary sentence with copula *is*. I call these transformations 'semantic' in the logician's sense, as involving the extralinguistic notions of existence and truth. And I add now a third semantic transformation: instantiation for predicates. The parallel between these three semantic transformations will help to explain why Greek writers make no type distinctions between uses of *on* and *onta* referring to things, events, and states of affairs. What these semantic transformations have in common is that they posit an extralinguistic item 'in the world', an item corresponding to a linguistic feature of the sentence (either subject, predicate, or the sentence as a whole). This notion of extralinguistic positing is, I claim, the essential function of *einai* in its absolute (noncopula) use. The transformational analysis is designed to show why it is *einai*, in virtue of its fundamental role in predication, that will also provide the verb for these three semantic, metapredicative transformations. Hence in place of the traditional copula–existence dichotomy, I propose this distinction between the elementary use of *einai* as copula and the second-order use of the same verb as semantic transform, where *esti/ên/estai* can represent either existence, instantiation, or truth. I suggest, in short, that what lies behind the copula–existence contrast is a more fundamental distinction between the syntactic role of the verb as copula and the semantic role of the verb as expression of extralinguistic reality or 'existence in the world', where the semantic use includes existence for subjects, instantiation for predicates, and truth or occurrence for the sentence as a whole. What I have previously described as existential and veridical uses can thus be more accurately seen as special cases of the semantic, extralinguistic function of the verb.

This analysis is syntactic, in that it recognizes transformational relations between two sentence forms, one elementary and one second-order. Just as the passive transformation derives *John is loved by Mary* from *Mary loves John*, so quasi-existential sentences of the form *There is an X that is Y* can be derived from copula sentences of the form

(An) X is Y. The pure existential form will then be derived from *There is an X that is Y* by a second transformation: zeroing the predication *is Y* will yield *There is an X,* or *X exists.* At the same time, a different set of semantic transformations from the same copula base *(An) X is Y* will give us either *Y is instantiated* (positing reality for the predicate) or *XY occurs* (positing reality for the sentence as a whole). All three of these transformation routes will produce the same formal outcome in Greek; namely, an absolute use of *einai*, whether veridical or existential (as illustrated in sections 7–12 of Essay 5). These three lines of transformation are all semantic, in that they posit extralinguistic reality for a component of the sentence or for the content of the whole sentence. These distinctions are erased in the surface outcome, which is normally an absolute or 'incomplete' use of the verb *einai.* The same form can represent existence for the subject, instantiation for the predicate, or truth and occurrence for the sentence as a whole. Thus this transformational analysis helps to explain why Greek philosophers regularly ignore our type distinctions between the 'being' of things, events, and states-of-affairs.

Although this analysis is syntactic, it makes use of conceptions that might be regarded as properly philosophical, such as the distinction between first-order and second-order sentences and the relevant notion of 'semantic'. When we are discussing the verb *to be*, such philosophical concepts come with the territory. I claim only that my transformational analysis is better linguistics and also better philosophy than the copula–existence dichotomy. As pointed out in Essay 5, the notion of predication cannot be understood as syntactic only. It is no accident that Aristotle's term *katêgoreisthai* means 'truly predicated'. We cannot give an adequate account of predication without relying on the notions of truth and existence. Although the syntactic use of *einai* as copula is logically prior, it cannot be fully understood without reference to the semantic notion of truth claim. This is the notion spelled out in the three semantic transforms of existence, instantiation, and fact or occurrence.

An additional point already mentioned (and quite independent of the transformational analysis) is the importance of the appearance of a verb *to exist* that does not take predicates. The availability of such a verb seems to be a precondition for the modern notion of existence, and hence for the copula–existence dichotomy. My guess is that such a verb first occurred in Arabic and gradually found its way into late medieval Latin, at some time in the period between Aquinas and Descartes. I hope that future research will either confirm my hypothesis or otherwise clarify this development. What is needed is a linguistic study that covers the same territory sketched by Etienne Gilson in *L'Être et l'Essence* (English translation as *Being in Some Philosophers*). This is part of the missing history of the concept of existence mentioned above under *Essay 2*.

Essay 6. 'The Thesis of Parmenides' (1969) is the first of three articles on the poem of Parmenides, its importance for later philosophy, and, more specifically, its impact on Plato. I analyze Parmenides' thesis primarily in terms of the veridical notion of truth and fact, and I argue against the traditional translation of *estin* as 'it exists'. The point of this controversy is partially blunted by my new account of the three semantic transformations, described in Essay 5. If we take Parmenides' thesis *esti* as asserting the semantic (extralinguistic) value of the verb quite generally, we can then explicate different parts of his argument by reference to more specific semantic functions. For interpreting 'you cannot know what-is-not' the relevant *estin* is propositional or veridical: you cannot know what is not the case; but for 'it cannot come into being from what-is-not' the relevant *is not* is what does not exist. Hence the subject described as ungenerated, imperishable, and indivisible is naturally understood as an object rather than a state-of-affairs. But if (as I suggest) Parmenides' thesis is interpreted as a general semantic claim, these type distinctions do not affect his argument.

So construed, Parmenides' assertion of *what-is* will posit whatever there must be in the world corresponding to true speech and true cognition. My critique of Owen and his followers will reduce to the charge that it is anachronistic in interpreting Parmenides to introduce the notion of existence as used by Descartes and Berkeley. For Parmenides, as for Plato and Aristotle, *to be* is to be something or other. It is ironical that Owen, who introduced this formula for Plato and Aristotle, never applied it to Parmenides. Thus the 'existential' reading of Parmenides' thesis does not take account of the fact that on the true road 'that *it is*' 'there *are* many sign-posts, that it *is* ungenerated and *is* imperishable, whole, unique, and perfect' (fr. 8. 2–3). The existential reading of *estin* does not do justice to the fact that Parmenides, in his punning manner, can make use of this repeated, emphatic use of the copula verb to allude to the same semantic notion: to posit the corresponding item in the extralinguistic world.

This new twist on the role of *einai* will not affect my account of Parmenides' argument, but it does require a correction in the formulation of his thesis. Instead of saying that existential and predicative uses of *to be* are both involved 'as partial aspects of the veridical use' (p. 154), I would now describe existential and veridical uses as aspects of the same semantic function, a function that presupposes the syntactic role of the verb as copula.

Until recently there has not been much discussion of my insistence on interpreting fragment 3 (and also 6. 1) in the most obvious way, as expressing an identity between *noein* and *einai*, as it was understood by Plotinus and others, and paralleled by the Aristotelian identification of *noêsis* in act with its object. I am happy now to welcome the partial agreement of Tony Long; but I resist Long's suggestion that the identification must go in both directions.[4]

It is one thing to hold that successful thinking should be identified with its object (as in Aristotle's view), and another thing to insist that Being, as object of knowledge, should also be a thinking subject that takes itself as object. That is roughly the view of *nous* in Plotinus, and apparently that of the Prime Mover in Aristotle. But I see no hint of that, nor of any form of panpsychism, in Parmenides—no reference to Being as a *subject* of thinking. On the contrary, if I am right in reading fragment 6. 1 as making the same claim for *legein* as for *noein*, that tells against taking identity here as symmetrical. For it is plausible for Parmenides to identify the intentional content of true speech, like the intentional content of true thought, with its object in the world, i.e. with Being. But that does not imply that Being is speaking, or that Being is talking about itself, any more than it implies that Being is thinking about itself. These consequences follow only if we attribute to Parmenides a strict (and, I claim, anachronistic) notion of logical

---

[4] See A. A. Long 'Parmenides on Thinking Being', in G. Rechenauer (ed.), *Frühgriechisches Denken* (Göttingen: Vandenhoeck & Ruprecht, 2005), 227–51. Long (p. 239) quotes a remark by Vlastos to the same effect.

identity. So I am unwilling to follow Long in taking the Parmenidean identification as symmetrical. Both of us would also have to deal with the parallel identity asserted between thought and body in fragment 17. That text is so difficult that it is not likely to decide the matter either way. But it seems easier to believe that the limbs are thinking (*phroneei*) than that Being is taking itself as object of thought.

Essay 7. 'Being in Parmenides and Plato' (1988) continues my interpretation of Parmenides' ontology and documents the Parmenidean elements in Plato's theory of Forms. Section I pursues the argument against the existential reading proposed by Owen and Barnes in favor of what I then called the veridical-predicative view, and would now describe as the semantic interpretation. Thus instead of saying that 'Parmenides begins with a veridical *esti*' (p. 176), I would now say that he begins with a general semantical or extralinguistic claim, an assertion presupposing the *is* of predication but going beyond any particular linguistic form to posit an object, event, or fact in the world. Section II responds to David Gallop's objections to my view. Section III traces the Parmenidean elements in Plato's theory of Forms as a confirmation of my reading of Parmenides. It is clear that Plato often has Parmenides' doctrine of Being in mind in his own use of *einai* and *ousia*, particularly for his introduction of the Forms in *Republic* 5. The one distinctively Platonic and non-Parmenidean formula for the being of the Forms is the definitional copula in *to ho estin X*, 'the what-X-is' (or 'what-is-X'), as a designation for the Form of X. (This terminology is more fully discussed in the appendix to Essay 4.)

In the appendix to Essay 7 I describe the various occurrences of the verb in Parmenides' poem and argue against the 'potential' reading of *einai* in fragments 3 and 6. 1. In both cases the natural interpretation of Parmenides' verses points to an identity between thought (*noein*) and being (or, in 6. 1, between both thought and speech and being). I suggest that it is only because of a philosophical reluctance to ascribe such a doctrine to Parmenides that the potential readings have been defended by many scholars, including Burnet and Owen. I submit that the potential reading for fragment 3 ('the same thing can be and can be thought') is linguistically strained and arbitrary, and that the corresponding reading for 6. 1 is even more unnatural—the least plausible of five possible constructions of this difficult verse. (When Zeller introduced the potential construal of fragment 3 he cited a text in which these words were still printed as the last verse in fragment 2; he was then misled by the potential construction in 2. 1.) I suspect that it is only the numbing force of repetition within the scholarly tradition that keeps these readings of fragments 3 and 6. 1 alive: commentators no longer approach the Greek text with an open ear.

As a student I was lucky in this regard. I once had a chance to discuss Parmenides with Karl Reinhardt, and I asked him what he thought of the potential reading of fragment 3. He stood up and spoke the verse aloud like a rhapsode: τὸ γὰρ αὐτὸ νοεῖν ἐστίν τε καὶ εἶναι. Then Reinhardt said: 'I could not say *this* and mean *that!*'. I was convinced.

Essay 8. 'Parmenides and Plato Once More' (2002) is my contribution to the Festschrift for Alexander Mourelatos; it emphasizes our agreement in recognizing the predicative function of *einai* as fundamental for the interpretation of Parmenides. I make use here of Lesley Brown's work on *einai* in Plato in order to clarify the discrepancy between the modern notion of existence and the Greek conception of being. I believe that the crucial difference is that in Greek the existential uses of *einai* are always potentially predicative, whereas the verb *to exist* in modern languages does not allow predicates. That is one reason why the copula–existence dichotomy tends to distort the Greek data, and why I propose to replace it with a distinction between the syntactic and semantic functions of *einai*, as explained above.

In an appendix to Essay 8 I originally offered arguments in favor of the traditional view of the chariot ride in Parmenides' proem as a movement from darkness to light, and against the more recent view of the proem as a *katabasis* or descent into the underworld. These arguments are transferred here to my concluding Postscript on Parmenides.

Charles Kahn
Philadelphia, 27 March 2008

1

The Greek Verb 'To Be' and the Concept of Being*

I am concerned in this paper with the philological basis for Greek ontology; that is to say, with the raw material which was provided for philosophical analysis by the ordinary use and meaning of the verb *einai*, 'to be'. Roughly stated, my question is: How were the Greek philosophers guided, or influenced, in their formulation of doctrines of Being, by the prephilosophical use of this verb which (together with its nominal derivatives *on* and *ousia*) serves to express the concept of Being in Greek?

Before beginning the discussion of this question, I would like to say a word about the implications of posing it in this form. I take it for granted that all thinking is conditioned to some extent by the structure of the language in which we express or formulate our thoughts, and that this was particularly true for the Greek philosophers, who knew no language but their own. However, I do not assume (as many modern critics seem to do) that such linguistic conditioning is necessarily a limitation, or a disadvantage. A partial disadvantage it may be, since a logical confusion can arise easily in one language which would

* This paper is based upon conclusions drawn from a larger study of *einai* which is being prepared for publication in one of the forthcoming volumes on *The Verb 'Be' and its Synonyms* in the supplementary series of *Foundations of Language* [*The Verb 'Be' in Ancient Greek* (Dordrecht: Reidel, 1973; repr. Indianapolis, Ind.: Hackett, 2003)].

This paper was presented on two occasions in December 1965, very nearly in the above form: to a philosophy colloquium at the University of Texas and to the Society for Ancient Greek Philosophy meeting in New York. It was also circulated in mimeograph form. As a consequence, I have made minor revisions in the text and added these afterthoughts. I am indebted to a number of friends and colleagues for helpful criticism, and in particular to Alexander Mourelatos and Anthony Kenny for their detailed comments.

be impossible in another. But a philosopher—even a philosopher ignorant of other languages—is always free to make a distinction which the language does not make for him, just as he is free to ignore a distinction built into the vocabulary or syntax of his speech, when he does not find this linguistic datum of philosophic importance. (A familiar example of the Greek philosopher's freedom in this respect is the irony which Socrates displays whenever he refers to Prodicus' practice of distinguishing between the meaning of near-synonyms.) The fact that Greek philosophy has been fruitfully translated into other tongues—notably into a language so different as Arabic—suggests that it is not language-bound in any very narrow sense.

On the other hand, it is clear that any given language permits the native speaker to formulate certain notions, or to make certain distinctions, more easily and more spontaneously than others. To this extent, one language—and I mean one *natural* language, of course— may be philosophically more adequate than another. In this sense, I would suggest that ancient Greek is one of the most adequate of all languages, and that the possession of such a language was in fact a necessary condition for the success of the Greeks in creating western logic and philosophy—and, I suspect, also for their success in creating theoretical science and rigorous mathematics, but this second point might be harder to defend. |

[246]   In any case, I do not intend to argue the superior merits of Greek as a language for philosophy, nor to maintain any general thesis about the relationship between philosophic thought and the structure of a given language. I mention these larger questions only to make clear that I wish to leave them open. All I hope to show is that some features of the use and meaning of *einai*—features which are less conspicuous or entirely lacking for the verb 'to be' in most modern languages—may cast light on the ontological doctrines of the Greeks by bringing out the full significance, and the unstated presuppositions, of the concepts expressed by *esti, einai, on,* and *ousia*. In other words, I propose to use the philological material in a purely instrumental way, not as a stick with which to beat the ancient thinkers for ignoring distinctions which we take for granted, but as a tool for the more adequate understanding of the Greek doctrines from their own point of view, including those ideas which the Greeks could take for granted but which we are inclined to ignore.

It is scarcely necessary to emphasize how important a role the concept of Being has played in the philosophical tradition which stretches from antiquity through the middle ages down into modern thought. Except perhaps for the concept of Nature, it would be hard to mention a philosophic idea which has enjoyed a comparable influence. The concept of Being is still very much alive today, at least in German philosophy: witness Heidegger's intensive study of what he calls the *Seinsfrage*, and Gottfried Martin's recent definition of 'Allgemeine Metaphysik' by reference to the classical question: *Was ist das Sein?* Yet we cannot blink the fact that, in English and American philosophy at any rate, the concept of Being is likely to be regarded with great suspicion, as a pseudoconcept or a mere confusion of several distinct ideas. The most obvious distinction which seems to us to be ignored in the notion of Being is that between existence and predication. The logician will go further, and point out that the word 'is' means one thing when it represents the existential quantifier, something else when it represents class inclusion or class membership, something else when it represents identity, and so forth.

I shall here leave aside the distinctions based upon the logic of classes and the strict notion of identity (as governed by Leibniz's law), because I do not find these distinctions reflected or respected in the actual usage of the verb 'to be' in Greek, or in English either for that matter.[1] But the distinction between the 'is' of existence and the 'is' of predication is now so well | established in our own thought, and even in the usage of our language, that it cannot be ignored in any discussion of Being. I begin, therefore, with the classic statement of this distinction by John Stuart Mill, who claimed that

[247]

many volumes might be filled with the frivolous speculations concerning the nature of being... which have arisen from overlooking this double meaning of the word *to be*; from supposing that when it signifies *to exist*, and when it signifies to *be* some specified thing, as to *be* a man,... to *be* seen or spoken of,... even to *be* a nonentity, it must still, at bottom, answer to the same idea.... The fog which rose from this narrow spot diffused itself at an early period over the whole surface of metaphysics (*Logic* I. iv. i).

---

[1] Of course both languages do have devices for making these distinctions, but they depend upon the use of definite and indefinite articles rather than upon that of the verb. And Greek is notably freer than English in the use (and omission) of both articles.

Mill's distinction has not only been built into the symbolism of modern logic; it has also been taken over, with remarkable unanimity, into the standard descriptive grammars of ancient Greek. Although the distinction was almost a new one for Mill, it has now become traditional.[2] I shall not question the use of this distinction in logic, but I have very grave doubts about its appropriateness in Greek grammar. For one thing, there is the practical difficulty of applying Mill's dichotomy. I can find no evidence for such a distinction in the usage of the classical authors, who pass blithely back and forth between uses which we might identify as existential and copulative. I have seen exegetes furrowing their brow over the question whether Plato in a given passage of the *Sophist* means us to take *einai* in the existential or the copulative sense, whereas in fact he shows no sign of wishing to confront us with any such choice.

But there is a graver theoretical disadvantage in the traditional dichotomy between the existential and the predicative uses of 'to be'. It confounds a genuine syntactic distinction—between the absolute and predicative constructions of the verb—with a further semantic contrast between the meaning 'to exist' and some other meaning or absence of meaning. This fusion of a syntactic and a semantic criterion into a single antithesis could be justified only if there were a direct correlation between the two; i.e. only if (1) the absolute use of the verb is always existential in meaning, and (2) the verb 'to be' in the predicative construction is always devoid of meaning, serving as a merely formal or grammatical device for linking the predicate with the subject. But these assumptions seem to me dubious for English, and false for Greek. In English the existential idea is expressed by the special locution 'there is' and not by the verb 'to be' alone. A sentence like 'I think therefore I am' is possible only in philosophy—or in poetry. There are, on the other hand, clear vestiges of an absolute use which was not strictly existential: | 'When will it be?' (= 'occur');   [248]
'Let be' (= 'remain as it is'); but such uses are marginal in comparison to the universal prevalence of the copulative use of 'to be' with

---

[2] Mill believed that his father was 'the first who distinctly characterized the ambiguity' (loc. cit.). See also the younger Mill's comments in the second edition of James Mill's *Analysis of the Phenomena of the Human Mind* (London: Baldwin & Cradock, 1869), i. 182 n. 54.

predicate nouns, adjectives, and prepositional phrases. In historical terms one may say that the rule that every sentence must have a finite verb has resulted in such an expansion of the predicative use of 'to be' that the original, semantically fuller use of the verb has been obscured or lost. But this decay of the absolute usage in most modern languages may give us a false idea of the original range and force of the verb. In Greek, by contrast, where the absolute construction of 'to be' is in full vigor, it does not necessarily mean 'to exist' (as we shall see). On the other hand, since nonverbal predicates in Greek do not automatically require a copulative *esti*, the tendency towards a purely formal use of the verb, devoid of semantic content, is not as far advanced. Because the predicative verb is never obligatory, it may be used with a certain variety of semantic nuances.

My position, then, is that Mill's dichotomy is applicable to Greek only as a syntactic distinction between the absolute and the predica- tive construction, and that even from the point of view of syntax the distinction is not as easy to define as one might suppose. But seman- tically the distinction is worse than useless, for it leads us to take the idea of existence for granted as the basic meaning of the Greek verb. Now if by a word for existence one means simply an expression which we would normally render into English by 'there is', then it is clear that the Greek verb *esti* often has this sense. But if we under- stand the phrase 'there is' as representing a univocal concept of existence for a subject of predication, as distinct from the content of the predication itself—as distinct from the 'essence' of the subject or the kind of thing it is (as we often do, for example, when we read the existential quantifier '(∃x)' as 'there is *something* of which the following is true')—if this generalized positing of a subject as 'real' is what we mean by existence, then I would be inclined to deny that such a notion can be taken for granted as a basis for understanding the meaning of the Greek verb. On the contrary, I suggest that a more careful analysis of the Greek notion of Being might provoke us into some second thoughts about the clarity and self-evidence of our familiar concept of existence.

Let me cite some evidence for what may seem the rather scandalous claim that the Greeks did not have our notion of existence. In the chapter of his philosophical lexicon which is devoted to the topic 'being' or 'what is', *to on* (*Met. Δ*. 7), Aristotle distinguishes four basic senses of 'to be' in Greek:

1. being *per accidens*, or random predication (i.e. 'X is Y', without regard to the logical status of subject and predicate);
2. being per se, or predication in good logical form according to the scheme | of the categories (e.g. when a quality is predicated of a [[249]] substance). Here *einai* is said to have as many senses as there are categories, and Aristotle points out that a construction with 'to be' may be substituted for any finite verb, e.g. 'he is walking' for 'he walks';
3. *einai* and *esti* may mean 'is true', and the negative means 'is false'. An example is 'Socrates *is* musical', if one says this (with emphasis) because it is true;
4. Finally, 'being' may mean either being in potency or being in act. 'For we say that something is seeing both when it is potentially seeing (capable of sight) and when it is actually seeing.'

Aristotle's procedure here is not purely lexical: he is analyzing ordinary usage in the light of his philosophical conceptions. But my point is that neither Aristotle's own conceptual scheme nor the normal usage of the verb obliges him to make any place for a sense of *einai* which we would recognize as distinctively existential. Furthermore, in every one of Aristotle's examples the verb is construed as predicative, although the general topic for the chapter is given in the absolute form, 'what is'.[3] The syntactic distinction between predicative and absolute construction is treated here as of no consequence whatever.

As a second illustration of the gap between Greek 'being' and our notion of existence, I take the famous opening sentence from

---

[3] How could the existential sense be fitted into Aristotle's analysis? There are two possibilities: (1) in the categorical use for primary substances, which 'are' in the most fundamental sense, and (2) in the use of *einai* for potency and act. But the category of substance is actually referred to by a formula for 'essence': *ti esti* (1017^{a}25), whereas the potency–act distinction can apply to any type of predication. One of the examples of potency is locational, and this approximates to our existential, as will be seen below: 'the statue of Hermes is (potentially) in the stone' (1017^{b}7).
The modern distinction between copula and verb of existence is really quite irrelevant to the analysis of *Met. Δ.* 7. But there are other passages in Aristotle which require more careful study in this connection. For example, Aristotle (like Plato before him) recognizes the possibility of sophistic fallacy involved in shifting from the predicative to the absolute construction, from *einai ti* to *haplōs einai* (*Soph. El.* 167^{a}2; *De Int.* 21^{a}18–28; cf. *Met.*

Protagoras' work *On Truth*: 'Man is the measure of all things, of what is, that it is, of what is not, that it is not' (τῶν μὲν ὄντων ὡς ἔστιν, τῶν δὲ οὐκ ὄντων ὡς οὐκ ἔστιν). This is as significant and emphatic a use of the verb as Greek can offer. Since the construction is absolute, we might be inclined to interpret the verb as existential here. But there are two difficulties in the way of such an interpretation. | In the first place, [250] Protagoras clearly intends to make men the measure of *all* things, i.e. of all matters of fact or alleged fact, not merely of questions of existence. His statement is more appropriate as the opening sentence of a work on truth if we give the verb a very general sense: 'Man is the measure of what is the case, that it is the case, and of what is not so, that it is not so'. The second objection to understanding the verb as existential here is that Plato, when he quotes this dictum in the *Theaetetus*, immediately goes on to explain it by means of the predicative construction: '*as* each thing seems to me, *such* is it for me; as it seems to you, such is it for you' (οἷα ἐμοὶ φαίνεται, τοιαῦτα ἔστιν ἐμοί). And he illustrates by the example of a wind which is cold for one man, but not for another. Unless Plato is radically misrepresenting Protagoras (which is at least unlikely), Protagoras himself must have intended his dictum to apply to facts stated in the predicative, and not merely in the existential form. Even if Plato *were* misinterpreting Protagoras, his interpretation would show that for a Greek philosopher the meaning of a strong use of *einai* in the absolute construction is not necessarily existential. Plato's exegesis becomes entirely natural and intelligible if we understand the absolute use of *einai* as I have suggested: as an affirmation of fact in general, as 'what is so' or 'what is the case'. The existential use, e.g. for an affirmation such as 'there are atoms and the void', would then be included as a special case of the general factual assertion intended by Protagoras' statement *hōs esti*. If man is the measure of all things, 'that they are so or not so', then he is the measure of the existence or

1030ª25–7). This led Grote to claim that Aristotle had anticipated Mill's discovery of 'the two distinct functions of the substantive verb'; see his *Aristotle*, 3rd edn., ed. A. Bain and G. C. Robertson (London: 1883). Since I hold Mill's distinction to be erroneous (at least for Greek), I am not inclined to claim it for Aristotle. For *haplōs einai* in Aristotle see the Postscripta.

The medieval-modern concept of the copula has its historical roots in *De Int.* 16ᵇ22–5 and 19ᵇ19–22, but I do not believe that our copula is what Aristotle himself had in mind. On this point further discussion is called for. (See Essay 2.)

nonexistence of atoms just as he is the measure of the being-cold or not-being-cold of the wind.

These remarks are intended to render plausible my claim that, for the philosophical usage of the verb, the most fundamental value of *einai* when used alone (without predicates) is not 'to exist' but 'to be so', 'to be the case', or 'to be true'. It is worth noting that this meaning of the verb, which appears among the four uses listed in the chapter of *Met. Δ* summarized above (where Aristotle recognizes the sense of truth even in the *predicative* construction, when *esti* appears in the emphatic initial position, 1017^{a}33–5), is elsewhere described by Aristotle as the 'strictest' or 'most authoritative' sense of 'to be' (*Met. Θ.* 10. 1051^{b}1: *to kuriōtata on*). Recent editors, notably Ross and Jaeger, are unhappy about this statement, and would like to 'emend' it in various ways. My argument suggests that they are wrong, and that the text is entirely in order. I understand Aristotle to be saying that, from a philosophic point of view, this use of *einai* is the most basic and the most literal meaning of the verb.

In any case, quite apart from the question of philosophic usage, there is absolutely no doubt that this meaning of 'to be' (namely 'to be so, to be true') is one of the oldest idiomatic uses of the verb in Greek, and indeed in Indo-European. In particular, the present participle **sont-* of the Indo-European verb **es-* forms one of the standard expressions for truth, or for what is the case, in many different languages. A derivative of this participle still serves as the normal word for 'true' and 'truth' in languages so far apart as Norwegian (*sann* and *sannhet*) and Hindi (*sac, satya*).[4] In English we have a cognate form of this old Indo-European participle of 'to be' in 'sooth', 'soothsayer'. When Gulliver's Houyhnhnms call a lie 'saying the thing which is not', they are not only speaking classic Greek (as Swift no doubt knew) but they are also speaking authentic Indo-European (which he could scarcely have guessed).

In Greek, this Indo-European idiom is represented in Attic by the frozen use of the participle in the dative, *tōi onti*, 'really, truly', by the equivalent adverbial form *ontōs*, and by the absolute use of the finite verb in *esti tauta*, 'these things are so'—one of the standard

⟦251⟧

---

[4] See H. Frisk, ' "Wahrheit" und "Lüge" in den indogermanischen Sprachen', *Göteborgs Hogskolas Arsskrift*, 41/3 (1935), 4 ff.

formulae of assent in the Platonic dialogues. The free use of the participle in this sense also occurs in Attic, but it is more characteristic of Ionic prose (as in the fragment of Protagoras). The fullest evidence is in Herodotus, where Powell's *Lexicon* lists ten instances of the idiom. For example, when Croesus asks Solon who is the happiest of mortals, the wise Athenian refuses to flatter the king but τῷ ἐόντι χρησάμενος, 'using verity'—sticking to the truth—he answers: Tellus of Athens (Hdt. 1. 30. 3).

Much more evidence might be cited, but this should suffice to show that the old Indo-European use of *es-* for 'to be true, to be so' is well preserved in Greek, and particularly in Ionic, the dialect in which the language of Greek philosophy first took shape. Some of the implications of this fact may be suggested if we briefly consider the possibility of interpreting the 'being' (*eon*) of Parmenides in this sense. His initial thesis, that the path of truth, conviction, and knowledge is the path of 'what is' or 'that it is' (*hōs esti*), can then be understood as a claim that knowledge, true belief, and true statement are all inseparably linked to 'what is so'—not merely to what exists but to *what is the case*. If we understand the verb and participle here as in Herodotus and Protagoras, Parmenides' doctrine of Being is first and foremost a doctrine concerning reality as *what is the case*. But if this is a valid interpretation, the familiar charge against Parmenides—that he confused the existential and the predicative sense of 'to be'—is entirely beside the point. For, as we saw in connection with Protagoras, both the existential and the predicative uses of the verb are special cases of the generalized usage for truth and falsity, for affirmation and denial.

Of course it may still be true that Parmenides' argument contains a fallacy | of equivocation. But the task of an interpreter is to show precisely *what* sense of *einai* the philosopher begins with, and how he inadvertently passes to another. This task is a delicate one, and it must not be short-circuited by introducing the modern dichotomy between existence and predication as a prefabricated solution. [252]

Before leaving this first, most general sense of *einai*—which I will refer to as the sense of verity or the veridical usage—I would call attention to two points. The first is the close logical connection between this usage and the grammatical function of the verb in predication. For every fact, every case of being-so, *can* be formulated by a predicative usage of 'to be' (even if this formulation happens to be logically misleading, as in a predication of existence: e.g. 'John is existent'). Without this unlimited flexibility of the predicative construction, it is hard to see how the verb *einai* could ever have acquired its very general sense of 'to be so'. Furthermore, any predication in the indicative normally implies an assertion, and an assertion means a claim to truth. (By 'normally' I mean when the indicative is used independently, not as part of a disjunction or a conditional. Even in such uses, however, the truth claim of the indicative remains a factor in the meaning of the compound proposition, since the truth-value of the latter is a function of the truth-values of the components, although truth is not actually *claimed* for the components taken separately.) Hence, although I have denied that the predicative use of *einai* forms a distinct pole in a basic dichotomy of usage, I do not mean to deny the fundamental role played by this construction in the total meaning of the verb, and most particularly in the sense of verity.

The second point I wish to make about the veridical usage is its essential ambiguity. 'To be true' is not quite the same thing as 'to be the case'. What is true or false is normally a statement made in words; what is the case or not the case is a fact or situation in the world. The veridical use of *einai* may mean either one (or both), just as our own idiom 'it is so' may refer either to a statement or to the fact stated. Now there is a one-to-one correspondence between what is the case and the truth of the statement that it is the case. The statement that the door is open is true if and only if the door is in fact open. This logical connection between truth and fact is no doubt the unconscious basis of the ambiguity of usage of *ta onta* in an expression like *legein ta onta*, which we may translate either as 'to tell the truth' or 'to state the facts' (although the second rendering is the more literal). In an expression like *ho eōn logos* in Herodotus, however, we can only render the phrase as 'the true account'. But of course the account is true precisely because it states the facts as they are; because it says *what is the case*. Because of this necessary connection between truth and fact, no confusion normally results from the ambiguity in the veridical use of *einai*. But this ambiguity | may   [253] nevertheless turn out to be of considerable importance in understanding the relationship between language and reality which the Greek philosophers take for granted. The relationship which this ambiguity reflects seems to me to play a fundamental role both in Plato's doctrine of Forms and in Aristotle's notion of essence (*to ti ēn einai*). It is not irrelevant to recall that Plato's description of the Forms as *ta ontōs onta* may be rendered equally well as 'what is truly true' or 'what is really real'. The language of Greek ontology naturally lends itself to the view that the structure of reality is such as to be truly expressed in discourse. For the Greek concept of truth is precisely this: *ta onta legein hōs esti, ta mē onta hōs mē esti*, to say of the things that are (the case) that they are, and of the things that are not that they are not.[5]

I said earlier, in criticism of Mill's dichotomy, that the absolute construction of *einai* is not necessarily existential in meaning. This claim has now been vindicated by our discussion of the veridical sense of the verb. For although this sense is quite distinct from the meaning 'to exist', it is normally expressed by the absolute construction. Of course it may be found in the predicative construction as well. Consider Aristotle's example: *esti Sokratēs mousikos*, Socrates *is* musical, he really is so. This sense of verity is actually implicit in every assertion, latent in every predicative use of 'to be' for a statement of fact. (That is why some philosophers claim that to say of a statement that it is true is simply to make the statement over again.) But in any given sentence, the latent veridical value of 'to be' may be brought out by emphasis, or by an unusual position early in the clause (as in Aristotle's example). A moment's reflection will show that this is to some extent true even for the English verb 'to be'. If we emphasize the verb in pronunciation we bring to light a veridical value which otherwise passes unnoticed: 'The man *is* clever, I tell you!'. A similar effect is obtained by contrasting 'The man is clever' with 'The man seems clever'. We may here leave open the question of whether this veridical value of the English verb could be considered part of its proper meaning, or whether it accrues to the predicative verb simply in virtue of the truth claim implicit in any predication in the indicative. There is at all events an intimate

---

[5] Plato, *Cratylus* 385b7, *Sophist* 263b; cf. Aristotle, *Met.* 1011[b]27. The formula is implicit in Parmenides, and explicit in the fragment of Protagoras quoted above. The translation given in the text reflects the natural syntax of ὡς ἔστιν, e.g. in Protagoras or Aristotle. Plato, however, often seems to play on the alternative construction (taking ὡς as adverb rather than as conjunction) and thus to take the formula as meaning: 'to speak of the things which are just as they are . . .'.

connection between the predicative usage, and the sense of verity, as I have already observed. But if the veridical value of 'to be' is almost never called to our attention in English, that is not the case for the predicative construction in Greek, where an emphatic use of the verb in this sense is often indicated by an unusual position, | or even by repetition.[6] When we recall that the usual formula for truth is absolute in form (as in *to on* or *esti tauta*), we see that here is one fundamental semantic value of *einai* which is quite indifferent to the syntactic distinction between absolute and predicative construction.

    In the remainder of this paper I will discuss two other features of the use and meaning of *einai* whose philosophical role is not as basic as that of the veridical sense which has concerned us thus far, but which nevertheless throw some interesting light on the development of Greek ontology. The first feature is what is known in comparative linguistics as the durative aspect. The second feature has not been generally noticed and seems to have no definite name. I shall call it the locative value of the verb.

    A. *The durative aspect.* Since the time of Meillet it has been well known to linguists (though, unfortunately, not always to Hellenists) that the stems of a Greek verb are characterized by a sharp aspectual contrast between the present-imperfect, the aorist, and the perfect. This aspectual distinction is to a large extent independent of tense, since both present- and past-imperfect tenses are formed from the 'present' stem, and the same temporal opposition occurs between perfect and pluperfect, again without change of stem. The aorist in turn is not necessarily a past tense, not even in the indicative (cf. the so-called 'gnomic aorist'). The difference of verbal stem corresponds to a difference in the point of view from which the action or state is considered: the present-imperfect stem represents action as durative, as a state which lasts or a process which develops in time; the aorist represents the action, by antithesis, as non-

---

[6] An extreme case, where repetition and initial position combine to turn the 'mere copula' into a strong asseveration of truth, is Euripides *IT* 721–2.

        ἀλλ' ἔστιν, ἔστιν, ἡ λίαν δυσπραξία
        λίαν διδοῦσα μεταβολάς, ὅταν τύχῃ.

It is worth noting that the *Oxford English Dictionary* lists the veridical use as one of the recognized meanings of 'to be' in English: viz. 'to be the case or the fact', as in 'so be it' (s.v. 'be', B. I. 3).

[254]

durative, either as the process pure and simple without regard to time (the unmarked aspect), or at the moment of reaching its end (the 'punctual' aorist). The perfect represents not the process itself but rather a present state resulting from past action.[7]

Most Greek verbs possess all three of these stems, or at least two; but the verb *einai* is one of a rather small class of verbs which have no aorist and no perfect.[8] All tenses of *einai* (present, imperfect, and future) are formed directly from the single, present-durative stem. The absence of an aorist stem is a feature which *einai* inherited from its Indo-European ancestor *es-. But | whereas the aspectual restriction has been faithfully preserved in Greek down to the present day (so that the modern Greek verb *eimai* 'to be' has no aorist and no perfect), in most languages the conjugation of *es- has been completed by introducing aorist or perfect forms from a different verbal root. Thus Latin incorporated *fui, futurum* into the system of *esse*, just as English acquired *be, been* from the same root, and *was, were* from another source (cf. German *war, gewesen*). As a result, the verb 'to be' in these languages has lost (or at any rate gravely weakened) the aspectual value which characterized the Indo-European stem *es-, whereas the Greek verb *einai* has faithfully preserved, or even strengthened, its durative character.

What is the philosophic significance of this morphosemantic fact? I think it may help us to understand (1) the Greek notion of eternity as a stable present, an untroubled state of duration, (2) the classical antithesis of Being and Becoming, and (3) the incommensurability already noted between the Greek concept of being and the modern-medieval notion of existence.

Let me illustrate these points briefly.

(1) The gods in Homer and Hesiod are *theoi aien eontes*, 'the gods who are forever'. In this and in a whole set of related uses *einai* has practically the sense 'to be alive, to survive'. The gods *are forever* because they

[255]

---

[7]   See e.g. A. Meillet, *Introduction à l'étude comparative des langues indo-européennes*, 8th edn. (Paris: Hackette, 1937), 195–7; P. Chantraine, *Morphologie historique du grec*, 2nd edn. (Paris: Klincksieck, 1947), § 172.

[8]   A. Meillet and J. Vendryès, *Traité de grammaire comparée*, 1st edn. (Paris: Champion, 1924), 169, § 270.

are deathless beings: their vital duration continues without end. Now, strictly speaking, the gods are not eternal. As the *Theogony* informs us in some detail, they have all been born: their vital duration had a temporal beginning. It is the philosophers who introduce an absolute *archē* or Beginning which is itself unbegun, a permanent and ungenerated source of generation. The initiator here is probably Anaximander, but we can see the result more clearly in the poem of Parmenides. His being *is forever* in the strong sense: it is ungenerated (*agenēton*) as well as unperishing (*anōlethron*). Limited neither by birth nor by death, the duration of *What is* replaces and transcends the unending survival which characterized the Olympian gods.

(2) Parmenides was also the first to exploit the durative connotations of *einai* by a systematic contrast with *gignesthai*, the verb which normally provides an aorist for *einai*, and which expresses the developmental idea of birth, of achieving a new state, of emerging as novelty or as event. In Parmenides as in Plato, the durative-present aspect of *einai* thus provides the linguistic underpinning for the antithesis in which Being is opposed to Becoming as stability to flux.[9]

(3) This intrinsically stable and lasting character of Being in Greek— | [256]
which makes it so appropriate as the object of knowing and the correlative of truth—distinguishes it in a radical way from our modern notion of existence, insofar as the latter has preserved any of the original semantic flavor of Latin *exsistere*. For the aspectual features of the Latin verb are entirely discrepant from those of *einai*, and actually closer to *gignesthai*. Etymologically *exsistere* suggests a standing out or a stepping forth, a coming-into-being, an emergence out of a dark background into the light of day. The linguistic structure of the verb reinforces this idea, since the preverb *ex-* implies the completion of a process while the aspect of the reduplicated present is punctual rather than durative (in contrast to *stare*).[10] Instead of an antithesis to Becoming, *exsistentia* provides as it were the perfect of *gignesthai*: the state achieved as a result of the process of coming-to-be. And in fact the sense of existence was originally acquired by the verb in the perfect: the existent was conceived literally

---

[9] e.g. *Theaet.* 152d: γίγνεται πάντα ἃ δή φαμεν εἶναι, οὐκ ὀρθῶς προσαγορεύοντες· ἔστι μὲν γὰρ οὐδέποτ᾽ οὐδέν, ἀεὶ δὲ γίγνεται.

[10] See Meillet and Vendryès, *Traité*, § 275.

as 'what has emerged', *id quod exstitit.*[11] Now what has emerged into the light of day is in a sense the contingent, what might not have emerged and what might easily disappear once more. Under the influence of the biblical notion of Creation, and the radical distinction between essence and existence which follows from it in the medieval doctrine of created beings, these linguistic connotations of *exsistentia* were preserved and developed at the theoretical level in the concept of a state of being which is intrinsically provisional and precarious, hovering on the verge of nothingness.[12] These connotations have even survived the separation from biblical theology and the translation into German, as one can see from Heidegger's account of *Dasein* as a foundationless *Geworfenheit*, a state of being thrown where one has no place to stand.

The connotations of enduring stability which are inseparable from the meaning of *einai* thus serve to distinguish the Greek concept of Being from certain features of the modern notion of existence. The final point | in our analysis of this meaning will help to bring the two notions together.   [257]

B. *The locative value of the verb 'to be'.* In considering what one may loosely call the expression for existence in a number of non-Indo-European languages—that is, the expression which serves to translate 'there is . . .' or *il y a*—I was struck by the fact that many (though not all) such expressions involve some allusion to place or location. Thus in the African dialect Ewe the verb which renders 'there is' or 'exists' means literally 'to be somewhere, to be present'. In Turkish, *var* and *yok* mean 'there is' and 'there is not', respectively, but *var* is also used

---

[11] See *Thesaurus Linguae Latinae* V², p. 1873, l. 31. For the beginnings of the usage see A. Ernout, '*Exsto* et les composés latins en *ex-*', *Bulletin de la société linguistique de Paris*, 50 (1954), 18. The aspectual contrast between *esse* and *exsistere* is partially preserved in the Spanish distinction between *ser* and *estar*.

[12] I must here leave open the question of the influence of Arabic vocabulary upon the medieval distinction between essence and existence. It is certainly of great importance that the Arabs rendered *to on* and *to einai* by passive forms of the verb 'to find' (root *WJD*), so that 'what is' in Greek becomes 'what is found' (= 'what exists') in Arabic. Since to find is to locate, or discover the place of, the idiom reorients 'being' in the locative-existential sense. (Cf. the parallel French idiom *se trouver*.) See the excellent remarks of A. C. Graham, '"Being" in Linguistics and Philosophy', *Foundations of Language*, 1 (1965)' 226–7. If a full history of the concept of existence is ever undertaken, it would also be important to study the use of ὑπάρχω, ὕπαρξις from the Stoics on, and of ὑπόστασις, ὑποστῆναι as well.

for statements of place and *yok* for absence. Now in Indo-European the situation is often comparable. Not only is *exsistere* itself a spatial metaphor, vaguely implying some local context, but expressions like '*there* is' and 'il *y* a' make explicit use of the adverb for definite place. It is interesting that in European languages where the old Indo-European *es- has been preserved in the expression of existence, it has retained its ancient existential force by the addition of such a local adverb: English 'there is'; Italian *c'è*, *ci sono*; German *dasein*. And in Russian, where the archaic forms *yest* and *nyet* (from *es-) serve by themselves for 'there is' and 'there is not', they *also* may mean 'is present' and 'is not here'. Our words 'present' and 'absent' themselves reflect the old locative use of the verb, derived as they are from the obsolete participle of *sum* which survives in historical Latin only in these forms: *ab-sens*, *prae-sens*. The corresponding Indo-European idiom is well represented in Greek: *apesti*, *paresti*.

Thus *einai* is quite normally used for 'to be somewhere' (with the place specified by an adverbial word or phrase), to be in the presence of, or remote from, some definite point of reference. The usual dichotomy between the existential and the predicative usage of the verb would require us to treat this locative use of the verb as merely 'copulative'. For the traditional doctrine assimilates the adverbial expression of place to a nominal predicate: it treats 'John is in the garden' as if it were syntactically parallel to 'John is a gardener'. But this assimilation, like the dichotomy on which it is based, seems to me radically mistaken. For grammatical and philological reasons which cannot be fully presented here, I am inclined to regard the locative as a distinct and fundamental use of 'to be', from which the truly copulative use (with predicate nouns and adjectives) might itself be derived. But regardless of whether or not the locative use is more fundamental than the predicative, I would insist that it is closer in meaning to what is usually called the existential sense of the verb. So intimate is the link between these two uses that I would myself prefer to speak in hyphenated terms of the existential-locative sense. For example, nearly all of the uses of the verb in Homer which we would recognize as existential are at the same time statements of place, and it might be urged that the distinctly existential value of the verb derives | merely from its emphatic position in the ⟦258⟧

sentence.[13] On this view a statement of existence is as it were an emphatic (or in some cases a vague and generalized) statement of place: 'There is an *X*' means 'Here, there, or somewhere in the world is an *X*'.

The importance of the locative associations of *einai* for an understanding of the ordinary existential use of the verb may be a matter on which philologists will disagree. But I think there can be no disagreement on the close connection between the ideas of existence and location in Greek philosophical thought. We have from Presocratic times the well-established axiom that *whatever is, is somewhere; what is nowhere is nothing.*[14] As Plato puts it (stating not his own view, but that of Greek common sense), 'we say that it is necessary for everything which is real (τὸ ὂν ἅπαν) to be somewhere in some place and to occupy some space, and that what is neither on earth nor anywhere in heaven is nothing at all' (*Tim.* 52b). If existence and location are not *identical* in Greek thought, they are at least logically equivalent, for they imply one another; that is, they do for the average man, and for the philosophers before Plato. Hence the *nous* of Anaxagoras, which is as spiritual or 'mental' a power as he could conceive, is nonetheless thought of as located in place; namely, in the same place 'where everything else is' (fr. 14). The principle of Love for Empedocles is an invisible force of attraction and a general law of combination by rational proportion, but it is also to be found 'swirling among' the other elements, 'equal to them in length and breadth' (fr. 17. 20–5). Even the Being of Parmenides, the most metaphysical concept in Presocratic thought, is compared to a sphere, and conceived as a solid mass extending equally in all directions. It is not merely that Greek thought was instinctively concrete: the very notion of *being* had local connotations. And so

---

[13]   The standard cases involve initial position for the verb:

ἔστι πόλις Ἐφύρη μυχῷ Ἄργεος ἱπποβότοιο (*Il.* 6. 152).
ἔστι δέ τις ποταμὸς Μινυήϊος εἰς ἅλα βάλλων
ἐγγύθεν Ἀρήνης, ὅθι μείναμεν Ἠῶ δῖαν (*Il.* 11. 722).

A less emphatic, but still unusual position

Κρήτη τις γαῖ᾽ ἔστι, μέσῳ ἐνὶ οἴνοπι πόντῳ (*Od.* 19. 172).

[14]   See *Gorgias* B. 3. 70, in H. Diels and W. Kranz, *Die Fragmente der Vorsokratiker* (Berlin: Weidmann, 1960), ii. 280. 26 [= D.-K.] the principle seems to have been used earlier by Zeno (Diels and Kranz, *Fragmente*, 29 A 24, Arist. *Phys.* 209ᵃ4). See also *Phys.* 208ᵃ29, ᵇ29 ff. (where it is traced back to Hesiod).

Plato, when for the first time he clearly introduced nonspatial entities into a philosophical theory, was careful to situate his new Forms in a new kind of place. What we are in the habit of calling the 'intelligible world' is presented by Plato quite literally as an intelligible region or place, the νοητὸς τόπος, conceived by analogy with the region known to sense-experience, but sharply contrasted with it, in order to serve as the | setting for Plato's radically new view of Being. (Cf. *Rep.* 6. 508c1, 509d2, 517b5.) ⟦259⟧

How did the new view of Being arise? There could be many answers to this question. I would like to end by suggesting one which may at the same time serve as a summary of the main points I have tried to make.

We began by admitting with Aristotle and Mill that 'to be' is not univocal, and that any doctrine of Being is obliged to reckon with a plurality of senses. Furthermore, the range of meaning of *einai* in Greek is likely to be wider and richer than that of the corresponding verb in any other language—and certainly richer than the verb 'to be' in most modern languages. For that very reason, the traditional dichotomy between the existential and the predicative use of the verb would have to be rejected for Greek as a hopeless oversimplification, even if it were not vitiated from the start by the confusion between a syntactic and a semantic criterion. The syntactic distinction between the absolute and predicative constructions is a problem for grammarians, and perhaps a difficult one. But I do not see that it is of any great importance for an understanding of the philosophic usage.[15] Even more negligible is the question of the omission of the verb *esti*, which is sometimes regarded as a characteristic feature of the copulative construction. (In fact the omission of the verb seems to be a purely stylistic feature, dictated by considerations of elegance or economy, and with no necessary relation to the syntax or meaning of the verb. The view that the predicative verb may be omitted, the existential not, is a pure myth. Democritus' famous statement in fr. 9, 'by custom (*nomos*) there is sweet, by custom bitter, by custom hot, by custom color, but in reality there are atoms and the void', is the very model of an existential assertion, but the verb 'to be' is omitted in every clause, including the last.[16])|

---

[15] The one important philosophic doctrine which seems to turn on the syntactic distinction is Aristotle's separation of the questions *ei esti* and *ti esti* in *Post. An.* 2. See the Postscripta.

[16] It has been suggested to me that instead of an existential ἔστι, one might suppose that some other term has been elliptically omitted in Democritus fr. 9 (= fr. 125): ἐτεῇ δὲ ἄτομα καὶ κένον; e.g. one might understand λέγεται or even the copula: 'things really are ...'.

[[260]]   What I have tried to do, then, is to clarify the semantic content and diversity of *einai* by concentrating on three features which are often neglected, and which are largely indifferent to the syntactic variation between absolute and predicative construction. These three features— which I call the veridical, the durative, and the locative (or locative- existential) values of *einai*—although they do not directly account for every particular usage of the verb, seem to point to what is most fundamental for its use in philosophy. The durative aspect, being inseparable from the stem, colors every use of the verb, including every philosophical use. Whatever the real entities are for a philoso- pher, these are the entities which endure. The locative connotation, suggesting as it does a concretely spatial and even bodily view of *what is*, inclines Greek philosophy towards a conception of reality as cor- poreal. This fundamental corporealism (which in Greek thought is not necessarily materialistic, but is compatible with hylozoism or even with panpsychism) is a persistent trend in Presocratic philosophy, as we have noted; it is not altogether absent from Aristotle; and it asserts itself with equal force in the rival Hellenistic cosmologies of the Stoics and the Epicureans. (It was still alive in the gnostic view of God from which St Augustine struggled to free himself.) To claim that the Greek view of reality was so persistently corporeal *because* their verb 'to be' had local connotations would no doubt be an exaggeration. But the two facts are related, and the relationship may be illuminating in both directions.

Neither the locative nor the durative values of *einai*, however, explain the peculiarly momentous role of this term in the development of western philosophy. Local concreteness and stable duration account

I doubt this. Even in the preceding clauses the adjectives represent the grammatical subject, not a predicate for some understood subject like 'things': νόμῳ γλυκύ means 'sweet (is, exists) by convention', not '(things are, are called) sweet by convention', since in the second case we would have the plural γλυκέα.

In any case, my point is not tied to this or to any other single example. For a striking double omission of the locative-existential see *Euthyphro* 12b (and ff.) ἵνα γὰρ δέος ἔνθα καὶ αἰδώς, 'Where fear is, there also is awe.' See also C. Guiraud, *La phrase nominale en grec de Homère à Euripide* (Paris: Klincksieck, 1962), p. 163–98. Typical examples from Homer are:

Ἀλλ' ἤτοι νίκη μὲν ἀρηιφίλου Μενελάου (*Il.* 4. 13)

and in the description of the Elysian field:

οὐ νιφετός τ', οὔτ' ἄρ χειμὼν πολύς, οὔτε ποτ' ὄμβρος (*Od.* 4. 566).

for certain characteristic features of the Greek concept of Being; they do not account for the concept itself. In order to understand what Being means for Plato, for Plotinus, and for Aristotle in the *Metaphysics*, we must above all bear in mind the double sense of verity and fact which I emphasized in the first part of my paper. Being for these philosophers as for Parmenides means what is or can be truly known and truly said. *To on* is first and foremost the object of true knowledge and the basis or the correlative of true speech. It is by reference to these two terms, *epistēmē* and *logos*, that the philosophical concept of Being has its unity and its importance. Thus for Plato the stable realm of Being is the proper object of knowledge as Becoming is of true opinion.[17] And it is in virtue of this relationship to knowing, and to the parallel concept of *noein*, that Plato is able to introduce a range of entities which are not bodily and not located in space.

[261] The entities which populate Plato's *noētos topos* are usually interpreted as | universal terms. But if 'term' means 'noun', it is clear that the Forms must be more than that, if their mingling and interconnection is to make discourse possible (*Sophist* 259e). Without entering upon an exegesis of the theory of Forms, I would like to suggest that the Forms could be thought of as analogous to 'predicates' in Quine's sense, not as terms alone but terms-plus-copula: not as Justice, for example, but as being-just. Whatever else it means for an individual thing to participate in a Form, it certainly means that the name of the Form is truly predicated of it, or in Quine's terminology that the Form as predicate *is true of* that particular thing. This is perhaps what Plato has in mind when he says that all Forms share in *to on* (*Soph.* 256e): they share in Being not simply as existent realities but as being-so in some determinate way, as being-what-they-are. (Here and throughout the *Sophist* Cornford's rendering of the strong or absolute use of *einai* as 'existence' seems to me systematically misleading.) The being of the Forms so understood also makes better sense of Aristotle's τὸ τί ἦν εἶναι—a strange formula which he never feels called upon to explain. The formula means quite literally a thing's *being-what-it-is*, not merely the content or character of *what-it-is* (τὸ τί ἐστι), the answer to the question, 'What is it?', but its being determinately so, as a man or a dog or a triangle.

---

[17] *Republic* 5. 478a–e. Cf. *Timaeus* 28a–c2.

The Forms of Plato and the essences of Aristotle are certainly not propositional in character, but they might thus be compared to open sentences, with an unfilled place for the subject. This comparison is far from satisfactory, since neither Form nor essence can be understood as a linguistic entity: they constitute the objective concepts or (in some sense) real entities which our linguistic predicates signify. What I mean to suggest is that the linguistic signs for Form and essence are best understood as predicates rather than as terms, as (open) statements rather than as general names. But even if this turned out to be false for the special doctrines of Form and essence, my main contention here would not be affected. For my contention is, first, that the terms *on* and *onta* are normally and idiomatically used for facts of a propositional structure, and, second, that just as *to eon* in Herodotus regularly constitutes the object of a verb of knowing or saying, so 'being' enters philosophy as the object of knowledge and true speech. Now it is only natural for the object of knowing to be conceived of after the pattern of propositions; for what can be known and truly stated is what is the case: a fact, situation, or relationship, not a particular thing or 'object' as such. The chief discrepancy between the Greek concept of Being and the modern notion of existence lies precisely here; for we normally assign existence not to facts or propositions or relations, but to discrete particulars: to creatures, persons, or things.

Of course the Greek use of *einai* for localized existence tends to blur this | distinction, since *what is somewhere* is normally an individual entity, precisely the kind of thing to which the modern notion of existence applies. When *what is* is used in this locative sense, it inevitably tends to be conceived as thing-like rather than as fact-like. It is not so much that the Greeks lack our notion of existence, as that they lack our sense of its distinctness from essence or from the being-so of fact and predication. This is true not only for the metaphysicians, but also (as we saw) for a philosopher of common sense like Protagoras.

To put the matter in a nutshell, the ontological vocabulary of the Greeks led them to treat the existence of things and persons as a special case of the *Bestehen von Sachverhalten*. It is remarkable that not only *onta* but every other Greek word for 'fact' can also mean 'thing', and vice versa. (Cf. *chrēmata* = *pragmata* in the fragment of Protagoras; *ergon* in the contrast with *logos*: 'in fact' and 'in word'; *gegonota* as the perfect of

[262]

onta, etc.) This failure on the part of the Greeks (at least before the Stoics) to make a systematic distinction between fact and thing underlies the more superficial and inaccurate charge that they confused the 'to be' of predication with that of existence.

It may be thought that the neglect of such a distinction constitutes a serious shortcoming in Greek philosophy of the classical period. But it was precisely this indiscriminate use of *einai* and *on* which permitted the metaphysicians to state the problem of truth and reality in its most general form, to treat matters of fact and existence concerning the physical world as only a part of the problem (or as one of the possible answers), and to ask the ontological question itself: What is Being?—that is, What is the object of true knowledge, the basis for true speech? If this is a question worth asking, then the ontological vocabulary of the Greeks, which permitted and encouraged them to ask it, must be regarded as a distinct philosophical asset.

POSTSCRIPTA

1. This paper does not pretend to offer a complete account of the philosophical usage of εἶναι. Perhaps the most important use which has been omitted here is what I would call the 'verb of whatness', the use made of εἶναι in asking and answering the question τί ἐστι; it is this use which underlines | the Platonic phrase ὅ ἔστι for the Forms (since this phrase reflects the Socratic question τί ἐστι; cf. *Phaedo* 75d1–3); the question of whatness is directly exploited by Aristotle in his concepts of τὸ τί ἐστι, τὸ τί ἦν εἶναι, and ὅπερ ἐστί (τι). This εἶναι of whatness corresponds in part to the modern 'is' of identity, but the ancient usage is oriented in a different, more ontological and 'essentialist' direction. In part, the peculiarities of this Greek usage are due to the pervasive influence of the veridical sense: 'what a thing is' means *what it really (truly) is*.

2. It might be (and has been) asked, what can be *new* in Mill's distinction between existence and the copula, since Aristotle not only notes the equivocation between εἶναί τι and εἶναι ἁπλῶς but also emphasizes the contrast between the philosophical questions τί ἐστι and εἰ ἔστι, on the basis of which the medievals erected the

[263]

systematic distinction between essence and existence. What then is new in Mill's dichotomy?

I answer that what is new in Mill is the assignment of the meaning 'exists' to 'is' when used alone, or when (as he says) it 'has a meaning of its own' in addition to performing the function of the copula. For both the terms of his dichotomy Mill was of course drawing on a traditional, indeed on a medieval analysis of 'to be'. (The explicit interpretation of 'to be' as 'to exist' is as old as the *esse existentiae* of Duns Scotus.) But Mill seems really to have been the first philosopher to offer just this *pair* of concepts—copula plus existence—as an adequate analysis of the meaning of the verb, and to correlate this antithesis with the syntactic distinction between the predicative and the absolute construction.

Aristotle's analysis of the sophistic shift from εἶναί τι to εἶναι ἁπλῶς (or conversely) bears only a superficial analogy to this dichotomy. One may, if one chooses, explicate εἶναί τι by reference to the copula; but εἶναι ἁπλῶς is not in general 'to exist'. On the contrary, it is either an indeterminate expression, since for Aristotle there is no one, single meaning of 'to be', or else it refers specifically to the being of *substances*, as the primary instance of being in general (τὸ πρώτως ὂν καὶ οὐ τὶ ὂν ἀλλ᾽ ὂν ἁπλῶς ἡ οὐσία ἂν εἴη, *Met. Z*. 1. 1028ᵃ30). Substances for Aristotle are, in the last analysis, living beings (ibid. 1040ᵇ5–10). Therefore ἁπλῶς εἶναι, as the being of substance, is ultimately synonymous with the old Homeric (and post-Homeric) use of ἔστι for 'is [264] alive'. (We may compare Hamlet's 'To be or not to be'.) Hence | the fallacy in passing from ὃ μηρός ἐστι ποιητής to ὃ μηρος ἔστιν: Homer is no longer (sc. a substance), for he is no longer alive (*De Int.* 21ᵃ18–28). The fallacy at *Soph. El.* 167ᵃ1–4 may be explained along similar lines: although it may be true to say τὸ μὴ ὂν ἐστι δοξαστόν, 'what is not (the case) is an object of belief', there is no sense whatsoever in which εἶναι can be predicated per se of 'that which is not (so)'. An existential nuance is possible here, but certainly not unambiguously required. We have an earlier example of the first sophism in Plato, *Euthydemus* 283d: Kleinias' friends want to make him wise, i.e. to make him what he is not, and to make him be no longer what he is now. But to make him be no longer is to *kill* him (ἀπολωλέναι). What kind of friends are these?

3. As for the distinction between εἰ ἔστι and τί ἐστι in *Post. An.* 2, there is no denying that it provides the foundation for the classical distinction between existence and essence. This distinction was systematically developed for the first time in Hellenistic philosophy, in regard to the knowledge of God: the standard formula is that we can know the existence (ὕπαρξις) of God, but not His essence (οὐσία). Philo seems to be the earliest extant author to put the distinction in this form, but he must have taken it over from earlier works which are lost. The terminology of 'existence' (ὑπαρκτός, ἀνύπαρκτος, ὕπαρξις), although unknown to Aristotle, is in current philosophical use from the time of Epicurus.[18]

The development of the concept of existence after Aristotle lies outside the scope of this paper: I will limit myself to two observations. The question εἰ ἔστι is not univocal for Aristotle, for he has no univocal concept of being or existence. But the situation is different for the Stoics, for whom 'to be (real)' means 'to be a body'. And nearly the same is true for the Epicureans. Even more momentous, however, is the change which occurs when the biblical doctrine of Creation and of the infinite distance between Creator and creatures is taken as a basic principle in a new ontology, i.e. in medieval metaphysics after Avicenna. For now existence in the case of created beings *is* in one respect univocal: it is that which God adds to the essences of things which he has, as it were, determined in advance. Thus existence comes to be thought of as something logically posterior, a kind of accident which supervenes to the essence of what does or can exist. To make the point by exaggerating the imagery: existence now tends to be thought of as the final push into actual being provided by the demiurge, as he sends things forth from his precosmic workshop of logical possibilities. It is in this reversal of logical priorities that I see the decisive shift away from Aristotle, and from | the   [265] Greeks. For when Aristotle makes *his* distinction between 'essence' and 'existence', he insists that the εἰ ἔστι question must be answered first: we cannot know *what* a thing is unless we know *that* it is, for only real things have essences (*Post. An.* 2. 7. 92ᵇ4–8).[19]

---

[18] For the texts see Fr. A.-J. Festugière, *La révélation d'Hermès Trismégiste, iv: le Dieu inconnu et la gnose* (Paris: Gabalda, 1945–54), ch. 1, esp. p. 11 n.

[19] For the development of existence as a philosophical idea distinct from the Greek notion of Being see E. Gilson, *L'être et l'essence* (Paris: Vrin, 1948), esp. chs. 3–5.

4. Since this paper was completed I have had a chance to consult
G. E. L. Owen's important study of the philosophical use of εἶναι in
Aristotle: 'Aristotle on the Snares of Ontology'.[20] Professor Owen
distinguishes what he calls being* (which has as many senses as there
are categories) from being**, 'the use which is rendered by "il y a" or
"es gibt", and represented in predicate logic by the formula "(∃x) Fx"'
(pp. 84–5). He points out that Aristotle nowhere distinguishes these
two uses of the verb. I would go further. Only being* is an explicit
philosophical concept for Aristotle: it is precisely his notion of 'being
proper', τὸ ὂν καθ' αὑτό. The second use, on the other hand (being**),
corresponds to *our* notion of existence as represented by the quantifier.
This second use certainly forms part of Aristotle's language: it is an
idiomatic use of ἔστι in Greek, and in Aristotle's Greek. But it occupies
at best a marginal position within his conceptual scheme. In the
Metaphysics, at any rate, it seems never to constitute a topic for philosophic discussion. In *Posterior Analytics* 2, where the question εἰ ἔστι
suggests that this usage *might* be articulated as a concept, the analysis
remains rudimentary. A mere oversight? Or a lack of interest which is
philosophically motivated? Perhaps the latter: for Aristotle, 'l'existence
d'une chose prise à part de son essence n'a pas de sens défini'.[21]

Thus I would like to see Owen's results as a confirmation of the
view presented here: that we have no reason to suppose that our
notion of existence—the notion rendered by the quantifier—can be
taken as the proper and fundamental meaning of the verb εἶναι as used
by the Greek philosophers. In Aristotle, at any rate, the 'existential'
interest in a question like εἰ ἔστι remains quite isolated within a
conceptual scheme almost wholly oriented in other directions: towards
the being of the categories, towards the veridical, towards οὐσία as
whatness, as substance, and as actuality.

---

[20] In R. Bambrough (ed.), *New Essays on Plato and Aristotle* (New York: Humanities,
1965).
[21] S. Mansion, *Le jugement d'existence chez Aristote* (Lonvain: Editions de L'Institut Supérieur de Philosophie, 1946), 243; cf. pp. 260–5.

2

On the Terminology for *Copula* and *Existence*

Dear Richard,

Here is my birthday offering: a note on two problems in the history of philosophical terminology, one of which we have often discussed. Since the history of both terms involves Islamic philosophy as well as the ancient and medieval material considered here, the Arabic texts will have to be discussed for any complete study of either problem. What I offer here is something more modest, only a preliminary gathering of data for the history of the terms *copula* and *existence* together with some remarks on the decisive contribution of Abelard to the classical theory of the copula.

The two terms are regularly paired off against one another in the traditional theory of the verb *to be*; for example, in Mill's *Logic* or in the classical handbooks of Greek and Indo-European syntax.[1] As far as I know, the earliest grammatical discussion to combine and contrast just these two terms in an analysis of *be* is Gottfried Hermann's *De Emendanda Ratione Graecae Grammaticae* (1801), where the concepts of copula and existence are imported from Christian Wolff's logic in order to provide a rational explanation (and 'correction') of the rules for the accentuation of ἐστί in ancient Greek.[2] Thus the use of just this

---

[1] See J. S. Mill, *A System of Logic, Ratiocinative and Inductive* (London: Parker, 1843), I. iv. § 1; R. Kühner and B. Gerth, *Ausführliche Grammatik* (Hanover/Leipzig: Hahn, 1904), *Satzlehre* I, § 345.3; B. Delbrück, *Vergleichende Syntax*, iii (= K. Brugmann and B. Delbrück, *Grundriss der vergleichenden Grammatik der indogermanischen Sprachen* (Strasbourg: Trübner, 1886–1900), v, § 5).

[2] G. Hermann, *De Emendanda Ratione Graecae Grammaticae* (Leipzig: Gerhard Fleischer, 1801), 84. For his rationalist motives see the preface, p. vi. For the philosophical influences on Hermann see Delbrück, *Vergl. Syntax*, I (= Brugmann and Delbrück, *Grundriss*, iii), 25–7.

brace of terms is established by the beginning of the nineteenth century. It may be older than that, but probably not much older. The standard terminology is at best embryonic in Kant's discussion of the relations between predication and existence in his criticism of the ontological argument (*Kritik der reinen Vernunft*, A 592 (= B 620) ff.). On the other hand, the distinction between the copulative and existential uses of *be* was drawn in antiquity, but without two terms corresponding to *copula* and *existence*. Of the authors I have looked at, Abelard is the one who comes closest to anticipating the dichotomy of Hermann and Mill, but even Abelard does not employ *existentia* as a technical expression for 'existence'.

I am concerned here not with the pairing of the terms *copula* and *existentia* in the eighteenth or nineteenth century but with their separate history in the earlier period. Both Latin terms are fixed in their standard uses in medieval | philosophy. The term *copula* occurs in Abelard and almost every later writer on logic. The technical sense of *existentia* (specifying the use of *esse* which contrasts with *essentia*, together with a connotation of actuality as opposed to potency) is perhaps not clearly attested before the *esse existentiae* of Duns Scotus. In both cases there are obvious roots for the medieval usage in classical Greek philosophy. Yet in both cases the connection between the ancient and medieval terminology is more problematic than one might suppose.

[[142]]

1. Copula

Prantl tells us that Abelard is the first extant Latin author to use *copula* as a technical term for *est* in the categorical proposition *homo est mortalis*.[3] The Kneales give this as the usual view, but suggest that the term may have appeared in earlier medieval discussions of the role of *est* in such propositions.[4] I do not venture any guesses about the terminology of

---

[3] C. Prantl, *Geschichte der Logik im Abendlande*, 2nd edn. (Graz: Druck, 1885, repr. 1955), ii. 197 with n. 370. Prantl cites from the *Dialectica* (p. 161 in the edition of De Rijk, 1956). He did not know Abelard's earlier work on logic, the so-called *Logica 'Ingredientibus'* (quoted below as '*LI*'), first published by Geyer in 1919–27, where the term *copula* appears in the relevant sense in at least two passages. See below.

[4] W. Kneale and M. Kneale, *The Development of Logic* (Oxford: Clarendon, 1962), 208.

unrecorded or unpublished discussions but, as we shall see, Abelard's early usage of the word suggests that *copula* was not yet a fixed term. If that is so, Abelard must be personally responsible for the classical terminology. It is clear that (as Prantl noted) the noun does not occur in the corresponding sense either in Boethius, who is Abelard's chief authority, or in the latter's translation of Aristotle. Boethius does use the verb *copulare* and its abstract noun *copulatio* to describe the function of *est*, following Aristotle's use of the terms σύνθεσις and συμπλοκή. It is easy enough to see how Abelard's use of the term *copula* develops in a natural way out of Boethius' language. But the impression remains that both the term *copula* and, in part, the theory it is designed to convey are Abelard's own.

We can surely neglect Prantl's suggestion that Abelard was indebted to a Byzantine terminology represented in the *Synopsis* attributed to Michael Psellus, since this work is now generally recognized as a Greek translation of the later *Summulae logicales* of Peter of Spain.[5] Furthermore, it is worth noting that in the passage quoted by Prantl from pseudo-Psellus the Greek equivalent of *copula* (namely σύνδεσμος) is introduced not as a technical term but as a simile: the verb ἐστί joins predicate with subject 'like a kind of link' τοῦτο τὸ ῥῆμα τὸ 'ἐστίν' συζεύγνυσι καθάπερ τις σύνδεσμος τὸ ἓν μετὰ τοῦ ἑτέρου.[6] This, as we shall see, is very close to the traditional language of the Greek commentators on Aristotle, and clearly shows that it was not in Greek usage that *copula* (or σύνδεσμος) had become a fixed term of logic.

On the other hand, we should take note of the fact that before | 　　[[143]] Abelard the Arabic equivalent of *copula* (namely *rābiṭa*) does seem to be fully established as a technical expression, judging from translations such as the following:

La troisième partie de la proposition est l'idée de rapport et le lien par lequel seulement une proposition est composée. Ce n'est pas que l'homme soit homme, mais qu'il soit sujet; ni que l'animal soit animal, mais qu'il soit

---

[5] Prantl, *Geschichte*, ii. 197 n. 370, with 273 n. 11. For the dependence of pseudo-Psellus on a Latin original see J. Mullally, *The 'Summulae logicales' of Peter of Spain* (Notre Dame, Ind.: University of Notre Dame Press, 1945), pp. ix–xi.

[6] Prantl, *Geschichte*, II. 273 n. 11, citing the edn. of Ehinger, I. 5. 13. The passage also seems to use τὸ συνδέν as translation of *copula*. In modern Greek the term is τὸ συνδετικόν.

prédicat. Or il en est ainsi par un lien entre eux deux, indiqué parfois par un troisième mot . . . et il s'appelle *copule*.[7]

I am told that this usage is fixed in Islamic philosophy at least from the time of Al-Fārābī in the early tenth century. Unless further evidence is forthcoming for Arabic influence on Latin authors of Abelard's period we seem obliged to suppose that the technical use of *copula* or its equivalent was established twice, first in the Arabic and then independently in the Latin tradition which derives from Aristotle. I shall suggest later why this may be so. But first I wish to show that the terminology did not crystallize in the ancient tradition running from Aristotle to Ammonius and Boethius, although the theoretical foundations for the concept of copula were largely prepared.

The origins of the medieval theory are to be found in Aristotle's analysis of the premisses of a categorical syllogism.

(1) *Pr. An.* I. 1. 24[b]16 ὅρον δὲ καλῶ εἰς ὃν διαλύεται ἡ πρότασις, οἷον τό τε κατηγορούμενον καὶ τὸ καθ' οὗ κατηγορεῖται, προστιθεμένου [ἢ διαιρουμένου secludit Ross] τοῦ εἶναι ἢ μὴ εἶναι.

'I call *term* that into which the premiss is resolved, viz. the predicate and that of which it is predicated, with *be* or *not be* added.'

Here εἶναι naturally suggests what we call the 'copula', in an analysis of the form *S is P*; but Aristotle uses no such term. Nor does Alexander in his commentary on this passage. And in fact in his technical statement of syllogistic premisses Aristotle rarely employs the form 'A ἐστί B'. He generally makes use of the converse formula κατηγορεῖται τὸ B κατὰ τοῦ A, or of its equivalent ὑπάρχει τὸ B τῷ A. It is true that Aristotle elsewhere suggests that sentences with finite verbs, like ἄνθρωπος βαδίζει, are in principle equivalent to sentences with copula and participle, like ἄνθρωπος βαδίζων ἐστί.[8] One might suppose, as the commentators did, that such an analysis in *S is P* form underlies Aristotle's treatment of categorical premisses, as reflected in (1) above. And the same analysis is explicitly presupposed in his doctrine that εἶναι has as many senses or uses as there are categories (*Met. Δ*. 7.

---

[7] Quotation from Avicenna in A.-M. Goichon, *Lexique de la langue philosophique d'Ibn Sīnā* (Paris: de Bronwer, 1938), 142.

[8] *De Int.* 21[b]9; cf. *Pr. An.* 51[b]13 ff.; *Met.* 1017[a]27–30.

1017^{a}22–30). But in his theory of declarative sentences in the *De Interpretatione* Aristotle treats the two-word sentence consisting of noun and verb (like ἄνθρωπος βαδίζει) as the elementary form, and mentions the copula sentence only as a special case, where ἐστί figures as 'third word added to the predicate' (ὅταν δὲ τὸ ἔστι τρίτον προσκατηγορηθῇ, *De Int.* 10. 19^{b}19). Hence the standard medieval designation of these sentences as *de tertio adiacente*. (So also in Greek, where ἐκ τρίτου προσκατηγορουμένου is cited as a technical term by Ammonius in *De Int.*, p. 160, 1.17.)

Thus both in his theory of syllogistic premisses and in his analysis of elementary propositions Aristotle avoids making any technical use of the sentence form *S is P*, probably because he wished to steer clear of the difficulties raised in earlier discussions of the role of ἐστί.[9] Nevertheless, in the course of his chapter on verbs in the *De Interpretatione* Aristotle makes some remarks which were to serve as the direct inspiration for the later theory of the copula.

(2) *De Int.* 3. 16^{b}19 αὐτὰ μὲν οὖν καθ᾽ αὑτὰ λεγόμενα τὰ ῥήματα ὀνόματά ἐστι καὶ σημαίνει τι,—ἵστησι γὰρ ὁ λέγων τὴν διάνοιαν, καὶ ὁ ἀκούσας ἠρέμησεν— ἀλλ᾽ εἰ ἔστιν ἢ μή οὔπω σημαίνει· οὐ (v.l. οὐδὲ) γὰρ τὸ εἶναι ἢ μὴ εἶναι σημεῖόν ἐστι τοῦ πράγματος, οὐδ᾽ ἐὰν τὸ ὂν εἴπῃς ψιλόν. αὐτὸ μὲν γὰρ οὐδέν ἐστιν, προσσημαίνει δὲ σύνθεσίν τινα, ἣν ἄνευ τῶν συγκειμένων οὐκ ἔστι νοῆσαι.

This passage is full of difficulties. Ackrill's translation runs:

When uttered just by itself a verb is a name and signifies something—the speaker arrests his thought and the hearer pauses—but it does not yet signify whether it is or not. For not even 'to be' or 'not to be' is a sign of the actual thing (nor if you say simply 'that which is'); for by itself it is nothing, but it additionally signifies some combination, which cannot be thought of without the components.

I mention the difficulties without attempting a full analysis. In his commentary Ackrill notices the possibility that εἰ ἔστι ἢ μή might be rendered 'whether anything is or is not the case', and that εἶναι and ὄν

---

[9] See the views cited in *Physics*, 185^{b}25–32, with the commentators on this passage. And compare the doctrine of the 'late-learners' at *Sophist*, 251–2, which implies that a sentence like ἄνθρωπος ἀγαθός ἐστι is illegitimate or always false. Aristotle deals with these problems in his own theory of categories and in the corresponding doctrine that εἶναι is 'said in many ways'.

here could represent either the existential or the copulative use of ἐστί. If I understood him aright, he concludes that εἰ ἔστι should be taken as existential, and that ὄν probably represents the copula, although the existential use (or some confusion between the two) cannot be excluded.[10] My own judgment is that Ackrill's first suggestion is the right one, that εἰ ἔστι here is what I called the veridical ('is the case'), as in the definition of truth and the various statements of the law of contradiction.[11] From this wider | use of ἔστι as mark of assertion   [145] or affirmation—as the expression for an arbitrary proposition— Aristotle naturally moves in (2) to the special case where ἐστί performs this role as the verb in a copula sentence. As far as I can see, there is no need here to bring in the existential idea either in the translation or in the literal exegesis of this passage. It is primarily, and perhaps uniquely, the veridical and copulative uses which Aristotle has in mind.[12]

Fortunately, these difficulties in the interpretation of (2) do not affect the concluding reference to σύνθεσίς τις, for there is no doubt that this concerns the copulative function of *is*. Aristotle's point is that whereas subject noun and predicate adjective (or predicate noun or participle) indicate the two components (συγκείμενα) of the proposition or judgment, ἐστί adds a meaning (προσσημαίνει) which is not another component but simply the propositional form that determines the combination of the two; i.e. ἐστί specifies *that* the predicate belongs to the subject. In paraphrasing this passage the Greek commentators employ συμπλοκή as a synonym for σύνθεσις, echoing Aristotle's use in the *Categories* and elsewhere, where he speaks of the union or junction of words in a sentence, and the union of concepts (νοήματα) in the

---

[10] *Aristotle's Categories and De Interpretatione*, trans. J. L. Ackrill (Oxford: Oxford University Press, 1963), 121–3.

[11] See *Met.* 1006ᵃ1, τὸ αὐτὸ εἶναι καὶ μὴ εἶναι, 1011ᵇ26, etc.; cf. ὅτι ἔστι at *Post. An.* 71ᵃ12–14. When Aristotle wants to specify the 'existential' use, he adds ἁπλῶς; e.g. τὸ δ' εἰ ἔστιν ἢ μὴ ἁπλῶς λέγω at *Post. An.* 89ᵇ33.

[12] This seems to be the view of Ammonius and of Porphyry as well, on whom Ammonius is often relying: ἀλλ' εἰ ἔστι, φησίν, ἢ μή, οὔπω δῆλον, σημαίνει δὲ αὐτῷ τὸ μὲν ἔστι τὴν κατάφασιν τὸ δὲ ἢ μὴ τὴν ἀπόφασιν, ἢ μᾶλλον τὸ μὲν ἔστι τὸ ἀληθὲς τὸ δὲ ἢ μὴ τὸ ψεῦδος (in *De Int.* 55. 11; cf. 56. 23–33). Similarly Boethius *in Peri Hermeneias*, ed. Meiser, 1. 65. 17: ergo nec si hoc ipsum 'est' purum dixeris, esse aliquid aut non esse significat, id est aut adfirmat aut negat. Compare *in Peri H.* 2. 75. 1–8.

corresponding judgment, as a συμπλοκή or σύνθεσις.[13] Thus the general notion of joining or 'copulating' subject and predicate terms, τὶ κατά τινος, is clearly Aristotelian. But neither a term equivalent to *copula* (as a designation of ἐστί) nor any further discussion of the function of the verb ἐστί in σύνθεσις is to be found in Aristotle.

Before passing to the later theory, there is one other Aristotelian text which must be noticed. In discussing the question of separate predicates which do not imply their combination for the same subject (as *Socrates is good* and *Socrates is a shoemaker* do not imply *Socrates is a good shoemaker*) and compound expressions which do not imply each component simply (as *That is a dead man* does not imply *That is a man*), Aristotle mentions the problem of *Homer is a poet*, which does not imply *Homer is* (i.e. *is alive*), and *What-is-not is an object of opinion*, which does not imply *What-is-not is* (i.e. *is real, is true*).

(3) *De Int.* 11. 21ᵃ25 ὥσπερ ὅ μηρός ἐστί τι, οἷον ποιητής· ἆρ᾽ οὖν καὶ ἔστιν, ἤ οὔ; κατὰ συμβεβηκὸς γὰρ κατηγορεῖται τὸ ἔστιν τοῦ ὁμήρου· ὅ τι γὰρ ποιητής ἐστιν, ἀλλ᾽ οὐ καθ᾽ αὑτό, κατηγορεῖται κατὰ τοῦ μήρου τὸ ἔστιν . . . τὸ δὲ μὴ ὄν, ὅτι δοξαστόν, οὐκ ἀληθὲς εἰπεῖν ὄν τι· δόξα γὰρ αὐτοῦ οὐκ ἔστιν ὅτι ἔστιν, ἀλλ᾽ ὅτι οὐκ ἔστιν.

('For example, Homer is something (say, a poet). Does it follow that he is? No, for the "is" is predicated accidentally of Homer; for it is because he is a poet, and not per se, that the "is" is predicated of | Homer. . . . It is not true to say [146] that what-is-not, since it is an object of opinion, is something that is; for the opinion of it is not that it is, but that it is not.') (Ackrill's translation, slightly modified.)

It is here, if anywhere, that Aristotle could have used the concept of a *copula* if he had one. Instead he is obliged to rely on the ambiguous

---

[13] In addition to *Cat.* 1ᵃ16 ff., 1ᵇ25, 2ᵃ6–10, 13ᵇ10, where συμπλοκή signifies the connection of words in a sentence, see *Met.* E. 4. 1027ᵇ19 and 30, where σύνθεσις and συμπλοκή are used interchangeably for the union of concepts in an affirmative judgment, in contrast to διαίρεσις for a negative judgment. Similarly *De Anima*, 3. 8. 432ᵃ11 συμπλοκὴ γὰρ νοημάτων ἐστὶ τὸ ἀληθὲς ἢ ψεῦδος (paralleled by σύνθεσίς τις νοημάτων in 3. 6. 430ᵃ28). The Aristotelian usage goes back of course to Plato's terminology in the *Sophist*, where συμπλοκή or συμπλέκειν occurs repeatedly not only for the mingling of Forms (259e6; cf. 240c1, 242d7) but also for the connection of noun and verb in the proposition (262c6, 262d4); so also σύνθεσις at 263d3, συνθείς at 262e12. And compare ὀνομάτων συμπλοκὴν εἶναι λόγου οὐσίαν at *Theaetetus* 202b4, where the context suggests that this use of συμπλοκή may not be original with Plato.

notion of 'accidental predication'. In later authors such as Abelard we find the theory of the copula developed by way of a commentary on passages (2) and (3), a commentary which is designed to explain precisely what is meant by the statement that *is* is predicated accidentally of Homer and of what-is-not.

We may turn now to the classical theory as we find it stated in full by Abelard or, more briefly, by J. S. Mill eight centuries later. The theory will be summarized in five or six propositions, each of which can be regarded as an explication or generalization of something said by Aristotle. In this sense, and in this sense only, the theory itself is 'Aristotelian'. Taken together, however, these propositions represent a coherent general account of the copula use of *is*, its relation to the existential use of *be* and to the ordinary use of other finite verbs, which is to my knowledge nowhere clearly formulated before Abelard.

1. Every simple declarative sentence can be rewritten in the form X *is* Y, and in particular every sentence of the form NV can be rewritten in the form N *is* V-*ing* (where 'N' stands for a noun form and 'V' for a verb).

2. In a sentence of the form X *is* Y, X and Y are terms (in the sense of the terms of a syllogistic premiss), whereas *is* is a meaningful third part which is not a term.

3A. In such a sentence, the meaning of *is* is that of a sign of affirmation, signifying that the predicate Y is affirmed of—said to belong to or to be true of—the subject X. Similarly, *is not* is a sign of denial.

3B. [The same point otherwise expressed.] In X *is* Y, the verb *is* serves to link Y to X and thus to combine them in a complete sentence (or proposition), i.e. one which can be true or false.

4. In such a sentence *is* serves merely as a link or copula (in the sense of 3A–B) and not also as a predicate which asserts the existence of the subject.

5. In the ordinary NV sentence the verb form serves twice: first as predicate term (like Y in X *is* Y) and again as *copulans* or linking element. The rewriting of NV sentences as N *is* V-*ing* according

to 1. above (e.g. rewriting *John runs* as *John is running*) serves precisely to bring out this double role of the verb.

Of these propositions numbers 1–3B are closely based on Aristotle's own remarks and can be found more or less fully developed in the ancient commentators. Propositions 4–5, which complete the theory, seem to be stated for the first time by Abelard. If this is true, Abelard is responsible not only for the introduction of the term *copula* but also for the perfection of a theory of sentence structure expressed by this term. Let me briefly cite evidence for 1–3A from Abelard and earlier commentators, before discussing his own original contribution. (In the citations which follow, '*D.*' is *Dialectica*, ed. Rijk, '*LI*' is *Logica 'Ingredientibus'*, ed. Geyer.)   [[147]]

1. *D.* 161. 33–162. 1: 'cum enim dicitur: "Socrates ambulat", tale est ac si dicatur: "Socrates est ambulans"'. Alexander (in *An. Pr.* 15. 17) gives the analysis of *Socrates is* into *Socrates is (a) being* as a special case of this rule: ἡ γὰρ λέγουσα πρότασις 'Σωκράτης ἔστιν' ἴσον δύναται τῇ 'Σωκράτης ὄν ἐστιν'.

2. *D.* 164. 32: 'Possumus quoque non incongrue verbum interpositum (i.e. *est*) partem propositionis, non terminum, appellare'. Since Abelard has just quoted a passage from Boethius which recognizes only *two* parts of the proposition, namely subject and predicate, he seems to be consciously innovating when he describes *est* as a distinct part. (Boethius tends to follow Aristotle's description of the copula as τρίτον προσκατηγορούμενον by regarding *est* only as a subpart of the predicate; he speaks sometimes of *duo predicata* in copula sentences: in *Peri Herm.* 1. 130.5; 2. 264. 21–4.) Abelard's insistence upon recognizing *est* as something distinct from the predicate is clearly related to the analysis of its role which is formulated above in propositions 4–5.

3A. *LI* 339. 22: ' "Est" verbum interpositum ad coniunctionem terminorum . . . nullius rei significationem ibi exercet, plus tamen ad vim affirmationis proficit . . . quam ipsi termini, similiter "non est" ad vim negationis'. Compare Alexander, in *An. Pr.* 15. 7: οὐ γὰρ ὅρος ἐν ταῖς τοιαύταις προτάσεσι τὸ 'ἐστίν', ἀλλὰ προστιθέμενον μὲν σύνθεσιν σημαίνει τοῦ κατηγορουμένου καὶ

τοῦ ὑποκειμένου καὶ ἔστι καταφάσεως δηλωτικόν. Compare
Boethius, op. cit. 2. 266. 1–3: 'est . . . qualis sit (propositio) id
est quoniam est adfirmativa demonstrat'.

3B. *D.* 161. 13–15: 'verbum interpositum praedicatum subiecto
copulat; et in his quidem tribus categoricae propositionis sensus
perficitur'. For the notion of completeness (which is more Stoic
than Aristotelian here) see Alexander, loc. cit. 15. 32 ὁ γὰρ
ἀφελὼν ἀπὸ τῆς προτάσεως τῆς 'Σωκράτης λευκός ἐστι' τὸ
'ἐστί' καὶ καταλιπὼν τὸ Σωκράτης λευκός' οὔτε ἀπόφασιν
πεποίηκεν οὔτε ἔτι πρότασιν τὸ καταλειπόμενον τετήρηκεν.
Notice the claim that the nominal sentence (with copula omitted) is grammatically or logically incomplete. This is combined
with the notion of the sentential | link in Ammonius, in *De Int.*   [148]
160. 10–15: ἐπεὶ γὰρ καὶ ὁ κατηγορούμενος ἐν ταῖς τοιαύταις
προτάσεσιν ὄνομά ἐστιν, οἷον τὸ δίκαιος, καὶ οὐ δύναται καθ'
ἑαυτὸν συνδυασθεὶς τῷ ὑποκειμένῳ τέλειον ἐργάσασθαι λόγον,
ἔδει αὐτοῖς ὥσπερ δεσμοῦ τινος τοῦ συνδέοντος αὐτοὺς πρὸς
ἀλλήλους καὶ τέλειον ποιοῦντος τὸν λόγον, ὃ ποιεῖ τὸ ἔστι.
(Compare ibid. 44. 13 where a similar point is made, on the
authority of Porphyry, in even more explicitly Stoic terms: ⟨τὸ
ἔστιν⟩ μετὰ μὲν τοῦ ὀνόματος αὐτοτελῆ ποιοῦν λόγον μετὰ δὲ
τῶν πτώσεων ἐλλιπῆ.) In Boethius we find this link imagery
(apparently derived from Ammonius' source, i.e. from the lost
commentary of Porphyry on the *De Interpretatione*) rendered in
Latin by *copulare*: 'duae res per ipsius verbi (sc. *est*) conpositio-
nem copulationemque iunguntur, ut est "homo animal est".
homo namque et animal copulantur atque iunguntur per id
quod dicitur "homo animal est"'. (In *Peri Herm*, 1. 65. 30–66. 4.
In the parallel passage at 2. 77. 13–26, where he speaks of *est* as
having *vis coniunctionis cuiusdam* and of contributing *conpositio-
nem aliquam copulationemque*, Boethius cites Porphyry by name as
his authority.)

Abelard's own contribution to the theory consists in a deepening
and generalizing of this notion of *est* as sentential link, so that he comes
to see it as the function not of the verb *est* in particular but of every
finite verb form. Thus he brings the post-Aristotelian discussion of the

linking role of *is* into connection with the original Platonic insight into the συμπλοκή of verb with noun as the minimal propositional form. Indeed, in his earlier work on logic Abelard makes use of the term *copula* for this more general notion of verbal link, and not specifically for the role of *est* (*LI* 351. 25, commenting on *De Int.* 16^{b}7): 'quandam proprietatem verbi supponit (sc. Aristoteles), ex qua vim maximam in propositione praedicativa de qua intendit, verbum habere monstrat.... Haec autem proprietas, quod verbum semper est nota, id est copula praedicatorum de altero, id est copulatorum praedicatorum'. A few lines later he remarks that a *verbum copulativum* may link itself as predicate to the subject (*sive se ipsum sive aliud copulet*), but that *est* in second position *copulat tantum et non copulatur* (351. 40). Here it is clear that the copula use of *est* is a special case and not the standard example of a *verbum copulativum*, which seems to mean any finite verb form. (Again, at 352. 15, Abelard uses the noun *copula* in a way which does not seem to refer exclusively or primarily to *est* as linking verb.) The double function of the ordinary finite verb is made explicit a few pages later, in his discussion of the predicative force (*vis praedicationis*) of the verb as such: 'personalia verba . . . per se ipsa praedicantur et geminatim funguntur, quia vim praedicati habent et copulantis, ut simul et praedicentur et se ipsa copulent. Sic enim dicitur "currit" quasi diceretur "est currens"' (*LI* 359. 23–8; for *vis copulandi* | *vel praedicandi* assigned specifically to the [149] substantive verb *est* see ibid. 362. 37).

This theory of the double function of the finite verb is of considerable interest in itself. But for Abelard it has the special merit of permitting him to deal with the problem raised in passage (3) of Aristotle (above p. 47): How can we clearly expose the fallacy involved in passing from *Homerus est poeta* to *Homerus est*? The problem seems to have been much discussed in Abelard's day, but the earlier solution which he mentions (and ascribes to 'magister noster', i.e. to William of Champeaux?) can scarcely have recognized the copula function as such, since it regarded *Homer is a poet* as a 'figurative and improper' use of *is* and proposed to rewrite the sentence as *The reputation of Homer survives through his poetry* (D. 135. 28–136. 36). The presupposition of this view seems to be that *Homer is a poet*, if taken properly and literally, would entail the present existence of the subject. Abelard radically modifies this view, since he resolves the problem not by rewriting the sentence but by generalizing the notion of an improper use so that every use of *is* in a sentence of the form *X is Y* is *per accidens atque impropria* (D. 134. 28 ff., 136. 37 ff.). That is to say, he regards *is* as properly used only to express the being or existence of the subject, when it occurs as an independent predicate (e.g. *Petrus est*, referring to himself), and as improperly used whenever it serves to link a further predicate (e.g. *Petrus est homo*). Thus *is* in its proper or 'original' use is a verb like other verbs, which copulates itself; it is improperly used whenever it serves 'only as copula', to link another predicate to the subject. (D. 138. 7: 'Neque enim inventum fuit in officio solius copulationis, verum simul, ut dictum est, in significatione existentium'. The terminology of the 'mere copula' appears here and elsewhere, e.g. 137. 1–2: 'cum non rem . . . praedicatam contineat, sed solius copulae officium habeat'.) This secondary use of *is* is of course most natural when the subject presently exists; but it is also natural to extend the use of the verb to nonexistent subjects (*chimaera est opinabilis*), just as we give *names* to nonexistent 'entities' in order to be able to speak of them in the way in which we normally speak of existing things (D. 137. 34 ff.). In neither case does the use of *est* as copula imply that the subject exists (D. 137. 3–6). By thus generalizing an earlier special view of the 'improper' use of *est*, Abelard may be said to have created the concept of the copula as such. And by combining this with a general insight into the predicative function of finite verb forms, he proposed a theory of the copula which is deeper than that found in later textbooks of logic. For his notion of the copula is what a contemporary philosopher might describe as the general notion of assertive tie or propositional link; and what we (following Abelard) call the *copula* is merely the expression | of this verbal function in canonical notation; that is, in the form *X is Y.*   ⟦150⟧

If we look back now at the Greek commentators, we can see that the elements of Abelard's theory were largely prepared for him, although the decisive points 4 and 5 (above, p. 48) are lacking. Thus in his comment on *De Int.* 16ᵇ24 Ammonius cites the following view from Alexander:

τοῦτο τὸ ἔστιν ἢ καὶ τὸ οὐκ ἔστιν) δύναμιν ἔχει προηγουμένως μὲν σημαντικὴν τῆς τοῦ ὄντος μεθέξεως ἢ στερήσεως, κατὰ δεύτερον δὲ λόγον καὶ κατηγορουμένου τινὸς πρὸς ὑποκείμενον συμπλοκῆς, οἷς προστιθέμενον τέλειόν τε ποιεῖ τὸν λόγον καὶ σημαντικὸν ἢ ἀληθείας ἢ ψεύδους· καὶ γὰρ ἂν ἀμέσως κατηγορῆται τοῦ ὑποκειμένου, καὶ τότε δυνάμει τὸ μὲν 'ἔστι' συμπλοκὴν αὐτοῦ πρὸς τὸ ὂν σημαίνει, οἷον Σωκράτης ὄν ἐστι' (in De Int. 57. 26).

Here the primary or principal use of ἔστι corresponds to Abelard's proper use of *est*; while the secondary use corresponds to the 'improper' use as copula: and the analysis of Σωκράτης ἔστι as Σωκράτης ὄν ἐστι prefigures Abelard's view of the double function of every verb which serves as independent predicate. All that is lacking is (1) a clear statement of the relation between the two uses, namely that the second use of *is* by itself never entails the primary use, and (2) the generalization of the copulative function to all finite verbs.

The terminology of the 'link' is also present in the Greek commentators, as we have seen in an earlier quotation from Ammonius (above, p. 50). But the term 'link' is employed there as a conscious simile (ὥσπερ δεσμοῦ τινος τοῦ συνδέοντος αὐτοὺς πρὸς ἀλλήλους), just as in the much later phrase of pseudo-Psellus: τὸ 'ἔστι' συζεύγνυσι καθάπερ τις σύνδεσμος τὸ ἓν μετὰ τοῦ ἑτέρου.[14] How far this language is from representing a fixed term for what we call the copula can be seen from another passage of Ammonius, where he speaks of the modal adverb 'necessarily' as the link between subject and predicate (with the *predicate* illustrated in this case by ἔστιν as independent verb): ὁ τρόπος οὐκ ἔστιν μέρος τῆς προτάσεως ἀλλὰ σύνδεσμος καὶ οἱονεὶ γόμφου χώραν ἐπέχει· συνδεῖ γὰρ τὸ κατηγορούμενον τῷ ὑποκειμένῳ. οἷον ἐὰν εἴπω 'ἄνθρωπος ἐξ ἀνάγκης ἐστίν,' ὁ τρόπος ὁ μεταξὺ καταφάσκει· συνδεῖ γὰρ καὶ συντίθησιν τὸ 'ἔστιν' τῷ 'ἄνθρωπος' (in An. Pr. 1. 24. 7).

We may say that the ancient commentators did not develop Abelard's theory of the copula either because they lacked his genius, or because they lacked his special logical interest in the problems represented by *Homer is a poet* and *The chimaera is imaginary*. And their failure to discuss the precise relationship between the *is* of predication and the *is* of existence | may also explain why they did not harden their talk of a link into a fixed term for *copula*. Insofar as they were concerned only with the form of copula sentences, they could make use of the Aristotelian term τρίτον προσκατηγορούμενον. But since historical developments (or nondevelopments) are always overdetermined and never

⟦151⟧

---

[14] See above, n. 6.

completely accounted for by any one explanation, we may add a consideration which is strictly terminological. As early as the time of Aristotle, the word σύνδεσμος ('link') had been selected as the proper term in grammar for what we call a 'conjunction'; and the corresponding term *copula* was used for a similar purpose in Latin grammar.[15] The tradition in such matters is very conservative, and to this day σύνδεσμος has kept this sense of grammatical 'conjunction' in modern Greek. (Hence the need for introducing a new term τὸ συνδετικόν for *copula* in post-Byzantine logic.) As long as the ancient tradition was intact, the term itself was scarcely free for another technical use, even if the need for one had been felt. But the concept of the copula was so largely prepared in the Greek commentators on Aristotle that it is not surprising to find it fixed in a technical expression as soon as logicians standing outside the ancient tradition began to reconsider the question from a more independent point of view. And so we can understand the fact (if it is a fact) that the term *copula* was invented twice, first by Alfarabi or one of his predecessors, and again by Abelard some two centuries later.

2. Existence

The terminology for existence is much more complicated, and I can only give a rough sketch of the problem. We have first to consider how ὑπάρχειν comes to be used as a synonym for εἶναι in its 'existential' use, and then to follow the history of *exsistere* as the Latin rendering of ὑπάρχειν in this sense. Either topic could supply a separate monograph.

ὑπάρχειν originally means 'to make a beginning', 'to take the initiative', 'to take the first step (in doing so-and-so)', e.g. to begin a guest-friendship (in the earliest occurrence of the verb, *Odyssey* 24. 286) or to initiate hostilities (frequently, e.g. in Herodotus ἀδικίης ὑπάρχειν, ἐμὲ ὑπῆρξαν ἄδικα ποιεῦντες; see LSJ s.v. ὑπάρχειν). The verb is a slightly less vivid variant of ἄρχω 'to initiate, take the lead', with the stylistic force of the verb muted by the preverb

---

[15] See e.g. Arist. *Poetics*, 1456ᵇ38, 1457ᵃ7, *Rhet.* 1407ᵃ20, etc. (though Aristotle classifies connecting particles like μέν and δέ as σύνδεσμοι); Steinthal, ii. 322 ff. The Latin grammarians render σύνδεσμος συμπλεκτικός (our 'coordinate conjunction') either as *copula* (cf. Varro, *De lingua latina*, 8. 10) or as *coniunctio copulativa* (Priscian).

ὑπο-, suggesting a fact that is not obvious or emphatic (cf. ὑποπέμπειν 'send secretly', ὑποφαίνειν 'shine a little', ὑπογελᾶν 'laugh slightly').

Perhaps the ὑπο- in ὑπάρχειν conveys the suggestion that the action described as 'initiating' certain consequences was not explicitly undertaken as a beginning, in order to lead to these | results (for example, to [[152]] reciprocal gift-giving or aggression in return); whereas the simplex ἄρχειν does normally imply that the subject has taken the lead *so that others will follow.* (The same idea of a beginning intended as such is also conveyed by the middle form of the simplex ἄρχεσθαι, although this usually describes an action which the subject *himself* will continue; e.g. ἄρχομ' ἀείδειν 'I begin my song' in the Homeric Hymns.[16])

In fifth-century prose and poetry ὑπάρχω is frequently used absolutely with no other verb such as ποιεῖν implied as its object or complement. In this absolute use ὑπάρχω means not 'to make a beginning' (in doing something) but 'to *be* a beginning', 'to be on hand (from the beginning, at the start)'. In this use ὑπάρχω is practically a synonym for πάρειμι 'to be present with', 'to be available for'. In the most natural or typical cases, the temporal sense of 'previously', or 'already, at the start' is clearly implied: Hdt. 7. 144. 2 αὗταί τε δὴ αἱ νέες τοῖς Ἀθηναίοισι προποιηθεῖσαι ὑπῆρχον, ἑτέρας τε ἔδεε προσναυπηγέεσθαι 'These ships had been constructed by the Athenians earlier and *were already on hand*, but it was necessary to build others in addition'. Similarly in Hdt. 2. 15. 2 εἰ τοίνυν σφι χώρη γε μηδεμία ὑπῆρχε 'If *there was* not even any land *available* for them *at the time*' (before the formation of the Nile delta), how could they claim to be the oldest nation? In this passage σφι . . . ὑπῆρχε is a paraphrase of the preceding Αἰγυπτίοισι οὐκ ἐούσαν πρότερον χώρην. Thus ὑπάρχω serves as an equivalent for εἰμί in its existential-possessive use (with the dative of 'owner'), but it adds the notion of temporal priority; that is, ὑπάρχειν τινί is a paraphrase-equivalent for εἶναι πρότερόν τινι, 'belong to earlier'. In other contexts this notion of temporal priority lapses or is replaced by the idea of present actuality, that is to say, by the notion of belonging-to or being on hand *from now on*, often with an

---

[16] An alternative explanation of the preverb in ὑπάρχω would be that it emphasizes the force of ἄρχω as *laying the foundation* (*underneath*) for whatever follows. Compare ὑποτίθεμαι 'to propose (a course of action)' and ὑποδέχομαι in the sense 'to promise'.

implied contrast to past or future deprivation: τῇδε ὑμῖν τῇ ἡμέρᾳ ἢ ἀγαθοῖς γενομένοις ἐλευθερίαν τε ὑπάρχειν καὶ Λακεδαιμονίων ξυμμάχοις κεκλῆσθαι 'on this day you will either show yourselves as brave men and gain your freedom and be called allies of Sparta' (or else be slaves of Athens as before) (Thuc. 5. 9. 9).

If we ignore the notion of temporal priority we see that the use of ὑπάρχειν with the dative in the last three examples makes it practically a synonym for εἶναι in the possessive construction, meaning 'belong to'. The verb may also be used without an expressed dative to mean 'on hand, available', just like εἰμί or πάρειμι (examples in LSJ s.v. ὑπάρχω B. 2). Since the use of ὑπάρχω comes to parallel that of εἰμί so closely, it is perhaps only a natural result of analogy that this verb too can be construed with a predicate adjective (even where it keeps its temporal-actual sense of 'being already available'): τὸ πλέον τοῦ χωρίου αὐτὸ καρτερὸν ὑπῆρχε καὶ | οὐδὲν ἔδει τείχους (Thuc. 4. 4. [153] 3), 'Most of the position was already (i.e. naturally) strong and required no fortification'. Thus before ὑπάρχειν becomes specialized as a verb of 'existence' we find it used in a predicative construction as an expressive equivalent for εἶναι as copula verb.

It is, however, not this copula use but the more frequent construction with the dative that accounts for the first technical use of the verb in philosophy: the use in which it expresses in logical terms the attributive relation which is normally expressed in grammatical form by the copula. Instead of 'A is B' Aristotle prefers to say τὸ B τῷ A ὑπάρχει 'B belongs to A' (Pr. An. 25ᵃ15 and throughout). Hence τὰ ὑπάρχοντα are 'attributes (of a subject)' e.g. at De Int. 16ᵇ10. (And see Bonitz, Index Arist. 789ᵃ29–ᵇ2; compare the more nontechnical use ibid. ᵃ12–28.) Since 'what belongs to a thing' includes not only its accidents but also essential or substantial attributes in the first category, ὑπάρχειν is said in as many ways as εἶναι, i.e. in as many ways as there are categories or combinations of categories (Pr. An. 48ᵇ2–4, 49ᵃ6–9). As we have seen, this use of ὑπάρχειν as equivalent in meaning to predicative εἶναι but of converse form is paralleled by κατηγορεῖσθαι (τὸ B κατὰ τοῦ A).[17] It is this attributive or predicative sense of

---

[17] Another formal equivalent to 'A belongs to B' is 'A is true of B', ἀληθεύεσθαι τόδε κατὰ τοῦδε (Pr. An. 49ᵃ6; cf. 48ᵇ2).

ὑπάρχειν which seems to underlie the later grammatical usage of the term ῥήματα ὑπαρκτικά to designate εἶναι and certain other verbs that take nominal forms as predicates. Since this class of verbs includes verbs such as ὀνομάζομαι ('I am named Charles'), it is clear that these are 'attributive' and not 'existential' verbs. Hence Priscian's decision to translate ῥῆμα ὑπαρκτικόν as *verbum substantivum* is, to say the least, misleading.[18]

Apart from this technical use in logic and grammar, the most common meaning of ὑπάρχω in later Greek seems to be that which we render as 'to exist' or 'to be real'. (This occasionally leads to rather ludicrous confusion, when a late commentator can no longer distinguish between Aristotle's technical sense and his own ordinary use of ὑπάρχειν.[19]) This later use has no special connection with the dative construction ὑπάρχειν τινί which underlies the attributive sense, although it is compatible with this construction in the early, pretechnical usage, e.g. in the passages already cited from Herodotus: αὗται αἱ νέες

---

[18] Priscian, *Inst. Gramm.* 8. 51, ed. Hertz, 1. 414. 14: ' "sum" verbo, quod ὑπαρκτικόν Graeci vocant, quod nos possumus 'substantivum' nominare'. The citation from Priscian given by Uhlig in the testimonia to Apollonius Dyscolus, *Syntaxis*, p. 29, 1 shows that Priscian regularly translated ὕπαρξις by *substantia*. The only explanation which occurs to me is the following: (1) Priscian regarded ὕπαρξις simply as equivalent to οὐσία (i.e. he had no precise grasp either of the terminological values of ὕπαρξις as 'attribution' and 'assertion' in the Greek grammarians or of the philosophical distinction mentioned below in n. 23), and (2) he was following an accepted rendering of οὐσία as *substantia*. His confusion may have been encouraged by a certain fluctuation in the use of ὕπαρξις by the Greek grammarians, illustrated in the next paragraph of this note.

Priscian aside, it is clear that ὑπαρκτικὴ σύνταξις in Apollonius is 'attributive' or 'predicative construction' (*Syntaxis*, 61. 24, Uhlig), and ὑπαρκτικὰ ῥήματα are verbs which take such a construction with nouns, pronouns, etc. There are two subclasses, verbs which say *what a thing is* (like εἶναι, γίγνεσθαι, πεφυκέναι) and those which say *what it is called* (like ὀνομάζεσθαι, καλεῖσθαι). The former make an attribution or assertion of being (ὕπαρξις οὐσιώδης), the latter an attribution of naming (ὕπαρξις ὀνοματική) (see Apoll. *Synt.* 112. 5). On the other hand, since ὑπάρχειν normally refers to attributes or properties and not to names, we find ῥήματα ὑπάρξεως used loosely for the first subclass, in contrast to ῥήματα κλήσεως (Apoll. *De Pronomine*, 52, 16). This looser terminology helps to explain Priscian's distinction between *verbum substantivum* and *verba vocativa* (*Inst. Gramm.* 1. 414. 19). The second class appears in Abelard as *verba nuncupativa*.

[19] Thus there seems to be an outright blunder in the reason Stephanus gives (in *De Int.* 14. 29–32) for rejecting ἀεὶ τῶν ὑπαρχόντων σημεῖον as a variant reading for ἀεὶ τῶν καθ' ἑτέρου λεγομένων σημεῖον in Aristotle's discussion of verbs (*De Int.* 16ᵇ7–10). The phrase would properly mean 'sign of the attributes of a subject', and is a correct paraphrase of Aristotle's text. But Stephanus takes it to mean that only verbs are a 'sign of existing things' and objects that this is not true: for substances exist too (ὑπάρχουσι γὰρ καὶ οὐσίαι), but verbs do not signify substances!

τοῖς Ἀθηναίοισι ὑπῆρχον, and εἴ σφι χώρη μηδεμία ὑπῆρχε. Although the natural translation of ὑπάρχειν here is 'be on hand', 'be available', or 'be in their possession', it is also possible to render the verb by 'be in existence'. And this nuance becomes more conspicuous (i.e. more acceptable as a translation) when the dative is lacking. Examples of ὑπάρχειν in this sense are to be found in Aristotle: ἀνάγκη τοιάνδε τὴν ὕλην ὑπάρξαι, εἰ ἔσται οἰκία 'It is necessary for matter of this sort to be present at the start (or 'to be in existence') if there is to be | a house'   [154] (*Part. An.* 639^{b}26; cf. Bonitz 789^{b}44–50; note also the predicate use with participles and adjectives, ibid. 50–7).

The hardening of this quasi-existential use of ὑπάρχειν into a fixed term seems to have occurred in the generation after Aristotle's death. The first definite example is Epicurus fr. 27 Usener (= DL X. 135) if the citation is literal: μαντικὴ οὖσα ἀνύπαρκτος, εἰ καὶ ὑπαρκτή, οὐδὲν παρ᾽ ἡμᾶς. Here the adjectives ὑπαρκτός and ἀνύπαρκτος can only be translated 'existent', 'nonexistent' (or 'real', 'unreal'). As Festugière has pointed out, this terminology is well attested in the surviving quotations from Hellenistic philosophy of the third and second centuries, and it is almost certainly a sheer accident (due to the loss of nearly all original sources for the period) if we have no example of ὕπαρξις in the sense of 'existence' or 'reality' before the time of Philodemus.[20] In philosophical Greek of the Roman period ὑπάρχειν (with its abstract nominalization ὕπαρξις) regularly serves as a synonym for εἶναι as verb of existence; for example, in Sextus' discussion of the question 'Do the gods exist?' (*Adv. Math.* 9. 29–194: the title is given as εἰ εἰσὶ θεοί, but the topic is immediately described as περὶ τῆς ὑπάρξεως τούτων σκέπτεσθαι). In Galen's *Institutio logica*, ch. 2 (p. 5 Kalbfleisch), existential statements are designated προτάσεις ὑπὲρ ἁπλῆς ὑπάρξεως and explicitly distinguished from questions of essence (= οὐσία?), in a very interesting bifurcation of Aristotle's first category. Thus the distinction between what a thing is and whether it is, first articulated in the *Posterior Analytics* but fully worked out only in the Hellenistic discussions of human knowledge of God's nature and existence, has now been incorporated into the rudiments of Aristotelian logic, and the stage is set for the medieval doctrines.

---

[20] A. J. Festugière, *La révélation d'Hermès Trismégiste* (Paris: Gabalda, 1945–54), iv. 11 n.

It should be pointed out that although this use of ὕπαρξις for real existence (in contrast to a mere word or an imaginary object) seems to be the dominant use in late Greek philosophy, the corresponding verb may still be construed both with paralocative and nominal predicates, as we can see from Sextus' discussion of the existence of the gods, e.g. 9. 143 τοῦτο δὲ παρὰ τὴν κοινὴν ἔννοιαν ὑπῆρχεν αὐτοῦ; 147 ἄτοπον δέ γε τὸ λέγειν τὸν θεὸν φθαρτὸν ὑπάρχειν. And the same predicative construction is normal for the corresponding verb *exsistere* in classical Latin (as will be seen in a moment). In neither case, then, would our familiar contrast between an existential and a copulative verb naturally arise.

I must leave open the rather difficult question of the relation between ὕπαρξις, ὑπάρχειν, on the one hand, and ὑπόστασις, ὑποστῆναι on the other in later Greek philosophy; for example, in Stoic and Neoplatonic authors.[21] And I have neither space nor skill to follow the history of *exsistere*, *exsistentia* in Latin. I note, however, that like other derivatives of *stare*, | *exsistere* serves in Varro, Lucretius, and later authors as a stylistic variant for *esse*, often with the nuance (suggested by *ex-*) of 'emerge', 'come into being', 'be produced'. As in the case of ὑπάρχειν, this quasi-existential sense of *exsistere* is fully compatible with the copulative construction: (*pecora*) *quae post tempus nascuntur, fere vitiosa atque inutilia exsistunt.*[22]

⟦155⟧

The noun *exsistentia* seems not to be attested before Marius Victorinus and Candidus in the fourth century AD. It is a learned invention, designed to render ὕπαρξις in metaphysical texts where the latter term is distinguished from οὐσία (*substantia*) as the more general concept, sheer being, without categorial determination, while οὐσία represents some determinate form of being, like 'substance' in the first Aristotelian category: 'Id est exsistentia vel subsistentia vel, si ... dicas ... vel exsistentialitatem vel substantialitatem vel essentialitatem, id est ὑπαρκτότητα,

---

[21] See H. Dörrie, 'Ὑπόστασις', *Nachrichten der Akademie der Wissenschaft zu Göttingen*, Phil.-Hist. Klasse 3 (1955), 35–92. The contrast between ὑπάρχειν and ὑφεστηκέναι is most explicit—and most problematic—in the Stoic contrast between the reality of the present and that of the past and future (Dörrie, 'Ὑπόστασις', pp. 51–2; von Arnim, *SVF* ii. 164. 26 and ii. 165. 32).

[22] Varro, *Rerum rust.* 2.1.7, cited by A. Ernout, '*Exsto* et les composés latins en *ex-*', *Bulletin de la société linguistique de Paris*, 50 (1954), 27.

οὐσιότητα, ὀντότητα'.²³ But this terminology was not taken up by Boethius, who apparently preferred *esse* to *exsistere* as a rendering of the technical use of ὑπάρχειν for pure, indeterminate being.²⁴ As we have seen, Priscian in the sixth century AD renders ὑπαρκτικόν as *substantivum*. Thus neglected by Boethius and Priscian, the technical use of *exsistentia* as contrasted with *substantia* in late Neoplatonism had no direct impact on early medieval terminology.

Abelard's usage is mixed. He often employs *exsistere*, *exsistens* for 'to exist', 'existing (thing)', but rarely uses the abstract noun and then in a rather surprising way: *exsistentiae rerum* seems to mean '(actual) states of affairs' in contrast to *res*, the existing thing, whose existence may be expressed by *esse*.²⁵ Aquinas' usage is even more Boethian: his normal expression for what we call 'existence' is *esse* or *actus essendi*. Only with the *esse existentiae* of Duns Scotus at the end of the thirteenth century do we find *existentia* firmly established as a technical term contrasted with *essentia*. Thus the modern terminology of 'existence' seems to derive from Scotus.

What connections (if any) can be traced between Scotus' use of *existentia* and the technical terminology of Victorinus nearly a millennium earlier, I do not know. In his translations of Proclus, William of Moerbeke renewed the ancient practice of rendering ὕπαρξις by

²³ *Adv. Arium*, 3. 7. 9, cited in P. Hadot, *Porphyre et Victorinus* (Paris: Études Augustiniennes, 1968), ii, p. 29, text 40. Professor Hadot calls my attention to Calcidius, in *Timaeum*, ed. Waszink, p. 289. 3, where *existentia* seems to reflect ὕπαρξις, although the Greek term is not mentioned (Calcidius is now dated later than Victorinus; Waszink, op. cit. p. xv). For the distinction between *exsistentia* and *substantia* see the citation from Candidus in *Thesaurus linguae latinae* s.v. *exsistentia*: 'exsistentia a substantia differt, quoniam exsistentia ipsum esse est et solum esse ... substantia autem non esse solum habet, sed et quale aliquid esse'. In this form the distinction can be found in Damascius (for the Greek terms ὕπαρξις and οὐσία), and is probably due to Porphyry. See the article of Hadot cited in the next note.

²⁴ Compare the key passage of Boethius' *De Hebdomadibus* with the corresponding citation from Damascius in P. Hadot, 'La distinction de l'être et de l'étant dans le "De Hebdo adibus." de Boèce', *Miscellanea Medievalia*, 2 (1963), 147, 151 n. 25. Boethius shows no trace of the *exsistentia–substantia* distinction we find in Victorinus and Candidus. It has been pointed out (by Graham, below, n. 28) that Boethius normally renders the substantival τὸ ὄν by the artificial form *ens*, but sometimes resorts to the more natural Latin form *exsistens* for the verbal-adjectival use of the Greek participle as predicate or attribute.

²⁵ *Dialectica*, 154. 11 and 156. 29. Compare Kneale and Kneale, *The Development of Logic*, p. 206.

existentia,[26] and these translations must have had some influence on the shaping of the medieval terminology. But ὕπαρξις for Proclus is not quite the same as either *exsistentia* for Victorinus or *existentia* for Scotus.[27] What role was played here by the concepts and terminology of Islamic philosophy I can only guess.[28] The history of 'existence' seems to consist largely of still unanswered questions.

---

[26] P. O. Kristeller, review article, *Journal of Philosophy* (1962), 77.

[27] For Proclus, ὕπαρξις is a preferred term for the reality of the divine principles which are beyond being (ὑπερούσιον, ἐπέκεινα τῶν ὄντων). See e.g. *The Elements of Theology,* ed. E. R. Dodds (Oxford: Clarendon, 1963), pp. 106, l. 10, and 108, ll. 25 and 32. Note that Dodds here renders ὕπαρξις by 'substance' and ὑπερούσιον by 'supra-existential'.

[28] For some remarks on the contrast between Arabic and Greek terminology for 'being', see A. C. Graham, ' "Being" in Linguistics and Philosophy', *Foundations of Language,* 1 (1965), 223 ff. For doctrinal contacts between Avicenna and Duns Scotus on the question of existence see E. Gilson, *L'être et l'essence* (Paris: Vrin, 1948), 128–31.

3

Why Existence Does Not Emerge as a Distinct Concept in Greek Philosophy[*]

In the extended discussion of the concept (or concepts) of Being in Greek philosophy from Parmenides to Aristotle, the theme of existence does not figure as a distinct topic for philosophical reflection. My aim here is to defend and illustrate this claim, and at the same time to suggest some of the reasons why it is that the concept of existence does not get singled out as a topic in its own right. Finally, I shall raise in a tentative way the question whether or not the neglect of this topic was necessarily a philosophical disadvantage.

Let me make clear that my thesis is limited to the classic period of Greek philosophy, down to Aristotle. The situation is more complicated in Hellenistic and Neoplatonic thought, for here we find two technical terms corresponding more or less to the notion of existence: the verb *hyparchō*, with its noun *hyparxis*, which renders 'existence' in modern Greek, and the verb *hypostēnai* with its noun *hypostasis*, which corresponds to the Latin verb *subsistere*, and is thus a rather close cognate of *exsistere*. I suspect that a careful study of these Greek terms would reveal that even in their usage we find no real equivalent for our concept of existence. In any case, this later terminology of *hyparxis* and *hypostasis* plays no part in the formulation of Plato's and Aristotle's ontology, and I shall ignore it here. My general view of the historical development is that existence in the modern sense becomes a

[*] This paper was originally delivered on 31 March 1976 in a session on Greek ontology in the International Philosophy Conference in New York.

central concept in philosophy only in the period when Greek ontology is radically revised in the light of a metaphysics of creation; that is
to say, under the influence of biblical religion. As far as I can see, this
development did not take place with Augustine or with the Greek
Church Fathers, who remained under the sway of classical ontology.
The new metaphysics seems to have taken shape in Islamic philosophy,
in the form of a *radical* distinction between necessary and contingent
existence: between the existence of God | on the one hand, and that of   [[324]]
the created world on the other. The old Platonic contrast between
Being and Becoming, between the eternal and the perishable (or, in
Aristotelian terms, between the necessary and the contingent) now
gets reformulated in such a way that for the contingent being of
the created world (which was originally present only as a 'possibility'
in the divine mind) the property of 'real existence' emerges as a new
attribute or 'accident', a kind of added benefit bestowed by God upon
possible beings in the act of creation. What is new here is the notion of
radical contingency: not simply the old Aristotelian idea that many
things might be other than they in fact are—that many events might
turn out otherwise—but that the whole world of nature might not
have been created at all: that it might not have *existed.*[1]

I leave it to the historians of Islamic and medieval philosophy to
decide how far my hypothesis is correct and to determine just when, or
in what stages, the new concept of existence was formulated. But, as
far as I can see, it is against the background of scholastic discussion of
the themes just mentioned that the modern concept of existence gets
separated out as a distinct topic for debate. By the modern concept
I mean the notion articulated in Descartes' doubts about existence and
in his proofs of his own existence, the existence of God, and the
existence of the external world, and further developed after Descartes
in the arguments about the existence of 'other minds'. The modern

---

[1] This is the conceptual basis for the intellectual pathos of contemporary 'existentialism', as
expressed for example by Jean-Paul Sartre in a famous passage of *La Nausée*: 'Aucun être
nécessaire ne peut expliquer l'existence: la contingence n'est pas un faux semblant, une
apparence qu'on peut dissiper; c'est l'absolu, par conséquent la gratuité parfaite. Tout est gratuit,
ce jardin, cette ville et moi-même. Personne n'a le droit; ils sont entièrement gratuits... ils
n'arrivent pas à ne pas se sentir de trop' (Paris: Gallimard, 1938; p. 185 of the *Édition de poche*).

concept of existence took a new, contemporary turn as a result of the development of quantification theory in logic. And it was applied to a new set of problems as a consequence of Russell's puzzles about denoting in the case of nonexistent subjects like 'the present king of France', as well as in the more directly puzzling case of negative existentials, like 'Santa Claus does not exist'. (It is interesting to note that although sentences of this form occur in classical Greek philosophy—'Zeus does not exist' or 'Centaurs do not exist'—their structure is never recognized as problematic. There seems to be little or no concern for the problem of reference as | such.[2]) We might summarize the modern concept of existence as the notion for which one analysis is suggested by Quine's dictum 'to be is to be the value of a variable'.

[[325]]

This brief survey of discussions of existence from Descartes to Russell and Quine is intended merely to identify what I mean by the concept of existence that does *not* emerge as a theme in Greek philosophy. It might be supposed that this nonemergence could be explained quite simply by the fact that classical Greek has no distinct verb meaning 'to exist' and hence must make do with the more general verb 'to be' (*eimi/einai*). But this explanation will not take us very far. On the one hand, it is perfectly possible to discuss questions of existence without relying on a special verb 'to exist', as Quine emphasizes in his essay 'On what *there is*', and as Descartes showed in his phrase 'Je pense, donc je *suis*'. And it seems clear that Aquinas has a theory of the existence of created things, although the verb he regularly uses to describe their existence is simply the verb 'to be' (*esse*). (Similarly, in Anselm's formulation of the ontological argument the expression for 'existence' is *esse in re*.) On the other hand, the Greek verb 'to be' has (from Homer on) a number of quite characteristic,

---

[2] There is an interesting approach to the problem of reference in Aristotle's discussion of the difference between contraries and contradictories in *Categories* 10, where he considers the different consequences for the truth-value of sentences about Socrates in the case where 'Socrates is not at all' (μὴ ὄντος ὅλως τοῦ Σωκράτους, 13ᵇ15–35). In this case it is only contradictories, and not contraries, of which one must be true and the other false. Aristotle's example is: 'Socrates is sick' will be false in this case, but 'Socrates is not sick' will be true (13ᵇ32). It is worth noting that he does not distinguish this from the parallel assertion 'Socrates is dead', which I believe he would regard as true. For I assume that what Aristotle has in mind here is the temporal existence or duration of individual living things and not existence in general, timelessly understood. See the distinction below.

idiomatic uses which we unhesitatingly recognize as 'existential'.[3] That is, ancient Greek has a set of idioms corresponding to our use of 'there is' in sentences like 'There is life on other planets' or 'There are no flying saucers'. Such idioms are used by Plato in arguing for the existence of the gods (in *Laws* 10) and by Aristotle in discussing whether or not there is an infinite or a void (in *Physics* III and v). So although the presence of a special verb 'to exist' may encourage or facilitate the emergence of existence as a distinct | philosophical topic,   [[326]] it is neither necessary nor sufficient for that development: not necessary for the reasons just given, and not sufficient because the Latin verb *exsistere* was in continual philosophical use (alongside of *esse*) from the time of Lucretius and Cicero until the end of classical antiquity without giving rise to this notion of existence—I mean, the notion which we find in Anselm and Aquinas *without* the use of a special verb. Here as elsewhere, the thesis of linguistic relativism, or linguistic determinism, tends to obscure more than it reveals.

Since I have just mentioned Plato's argument for the existence of the gods and Aristotle's discussion of the existence of the infinite and the void, I must make clear that my thesis about the nonemergence of existence as a distinct topic is not intended as a denial of the obvious fact that the Greek philosophers occasionally *discuss* questions of existence. My thesis is rather that the concept of existence is never 'thematized': it does not itself become a subject for philosophical reflection. We might say: the notion of existence is used, but never mentioned. Even this statement has to be qualified, since there are several passages in Aristotle where he shows that he is on the verge of isolating off existence as a distinct topic. For example, he distinguishes in passing between the use of 'to be' in 'Homer is a poet' and the 'absolute' use of the verb in the sentence 'Homer is' (in *De Int.* 11); and he repeatedly distinguishes in *Posterior Analytics* 2 between the questions 'What is x?' (τί ἐστι) and 'Whether x is or not?' (εἰ ἔστιν ἢ μή). Since his initial examples of this second question are 'whether there is a centaur or not' and 'whether there is (a) god' (89ᵇ32), the point of the

---

[3] I have documented these uses in some detail in Chapter 6 of *The Verb 'Be' in Ancient Greek* (Dordrecht: Reidel, 1973) (vol. vi of J. W. M. Verhaar, (ed.), *The Verb 'Be' and its Synonyms*).

εἰ ἔστι question seems clearly existential in our sense. But such passages are almost the exception that proves the rule. In the first case the sentence 'Homer is' (Ὅμηρός ἐστιν) is apparently taken to mean 'Homer is alive (now),' so that the existential sense is at best very limited and specific. And in the more systematic distinction between types of questions in *Posterior Analytics* 2, it is not at all clear that the question of existence as such (εἰ ἔστιν), ('whether X is or not') is carefully kept separate from the question of propositional fact (ὅτι ἔστι) ('whether or not X is Y' or 'whether XY is the case'). As Ross says (in commenting on 2. 1), 'the distinctions become blurred in the next chapter'.[4] Aristotle's interest seems to shift, inevitably and almost imperceptibly, | from the existence of individual substances like cen-   [327] taurs or gods to the 'existence' of states of affairs, like the moon being eclipsed. Now the interpretation of these chapters in the *Analytics* is extremely difficult, and I am not at all sure I know just what Aristotle has in mind. What does seem clear is that our difficulties of interpretation are in part due to the fact that Aristotle does not consistently regard the 'whether-X-is-or-not' question as a question about the existence or nonexistence of individual entities of a specified kind, such as centaurs or gods. Even in this passage, then, which seems to be the nearest thing to an explicit distinction of the topic of existence in Aristotle, the distinction does not quite come off.

The upshot is that, although we can recognize at least three different kinds of existential questions discussed by Aristotle, Aristotle himself neither distinguishes these questions from one another nor brings them together under any common head or topic that might be set in contrast to other themes in his general discussion of Being. The three kinds of questions (which have been carefully catalogued by G. E. L. Owen[5]) are (1) questions of individual existence over time, in the sense in which we say that a man or a block of ice comes into existence and goes out of existence (i.e. that the man dies or the ice melts); (2) questions of sortal existence, timelessly understood: whether there are

---

[4] See Ross' edition of *Aristotle's Prior and Posterior Analytics* (New York: Oxford University Press, 2003), 610–12.
[5] G. E. L. Owen, 'Aristotle on the Snares of Ontology', in R. Bambrough (ed.), *New Essays on Plato and Aristotle* (New York: Humanities, 1965), 69–95.

such things as centaurs (which Owen identifies with the modern use of the existential quantifier); and (3) more abstract or conceptual questions of existence in connection with items like the infinite, the void, and the subject matter of geometry: in what sense we want to say that such things do or do not exist. What is important to note for our purposes is that although these three topics may quite reasonably be grouped together from the point of view of the modern notion of existence, there is nothing in Aristotle's own conceptual scheme that serves to bring them together. The closest correlate to the notion of existence within Aristotle's own scheme is the concept of potency and act. And that, I suggest, is not very close.

What is true for Aristotle is true a fortiori for Parmenides and Plato. And here I will turn from documenting the absence of existence as such to the more constructive task of identifying the decisive concept that in fact dominates the view of Being in classical | Greek ontology.   [[328]]
More precisely, I want to point to the concept that determines the meaning or sense of 'Being' (τὸ ὄν) when the term is first introduced into philosophic discussion, in the poem of Parmenides and the early statement of Plato's theory of Forms.

My claim, then, is that the concept of Being in Parmenides and Plato—and to some extent in the later tradition as well—is understood primarily by reference to the notion of truth and the corresponding notion of reality. The question of Being is first of all the question of the nature of reality or the structure of the world, in the very general sense of 'the world' which includes whatever we can know or investigate and whatever we can describe in true or false statements. The question of Being, then, for the Greek philosophers is: How must the world be structured in order for inquiry, knowledge, science, and true discourse (or, for that matter, false discourse) to be possible? In linguistic terms, this means that the decisive usage of the verb in the creation of Greek ontology is what I call the veridical use, in which the verb *esti* means 'is true' or 'is the case'.

Before pursuing this thesis I must pause for a few linguistic remarks. Plato and (even more) Parmenides have often been accused of confusing or conflating the copula and the existential uses of 'to be', and hence of producing the pseudoconcept of Being by the mistaken assumption that the verb had a single meaning when used for

predication and for statements of existence. I do not wish to deny that such confusions sometimes arise in Greek philosophy: I insist only that they play no essential role in the creation and articulation of the concept of Being by Parmenides and Plato. They play no essential role because both predication (with a copula use of 'to be') and statements of existence (with an existential use of the verb) may be regarded as special cases of the more general and more fundamental use of 'to be' to express the content of a truth claim as such: the so-called veridical use to affirm a propositional content or an objective state of affairs. Since I have illustrated this use in detail elsewhere, and have pointed to its archaic origins in the prehistoric use of the Indo-European participle *sant- (corresponding to Greek ὄν, ὄντος), in the common Indo-European usage represented in the old English word 'sooth', and the Sanskrit forms *sat* and *satya*, I need here only remind you that this prehistoric idiom is alive and well in colloquial American English today, in the locution 'Tell it like it *is*'. The 'is' here is a pure veridical. The peculiar grammatical features of the veridical | use are   [329]
(1) that its understood subject is propositional in form—a fact or a state of affairs asserted to obtain, and not an object or concept whose existence is affirmed—and (2) that it is typically construed (without any predicate) in a clause of comparison with verbs of saying or knowing (*verba sentiendi et dicendi*): '*Tell* it *like* it is'. Thus the canonical form of the veridical construction of 'to be' in Greek, from Homer on, is as follows: 'Things are (in fact) as you say (or think or know) them to be' ἔστι ταῦτα οὕτω ὥσπερ σὺ λέγεις. As this locution shows, the prephilosophic conception of truth in Greek (and in Indo-European generally, if not in all languages) involves some kind of correlation or 'fit' between what is said or thought, on one side, and *what is* or *what is the case* or *the way things are* on the other side. Let us call this the correlation between assertion and reality, where 'assertion' is used neutrally both for *saying that it is so* and *thinking that it is so*; and 'reality' is used simply as a convenient abbreviation for *the fact that it is so* or *what happens to be the case*.

My claim, then, is that in the formation of the Greek concept of Being, the key notion is that of truth—the goal of science and the proper aim of declarative speech. If we bear in mind the structure of the veridical use of the verb, we will easily see how the philosophers' interest in knowledge and truth, taken together with this use of 'to be', immediately leads to the concept of Being as reality. I repeat, I am using 'reality' here not in any large metaphysical sense but simply as a convenient term for the facts that make true statements true and false statements false, or for whatever it is 'in the world', for whatever 'is the case', that makes some assertions and some judgments correct and others mistaken. If I assert—either in thought or in speech—that the sun is shining, and if what I assert is true, then the corresponding 'reality' is simply the fact that the sun is shining.

So far I have said nothing about *be* as verb of existence or as copula. I have shown only that starting from the veridical locutions and the notion of Being as truth, we immediately get to the related notion of Being as reality, in a suitably loose and generalized sense of 'reality'. Of course, we can easily see how the existential and copula uses of *be* will also turn up, if we think of the reality in question as expressed by a subject–predicate sentence—for instance by the sentence 'The sun is shining'. For if this sentence is true, then its subject (the sun) must exist. And the sentence uses the copula verb *is* to predicate something of this subject; namely, *that* | *it is shining*, or *that its light reaches us*. So when we are talking [330] about truth and reality, the existential and copulative uses of *be* are never far away. But I insist that if we *begin* to interpret the concept of Being by looking for existential or copula uses of the verb, we will not only make unnecessary trouble for ourselves; we may miss the real point. We will fail to grasp the essential features of the Greek concept of Being.

Consider now what Parmenides says about Being or *what is*, τὸ ἐόν. He introduces it (in fragment 2) as the object for knowledge and the territory or homeland of truth. 'These are the only ways of inquiry there are for knowing (*or* 'for understanding', *noēsai*): the one, *that it is* ... the other *that it is not.*' The former he calls 'the path of Persuasion, for she follows upon Truth'; in other words, Being, or *what is*, is what we can and should believe (be persuaded by), because it leads to (or is identical with) truth. The other path (*that it is not*) he rejects as 'unheard of' or 'uninformative' (*panapeuthēs*), a way that cannot be trusted, 'for you cannot know *what is not* ... nor can you point it out'. Parmenides' explicit reason here for rejecting *what is not*, τὸ μὴ ἐόν is that it cannot be an object of knowledge (*gnōnai*), a path for understanding (*noēsai*), or a topic of informative discourse (*phrazein*).

Since in Greek the expressions τὸ μὴ ὄν and τὰ μὴ ὄντα would normally designate the content of lies and false belief, it is obvious why these labels will not signify an object of knowledge or reliable information. The peculiarly Parmenidean touch is to identify 'the thing that is not', as the content of falsehood and error, with *nothing* or nonentity (μηδέν at Parmenides 8. 10: cf. 6. 2).

I submit: The guiding thought at the outset of Parmenides' poem, the thought which motivates his articulation of the concept of Being, is the idea of Truth as the goal of knowledge and inquiry. But of course the 'being' which is known and truly asserted must be a 'reality' in the very general sense indicated earlier. So for Parmenides the veridical notion of Being leads directly to the concept of Reality as opposed to Appearance or false Seeming: Being and Truth—*to eon* and *Alētheia*—are explicitly contrasted with the erroneous Opinions (or Seemings, *doxai*) of mortals. By setting this contrast between true Reality and false or mistaken Appearance at the center of his doctrine, Parmenides passes beyond the commonsense, pretheoretical notion of 'reality' implied by the ancient locutions for truth, and articulates for the first time a metaphysical concept of Being. |

[331]   Parmenides' theory of Being has many other aspects which are not directly accounted for by the veridical sense of the verb: its contrast with Becoming, for example—that is to say, its eternal and perfectly static character as an entity that cannot change or move—and also its spatial extension and indivisible bodily mass. My aim here is not to offer a complete account, not even a general sketch, of Parmenides' ontology, but simply to identify the concept that gives meaning to his quest, the concept that can permit us to understand what the Greek project of ontology was all about. Now aside from the properties of spatial location and bodily mass, the Eleatic attributes of Being are all preserved in the ontology which Plato develops for the Forms in the middle dialogues. A brief look at the *Phaedo* (65–6), where the general doctrine of Forms is introduced for the first time by a systematic use of the terminology of Being (ὄν, οὐσία)[6], or a glance at the even more

---

[6] See, for example, Burnet's comments on *Phaedo* 65c3 and 65c9 (in his edition of the dialogue), and my own fuller statement of these remarks about Parmenides and Plato in 'Linguistic Relativism and the Greek Project of Ontology', in G. M. C. Sprung (ed.), *The Question of Being* (University Park, Pa.: Pennsylvania State University Press, [1977]).

Parmenidean passage in *Republic* 5 (478–80), where τὸ ὄν as stable object of knowledge is contrasted with the many sensible particulars that are object of *doxa*, would suffice to show that here too the initial clue, the key to the concept of Being in Plato as in Parmenides, is provided by the notions of truth and knowledge, and by the very general concept of reality or what is so that is required by these two notions.

In the first instance, then, Being for Plato is characterized as the reality which is sought after in intellectual inquiry, apprehended in noetic cognition, and described or defined in true discourse. But when we pass from these general 'veridical' contours to a more detailed analysis, the copula construction emerges as the primary formula for the articulation of the concept of truth and its grounding in the reality of the Forms. Every truth for Plato can properly be expressed in the copula form 'X is Y'. Even the existential proposition can be so expressed: 'Justice exists' is expressed as 'Justice is something (*ti*)'. Now the copula proposition in turn is to be interpreted ontologically in terms of participation: 'X is Y' is true only if and because X participates in Y-ness or in the Y. In the last analysis, I suggest, Plato's concept of Being is the being-of-a-Form, or the being-related-to-a-Form by way of participation. | The concepts of truth and predication,   〚332〛 which concern statement and knowledge, are grounded upon these more fundamental notions of Being which concern the nature of things: Forms and participation.

Summarizing our positive results so far, we can say: in Greek ontology, from Parmenides on, the question of Being is a question as to what reality must be like—or what the world must be like—in order for knowledge and true (or false) discourse to be possible. It is, in effect, the first question which Wittgenstein set out to answer in the *Tractatus*: How must the world be structured if logic and scientific language are to be possible? Since for Plato knowledge is assimilated to discourse, and discourse is analyzed in the predicative form 'X is Y', the problem of knowledge and true discourse becomes, in part at least, the problem of predication: What must reality be like if predications like 'X is Y' are to be possible, and sometimes true? What will X be like? What will Y be like? And how can the two be related to one another?

In Aristotle the concept of Being becomes more complex—too complex for summary statement here. We would have to begin by analyzing the doctrine of the categories, and go on to consider the concepts of potency and act. Let me remark only that the scheme of the categories, which is formulated as a device for distinguishing types of predication, serves in effect for analyzing types of existence as well. To the various forms of predication recognized by the division into categories correspond so many different modes of existence. The most fundamental mode is of course that of the primary category, the being of substances; that is to say, the existence of individual entities of a definite kind—which in the paradigm case means the existence of a living organism belonging to a definite species: a human being, or a horse, or a pine tree. For Socrates *to exist* is for him *to be a (living) man*, to live a human life; for a particular tree to exist is for it to be a living oak or chestnut. For white *to exist* is *to be a color*; that is, a quality, belonging to some particular substance. For walking *to exist* is *to be an action* performed by some man or animal. Thus the general tendency of this Aristotelian method in ontology is for the existential idea to be absorbed into the theory of predication, and to be expressed linguistically by copula uses of the verb. So we find that the key ontological formula of Aristotle's metaphysics, the τὸ τί ἦν εἶναι, defines the mode of existence for any subject whatsoever, but it does so without any existential use of the verb. The concrete being of Socrates is a | [333] compound of matter and form, body and psyche; but the matter itself is determined by the essence, the τὸ τί ἦν εἶναι for man, the being-what-it-is. Socrates' being or existence is his being-human, his being-what-a-man-is; that is to say, his being that particular kind of thing that is specified in the definition which answers to the question: What is X? What is a human being (τί ἐστιν ἄνθρωπος)? Thus for Aristotle, as for Plato, existence is always εἶναί τι, being something or other, being something definite. There is no concept of existence, as such, for subjects of an indeterminate nature.

To return now to the question with which we began: that of why existence does not emerge as a distinct concept in Greek philosophy. In principle the answer is clear. My explanation is that in Greek ontology in its early stages, in Plato and Parmenides, the veridical concept was primary, and the question of Being was the question of 'reality', as determined by the concept of truth. Since this conception of reality is articulated in Plato by copula sentences of the form 'X is Y', it turns out that even the concept of existence gets expressed in this predicative form: as we have seen, Platonic Greek for 'X exists' is 'X is something', εἶναί τι. In the scheme of categories which Aristotle takes as the starting point for his own investigation of being, this same predicative pattern serves as the primary device for analyzing τὰ ὄντα, *what there is*, and for showing how the various kinds of being are related to one another. So it is naturally the theory of predication, and not the concept of existence, that becomes the central and explicit theme of Aristotle's metaphysics, as it was the implicit theme of Plato's discussion of Being in the *Sophist*.

If we conclude, now, by raising the question whether it was a philosophical disadvantage for Greek ontology to begin with the concept of truth and reality (as object of knowledge and the content of true statement), and whether it was a mistake to proceed by developing a theory of predication and neglecting the concept of existence as such, we cannot hope to answer such a question with any brief statement. I will simply hint at the line which a defense of Greek ontology might pursue. Let us imagine Parmenides, Plato, and Aristotle responding as follows.

Granted that our starting point in ontology does not provide a theory of reference or denotation, and hence does not confront the problems of negative existentials or statements about nonexistent subjects. After all, a discipline in its initial stages cannot hope to deal with *all* of the problems. But by articulating our own | doctrines of being around the topics of truth and   [334] predication we pointed to the notions of propositional analysis and truth for sentences or statements (λόγος) that provide the conceptual framework within which a theory of reference and a clear account of existence becomes possible. It is scarcely necessary to defend our achievements by pointing to the contemporary relevance of a Platonizing ontology for the discussion of universals and the theory of mathematical objects (numbers, sets, etc.), or to the obvious role which Aristotelian ideas about individuals, predication, and natural kinds continue to play in modern work in ontology, logic, and theory of language. We should perhaps emphasize what is less obvious: that the veridical starting point for Greek theories of Being or reality anticipates in a rather striking way the contemporary standpoint which (following and developing certain ideas of Tarski) takes the notion of truth for sentences as basic in any theory of meaning and knowledge. (Consider the view of Donald Davidson in his presidential address 'On the Very Idea of a Conceptual Scheme',[7] or the parallel doctrine which Henry Hiz calls 'aletheism'.) Above all, we would insist that the articulation of Greek theories of reality around the topics of truth and predication or λόγος guarantees that philosophical speculation—as long as it is faithful to this starting point—will remain in close contact with genuine problems of knowledge in the sciences and with careful work in logic.

Now we must admit (these philosophers will conclude) that our neglect of the topic of existence as such does leave us without any ready means of formulating Cartesian doubts about the existence of the external world, just as it also leaves us without the concept of existence that provides the nerve of Anselm's ontological argument. From the standpoint of our ontologies, no one could ever have formulated either Anselm's argument or Descartes's radical doubts about existence. But, depending upon one's view of the value of the ontological argument and the philosophical importance of skepticism concerning the external world, these deficiencies in our standpoint could perhaps be counted as assets rather than as liabilities.

---

[7] *Proceedings and Addresses of the American Philosophical Association*, 47 (1973–74), esp. pp. 16 ff.

4

Some Philosophical Uses of 'To Be' in Plato[*]

I here discuss two sets of passages where Plato uses the verb εἶναι (and its nominal forms ὄν and οὐσία) in a philosophically loaded way, in connection with the notion of truth. I suggest that the systematic nature of this connection has not been recognized and hence its philosophical significance has not been properly understood.

Syntactically, the passages in question are a mixed bag. In a few cases we have what I call the *veridical construction* with a subject of sentential rather than nominal form: the verb is construed absolutely (no further predicate is expressed or understood), and it is syntactically linked to a clause of thinking or saying.[1] In other cases, where the subject (or implied subject) is a noun phrase, an absolute construction of the verb may bear an existential sense. Most often, however, εἶναι will function as copula with predicate adjective, noun, or prepositional phrase.

In cases where no predicate is expressed there has been a tendency of late to describe the use of the verb as 'incomplete' and to construe it as an elliptical copula, i.e. to interpret an expression of the form *X is* as elliptical for *X is Y*, where the value of *Y* is either specified by the

---

* The first version of this paper was presented to Professor Aubenque's seminar on Greek ontology at the Sorbonne in February 1980. I want to thank Pierre Aubenque for his kind invitation to address the seminar, and for thus inducing me to return to some unfinished business on *to be*. I am also grateful to Jonathan Barnes, Lesley Brown, and Christopher Kirwan for detailed comments on an early draft.

[1] The full veridical construction involves a clause of comparison with the verb of thinking or saying: ἔστι ταῦτα οὕτως ὡς σὺ λέγεις ('Things are just as you say'), or in English, 'Tell it like it is!'. See my *The Verb 'Be' in Ancient Greek* (Dordrecht: Reidel, 1973), 334–6.

context or left quite general.[2] I do not want to deny the appropriateness of such an interpretation in many cases, perhaps in most. But I want to insist that the uses of εἶναι in Plato (as in Greek generally) are often *overdetermined*: several grammatical readings of a single occurrence are not only possible but sometimes required for the full understanding of the text. (Whether or not fallacy arises from such ambiguity is a question that must be considered separately for each case.)

Even where the syntax is unambiguous, a copula use of the verb may bear a veridical value; that is to say, it may serve to call attention to the truth claim that is implicit in every declarative sentence. This function of the verb, which I have elsewhere called the veridical *nuance* or veridical *lexical value*, is not so clearly defined a notion as the veridical construction. It is unmistakable in those cases where a use of εἶναι is naturally translated as 'is true', 'is so', or 'is the case'; but these are typically not copula constructions. In the copula use a veridical nuance emerges whenever there is any contrast between being so and seeming so, between being *really* such and such and being only *called* such and such or *believed to be* such | and such. Just as in the veridical construction [106 proper there is an explicit comparison between a clause with εἶναι and a clause with a verb of saying or thinking, so in the wider range of uses with veridical nuance there is a contrast, expressed or implied, between how things *are* and how they *seem*, i.e. how they are said or believed to be. The classical example of this is a line from Aeschylus:

οὐ γὰρ δοκεῖν ἄριστος, ἀλλ᾽ εἶναι θέλει.

('He wants not to appear but to be the noblest.')

(*Septem* 592)[3]

Parallels from other languages make clear that this veridical value for εἶναι is an inheritance from Indo-European, where the verb and its participle *⋆sant-* seem to have been used in juridical contexts for 'the facts of the case' or the person who is *really the culprit* and not merely accused or suspected.[4] So in a context of inquiry τὸ ὄν signifies 'the fact'

---

[2] See e.g. John McDowell, *Plato: Theaetetus* (Oxford: Clarendon, 1973), 118; David Gallop, *Plato: Phaedo* (Oxford: Clarendon, 1975), 92, following G. E. L. Owen and others.

[3] For this and other examples of copula with veridical value see *The Verb 'Be'*, pp. 356–60.

[4] *The Verb 'Be'*, pp. 332 with n. 2, 355 with n. 6, 359 n. 28. Thus *sons* (= ὤν) in Latin means 'guilty', *insons* 'innocent'. See A. Ernout and A. Meillet, *Dictionnaire étymologique de la langue latine*

or the truth one is trying to get at. The range of idomatic uses reflects (or explains) the role of εἶναι as privileged signal for the truth claim that is implicit in the indicative form of every declarative sentence.[5] Thus the minimal case of a veridical value for ἐστί is simply an emphatic assertion. Let me briefly illustrate these points from Aristotle, before turning to Plato. We have the veridical construction proper in *Met. Γ.* 7, where Aristotle defines truth as saying of what-is *that it is* and of what-is-not *that it is not*, and falsehood conversely:

τὸ μὲν γὰρ λέγειν τὸ ὂν μὴ εἶναι ἢ τὸ μὴ ὂν εἶναι ψεῦδος, τὸ δὲ τὸ ὂν εἶναι καὶ τὸ μὴ ὂν μὴ εἶναι ἀληθές (101. 1ᵇ26–7).

Here the participial forms ('what-is' and 'what-is-not') refer to states of affairs in the world, to positive and negative facts as it were, while the infinitival clauses ('that it is', 'that it is not') represent the propositional content asserted: what is *said* to be the case. I see no trace of the copula construction here, no suggestion that a predicate is to be supplied or understood for 'to be'.

In *Met. Δ.* 7, on the other hand, the use of εἶναι to signify truth (ὅτι ἀληθές) is illustrated by an ordinary copula construction, with the verb in the emphatic initial position: ὅτι ἔστι Σωκράτης μουσικός, ὅτι ἀληθὲς τοῦτο. Word order is of rhetorical rather than grammatical significance in Greek, and an initial ἔστι does not in general call for a veridical interpretation.[6] What Aristotle tells us (and what we might not otherwise guess) is that he recognizes the veridical idea, the distinct expression of a truth claim, in a standard copula use of ἐστί, at least when that use is sufficiently emphatic. Or perhaps we should say that Aristotle reads ἐστί here twice: once as | copula ('Socrates is musical')   [[107]] and once as veridical sentence-operator ('*It is true that* Socrates is musical'). For in his negative example τὸ δ' οὐκ ἔστιν ἡ διάμετρος σύμμετρος, ὅτι ψεῦδος, where the negation can be read either internally ('the diagonal is not commensurate') or externally ('it is not the case that the diagonal is commensurate'), the latter reading seems to be indicated

---

(Paris: Klicksieck, 1985), s.v. *sons*. Compare the impersonal use in Greek: τὰς δίκας ἀποβαίνειν κατὰ τὸ ἐόν, 'to render justice according to the facts', in Hdt. 1.97.1. Other Herodotean examples of τὸ ἐόν for 'the facts' under investigation are cited in *The Verb 'Be'*, pp. 352–3.

[5] For further discussion see *The Verb 'Be'*, pp. 186–91, 369–70, 407–8.

[6] *The Verb 'Be'*, pp. 424–5.

by Aristotle's own statement ὅτι ψεῦδος: ('this means) that it is a falsehood (sc. to say *that it is commensurate*)'. If, following this clue, we read the veridical sentence operator into the copula construction here, we have a clear case of what I call overdetermination: a single occurrence of the verb that requires two readings for a full understanding.

I

My first set of Platonic passages involves the terminology of the doctrine of Forms in four different dialogues. In the first example, from the *Lysis*, that doctrine is itself not stated but some of the relevant terminology is introduced, probably for the first time.

(1) At *Lysis* 219c the regress of one-thing-dear-for-the-sake-of-another is broken by the prospect of reaching 'an ἀρχή which will no longer refer us to something else dear, but we will arrive at *that which is primarily dear* (ἐκεῖνο ὅ ἐστιν πρῶτον φίλον), for the sake of which we say all other things are dear'. The pronoun ἐκεῖνο with the phrase ὅ ἐστιν introducing the name or predicate for a Form will become a familiar part of the later terminology, which is also anticipated here in the comparison of many other dear things to images (εἴδωλα) of the one primary φίλον (219d3). Our present interest lies, however, less in the anticipation of things to come than in the veridical value placed upon the copula construction ὅ ἐστιν. This value would not be clear from the first occurrence just cited from 219c7; but it is brought out in the sequel by the contrast between the deceptive images and their original, 'that primary thing, which is truly dear' (ἐκεῖνο τὸ πρῶτον, ὃ ὡς ἀληθῶς ἐστι φίλον, 219d4–5).[7] And the same value is reasserted in the opposition between 'what is really dear' (τὸ τῷ ὄντι φίλον, 220b1 and b4) and those things which are dear for the

---

[7] Readers have objected (1) that ὡς ἀληθῶς (like τῷ ὄντι in what follows) can be rendered 'really' or 'genuinely' instead of 'truly', and (2) that hence all connection with the notion of truth is lost. I agree with (1) but not with (2). The notion of a genuine *F* is logically dependent upon the claim that something is truly (and literally) *F*. Thus fake diamonds and decoy ducks are not truly diamonds and ducks; i.e. it is not (literally) true to say that they are diamonds and ducks. A thing is really *F*, or is a genuine *F*, if and only if it is truly *F*; i.e. if and only if it is (literally) true to say of the thing *that it is F*.

sake of something else and hence only nominally dear (ῥήματι φαινόμεθα λέγοντες αὐτό, b1). Plato's future doctrine of eponymy, that particulars are 'named after' the Forms in which they participate (*Phaedo* 78e2, 102b2), is here adumbrated, and the notion of truth is introduced in a way that is also characteristically Platonic: to a descriptive term or predicate 'F' (in this case 'φίλον') there corresponds a unique entity of which this term is true without qualification; the term applies to other things derivatively, in virtue of their | relation to this   ⟦108⟧ privileged paradigm (which is here called 'the primary F'; in later dialogues it will be 'the F itself').

(2) *Symposium* 210e. In his first dazzling but sharply focussed statement of the standard doctrine, Plato introduces us to a single Form, in a sudden vision of 'something beautiful of a marvelous nature, that very thing (τοῦτο ἐκεῖνο) *for the sake of which* our previous labors were undertaken'. The description opens with a good example of the overdetermined or overworked use of εἶναι: πρῶτον μὲν ἀεὶ ὄν... ἔπειτα οὐ τῇ μὲν καλόν, τῇ δ' αἰσχρόν, οὐδὲ τοτὲ μέν, τοτὲ δὲ οὔ. The participle ὄν naturally takes the strong 'existential' value with ἀεί ('is eternally', 'is forever') echoing the Homeric formula θεοὶ αἰὲν ἐόντες and immediately paralleled not only by οὔτε γιγνόμενον οὔτε ἀπολλύμενον but also by οὔτε αὐξανόμενον οὔτε φθίνον, which do not take the predicative construction. Initially, then, there is no reason to construe the participle as copula, incomplete or otherwise. But of course it does provide the verb of predication on which to hang the following antithetical phrases (and so we have ὡς τισὶ μὲν ὂν καλόν at 211a5). Hence the predicative phrases τῇ μὲν καλόν, πρὸς μὲν τὸ καλόν, etc. in the rest of the sentence do permit us to go back and see that ἀεὶ ὄν can be read not only as 'this beautiful thing is forever' but also as 'this thing is forever beautiful'. The existential use in ἀεὶ ὄν is pregnant with the incomplete copula. But it would be a mistake to *eliminate* the first construal in favor of the second, since we would then lose not only the Homeric overtones but the rhetorical balance with the immediately following participles. We must recognize both the absolute construction (explicitly) and the copula syntax (implicitly) as part of the total meaning of the text. And so likewise for αὐτὸ καθ' αὑτὸ μεθ' αὑτοῦ μονοειδὲς ἀεὶ ὄν at 211b1–2: both 'it is always uniform' and also 'it is eternal, exists forever'.

At 211c7–d1 we encounter the ἐκεῖνο ὅ ἐστι formula familiar from the *Lysis*: ἐπ' ἐκεῖνο τὸ μάθημα τελευτῆσαι, ὅ ἐστιν οὐκ ἄλλου ἦ αὐτοῦ ἐκείνου τοῦ καλοῦ μάθημα, καὶ γνῷ αὐτὸ τελευτῶμ. ὅ ἐστι καλόν:[8] '(One passes from beautiful studies) to come finally to *that very* study *which is* study of nothing but *that very Beautiful itself*, and one ends by knowing this, (namely) what *is* beautiful', or perhaps: '*what beautiful is.*' There is an ambiguity in the syntax of ὅ ἐστι καλόν which we shall find again in the *Phaedo*: καλόν may be construed either as subject or as predicate with ἐστί. The predicate syntax is favored by the parallel with μάθημα above and by the absence of the article with καλόν. (But compare *Phaedo* 65d4, cited below, where δίκαιον αὐτό without the article must be subject.) Since we have, in effect, an 'is' of definitional equivalence, the distinction between subject and predicate is of no logical significance.[9] It is important that the | term following ἐστί does *not* take the article, and thus preserves its form as a predicate (as G. E. L. Owen has pointed out); and this remains true even if one wanted to construe it here as grammatical subject, on the analogy with the what-is-X question: 'to know what beautiful is' would be to know the full sense of the term, and perhaps its privileged reference as well (i.e. the entity of which it is uniquely true). If καλόν is taken as predicate, ἐστί should carry a strong veridical charge: 'to know (the beautiful) itself, the one thing that is *truly* beautiful'. (Compare ὃ ὡς ἀληθῶς ἐστι φίλον above from *Lysis* 219d5.) The account of the vision ends in any case with an emphasis on the notion of truth: the philosophical initiate 'begets not images of virtue, since he has not been in contact with an image, but true virtue, since he has been in contact with truth' (τὸ ἀληθές, 212a5).

(3) In the fuller statement of the doctrine of Forms in the *Phaedo*, the first mention of Forms is preceded by the question: 'When does the soul grasp truth?' (ἀλήθεια, 65b9). The veridical value of the participles which follow (τὰ ὄντα, 65c3, τὸ ὄν, c9), and the systematic exchange

[[109]]

---

[8] Here and in what follows I ignore the orthotone accent which Burnet prints for ἐστί, presumably in those cases where he regards its use as particularly emphatic. On the accent of ἐστί see *The Verb 'Be'*, app. A.

[9] See below, Appendix on the grammar of ὅ ἐστι F. I leave open the question whether or not it is appropriate to speak here of the 'is' of identity, and thus to construe the two terms as *names*. But since in a definition the two designations of the same concept are at least logically equivalent, the subject–predicate relation can go either way.

between τὰ ὄντα (66a3), τὸ ὄν (66a8, c2) and ἀλήθεια (66a6), τὸ ἀληθές (66b7, d7, 67b1) in this connection was correctly noted by Burnet and has been discussed elsewhere.[10] Throughout this passage the participle is construed absolutely, with the sense of 'truth' or 'true reality', as the object sought in the philosopher's quest for knowledge (cf. ζήτησις at 65a10, σκοπεῖν at b10, ζητεῖ at d1, etc.). This is the ordinary notion of truth associated with any inquiry into 'the facts'; Plato's terminology here differs from Herodotus' use of τὸ ἐόν only by the strongly theoretical context in which it is embedded. A more technical formulation begins to appear at 65d4: φαμέν τι εἶναι δίκαιον αὐτὸ ἢ οὐδέν; 'Do we say that (the) just itself is something or nothing?'.[11] Note that the claim of existence is expressed by the grammatical copula: to exist is to be *something*. Veridical idea, existence claim, and predicative syntax are all taken up in the nominalization of the verb οὐσία at 65d13, in Plato's first generalized reference to the Forms: '(I am speaking) of the being (οὐσία) of all those things, what each one really is', (περὶ) ἁπάντων τῆς οὐσίας ὃ τυγχάνει ἕκαστον ὄν. The phrase ὃ τυγχάνει ὄν is a strengthened version of ὅ ἐστι which seems to underscore its veridical force ('what a given thing really is', Burnet; 'what each one actually is', Gallop). The question whether ἕκαστον is subject or predicate of the copula is probably as unanswerable here as at *Symp.* 211c8. To speak of *what F is* or of *what is (truly) F* is, for Plato, to speak of the same thing.

We can say that the formula ὅ ἐστι represents an 'is' of equivalence in a formula for essence, an answer to the Socratic request for a definition, like | Aristotle's τὸ τί ἐστι or τὸ τί ἦν εἶναι. But it would be misleading to say that οὐσία here means 'essence'; it is simply a nominalization for the various uses of εἶναι, among which ὅ ἐστι will emerge as the most important. [110]

[10] See 'Linguistic Relativism and the Greek Project of Ontology', in G. M. C. Sprung (ed.), *The Question of Being: East–West Perspectives* (University Park, Pa.: Pennsylvania State University Press, 1977).

[11] Gallop's translation 'Do we say that there is something *just*, or nothing?' renders the sense correctly but it is not plausible as a reflection of the syntax. ('There is something just' would presumably be εἶναι δίκαιόν τι.) The construction is clear from the parallel at 74a12: φῶμέν τι εἶναι (sc. αὐτὸ τὸ ἴσον) ἢ μηδέν, 'Do we say that it is something or nothing?'. In this case Gallop's translation 'Are we to say that there *is* something or nothing?' seems to me wrong.

The doctrine stated at 65d is developed systematically from 74a–b with the introduction of αὐτὸ τὸ ἴσον. We begin by recognizing the existence of such an entity (with the copula construction as at 65d4: φῶμέν τι εἶναι ἢ μηδέν; 74a12 'Do we say it is something or nothing?'), followed by the indirect question with ὅ ἐστι: 'And do we know what it is?' ἦ καὶ ἐπιστάμεθα αὐτὸ ὅ ἐστιν.[12] The phrase 'what it is' (ὅ ἐστιν) is then used with the article as a technical label for the Form: 'do equal sticks and the like seem to us to be equal in the same way as the *what-it-is* itself?' (οὕτως ἴσα εἶναι ὥσπερ αὐτὸ τὸ ὅ ἐστιν, 74d6). And so in a second technical or frozen use at 75b1: the sensible equals strive after ἐκείνου τοῦ ὅ ἐστιν ἴσον, 'that very *what-is-equal*', in a phrase where the subject–predicate construction of ἴσον is again indeterminate. But the underlying syntax of an indirect question after 'to know' immediately reappears at 75b6: 'having acquired knowledge of the equal itself (sc. knowledge of), what it is' (εἰληφότας ἐπιστήμην αὐτοῦ τοῦ ἴσου ὅτι ἐστίν).

Plato thus moves deliberately back and forth between idiomatic and quasi-technical uses of the phrase ὅ ἐστι before focussing on it as the official designation for the Forms at 75d2: 'Our argument now does not concern the equal more than the beautiful itself and the good itself and just and holy and, as I say, it concerns all those things on which we set this seal of the *what-it-is* (τὸ ὅ ἐστι), both in the questions that we ask and in the answers that we give' (75c10–d3).[13] Here the formula with the frozen veridical-copula ἐστί is explicitly set within the framework of dialectical inquiry, pursued in questions like 'What is the equal?', 'What is the pious?'. And we have the same framework in our final passage from the *Phaedo*, the summary reference at 78d1–4 to

---

[12] This is Burnet's text, based on BT, representing a standard form of indirect question, as in *Symp.* 211c8. (For the use of the simple relative ὅς instead of the indirect relative ὅστις in indirect questions see H. W. Smyth, *Greek Grammar*, rev. G. Messing (Cambridge, MA: Harvard University Press, 1956), 601, § 2668; R. Kühner and B. Gerth, *Ausführliche Grammatik* (Hanover/Leipzig: Hahn, 1904), 438, § 562.4.) The variant αὐτὸ ὅ ἐστιν ἴσον (in W and in margins of B and T) would be less natural, but exactly parallel to αὐτὸ ὅ ἐστι καλόν at *Symp.* 211c8; cf. τὸ ὅ ἐστιν ἴσον at *Phaedo* 75b1. Such parallels explain the variant, but are not evidence for what Plato wrote here. We have the same variant at 74d7, with ἴσον after τὸ ὅ ἐστιν in T and a second hand of B: here Robin prints αὐτὸ τὸ ὅ ἐστιν ἴσον.

[13] Burnet reads τὸ αὐτὸ ὅ ἐστι 'the what-it-is itself', where the MSS have τοῦτο, Iamblichus τό. I prefer to read τοῦτο τὸ ὅ ἐστι (proposed also by Gallop: *Plato* 230). Loriaux keeps τοῦτο ὅ ἐστι, with the MSS (see R. Loriaux, *Le Phédon de Platon* (Namur: Secretariat des publications, facultés universitaires, 1969), i. 151).

the whole range of Forms as a privileged mode of being: 'this very reality (αὐτὴ ἡ οὐσία) of whose being (τοῦ εἶναι) we give an account in questions and answers ... the equal itself, the beautiful itself, each what-it-is (ὅ ἐστι) itself, true being (τὸ ὄν)'. Here in four lines we have four verbal or nominalized occurrences of εἶναι: (i) the abstract nominalization οὐσία, which has no value over and above the range of meanings for the verb throughout this passage (as in 65d13, above), where the implicit 'What-is-it?' question with veridical-definitional force (What is it *really*?) prepares for the sense of 'essence' or 'what-ness', as in the phrase λόγος τῆς οὐσίας for 'definition' (which we will encounter in *Republic* 7, but can see emerging here in λόγον δίδομεν τοῦ εἶναι); (ii) the infinitive τὸ εἶναι of which one gives an account, i.e. the 'What-is-it?' | that figures as question and answer in dialectic; (iii) [[111]] the frozen version of the question (or answer) as a designation for the Form: αὐτὸ ἕκαστον ὅ ἐστιν (at 78d4, repeated without αὐτό in the next line); and (iv) the veridical participle τὸ ὄν, originally introduced as a general designation for truth (or true reality) as the object of which philosophers are in search, but now given more precise content by the systematic use of the verb in articulating the notion of Forms in 74–6.[14] (Looking back, we can see that this more specifically Platonic sense of τὸ ὄν was implicit in τῆς οὐσίας ἁπάντων ὃ τυγχάνει ἕκαστον ὄν at 65e1, though we did not yet have the distinction drawn between Forms and particulars. The phrase just quoted from 65e1 is a good example of Plato's technique of signalling to the reader in advance a doctrine which he will then proceed to develop methodically.)

Burnet (on 78d4) claims that τὸ ὄν is added here 'to suggest the opposition of εἶναι and γίγνεσθαι'. Now it is true that the opposition between what is invariable and what is changing will be formulated in the following words. But, unlike the context at *Symposium* 211a–b, in our *Phaedo* passage the verb γίγνεσθαι is not to be found; and what is directly suggested by τὸ ὄν is not so much the static or durative value of the verb as the veridical idea that has been constantly in play since the

---

[14] I follow Burnet in punctuating after ὅ ἐστι at 78d4, thus taking τὸ ὄν in apposition to all that has gone before. One might be tempted to drop the comma and read αὐτὸ ἕκαστον ὅ ἐστιν τὸ ὄν as 'each very *entity that is*'. But Plato regularly avoids the article with a term following (and completing) ὅ ἐστι. Thus αὐτὸ ὅ ἐστιν κερκίς, αὐτὸ ἐκεῖνο ὅ ἐστιν ὄνομα, at *Crat.* 389b5, d6–7; ὅ ἐστι κλίνη, at *Rep.* 10 597a2, c3, c9; τὴν ἐν τῷ ὅ ἐστιν ὂν ὄντως ἐπιστήμην οὖσαν, *Phaedrus* 247e1–2; τὸ ὅ ἐστιν ζῷον, *Timaeus* 39e8.

phrase was first introduced at 65c9. The Platonic–Eleatic conception of Being is defined by the convergence of two antitheses: (1) the opposition of Being and Seeming (εἶναι and φαίνεσθαι) which exploits the veridical value of εἶναι, and (2) the opposition of Being and Becoming which exploits the static value of the verb (in contrast to γίγνεσθαι as 'mutative' copula),[15] the value which serves to express the idea of eternal constancy and uniformity. In characterizing the realm of change as unreliable appearance, while identifying immutability with true Reality, Plato is of course following in Parmenides' footsteps. What he has added to this Eleatic dualism (besides the much higher level of conceptual clarity in stating the theory) is to locate the point of convergence between truth and changelessness in the predicative formulae for εἶναι corresponding to the 'what-is-it?' question and reflected in the phrase ὅ ἐστι. The definitional copula, or 'is' of whatness,[16] thus serves as the focus for the two converging constituents of the Platonic notion of Being: the idea of true reality (as opposed to appearance) and the idea of immutable uniformity (as opposed to change or Becoming).

Hence three of the four primary linguistic functions of εἶναι in Greek—the predicative construction, the static aspect, the veridical nuance—provide essential instruments for the articulation of Plato's ontology of Forms: for a theory of οὐσία as *the reality which is truly and immutably | what-it-is*. The fourth primary function of the verb, in the [112] existential uses, is likewise relevant; but an *explicit* statement of existence is relatively rare, and the most technical examples of such a statement are actually copulative in form: being something (τι εἶναι) rather than nothing.[17]

---

[15] For the static–kinetic (or stative–mutative) contrast see *The Verb 'Be'*, pp. 194 ff., following John Lyons.

[16] For my ' "is" of whatness' see n. 9 above. Grammatically speaking, it is clear that we need the copula construction of ὅ ἐστι to support the contrast between the 'is truly *F*' of the Forms and the 'is and is not (*F*)' of particulars. See below on *Rep.* 5 478d–479c.

[17] See 74a10 φῶμέν τι εἶναι ἢ μηδέν, discussed above. So in earlier dialogues in introducing a concept for analysis: *Gorgias* 495c3–5 ἐπιστήμην που καλεῖς τι ... οὐ καὶ ἀνδρείαν νυνδὴ ἔλεγές τινα εἶναι μετὰ ἐπιστήμης; *Prot.* 330c1 ἡ δικαιοσύνη πρᾶγμά τί ἐστιν ἢ οὐδὲν πρᾶγμα; d3 οὐκοῦν φατὲ καὶ τοῦτο (sc. ὁσιότητα) πρᾶγμά τι εἶναι. Occasionally an absolute (or quasi-absolute) existential use serves this function: *Gorgias* 450c4 εἰσὶν ἡμῖν τέχναι· ἢ γάρ. So in *Prot.* 330d2 οὐκοῦν καὶ ὁσιότητά φατε εἶναι ('there is some such thing as piety'), with the same construction as in *Gorgias* 495c5.

(4) The use of 'to be' in the doctrine of Forms in *Republic* 5–7 could only be adequately treated in an analysis of that doctrine itself. I limit my remarks here to three points noted for the *Phaedo* which we find more fully elaborated in the *Republic*: (a) the oscillation between predicative and absolute syntax for expressions of the veridical contrast between Forms and particulars; (b) the convergence of veridical and static values in the οὐσία of the Forms as true and unchanging 'reality'; and (c) the copula of whatness (the οὐσία of τί ἐστι; and ὅ ἐστι) as a characterization of Forms.

(a) As in *Phaedo* 65, so in *Republic* 5. 476e ff., it is the veridical notion which predominates in Plato's use of τὸ ὄν to introduce the theory of Forms. That notion is first presented in the description of true philosophers as 'lovers of the spectacle of truth' (475e4). The distinction between Forms and particulars, the one and the many, is then correlated with the opposition between Being and Seeming: each Form is really one, but *appears* as many: αὐτὸ μὲν ἓν ἕκαστον εἶναι, τῇ δὲ ... κοινωνίᾳ πανταχοῦ φανταζόμενα πολλὰ φαίνεσθαι ἕκαστον (476a5–7). As in the verse from Aeschylus cited above, the veridical nuance of the copula εἶναι is brought out by antithesis with φαίνεσθαι, reinforced here by φανταζόμενα. But it is only at 476e10 ff., with the use of the participial forms as objects of 'to know', that the veridical proper makes its appearance as the general designation for the Forms. (Compare *Phaedo* 65c3, c9 ff. and 78d4, cited above.) Opinions may differ, but at any rate it seems clear to me that the veridical construal gives the best sense at 477a1: πῶς γὰρ ἂν μὴ ὄν γέ τι γνωσθείη, 'How could anything that is not (the case) be known?'. The Parmenidean echo is unmistakable, and those readers who take ἔστι in Parmenides fr. 2 as 'exists' may be inclined to do the same for τὸ ὄν in this section of *Republic* 5. Hence I must briefly give my reasons for preferring the

For more straightforward (and less technical) existential uses in connection with the Forms see e.g. *Phaedo* 76d7 εἰ μὲν ἔστιν ἃ θρυλοῦμεν ἀεί, e2 οὕτως ὥσπερ καὶ ταῦτα ἔστιν, e4 εἰ δὲ μὴ ἔστι ταῦτα, 77a3 πάντα τὰ τοιαῦτ᾽ εἶναι ὡς οἷόν τε μάλιστα.

In the echo of the 'seal of ὅ ἐστιν' phrase at 93d8–9, ὥσπερ αὐτῆς (or αὐτή?) ἐστιν ἡ οὐσία ἔχουσα τὴν ἐπωνυμίαν τὴν τοῦ ὅ ἐστιν, the translation of the first ἐστίν is uncertain between 'belongs to it' (Burnet, Bluck) and 'exists' (Hackforth, Gallop). I suspect overdetermination. But Loriaux's argument (*Le Phédon*, i. 155) that ὅ ἐστιν too must therefore imply 'une affirmation d'existence' is unconvincing—except in the sense that any true use of a copula may be thought to imply the existence of its subject.

veridical reading. (1) It is linguistically the more natural: γιγνώσκειν τὸ ὄν is essentially the same idiomatic construction as ἐκμαθεῖν or συμβαλέσθαι τὸ ἐόν in Herodotus (9. 11. 3; 7. 209. 1) and εἰδέναι τὰ ἐόντα in Homer (*Iliad* 1. 70). (2) It is also philosophically preferable, since it gives Plato a true and noncontroversial premiss ('What is known must be the case', or S *knows that p* implies *p*) instead of a premiss that is dubious, if not false: 'One cannot know what does not exist'. And why should Plato characterize knowledge as essentially or primarily *knowledge of existence*: ἐπιστήμη ἐπὶ τῷ ὄντι πέφυκε, γνῶναι ὡς ἔστι τὸ ὄν (477b10)? (3) It seems to me | that the reading here of ὡς ἔστι as 'that it exists' is in fact ruled out by Plato's own paraphrase at 478a6: τὸ ὂν γνῶναι ὡς ἔχει. Finally, (4) the shift to a predicative construction at 479a7 ff. (for φαίνεσθαι) and 479b9–10 (for ἐστί and εἶναι) would be not only unjustified but wholly unexpected if the verb had been understood existentially up to this point; whereas between the veridical and the copula the move is an easy one in both directions: from *X is (really) F* to *It is the case (that X is F)* and also from τὸ ὄν as *what is the case* to τὸ ὄν as *what is the case concerning X* (cf. τὰ ὄντα περί τινος at *Soph.* 263b4–d2). In either direction the shift involves a type ambiguity between things (as subjects of predication) and states of affairs (as 'what is the case', absolutely speaking). But this is not an ambiguity to which Plato is particularly sensitive, any more than Parmenides was.[18]

[113]

Thus I understand Plato to be saying that 'knowledge naturally takes *what-is(-so)* as its object, to know (of) what is (so) that it is (so)', ἐπιστήμη ἐπὶ τῷ ὄντι πέφυκε, γνῶναι ὡς ἔστι τὸ ὄν (447b10). In γνῶναι ὡς ἔστι τὸ ὄν we have the double use of the verb noted in Aristotle's definition of truth: λέγειν τὸ ὂν εἶναι, 'to say of what is (so) that it is (so)', where the participle refers to the fact and the infinitive

---

[18] I suggest that, for both Parmenides and Plato, the veridical ἐστί and τὸ ὄν ('what is the case') be understood as a conjunction of 'X exists' and 'X is F', for unspecified values of X and F, so that the veridical unfolds naturally and nonfallaciously into the existential plus the incomplete copula. The negative τὸ μὴ ὄν here (and οὐκ ἔστι in Parmenides) is to be understood as equivalent to the conjunction of two corresponding negations: what does not exist and is not F, for any value of F; i.e. what has no properties at all. (This is the view of τὸ μὴ ὄν that Plato will reject in the *Sophist*.)

A different 'veridical' reading of τὸ ὄν in this passage (understood as 'is true' and applied to propositions known or believed rather than to objective states of affairs) is defended by Gail Fine in 'Knowledge and Belief in *Republic* V', *Archiv für Geschichte der Philosophie*, 60 (1978), 124 ff.

expresses our statement or judgment of the fact. But Plato's γνῶναι ὡς ἔστι τὸ ὄν is ambiguous in a way that Aristotle's λέγειν τὸ ὂν εἶναι is not: it can mean either 'to know (of) what is *that it is*' (as in Aristotle's formula), or 'to know what is *as* it is', with ὡς introducing a comparative construction as in the standard veridical ('Tell it *like it is*'). The second construction seems to be favored at 478a6, τὸ ὂν γνῶναι ὡς ἔχει, though both readings remain possible.[19]

Initially, then, the veridical object of knowledge is represented by an absolute use of εἶναι,[20] and likewise for the initial characterization of particulars as objects of δόξα: ἅμα ὄν τε καὶ μὴ ὄν . . . τὸ ἀμφοτέρων μετέχον, τοῦ εἶναί τε καὶ μὴ εἶναι (478d5–6, e1–2), 'both being (so) and not being (so)', 'participating both in being (so) and in not being (so)'. As we have noted, however, as the argument proceeds the construction becomes predicative, first with φαίνεσθαι and then with εἶναι: the many καλά will also appear αἰσχρά, the many doubles will also turn out to be halves (479a6 ff.). So for the many particulars generally 'each one of them no more *is* than *is not* what one says it to be' (πότερον οὖν ἔστι μᾶλλον ἢ οὐκ ἔστιν ἕκαστον τῶν πολλῶν τοῦτο ὃ ἄν τις φῇ αὐτὸ εἶναι; 479b9). The pure being-so (τὸ εἰλικρινῶς ὄν) of the Form *F* lies in its being just 'what *F* is' (τὸ ὅ ἐστιν) and nothing else; the mixed halfway being of beautiful or just particulars lies in their being such that it is both true and false to say of each one *that it is F* (that it is beautiful or just). The particular is beautiful in | some respects, ugly in others; each one participates in the eponymous Form but also   ⟦114⟧

---

[19] Another possibility is to read ὡς ἔστι (or ὡς ἔχει) as an indirect question: 'to know (of what is) *how* it is', where ἔστι might be understood as the incomplete copula with τὸ ὄν as existential. This would be a partial reading ('to know of an existing *X*, that it is *F*') of the full veridical, as explained in the preceding note. In this case we may speak of *under*determination in the use of εἶναι, since the context leaves us free to choose between alternative readings.

For similar ambiguities see *Cratylus* 385b7–8, *Sophist* 263b4–9. At *Euthydemus* 284c7 the comparative construction is required: the liar τὰ ὄντα μὲν τρόπον τινὰ λέγει, οὐ μέντοι ὥς γε ἔχει.

[20] Absolute despite the adverbs in τὸ παντελῶς ὄν, εἰλικρινῶς ὄν, μηδαμῇ ὄν at 477a, etc. Lesley Brown has called my attention to an inadequate definition of absolute construction in *The Verb 'Be'*, p. 240, where I admit adverbs of time but exclude adverbs of manner. (I had in mind adverbs with adjectival or predicative force, as illustrated there on pp. 150 ff.) The best test for an absolute construction with adverbs would be whether the adverb is optional; i.e. whether we can recognize the same value and construction *for the verb* if the adverb is omitted. But perhaps the notion of absolute construction has a clear sense only by contrast with the nominal and locative copula, and does not admit of more precise definition.

in the opposite Form. Whatever else one may find to complain of in this argument, the shift from absolute (veridical) to predicative εἶναι need not be fallacious, since the veridical value of τὸ ὄν ('what is so') is an operator on an arbitrary sentence; and the copula use now specifies the sentence.[21] A particular *F* participates both in being-so and not-being-so (with ὄν absolute) just because it both is and is not *F*, in other words just because it is both true and false to say that it is *F*; whereas for a Form such a predication is true without qualification.[22]

(b) When the Forms re-enter the discussion in book 6 they are identified by the 'what-it-is' formula that was used as seal or signature in the *Phaedo*: for each class of particulars we posit a single Form (ἰδέα), each of which we call 'what it is' (ὃ ἔστιν ἕκαστον προσαγορεύομεν, 507b7).[23] On my view, the verb in ὃ ἔστιν represents a copula of definitional equivalence, charged with the special veridical values of (a) what a thing really is, in contrast to what it seems, and (b) what is really (unqualifiedly) *F*, as opposed to what is partially or imperfectly *F*. These values fit neatly into the epistemic context in *Republic* 6, where the one–many or Form–particular antithesis is immediately taken up by the opposition between intelligible and visible objects in the next sentence (507b9), and developed at length in the following sections on the Divided Line and the Cave. But this veridical and epistemic contrast between

---

[21]   This is an example of the veridical unfolding into the incomplete copula. I understand the argument to go as follows:

1. One cannot know that *p* if it is not (fully) the case that *p*.
2. It is not fully the case that the many *F* are *F*.
3. One cannot know of the many *F* that they are *F*.
4. One cannot know the many *F*.

The move from 3 to 4 is not explicitly made, much less argued for. But it *can* be argued for, if knowing a thing is always knowing that something is true of it. (The type shift from state of affairs to thing as object of 'to know' also occurs in the move from 3 to 4.)

[22]   Fallacy threatens, however, in the ambiguous use of negation. Some negative statements must be true of Forms, but Forms cannot participate in the Not-Being of τὸ μηδαμῶς ὄν, which would make them *indeterminate*. Plato himself became aware of this ambiguity, and in the *Sophist* he rejects τὸ μὴ ὄν αὐτὸ καθ' αὑτό as wholly indefinite and unintelligible (238c9, 239c4, 258e6 ff.) and instead redefines τὸ μὴ ὄν in terms of (true) negative predication.

[23]   Or 'which we call "what each one is"', with ἕκαστον as subject of ἐστίν. This familiar syntactic ambiguity is independent of the textual controversy (where I accept Burnet's text and read αὐτὸ καλὸν καὶ αὐτὸ ἀγαθόν as object of τιθέντες).

Note the earlier, unemphatic use of εἶναι as existential (or existential-copula) applying to particulars: πολλὰ καλά... ἕκαστα οὕτως εἶναί φαμεν at 507b2–3: 'We say that there are many beautiful things ... and that in each case they exist in this way (sc. as many)'.

Being and Seeming, Knowledge and Opinion is soon fused with the
more properly ontological antithesis of Being and Becoming: at 508d the
region illuminated by truth and Being (ἀλήθειά τε καὶ τὸ ὄν) is contrasted
with the darkness of Coming-to-be and Perishing (τὸ γιγνόμενόν τε καὶ
ἀπολλύμενον), where the soul is perplexed by fluctuating δόξαι in place of
clear knowledge and intelligence. And so throughout the following
discussion: the terms Being (οὐσία, ὄν) and Becoming (γένεσις) serve
as a standing reference to the two classes of Forms and particulars
(e.g. at 525b5: φιλοσόφῳ δὲ διὰ τὸ τῆς οὐσίας ἁπτέον εἶναι γενέσεως
ἐξαναδύντι). Thus the terminological contrast is stative-mutative; but the
interpretation of the contrast is regularly slanted towards the greater cognitive clarity and 'truth' of intelligible Being (e.g. 518c8 ff., 519a9–b4,
523a3, 525c5–6, 526e6, 527b5).

It is worth noticing that this convergence of veridical and static-
immutable values finds a natural justification in the predicative construction. A particular *F* which comes to be, perishes, and changes in
the meantime is only provisionally and fitfully *F*. For Plato these time-
qualifications on 'is *F*' are just as damaging to the epistemic and
ontological credentials of particular *F*s as are the relative or perspectival
conditions on 'appearing | *F*' that were emphasized in the previous   [[115]]
discussion (5 479a–b; cf. *Phaedo* 74b–c). Both types of disability were
mentioned together in Plato's initial statement of his neo-Eleatic
dualism at *Symp.* 211a–b.

(c) To conclude these remarks on *Rep.* 6–7, I note the conspicuous
reappearance of the 'What-is-X?' formulation in the final description
of dialectic. The kind of inquiry which 'draws the mind toward οὐσία'
is illustrated at 524c11 by the question 'What in the world is the great
and the small?' (τί οὖν ποτ᾽ ἐστί . . .), and completed by 'giving and
receiving an account (λόγος)' in an investigation directed towards 'just
what each thing is' (ἐπ᾽ αὐτὸ ὅ ἐστιν ἕκαστον), and in particular
towards 'just what good is' or 'just what-is-good' (αὐτὸ ὅ ἐστιν
ἀγαθόν) (531e5, 532a7–b1). Dialectic is the only discipline which
attempts systematically to grasp in every case, 'concerning each thing
itself, what each one <truly> is' (αὐτοῦ γε ἑκάστου περὶ ὅ ἐστιν
ἕκαστον, 533b2). The dialectician is the one who gets hold of the
λόγος τῆς οὐσίας of each thing, the definition or explanation of *what it
is*, and is able to give an account of this both to himself and to someone

else (534b3–5). Here as elsewhere, οὐσία as object of knowledge is ultimately defined by reference to the whatness-questions of dialectic. In this culminating account of philosophic knowledge, the copula syntax of the ὅ ἐστι formula thus bears the whole weight of Plato's ontology.

II

I turn now to uses of εἶναι in three passages where there is no mention of Forms and no emphasis on the stative-mutative contrast of Being and Becoming. The first text is a section of the *Parmenides* where the veridical value of 'to be' is treated for its own sake. The other texts are two major passages in the *Theaetetus* where an absolute or incomplete use of εἶναι plays a crucial role.

(1) At *Parmenides* 161e–162b the use of εἶναι for *being-so*, as the correlate of true statement, is recognized as one sense of the phrase μετέχειν τῆς οὐσίας 'to participate in being'. The passage occurs in the paradoxical derivation of contrary conclusions from the hypothesis 'if the One is not', 'if the One does not exist', εἰ μὴ ἔστι τὸ ἕν (160b5). For the sake of clarity I shall regularly use 'exists' to translate an ἔστι which represents the predicate in this hypothesis, in order to distinguish it from uses of εἶναι that emerge in the course of the argument, and which may or may not have the same sense as the verb of the hypothesis. Our section begins with the claim that if the One does not exist, it must nonetheless participate somehow in being. The reason given is: 'It (the One) must be as | we say; for if it is not so, we would not be telling the truth in saying *that the One does not exist*. But if this is true, clearly we say what-is(-so). Now since we claim to be telling the truth, we necessarily claim also to say what-is(-so)': ἔχειν αὐτὸ δεῖ οὕτως ὡς λέγομεν· εἰ γὰρ μὴ οὕτως ἔχει, οὐκ ἂν ἀληθῆ λέγοιμεν ἡμεῖς λέγοντες τὸ ἓν μὴ εἶναι· εἰ δὲ ἀληθῆ, δῆλον ὅτι ὄντα αὐτὰ λέγομεν. . . . ἐπειδὴ δέ φαμεν ἀληθῆ λέγειν, ἀνάγκη ἡμῖν φάναι καὶ ὄντα λέγειν (161e4–162a1). Slightly schematized, the argument is as follows:

(i) If we speak truly, what we say must be the case (οὕτως ἔχειν).
(ii) If what we say is the case, we say things-that-are (ὄντα), i.e. things that are in fact as we say.

In step 1 we have a general statement of the form 'If *p* is true, then *p*'. This is expressed by an idiomatic variant on the veridical construction with οὕτως ἔχει in place of οὕτως ἔστι, thus making the point first without introducing the verb 'to be'. Step 2 provides the verb in the participial form ὄντα, 'what is the case' (like ὄν in γνῶναι τὸ ὄν, 'knowing what is so', in *Rep.* 5. 477b10; cf. λέγειν τὸ ὂν εἶναι in Aristotle's formula for truth).

In the standard veridical construction, the subject of εἶναι (or τὸ ὄν) is a sentential content or proposition; and ὄντα in *Parmenides* 161e6, 162a1 seems likewise to represent an entire sentence ('whatever we say'). But Plato's use of οὕτως ἔχει in this context, although idiomatic, is veridically nonstandard, since it takes as subject not a proposition but the One (αὐτό 161e4). This gives us a copula (subject–predicate) variation on the veridical construction: 'If we say something true about X, we say how X is', or 'we say something-that-is(-so) about X'. The formal variation (and approximation to Aristotle's example of ἔστι as 'is true') is clear in the next sentence, with ἔστι as emphatic ('veridical') copula:

ἔστιν ἄρα, ὡς ἔοικε, τὸ ἓν οὐκ ὄν (162a1–2).

The One truly *is* then, as it seems, nonexistent.

In order to produce the paradox of an apparent contradiction, Plato then develops the veridical copula in both directions, affirmative and negative, so that by the principle of double negation it would follow that if the One *were not* nonexistent, it would have to exist, which is excluded by hypothesis.

εἰ γὰρ μὴ ἔσται μὴ ὄν, ἀλλά πῃ τοῦ εἶναι ἀνήσει πρὸς τὸ μὴ εἶναι, εὐθὺς ἔσται ὄν (162a2–3).

For if it *is not* nonexistent, but somehow slips from *being* [i.e. from the copula 'being x'] to *not being* [i.e. to 'not being x'], it will immediately be existent.

To prevent this slippage a copulative 'bond' is required, tying the One | [117] to nonexistence, just as there must be a negative bond to tie the existent (τὸ ὄν) to nonexistence.

δεῖ ἄρα αὐτὸ δεσμὸν ἔχειν τοῦ μὴ εἶναι τὸ εἶναι μὴ ὄν, εἰ μέλλει μὴ εἶναι, ὁμοίως ὥσπερ τὸ ὂν τὸ μὴ ὂν ἔχειν μὴ εἶναι, ἵνα τελέως αὖ ᾖ (162a4–6, omitting εἶναι before ᾖ, with Shorey and Burnet).

Hence the One must possess as a bond for nonexistence (its) *being* nonexistent, if it is not to exist, just as what exists (τὸ ὄν) must possess not-being (μὴ εἶναι), <sc. not being> *what does not exist* (τὸ μὴ ὄν).

This duplication of the veridical copula in negative form seems logically superfluous; but Plato's argument aims at a formal contradiction (or apparent contradiction) between properties of the One. And for this result he needs to define not only an οὐσία corresponding to the copula in a true affirmation but also a μὴ εἶναι and μὴ οὐσία corresponding to the copula in a true negation. In what follows the text is uncertain, but the line of reasoning seems clear:

In this way the existent will surely exist and the nonexistent not exist, if (a) the existent participates in *being* (οὐσίας), namely in being existent (τοῦ εἶναι ὄν), and in *not being* (μὴ οὐσίας), i.e. not being nonexistent, if it is to be wholly existent, whereas (b) the nonexistent participates in the *not being* (μὴ οὐσίας) of not being existent, and in the being (οὐσίας) of being nonexistent (162a6–b2, the Burnet-Shorey text).

If we now drop my stipulated translation 'existent' or 'exists' for the predicate of the hypothesis, and render εἶναι by 'to be' throughout, we see that the argument has reached a conclusion similar in form to that of the *Sophist*, though based upon different premises: 'What-is has a share in not-being and what-is-not has a share in being' (162b3–4). What follows for the One here is that both Being (οὐσία) and Not-Being (μὴ οὐσία) belong to it, since (i) it *is not* by hypothesis ('it does not exist'), but (ii) the argument shows that it must also have a share in *being* something, namely, being nonexistent (τῷ ἑνί, ἐπειδὴ οὐκ ἔστι, τοῦ εἶναι ἀνάγκη μετεῖναι εἰς τὸ μὴ εἶναι 162b5–6). Since for the One in this hypothesis the positive being is that of the (veridical) copula, whereas the negative being is that of the predicate 'exists', there is no real contradiction.[24]

---

[24] The *appearance* of contradiction is strengthened by an equivocation on οὐσία in the conclusion: at 162b6 ('Being turns out to belong to the one') οὐσία represents the veridical copula, as throughout the preceding argument; but in the next sentence ('and Not-Being must belong to it also, if it is not', καὶ μὴ οὐσία ἄρα, εἴπερ μὴ ἔστιν), οὐσία is most naturally taken as nominalization for the verb of the hypothesis (conventionally rendered here as 'it does not exist').

The same conclusion can be reached with the copula value of οὐσία maintained throughout if one thinks of the last sentence as elliptical: 'The One must share in not-being <sc. in not-being existent, with ὄν as the verb of the hypothesis>, if (by hypothesis) it does not exist'. Precisely this inference was prepared at 162b1–2 (τὸ δὲ μὴ ὂν μὴ οὐσίας μὲν <sc.

Note that throughout this section the veridical idea is expressed by a grammatical copula. Only in the participle ὄντα at 161e6 and 162a1 is the verb used absolutely, as in a standard veridical construction.

(2) At *Theaetetus* 152a, on the other hand, where Plato quotes the opening sentence of Protagoras' work on Truth, it seems natural to recognize the veridical proper, with the verb construed absolutely as in the formulae for 'Yes, it is so': ἔστι ταῦτα, ἔστιν οὕτω. | [118]

πάντων χρημάτων μέτρον ἄνθρωπον εἶναι, τῶν μὲν ὄντων ὡς ἔστι, τῶν δὲ μὴ ὄντων ὡς οὐκ ἔστιν.

Man is the measure of all things, of what is (so) that it is (so), of what is not that it is not.

We have a clear precursor for Aristotle's own formula for truth in *Met.* Γ. 7, with bivalent symmetry for affirmation and denial, and the double use of the verb: for the facts (in participial form) and for the corresponding judgment (in the finite verb).

In the excellent commentary to his translation of the *Theaetetus* John McDowell has interpreted these four occurrences of εἶναι as instances of the incomplete copula: 'a man is the measure of things which are *f*, that they are *f*, and of things which are not *f*, that they are not *f*'.[25] Such an interpretation can be defended on the basis of the next sentence, where ἐστί occurs as copula (with veridical force implied by the contrast with φαίνεται):

ὡς οἷα μὲν ἕκαστα ἐμοὶ φαίνεται τοιαῦτα μέν ἐστιν ἐμοί.

(This is I suppose what he means:) that such as things appear to me in each case, just such are they (really) for me (whereas for you they are such as they appear to you.)

And in the example which follows, the question is whether or not a given wind *is cold* (152b6). So it is clear that in giving a philosophical exegesis of Protagoras' formula Plato will spell out the veridical 'is' in a copula

---

μετέχειν> τοῦ μὴ εἶναι ὄν). On this reading of καὶ μὴ οὐσία ἄρα, there is no equivocation in the conclusion, though still no contradiction. The syntax, and hence the logic, is here underdetermined. (I owe a recognition of this last point to Christopher Kirwan, though he might not approve my formulation of it.)

[25] *Plato: Theaetetus* (Oxford: Clarendon, 1973), 118. Similarly for αἴσθησις ἄρα τοῦ ὄντος ἀεί ἐστιν at 152c5, 'perception is always of what is really so', McDowell recognizes an incomplete 'is', with complement omitted (*Theaetetus*, p. 120, on 152b1–c7).

construction. But that is no reason to suppose that Protagoras himself, or Plato in quoting him, understood τὰ ὄντα ὡς ἔστι as an incomplete use of the verb, requiring some completion by a predicate word or phrase. Protagoras speaks the language of Herodotus, where the absolute use of the veridical participle is quite common. And we have seen how easily Plato oscillates back and forth between absolute and predicative constructions of εἶναι when the veridical idea is in play. In a context like *Theaetetus* 152a–c it is easy to understand why Plato, like a contemporary philosopher, should prefer to explicate the veridical notion by using 'is' as copula. For the absolute 'is' of the veridical construction is metasentential: like the adverbs 'possibly' and 'necessarily' it functions as syntactic operator on an entire sentence. The use of ἐστί in this construction presupposes some more elementary sentence to be endorsed, and any detailed discussion will have to provide a sample sentence. But the absolute use gives us no clue as to what sentence we are talking about. The incomplete copula, on the other hand, although it does not provide the whole sentence, will specify the sentence form *S is P*, and thus point the way to concrete examples. So there | is a justifiable philosophic preference for formulating the veridical idea in copula form.[26] If one assumes (as Plato probably and Aristotle certainly did) that every sentence can be put into *S is P* form, then the veridical ἐστί and the copula construction become logically equivalent, just as '*p*' *is true* is logically equivalent to *p*. The movement back and forth between the two forms is all the more natural if, as I have suggested, the absolute use of ἐστί in the veridical construction is to be understood as a generalizing abstraction from, and thematization of, the truth claim implicit in normal declarative uses of the copula.[27]   [119]

Assuming, then, that every relevant instance of the absolute veridical can be mapped onto a copula construction, it makes no substantive difference for the philosophic analysis whether or not the verbs in the *homo mensura* formula are read as incomplete uses of the copula.[28] If

---

[26] Compare Fred Sommers's proposal to interpret Aristotle's formula for truth (λέγειν τὸ ὂν εἶναι) as containing an incomplete copula: 'saying of what-is-P *that* it is P . . . for instance saying of snow (what-is-white) that it is white' ('On Concepts of Truth in Natural Languages', *Review of Metaphysics*, 23 (1969), 282, cited in *The Verb 'Be'*, p. 336 n. 7).

[27] See *The Verb 'Be'*, pp. 407–9.

[28] It would of course make a difference if one took account of complex sentence forms (such as conditionals and disjunctions) which cannot be put into *S is P* form. This discrepancy, if pressed, would tell against the copula construction as a reading for the claim that man is 'the measure of *all* things'. But probably neither Plato nor Protagoras has such complex sentence forms in view.

I have taken the trouble to reassert my view of this text as an idiomatic, absolute use of ἐστί, that is because the veridical value of ἐστί emerges more clearly on this reading.[29] And this veridical idea is crucial for any interpretation of our second passage from the *Theaetetus,* Plato's final refutation of the definition of knowledge that was initially supported by this quotation from Protagoras.

(3) The refutation of the thesis that knowledge is sense perception is completed at 186c–e with the argument that knowledge requires truth, and truth requires being (οὐσία); but sense perception cannot attain to being, and hence not to truth. Therefore knowledge must be sought not in sense-experience but in reasoning and reflection concerning such experience; for it is only in this rational activity of comparison and judging (κρίνειν) that being and truth can be reached (186b8, d2–5).

What is the οὐσία required for truth and knowledge, accessible not to sensation but only to reasoning (ἀναλογίσματα, συλλογισμός)? The Protagorean formula for truth, with which the discussion began, offers a natural interpretation: 'being' represents (a) the facts in the world, τὰ ὄντα, the way things really are, and (b) the assertion of these facts in (true or false) judgments to the effect that things are so (ὡς ἔστι) or not so (ὡς οὐκ ἔστι). Both modes of being are required for the concept of truth as it operates in the dialogue. There must be a way the world is, and there must be a propositional reflection (correct or incorrect) of this fact in statement or judgment. (The Protagorean thesis takes the distinction for granted, in order to claim that the two modes of being will necessarily coincide.) It would be reasonable to insist that οὐσία in either sense is indispensable for truth and knowledge. But in the context of a rejection of sensation as incompetent here, and in view of the grounds cited for that rejection, it is | more appropriate to interpet [[120]] οὐσία in the second sense: as a shorthand expression for the propositional structure of thought, provided by modeled on language, and entailing reference, predication, and assertion. It is this structure that is required for thought to be true or false, for judgment either to tell it like it is or to tell it otherwise. And it will be appropriate to look for

---

[29] This reading also connects the *Truth* of Protagoras directly with the Way of Truth in Parmenides' poem, at least on my interpretation of ἔστι in Parmenides fr. 2 as a reflection of the veridical idiom.

such a structure not in sense perception as such but in the thinking or reasoning by which we compare, calculate, and reflect upon the items in our sense experience.

On this natural interpretation, the final argument at 186c–e is one of considerable scope and power. It bears a strong analogy to Kant's critique of empiricism, but without the burden of Kant's elaborate metapsychology. Plato's conception of thought and judgment sticks refreshingly close to the model of silent speech (189e–199a; cf. *Sophist* 263d–264b). Why, then, has such an interpretation not been generally accepted, or even recognized?[30] The answer must lie in the rather obscure way in which the notion of οὐσία enters the argument, beginning with a problematic use of the verb at 185a. We need to show that the interpretation just proposed for οὐσία will fit the concept denominated by ἔστι and οὐκ ἔστι at 185c. And this requires a step-by-step analysis of the text. The passage falls into three parts:

A. 184b–185e: the argument to show that τὰ κοινά are not perceived through the senses.

B. 186a–c: the application to οὐσία.

C. 186c 7–e12: the inference that since sensation cannot attain Being and truth, it cannot be knowledge.

Section A concerns the whole range of 'common' properties; Being enters only as one among the rest. It is in the short transitional passage B that the concept of οὐσία is most fully articulated. But that should of course be the same concept that was introduced in section A.

A. 184b–185e. In order to show that the common properties are not accessible through the senses, Plato makes use of the principle of a unique one-to-one correlation between sense and object, so that 'it is impossible to perceive through one power what one perceives through another, for example to perceive through sight what one perceives through hearing' (184e8–185a2). This is not an ad hoc assumption, but the direct application of a standard principle of individuation for capacities or modes of cognition: if two cognitive capacities are distinct

---

[30] It has in fact been recognized by Myles Burnyeat ('Plato on the Grammar of Perceiving', *Classical Quarterly*, 26 (1976)), who, in a final footnote (p. 50), stresses the Kantian parallel from a point of view that reinforces the interpretation proposed here.

from one another, the range of phenomena studied by each will be distinct; and conversely.[31] As applied here, the principle effectively rules out common sensibles of the Aristotelian type, defined as the object of more than one sense. |

Plato's argument begins with a distinction between (a) the various   [[121]] bodily organs or instruments 'through which' we perceive colors, sounds, and flavors, and (b) the single psychic principle on which these bodily channels converge and 'by which' we perceive the corresponding qualities (184c–d).[32] The latter is, in effect, the mind, conceived here as including (but not as limited to) the unified psychic power of qualitative sense perception. When Plato goes on to contrast the qualities perceived through individual organs with certain common properties (κοινά) applying to more than one sense, one might at first suppose he has in view something like Aristotle's distinction between proper and common sensibles.[33] But, as we have seen this cannot be right. For Aristotle's κοινὰ αἰσθητά are perceived through bodily organs just like any other sense qualities: they are simply qualities perceived *by more than one sense* (*DA* 418ª18–20). For Aristotle, the list of such common qualities includes motion, rest, shape, size, number, and unity. Plato says nothing here about motion, shape, or size. But on unity and number he flatly disagrees with Aristotle: these are not properties perceived through bodily organs at all (185e1, e6–7). From Aristotle's point of view, Plato conflates two distinctions: (1) between proper sensibles, accessible to a single sense, and common sensibles, accessible to more than one, and (2) between strictly sensible input, received through bodily organs, and nonsensible input contributed by the mind or rational psyche. Since Plato's discussion comes

---

[31] See *Ion* 537d5 ff., 538a; *Rep.* 5 477d. The principle is not as implausible as some may think, if one is careful to distinguish the intentional *object* of a capacity or science, defined in terms of some theoretical description, from the *physical objects* studied, since of course the latter may overlap. Anatomists, biochemists, and students of learning theory (as well as butchers and stockbreeders) may all deal with the same animals; but one studies its bone structure, another its molecular composition, its behavior, etc. Similarly, one may both see and hear a bell; but one sees its visual appearance and hears its ring.

[32] For the nature and importance of this distinction see Burnyeat's article cited in n. 30.

[33] See *DA* 2. 6. 418ª10–20; 3. 1. 425ª14 ff., with my discussion in 'Sensation and Consciousness in Aristotle's Psychology', *Archiv für Geschichte der Philosophie* 48 (1966), 52–4, 64 nn. 48–9 (= J. Barnes, M. Schofield, and R. Sorabji (eds.), *Articles on Aristotle*, iv (London: Duckworth, 1979), 8–9, 17).

first, he has no occasion to refer to Aristotle's view. Hence we cannot be sure whether he simply overlooked the possibility of an overlap between the objects of sight and touch or whether, like Berkeley, he would have denied that perceptions of tactile and visual space (and hence of tactile and visible shape, size, and motion) were actually perceptions of the same quality. The second interpretation is the more charitable: it implies that, for Plato, Aristotle's common sensibles are not properly sensed at all, but constructed by the mind out of its own resources. In either case it is clear that the κοινά of the *Theaetetus* are much less like Aristotle's common sensibles than they are like Kantian 'concepts', contributed by the mind for the organizing of sense experience. And this is just what we would expect in the light of Plato's earlier doctrine of Recollection and the strongly Kantian slant given to this doctrine in *Phaedrus* 249b.[34]

The argument of section A runs as follows (184e8–185e):

1. It is impossible to perceive through one sense what one perceives through another sense.

2. If you think some one thing concerning both what you hear and what you see, this common thing cannot be perceived either through hearing or through sight (from 1).[35] | [122]

3. Concerning sound and color, one of the things you think about them is *that they both are* (ὅτι ἀμφοτέρω ἐστόν).

4. And also you think that each is *different* from the other but the *same* as itself.

5. And that both are *two*, and each is *one*.

---

[34] δεῖ γὰρ ἄνθρωπον συνιέναι κατ᾽ εἶδος λεγόμενον, ἐκ πολλῶν ἰόντ᾽ αἰσθήσεων εἰς ἓν λογισμῷ ξυναιρούμενον, 'it is necessary for a human being to understand what is said by reference to a form (or kind of thing), passing from a multitude of sensations to a unity gathered together by reasoning' (*Phaedrus* 249b6–c1).

[35] In order to get from (1) 'You cannot perceive through sense₁ what you perceive through sense₂' to (2) 'if you *think* something both about the object of sense₁ and also about the object of sense₂, this common item cannot be perceived either through sense₁ or through sense₂', another premiss is required that is not easy to spell out. McDowell (*Theaetetus*, p. 186) refers simply to 'an implicit assumption about the unity of the act of thinking'. Lesley Brown (in a letter) suggests something more precise: 'What applies to the object of a given sense (e.g. something *about* the object of vision or hearing) can be sense-perceived, if at all, only through the corresponding sense'. Thus the brightness of a color could be seen, the loudness of a sound could be heard, but the *intensity* of each—conceived as a common property of both, for example as a ratio over an arbitrary unit—would, like number itself, not be an object of either sense.

6. You are also able to inquire whether they are *like* or *unlike* one another.

7. For all the properties mentioned in 3–6, it is impossible to perceive them either through sight or through hearing (from 2).

8. Nor can they be perceived by some third sense, as for example if it were possible to inquire of color and sound whether or not they were both bitter (ἆρ' ἐστὸν ἀλμυρὼ ἢ οὔ), using the sense of taste.

9. Therefore such common properties cannot be perceived through any organ of bodily sense; it is the mind (ψυχή) by itself which considers these properties in relation to all things.

The soundness of this argument depends upon the truth of premiss 1, which Aristotle and other philosophers would deny. The truth of the conclusion, however, insofar as it concerns οὐσία, does not depend upon this premiss. For even philosophers who believe that some properties (like shape and motion) are perceived by more than one sense may not wish to include Being among the common sensibles.

The question now arises: What exactly does Plato mean here by this property 'which is common to all things, including these (viz. sound and color), and to which you give the name "is" (ἔστι) and "is not" (οὐκ ἔστι)'? (184c5; at c9 it is called οὐσία καὶ τὸ μὴ εἶναι; from 186a2 on it is simply οὐσία). The verb itself appears twice in the argument, first in 3 with an apparently absolute construction ('that both color and sound *are*'), and then in 8 as the ordinary copula: 'whether color and sound are both bitter or not'. In premisses 4–6 no verb appears, but the copula ἐστί (or ἐστόν) must be understood throughout. Since the subject remains substantially the same (color or sound or both), and since the two occurrences of the verb are identical in form (ἐστόν), it is natural to suppose that the first occurrence has some strong connection with the implied copula in 4–6 and the explicit copula in 8. We expect the connection to be close enough for there to be a *single* concept or function of Being named by ἔστι and οὐκ ἔστι, and referred to in the list of common properties at 185c–d. Hence a thoughtful interpreter will be tempted to explain the apparently absolute construction of ἐστόν in 3 as some kind of incomplete copula, in order to impose a single interpretation on the verb throughout the argument.

But this is to read the passage backwards. Read in its place, the statement that sound and color both *are*, with no predicate in sight, must mean that both *exist*, that both are something rather than nothing. By way of introduction, the sentence with existential ἐστόν serves to posit sound and color as legitimate subjects of discourse, or (in a different technical jargon) to | claim that both terms have a genuine ⟦123⟧ reference. This is the natural preliminary to any further comments about them, such as the claim in 4 that each is different from the other but the same as itself. The existential reading of ἐστόν in 3 is not only linguistically the easiest but logically the most appropriate as a starting point for the argument.[36]

At the same time, if I am correct in suggesting that the basic function of the existential use of εἶναι is to introduce a subject for further predication,[37] a Greek reader would normally *hear* the existential verb as pregnant with the incomplete copula: 'there is an X' invites us to expect more, namely, 'There is an X *which is such and such*'.[38] And in fact the 'existential' ἐστόν in 3 also provides the copula for the verbless predications in 4–6. (Another case of overdetermination.) Hence Plato can return to ἐστόν as copula in 8, with no feeling of equivocation, and then speak of ἔστι and οὐκ ἔστι as if they named a single concept from beginning to end (from 3 to 8). And in a sense there is only one concept represented by εἶναι throughout the argument; namely, being a subject equipped with predicates. The notions of existence and predication, which we distinguish as two separate logical or linguistic functions, are conceived in Greek as two sides of

---

[36] Compare the existential assumption that frequently introduces the dialectical consideration of a concept of Form. In addition to the examples cited above in n. 17 see *Gorgias* 454c7 καλεῖς μεμαθηκέναι . . . τί δέ; πεπιστευκέναι.

It might be objected that the existential construal of ἐστόν at 185a9 is ruled out by the introduction of the negative forms in what follows (οὐκ ἔστι at 185c6, μὴ εἶναι at c9). But by then we have shifted to the copula construction (ἆρ᾽ ἐστὸν ἁλμυρὼ ἢ οὔ at 185b10) and there is no focus on negative existentials. The negative forms stand for negative predications and negative propositions (or judgments), which may of course be true. But in the final discussion of οὐσία as propositional truth or reality in 186a–c the negation would be misleading and is silently dropped.

[37] *The Verb 'Be'*, p. 257; cf. pp. 249, 252 ff.

[38] This is a characteristic feature of the existential ἐστί, which we lose by translating it as 'exists'. Thus in a Greek sentence of the form *There is an X which is F* we rarely if ever find ἐστί repeated in the second clause (see *The Verb 'Be'* p. 281 with n. 47).

For the double reading of ἐστόν at 185a9 compare the remarks of McDowell (p. 187) and Burnyeat (*CQ* (1976), p. 45 n. 46); in effect, Burnyeat anticipates my analysis of the syntax as overdetermined.

a single coin. The οὐσία which is introduced by the argument of section A is just the notion of Being as propositional structure that is needed for the argument of section C. The notions of reference (in the existential use) and of predication (with the copula) combine to flesh out the bare ἔστι of assertion or truth claim with the fuller sentential structure *S is P*, where *S* is given by the existence claim for color and sound, *is* represents ἐστί or ἐστόν as copula, and the variable *P* takes as substituends 'same' and 'different', 'two', 'one', 'like', 'unlike', etc. Existence-with-predication, or being a subject for attributes, is indeed the *most* common property, which applies to everything there is (186a2: τοῦτο γὰρ μάλιστα ἐπὶ πάντων παρέπεται).

B. 186a–c. Taking both the existential and copula uses in section A at their face value, then, we find that together they provide the notion of propositional structure capable of carrying a truth claim, which is what was required for the quasi-veridical *being-so* that fits the argument in section C. What remains to be seen, then, is whether this view can account for the characterization of οὐσία in the transitional section B, where οὐσία and its verb occur six times, and the linguistic functions of the verb seem to be more diverse.

(i) At 186a2 οὐσία is said to be the most common of all the κοινά. But this poses no problem for an account of Being as existence, predication, and the subject–predicate fusion of the two. As Plato notes elsewhere, even | Not-being must *be* in this sense, as a subject ⟦124⟧ of which predicates can be true. (See *Parmenides* 162a1–b7, discussed above; and cf. *Met.* Γ. 2. 1003ᵇ10.)

(ii) After repeating some of the κοινά previously mentioned, Socrates asks about 'noble and shameful, and good and bad' (καλόν, αἰσχρόν, ἀγαθόν, κακόν), to which Theaetetus replies: 'They, too, seem to me to be pre-eminently things whose being (οὐσία) the mind considers in relation to one another, calculating in itself things past and present in relation to things in the future' (186a9–b1, trans. McDowell). Here οὐσία functions as a vague nominalization for *any* relevant use of the verb. On the one hand, we could almost disregard it in translation, taking 'the οὐσία of noble and base' as periphrastic for 'the noble and the base' (or for 'what is noble and what is base'). On the other hand, as object of the verb 'to consider, investigate' (σκοπεῖσθαι), the circumlocution has the force of a phrase like '(to investigate) *the nature* of good and bad', 'to inquire *what good is*'. The verb underlying οὐσία is thus loaded not only with the existential sense ('inquiring whether there is such a thing') but also with the (veridical) copula of whatness: 'investigating their nature, i.e. trying to find out *what they really are*'. There seems to be an echo here of the Protagorean thesis formulated at 172a–b, concerning 'things noble and base, and just and unjust, and pious and impious', that such things have no real being or truth, beyond their customary acceptance in a given society: ὡς οὐκ ἔστι φύσει αὐτῶν οὐδὲν οὐσίαν ἑαυτοῦ ἔχον (172b4), 'that none of them exists by nature, possessing its own οὐσία'. The associated claim, that wisdom consists not in truer judgments but in having and producing more *useful* or *beneficial* perceptions (first formulated at 166d–167c, echoed at 177d ff.), was criticized by reference to judgments concerning the future (178a–179b). It is this entire discussion which Theaetetus seems to have in mind in referring here to calculations about the future in the consideration of good and bad, noble and base.[39]

After pointing out that the hardness (or hard quality, σκληρότης) of something hard and the soft quality of something soft are perceived through touch, Socrates adds: 'But their οὐσία and that they are (ὅτι ἐστόν) and their opposition to one another and the οὐσία in turn of the opposition, all this our psyche tries to judge by reviewing and comparing these things with one another' (186b6–9). This gives us three more occurrences of οὐσία and its verb; (iii)–(v).

(iii) The οὐσία of the tactile qualities and hardness and softness might be their *existence* (as nominalization of the existential use of ἐστόν we found at 185a9, and perhaps will find again in the next words here). But the term is | more naturally taken in the sense of [125]
'nature' or 'what they are' given in the immediately preceding occurrence of the noun at 186a10. (See under (ii), above.) The point may be that bodily sensation *feels* these qualities but only rational thought can

[39] McDowell (*Theaetetus*, p. 190) sees a reference to 177c–179 in Theaetetus' remarks at 186a8–b1. I suggest that the allusion is not only to this final argument but to the whole topic of moral and prudential judgments raised at 166d. Hence the reference to καλόν and αἰσχρόν on the one hand (186a8), ὠφέλεια on the other (186c3).

say what they are, i.e. can label them as 'hard' or 'soft', since such conceptualization, crystallized in words, implies a range of contrast and comparison and a generalization over many cases, which go beyond the momentary tactile experience as such.[40] In the absence of further clues, however, it seems best to take 'the *οὐσία* of hardness and softness' quite generally, for *anything* that can be said about the nature of these qualities, including what is going to be said in the rest of this sentence.

(iv) *καὶ ὅτι ἐστόν*: either (a) 'and that they both are', which should mean 'that they exist', 'that they really occur', as at 185a9, or (b) 'and *what* they both are' (reading *ὅ τι*, as McDowell suggests, p. 111), the latter giving us either the narrow or the broad view of whatness suggested for (iii). McDowell takes the narrow view (identifying 'a quality which one perceives as the quality it is', p. 191), and understands *καί* here as 'i.e.'. I prefer to think Plato is not making the same point twice, and hence would take *οὐσία* as whatness (broadly construed) and *ὅτι ἐστόν* as primarily existential. But it would be unreasonable to insist on a choice between possible interpretations here, where the basis for excluding any plausible reading is likely to be arbitrary. If Plato had wanted to *impose* a particular understanding of *οὐσία* and *ἐστόν*, he would presumably have given us more clues.

---

[40] See John Cooper, 'Plato on Sense Perception and Knowledge: *Theaetetus* 184 to 186', *Phronesis*, 15 (1970), 130 ff. for an interpretation along these lines. I agree with Cooper that Plato does not here make clear the status of sensory concepts like 'red', 'warm', or 'sweet', and sometimes speaks *as if* these were directly available to perceptual awareness through the body, so that labeling a color as red, for example, would not require the *independent* contribution of the psyche (Cooper, 'Plato', pp. 130–4). I doubt, however, that he tended 'to assimilate or confuse with one another sensory awareness and the conceptual labelling of its objects' (p. 134). In principle, that distinction is clearly drawn in the passage from the *Phaedrus* quoted in n. 34. Plato shows no special interest in sensory concepts as such, but that is presumably because they provide the weakest case for the point he wishes to make: the need for an independent contribution of the mind to any perceptual judgment that might be a candidate for knowledge. There is no clear indication in this context that Plato is considering whether a minimal sensory judgment such as 'This is red' requires a concept like *εἶναι*; but I think his answer would certainly have been 'yes'. Cf. *Theaet.* 183a6–b5, *Crat.* 439d9. If applying the concept of hardness means more than *feeling* hardness, or being able to discriminate hard things from soft, it must involve a judgment *that this is hard*. So the concept of hardness, like any sensory concept, will not be available in the absence of predication and judgment, i.e. without *εἶναι*.

(v) 'And the opposition (of hardness and softness) to one another and the οὐσία in turn of their opposition.' The expression 'in turn' (αὖ) suggests that the οὐσία of their opposition is related to that opposition itself just as the οὐσία of the two tactile qualities is related to these qualities. Since the opposition itself is already a conceptual κοινόν, not a bodily sensation, the relation in this case cannot be the mere conceptual labeling of the opposition, as in the narrow notion of whatness proposed under (iii) and (iv). This tells (though perhaps not decisively) in favor of the broader understanding of whatness both here and in (iii). Judging the opposition of hardness and softness is just comparing them and recognizing *that they are opposed to one another.* Considering the οὐσία of their opposition is asking or answering questions about the nature of this opposition: Is it a matter of degree? Is one term positive, the other negative? Can the opposition be explained in terms of physical microstructures? and so forth.

(vi) The last occurrence of οὐσία in section B is the most general and the most emphatic. It appears at 186c3, in the summing up of points made in sections A and B, before the final argument of section C. On pain of fatal | fallacy, the notion of οὐσία here should be the one which figures in the final argument, since that argument begins in the very next sentence: 'Can anything attain truth, if it does not even attain οὐσία?'   [126]

The context is a restatement of the dichotomy between (a) those items which human beings and animals can perceive from birth, as 'experiences (παθήματα) which pass through the body and reach the mind (ψυχή)', and (b) the reasonings or calculations (ἀναλογίσματα) concerning these experiences 'with respect to οὐσία and benefit (ὠφέλεια), reasonings which are acquired, by those who do acquire them, with difficulty and over a long period of time, through education and much trouble' (186c1–5). In what sense does οὐσία belong here next to benefit or advantage, as the goal of long and difficult training and reasoning? If I am right in suggesting that this reference to ὠφέλεια echoes the nontheoretical basis for wisdom (in what is better, advantageous, useful) proposed on behalf of Protagoras at 168d ff.,[41] then οὐσία must represent

---

[41] In addition to ἀγαθά, ἀμείνων, χρηστός at 166d–167c see τὸ συμφέρον at 172a and τὸ ὠφέλιμον at 177d–178a, 179a5.

the alternative, theoretical standard of *truth* or *reality*, which has been in
dispute throughout the dialogue, ever since Protagoras' Measure formula
was first introduced. (For the contrast between the two criteria, see e.g.
167a–d, esp. 167b4: ἐγὼ δὲ βελτίω μὲν τὰ ἕτερα <sc. φαντάσματα> τῶν
ἑτέρων <καλῶ>, ἀληθέστερα δὲ οὐδέν.) But if οὐσία simply *meant*
'truth' here, the first stage of the following argument could do no
work. Now what wisdom, training, and reasoning are needed for is *to
get things right*, to judge things *as they really are*. So it is the objective
standard of *how the world is*, the standard whose meaningfulness Protagoras wished to deny, that is most plausibly referred to here by οὐσία.
When thought succeeds in representing this οὐσία correctly, we have
truth. The οὐσία which is necessary but not sufficient for truth should be
the representational effort itself; that is, the content of the judgment or
statement which *claims* to say *how things are*. In order to preserve continuity between the arguments in A and in C we must recognize that
Plato does not always sharply distinguish between οὐσία as reality, or
being-so in the world, and οὐσία as content of a description of reality, the
being-so in a truth claim. He seems to slide here (in πρὸς οὐσίαν at 186c3)
from the intentional to the objective *being-so*, just as he sometimes slips
from knowing or saying of what-is *that* it is (ὡς ἔστι intentionally
understood) to knowing or saying it *as* it is (ὡς ἔστι objectively understood).[42] The slide is a natural one, since on a realistic (correspondence)
view of truth the intentional or judgmental being-so is a direct mirroring
of the objective facts. It is not obvious from the text that Plato is clearly
aware of this distinction, or of the need for drawing it here. But if we do
draw it for him, the argument becomes perspicuous: | ⟦127⟧

1. Having knowledge entails grasping truth.

2. Grasping truth entails grasping how things are ('attaining οὐσία'
   objectively understood).

[42] The slide is hard to locate precisely. At 186a2, οὐσία presented as the most general
κοινόν seems to me clearly intentional: the existential-predicative content of judgment
illustrated in 185a–d. At 186c3 the οὐσία which stands next to ὠφέλεια should be objective
truth or reality. The intermediate occurrences at 186a10, b6–7 can perhaps be read either
way.
   The judgmental and objective interpretations of οὐσία are explicitly distinguished from
one another in John Cooper's paper (*Phronesis* (1970), pp. 140–4), though he regards them as
alternative rather than complementary.

3. Grasping how things are entails judging that things are so ('attaining οὐσία' intentionally understood).

4. Judging that things are so ('calculating πρὸς οὐσίαν' at 186c3) entails a whole range of concepts, including existence (being something, as a subject of attributes), predication (being *x*, having an attribute), and truth claim (putting subject and attribute together in being-so, as a mirror of the world).

The range of concepts in 4 are all represented in the uses of οὐσία in sections A and B. In order to see how Plato could refer to them by the single term οὐσία or ἔστι, I would suggest a unifying title like 'intentional being-so' or 'propositional structure as a representation of reality', where 'reality' refers to being-so in the world, the objective οὐσία that figures in step 2. Since the οὐσία of step 4 (together with the other κοινά: 'same', 'different', etc.) can be found 'not in bodily sense experiences (παθήματα) but in our reasoning (συλλογισμός) concerning these', it is in the latter and not in the former that knowledge itself must be located (186d2–5).

Appendix: on the grammar of ὅ ἐστι F

Gregory Vlastos, developing some remarks of A. R. Lacey,[43] has recognized three possible construals of a phrase like ἐκεῖνο τὸ ὅ ἐστιν ἴσον at *Phaedo* 75b1–2, depending on whether (i) the verb is taken absolutely with ἴσον as subject; (ii) it is taken as copula, again with ἴσον as subject; (iii) it is taken as copula with ἴσον as predicate. These are certainly the three grammatical possibilities. I am less happy about the way Vlastos represents the alternatives. (In what follows, the words in parentheses are added by Vlastos to Lacey's formulation.)

   (i) That F which is (i.e. which really is, which is real).
   (ii) That thing which F is (i.e. that thing with which F is identical).
   (iii) That thing which is (an) F (or 'which really is F').

Here the issue of grammatical construal is confounded with problems of philosophical exegesis. In (i) the absolute construction is presented neither as the idiomatic veridical nor as the existential but as a specifically philosophic existential-veridical: 'really is', 'is real'. In (ii) the

---

[43] Vlastoz, *Platonic Studies* (Princeton, NJ: Princeton University Press, 1973), 261 n. 102, citing A. R. Lacey, 'Plato's *Sophist* and the Forms', *Classical Quarterly*, NS, 9 (1959), 51.

notion of identity imposes a particular logical straitjacket on a copula that may be more loosely definitional (my 'is of whatness'). And in (iii) the insertion of 'an' before 'F' prejudges the interpretation of self-predication in a way that Plato would not allow. It is clear that the Form F is in some sense the privileged bearer of the name 'F', so that it is conspicuously true to say of such a Form *that it is F*. But the philosophical | problem of self-predication is not to be resolved by   ⟦128⟧ fixing the syntax of ὅ ἐστιν ἴσον or ὅ ἐστι καλόν.

I propose here to ignore the philosophical exegesis and consider only the grammatical construction. I doubt whether this is of great philosophical interest, but it is just as well to make clear what I take the situation to be. We must distinguish between (A) those passages where the relative clause is used in an idiomatic way, blended with the grammatical context, and (B) those texts where it has become a fixed formula.

Considering first (A), I do not believe there are any examples where the absolute construction (i) is the more natural reading, taken in context. There are a few examples, such as αὐτὸ τὸ ὅ ἐστιν at *Phaedo* 74d6 and ἐκείνου τε ὀρέγεται τοῦ ὅ ἐστιν ἴσον at 75b1, where an absolute reading ('the Equal which is real') is possible, and might well be included by grammatical overdetermination. But since a copula construction is indicated both before (at 74b2) and after (ὅτι ἐστίν at 75b6) this passage, it seems natural to preserve the continuity of a copula reading throughout. Thus I take τὸ ὅ ἐστιν (ἴσον) here as literally 'what is (really) equal' or 'what equal really is', leaving open the choice between syntax (ii) and (iii).

Construction (ii), with the nominal term as subject of the copula, is illustrated by at least one unambiguous example, at *Meno* 72c9–d1: τὸν ἀποκρινόμενον τῷ ἐρωτήσαντι ἐκεῖνο (sc. τὸ εἶδος) δηλῶσαι, ὅ τυγχάνει οὖσα ἀρετή, 'the answerer will point out to the questioner (who asks "What is virtue?") that form (εἶδος) which virtue really is'. (It is interesting, but grammatically irrelevant, that we do not have the standard form ὅ ἐστι in this example.) The same syntax seems plausible whenever the relative clause can be construed as an indirect question: 'to know what F is'.[44] So perhaps at *Symp.* 211c8 (γνῷ ... ὅ ἐστι καλόν, 'knows ... what beautiful is') and almost certainly at *Phaedo* 74b2

---

[44] Ernst Kapp, *Ausgewählte Schriften* (Berlin: de Gruyter, 1968), 64, suggests that this is the origin of the ὅ ἐστι formula, and that a decisive change takes place once the nominal term is construed as predicate, as in (iii).

108   CHARLES H. KAHN

(ἐπιστάμεθα αὐτὸ ὅ ἐστιν, 'we know what it is') and ἐπιστήμη αὐτοῦ τοῦ ἴσου ὅτι ἐστίν at 75b5.

Clear examples of (iii), with the nominal term as predicate, are found in *Lysis* 219c–d (ἐκεῖνο ὅ ἐστιν πρῶτον φίλον... ὃ ὡς ἀληθῶς ἐστι φίλον), and in the *Symposium* in connection with knowledge of the Form of Beautiful (211c7 ἐκεῖνο τὸ μάθημα... ὅ ἐστιν... ἐκείνου τοῦ καλοῦ μάθημα). But the first unmistakable use of this expression for a Form, in the very same context, is grammatically ambiguous, as we have seen: ὅ ἐστι καλόν at 211c8 may be 'what *is* beautiful' as easily as 'what beautiful is'. And, as we noted earlier, most of the *Phaedo* examples are similarly ambiguous (above, pp. 107 ff.). The most striking fact is how often the subject–predicate syntax of the ὅ ἐστι clause is *under*determined. But that is natural enough if the formula is thought of as a definitional equivalence, an answer to the question 'What is X?'.

When we turn to (B) passages, where ὅ ἐστι F has become a fixed designation for the Forms, the situation is rather different. Some cases seem to admit either subject or predicate syntax for the noun, e.g. *Rep.* 10 597a2: (τὸ εἶδος) ὃ δή φαμεν εἶναι ὅ ἐστι κλίνη, either 'the Form which bed is' or 'the Form which *is* bed'. But another example from the same context actually excludes both constructions: *Rep.* 10. 597c3 μίαν μόνην (κλίνην) αὐτὴν ἐκείνην ὅ ἔστιν κλίνη, where on any grammatical reading we ought to have ἥ ἐστι κλίνη. What such a passage shows is that ὅ ἐστι κλίνη (or at 597a4 ὅ ἐστι alone) has become a frozen formula, sealed off from the syntactic context. And the same is true for the example at *Timaeus* 39e7: ἐνούσας ἰδέας τῷ ὅ ἐστιν ζῷον, 'Forms being present in the Real Animal', where τὸ ὅ ἐστιν ζῷον functions as a syntactic unit like τὸ τί ἦν εἶναι in Aristotle. |

[129]   Vlastos (*loc. cit.*) has argued that at *Rep.* 597a4 the verb in ὅ ἐστι must be used absolutely, with the sense 'is real'. I confess that I see nothing in the context to exclude a copula reading throughout. On the other hand, since the syntax of ἐστί in these frozen, formulaic examples is even more underdetermined than in the contextual uses mentioned under (A), there is no reason to rule out the absolute (veridical-existential) reading as a possible overtone. The Forms are, after all, real existent entities, as well as being truly and essentially what-they-are. But it is Plato's general doctrine and not the grammar of the clause which justifies us in reading this meaning into ὅ ἐστι F.

5

A Return to the Theory of the Verb *Be* and the Concept of Being

The recent reprinting of my book *The Verb 'Be' in Ancient Greek* by Hackett, thirty years after its appearance in 1973, gave me the opportunity to rethink and reformulate the theoretical framework for my description of the Greek verb. Since the audience for the reprinted book will inevitably be restricted, I present here a more accessible, slightly revised version of the new (2003) introduction. In the original 1973 book the theoretical discussion was far too long and not always consistent. What follows is a more concise and, I hope, more coherent version of my theoretical account of *einai*.

1. My original aim, beginning as early as 1964, was to provide a kind of grammatical prolegomenon to Greek ontology. The notion of Being, as formulated by Parmenides, seems to come from nowhere, like a philosophical meteor with no historical antecedents but profound historical consequences. It would be difficult to overstate the influence of this new conception. On the one hand, Plato's doctrine of the eternal being of the Forms as well as his struggle with Not-Being both clearly derive from Parmenides' account of *to on*. On the other hand, not only Aristotle's doctrine of categories as 'the many ways that things are said *to be*' but also his definition of metaphysics as the study of 'being qua being' provide deliberate alternatives to Parmenides' monolithic conception of *what is*. And that is not all. There is a well-known line of development in Greek natural philosophy that leads to Anaxagoras, Empedocles, and the atomists, and that can only be understood as a response to the Parmenidean challenge. But where

did such a powerful conception come from, and how are we to understand it? Since there is no clear anticipation of the concept of Being in Parmenides' predecessors, our only clue is the linguistic material that Parmenides had at his disposal; that is to say, the usage of the verb *to be* in early Greek. So I set out to catalogue these uses, in the hope that a better grasp of this material could contribute to a better understanding of the ontological doctrines of Parmenides, Plato, and Aristotle.

Thus my original project was philological and hermeneutical. However, this project was altered by my concern with the attacks on this concept from relativists and positivists, who claimed that the metaphysics of Being resulted simply from linguistic confusion or from the reification of local peculiarities of vocabulary. Since the question of Being was of such fundamental importance for the Greek philosophers, I felt obliged to defend their theoretical concern with Being as a valid philosophical enterprise. The outcome is my counterclaim that the | variety of uses for *einai* form a significantly unified conceptual [382] system, a network of interdependent concepts clustering around the notion of predication, and that these concepts provide a proper subject for ontology both ancient and modern.

Hence the argument of my book reaches two conclusions, one linguistic and one philosophical. The philosophical conclusion, my defense of Greek ontology, rests on my account of the system of *einai* but does not follow from it. Greek ontology might be defended on different grounds, and a reader might accept my account of the system of *einai* but doubt its value as a defense of ontology. Furthermore, I have not tried to demonstrate the fruitfulness of my linguistic results for the interpretation of Greek philosophy. That could be done only by a detailed analysis of Platonic and Aristotelian texts.[1] My study of *einai* remains, after all, essentially a grammatical prolegomenon to the history of Greek ontology.

2. Thirty years ago the theory of the verb *to be* in Greek, and in Indo-European languages generally, was a simple one. There was a verb **es-* whose original meaning was 'exists', or perhaps something

---

[1] For the application of my account of *einai* to Parmenides see Essay 8 below with references there to earlier publications. For Plato's usage see Essay 4 above.

more concrete like 'be present', that came eventually to be used as dummy verb with nominal predicates, so that it lost its original mean-ing and degenerated into the role of 'mere copula'. This distinction between *be* as copula and *be* meaning 'exists' was first made famous by John Stuart Mill, who claimed that the entire metaphysics of Being was based upon a confusion between these two uses of the verb. Linguists and philologists have generally taken over this dichotomy for their own purposes. I note as a mark of its pervasive influence that Kirk and Raven could refer without question to 'the ambiguity, of which Parmenides himself was unconscious, between the predicative and the existential senses of the Greek word *esti*'.[2] Malcolm Schofield corrected this view by denying that Parmenides himself was confused; but Schofield agreed that the Parmenidean use of *esti* 'is simultaneously existential and predicative'.[3] I think this change reflects our greater sophistication in dealing with the Greek verb *einai*. At least we no longer take for granted Mill's deflationary account of Greek theories of Being as based upon a linguistic confusion. But I suggest that we need to go a step farther and call into question the fundamental nature of the contrast between copula and existential verb.

A radical critique of this dichotomy is easier today than it was thirty years ago, because others have shown the way.[4] G. E. L. Owen's formula that, for Plato and Aristotle, to be is always to be something or other, was one way of undermining this distinction by showing that existential uses in Aristotle were also predicative. And Owen's approach has been decisively advanced by Lesley Brown's work on the syntax of *einai* in Plato's *Sophist*.[5] I will not reargue here my old

[2] G. S. Kirk and J. E. Raven, *The Presocratic Philosophers* (Cambridge: Cambridge University Press, 1957), 269.

[3] G. S. Kirk, J. E. Raven, and M Schofield, *The Presocratic Philosophers*, 2nd edn. (Cambridge: Cambridge University Press, 1983), 246.

[4] See e.g. Hintikka's attack on what he calls the Frege–Russell claim of ambiguity for the verb *is* ('The Varieties of Being in Aristotle', in S. Knuuttila and J. Hintikka (eds.), *The Logic of Being: Historical Studies* (Dordrecht: Reidel, 1986)).

[5] G. E. L. Owen, 'Aristotle on the Snares of Ontology', in R. Bambrough (ed.), *New Essays on Plato and Aristotle* (New York: Humanities, 1965) and *Logic, Science, and Dialectic: Collected Papers in Greek Philosophy*, ed. M. Nussbaum (Ithaca: Cornell University Press, 1986); L. Brown, 'Being in the Sophist: A Syntactical Enquiry', *Oxford Studies in Ancient Philosophy*, 4 (1986), 49–70.

objections to the dichotomy between copula and existential | uses;   [[383
namely, (a) that there are important uses of *einai* that are neither,
such as the veridical; (b) that there are other uses that are both, such
as existential-locative sentences; and (c) that the distinction itself is
problematic, since the copula use is defined syntactically while existence is a matter of the lexical meaning of the verb.

3. Acknowledging all of these deficiencies, we may still find the
copula–existential distinction useful for organizing the data, as I did in
my book. However, what I did not do was reflect critically enough on
the distinction itself in order to recognize that the copula use is
implicitly existential, and that most if not all existential uses of *einai*
are potentially predicative. The syntactic distinction between copulative and absolute constructions is real enough but superficial, a feature
of surface structure only for the Greek verb. This is how I interpret the
results of Lesley Brown's study of Plato's *Sophist*. She shows that the
relation between the verb *einai* in sentences of the form *X is* and *X is Y*
is like that between the verb *teaches* in *Jane teaches* and *Jane teaches
French*. This seems true not only for Plato but also for Aristotle and
for the language generally. Adding a predicate to *einai* does not change
the meaning of the verb any more than adding a direct object to *teaches*
changes the meaning of the verb *to teach*. From the point of view of
transformational grammar, the longer form is more basic: *X teaches* is
derived from *X teaches something* by zeroing the direct object. Similarly,
I suggest, *X is* can be derived from *X is Y* by zeroing the predicate. This
is one way of formulating the thesis that I have modestly referred to as
my version of the Copernican Revolution: replacing existence by
predication at the center of the system of uses for *einai*. Logically
speaking, every absolute or existential use of *einai* can be seen as an
abridged form of some predication. *X is* is short for *X is Y* for some *Y*.[6]
That is the full meaning of the formula: to be is to be something or
other.

Let me say a bit more on the interdependence of predicative and
existential uses.

---

[6] Hence the existence of the subject is entailed by basic predications, as I argue below. But
the syntactic derivation will vary for the different existential sentence forms. See below,
Sects. 8–11.

(i) *A copula use of einai is implicitly existential.* Take an ordinary use of *esti* as copula, with nominal or locative predicates. If you bring *esti* to the front of the sentence, you will often get a strong existential nuance that justifies a translation as 'There is such and such': ἔστι πόλις Ἐφύρη μυχῶι Ἄργεος 'There is a city Ephyre in the corner of Argos'.[7] But word order has no syntactic significance in Greek. In the initial position the syntax of the verb is still that of the copula, as in 'Ephyre is a city' (Ἐφύρη πόλις ἐστί). The initial position gives rhetorical emphasis, but it could not give the copula verb an existential sense if the verb itself did not possess existential import. This implication of existence for the subject is generally stronger when the copula verb is construed with a locative complement, as in the sentence just cited. (Thus we can identify a whole class of locative-existential sentence types.[8]) | But the existential implication of the copula does   ⟦384⟧ not depend upon locative complements.[9] I argue that positing the subject as something to talk *about* is an essential element of subject–predicate assertions, so that some claim of existence for the subject is implicit in all affirmative subject–predicate sentences. (I leave aside the case of negative sentences as more problematic. We may think of the negation as potentially nullifying any claim of existence for the subject.) In copula sentences this claim is carried by copula *esti* as sign of the subject–predicate relation. Such existential import for the copula can explain why, in Aristotle's square of opposition, 'All Greeks are human' entails 'Some humans are Greeks', although the usual quantified version of this rule is not valid in formal logic.[10] In a natural language like Greek, a predicative assertion implies a subject of which something is true, and (in normal cases) for the predication to be true the subject must exist. If there is no subject to begin with, it cannot have positive attributes.

[7] From sentence 27 in my *The Verb 'Be' in Ancient Greek* (Dordrecht: Reidel, 1973; repr. Indianapolis, Ind.: Hackett, 2003), 246.

[8] See my *The Verb 'Be'*, 164–7, 245–65.

[9] For examples of nominal copula with existential nuance see *The Verb 'Be'*, sentences 40 (p. 250), 45, and 46 (p. 259).

[10] In a Fregean scheme the plural grammatical subject in 'All Greeks are human' would suggest a different analysis in terms of classes or concepts, not a straightforward *S is P* sentence. I am assuming, however, that for an Aristotelian interpretation an expression like 'all Greeks' refers not to classes or concepts but to Greeks taken individually, just like 'some Greeks'.

The abnormal cases are those where, for nongrammatical reasons, the predicate expression does not assign a real attribute and hence the existence of the subject is problematic. That is why, in the time of Abelard, logicians began reparsing sentences with *chimaera* and *centaurus* as subject term of the copula *est*. Sentences like *Chimaera est opinabilis* 'The chimera is a subject of opinion' were then analyzed as 'Someone imagines chimeras'.[11]

This view of the copula is systematically developed by Allan Bäck. He presents this as Avicenna's interpretation of the copula, which he endorses: 'The copula *is* asserts the claim of existence', so that *S is P* is to be read as *S is existent as a P*. Thus for Aristotle (according to Avicenna and Bäck) an ordinary copula sentence *S is P* makes two claims: 'S exists', and 'S is a P'.[12] Because they did not thematize existence in our sense, the Greek philosophers do not seem to have worried much about negative existentials. (Some interpreters have claimed to recognize the modern problem of negative existentials in Plato's concern with Not-Being, but I believe they are misguided by the desire to modernize Plato's problems in order to make them seem more interesting for a contemporary reader.) Nor do I see any explicit concern in Plato or Aristotle with predication for imaginary entities, as in Mill's example: 'A centaur is a fiction of the poets'.[13]

So much for the existential force of the copula. Now for the converse claim.

(ii) *Existential uses of einai are potentially predicative.* In English *to exist* | [385] does not take predicate nouns or adjectives, and it does not normally take locatives either. (*Socrates exists wise* is not an acceptable sentence,

---

[11] K. Jacobi, 'Peter Abelard's Investigations into the Meaning and Functions of the Speech Sign "Est"', in S. Knuuttila and J. Hintikka (eds.), *The Logic of Being: Historical Studies* (Dordrecht: Reidel, 1986), 157–8; see also S. Ebbesen, 'The Chimera's Diary', in Knuuttila and Hintikka, *Logic of Being.*

[12] A. Bäck, *Aristotle's Theory of Predication* (Leiden/Boston/Köln: Brill, 2000), 3, 11, and *passim.*

[13] Aristotle does mention centaurs once (*Post. An.* 2. 1) and goatstags several times (Bonitz *Index* s.v. τραγέλαφος) as examples of 'what is not' (τὸ μὴ ὄν). For commentary see L. Brown, 'The Verb "To Be" in Greek Philosophy: Some Remarks', in Steven Everson (ed.), *Companions to Ancient Thought*, iii (Cambridge: Cambridge University Press, 1994), 233–5. For the claim that questions of existence are not thematized in Greek philosophy see Essay 3 above.

and *Socrates exists in the marketplace* is not acceptable without a special context.) In this respect, *exists* is never a good translation for *esti*, since there is hardly any use of the Greek verb that cannot be completed by a predicate expression. The most explicit Greek formula for asserting existence is in fact predicative in form: *einai ti* 'to be something (rather than nothing)'. This is a paradigmatic illustration of the point that *einai* does not lose its existential force when it gains a predicate.

Lesley Brown has shown how the absolute or 'existential' uses of *einai* in the *Sophist* are regarded by Plato as so closely related to the predicative use that he treats 'such and such is' as interchangeable with 'such and such is something'. And the same is true for a crucial argument introducing the doctrine of Forms in *Republic* 5, where Socrates begins by construing *what is* absolutely in his identification of the Forms as 'what is completely' (*to pantelôs on*, 477a3) but ends by contrasting this with 'the many beautiful things' each of which 'will also appear ugly' (479a), and hence 'oscillates between not being and purely being' (479d). Here again it is clear that Plato draws no distinction between *einai* with and without an additional predicate.[14]

Both in the *Sophist* and in the *Republic*, then, we can say that Plato has only one concept of Being, expressed by *einai*, *ousia*, and *on*, a concept that will cover the notions of existence, predication, identity, truth, and perhaps more. That is why many scholars have wanted to speak of a 'fused' meaning for the verb, where existence and predication come together. I think this term is misleading, since the idea of fusion implies that the constituents were previously separate from one another. Of course for analytical purposes we need to introduce such distinctions into our hermeneutical metalanguage in commenting on Plato's text. But we must be alert to the discrepancy between such modern distinctions and what is actually under discussion in the

---

[14] In a letter Lesley Brown cites a passage from Plato, *Laws* 10. 901c8–d2, where a single occurrence of *einai* provides the verb for three clauses, although in the first clause (where the verb occurs) the syntax is absolute and the meaning existential, whereas in the second and third clauses (where the verb is absent and must be supplied) the syntax is copulative with an adjectival predicate. This shows, as Brown points out, 'that for Plato they are one and the same verb, which can be both complete and incomplete'.

ancient texts. It is we who are fusing the two meanings, not Plato or Aristotle.[15]

Putting the predicative use in the center of the system, then, means reinterpreting the so-called existential uses as a secondary or derivative phenomenon. When we come to the syntactic analysis, we will see that both existential and veridical uses are best construed as second-order forms, as a semantic sentence operator on a first-order sentence. I shall suggest that these second-order, explicitly semantic uses of *einai* are to be explained by reference to the implicitly semantic functions | of the verb in its first-order use as copula.   [386

4. I claim, then, that it is precisely the predicative function of *einai* that serves as logical foundation for the system of uses for *einai*, and that it is the conceptual unity of this system that justifies the theme of Being as a subject for philosophical research. More generally, I claim that the three notions of predication, existence, and truth belong together in any theory of how language functions as an attempt to depict reality— or, more neutrally, as a medium for conveying information. It is this network of interdependent concepts that explains why ontology, the theory of *to on*, emerged as a branch of Greek philosophy. And the conceptual coherence of the Greek discussions of Being will emerge most clearly if the predicative function of the verb is recognized as fundamental.

Before developing the syntactic argument for this thesis, I want to support it with a strictly philosophical consideration. In earlier presentations of the case for the priority of the predicative construction I failed to take into account an important piece of evidence. This is the famous doctrine of Plotinus that Being (*einai*, *on*, or *ousia*) does not belong to his supreme principle, called the One and the Good. If by Being Plotinus understood what we call existence, it would be absurd for him to deny it so categorically of the One. For if the One did not exist, nothing else would exist—there would be no world at all, neither a noetic cosmos nor a sensible cosmos, since everything else depends for its reality upon the One. By denying *einai* of the One, Plotinus denies it not reality but

---

[15] For those passages where Aristotle distinguishes between being *simpliciter* and being such and such (*Sophistici Elenchi* 167ᵃ1, 180ᵃ36; *Post. An.* 2. 1.89ᵇ32) see the discussion in Brown's 'The Verb "To Be"', that shows that Aristotle is not making Mill's distinction.

predicative structure, on the grounds that the being of predication implies plurality; namely, the conceptual distinction between the subject (*hypokeimenon*) and what is predicated of it.[16] That is why 'One' and 'Good' do not represent attributes of the supreme principle, but only names that somehow refer to the One but do not describe it. I submit that Plotinus is relying here on his acute philosophical sense for the fundamental function of the verb *einai* in Greek.

Since I now insist that copula uses of *einai* will normally imply existence for their subject, my proposed revolution in favor of the predicative function should seem less objectionable to those scholars who, like Rijk, regard existence as fundamental for the philosophical meaning of the verb.[17] These two apparently competing conceptions of *einai*—whether the predicative or the existential use belongs at the center—are ultimately not in conflict with one another, since their concerns are so different. My claim is that the syntactic function of predication is more basic for comprehending the uses of *einai* as a unified system, and also for understanding the role of the verb in philosophy. If, on the other hand, we are looking for the lexical content or *meaning* of the verb, as given in translation and paraphrase, the copula *syntax* will not even be a candidate. We discuss this question below, in section 12.

5. Before turning to the syntactic description, I need to borrow some concepts | from the philosophy of language, and in particular the concepts of predication and existence. These will be needed not only to describe the data adequately but also to formulate my argument for the coherence of the Greek system. In addition I need the method of transformational grammar in order to provide a rigorous syntactical description of the sentence types exemplifying the copulative, existential, and veridical uses. I have adopted the transformational grammar of Zellig Harris in the version that includes a theory of elementary or kernel sentences, from which more complex sentences can be formed or into which they can be decomposed. This theory of elementary

[387]

---

[16] For Plotinus' denial that the One is a being (*on*) 'so that it would not be predicated of something else' see *Ennead* 6. 9. 5, 30–3. But I do not mean to suggest that Plato has the same thought in mind in the uniquely puzzling passage at *Republic* 6. 509b where Socrates describes the Good as 'beyond Being (*ousia*), exceeding it in dignity and power'.

[17] L. M. de Rijk, *Aristotle: Semantics and Ontology*, i (Leiden: Brill, 2002), 30–3 and *passim*.

sentences provides a fully worked-out contemporary model for the kind of first-order descriptive language that is sketched by Aristotle in the *Categories*; while Harris's theory of transformations permits us to see how, at least in principle, the rest of the language can be constructed on such a base. I take this to be the independent philosophical interest of such a system of transformational grammar, over and above my use of it for a description of the Greek verb. Here is a system that actually displays the underlying grammatical structure of sentences in a natural language. By way of contrast, such a system makes clear the distance between a properly grammatical analysis and Aristotle's logical-ontological project in the *Categories*.

For our syntactic analysis we need the notion of elementary or first-order sentence structure. This will be specified theoretically by the kernel sentence forms of our transformational grammar.[18] Here I list a few simple forms, where N stands for noun, V for verb, A for adjective, P for preposition.

1. NV: *Socrates walks*
2. NVN: *Socrates sees Plato*
3. N is A: *Socrates is wise*
4. N is N: *Socrates is a man*
5. N is PN: *Socrates is in the marketplace*; *Socrates is in trouble*.

Sentence forms 3–4 represent the nominal copula; sentence form 5 represents the locative and paralocative copula.

In first-order sentences the subject term N may be a proper name, but it may also be a common noun referring to persons or to individual things (animals, plants, places, etc.). I count as syntactically first-order such sentences as *A man speaks*, *The cat sees the mouse*, *The tree is tall*, *The tree stands in the yard*. Because these subject nouns can also appear in predicate position, some theorists might prefer not to count them as elementary but instead derive them transformationally from the corresponding predicate (*is a man*, *is a cat*, etc.). In order to avoid this theoretical debate as to what can count as elementary, I prefer to rely on the more generous notion of first-order nouns, referring to

---

[18] For the full theory refer to *The Verb 'Be'*, pp. 10–22.

persons, places, and particular things. Whether the class of first-order nouns can be defined in purely grammatical terms is unclear.[19] Here I simply take for granted this distinction between 'concrete' nouns on the one hand, referring to individuals, and, on | the other hand [[388]] 'abstract' nouns that are formed from nominalized predicates, e.g. *wisdom*, transformationally derived from *(he) is wise*, or *outcry*, transformationally derived from *(they) cried out*. The syntactical level of the sentence will depend upon the level of the subject noun. Thus *Socrates is wise* is a first-order use of the copula verb. On the other hand, in *Wisdom is a virtue* and *The outcry was far away*, the syntax of the copula is second-order, since these sentences have second-order (abstract) nouns as their subject.

Some explanation is required for the terminology of subject and predicate. Predication can be defined (without reference to the verb *be*) in terms of the basic noun–verb sentence *John runs* or (to take the example by which Plato first introduced this analysis) *Theaetetus sits*. By grammatical subject I mean the noun (or noun phrase) in sentences of this form, and by grammatical predicate I mean the verb or verb phrase in such sentences. By predication I mean, first of all, the relation between noun and verb (or subject and predicate) that constitutes sentencehood. Here predication is a purely syntactic notion, equivalent to sentencehood for a noun–verb sentence.

Initially, then, the terms *subject* and *predicate* are defined syntactically, and identified with the two sentence components that Plato and Aristotle referred to as noun (*onoma*) and verb (*rhêma*) respectively. However, when Aristotle introduced the term 'subject' (*hypokeimenon*) into his own theory of predication, he did not refer it to the *onoma*, the nominal sentence-component, but rather to the object or individual that the sentence is about. The original meaning of the term *subject* is thus what we sometimes call the understood subject or the logical subject: the subject in the sense in which the subject of the sentence *Socrates died in 399 BC* is not the name *Socrates* but Socrates himself. This original (but from the modern point of view secondary) use of the term 'subject' for an entity that is not a linguistic part of the sentence is essential for Aristotle's notion of predication, and it is also required for

---

[19] For discussion of this question see *The Verb 'Be'*, pp. 76–7, 290.

the analysis to be given here. We have already relied on the notion of (extralinguistic) subject of reference in defining first-order nouns as those that refer to persons or particular things. I call attention here to this double sense of the term 'subject', because I will use it systematically in both senses. In regard to the sentence *Socrates died in 399 BC* I will call the name *Socrates* the syntactic or grammatical subject of the sentence, whereas it is Socrates himself who is the ontological or semantic subject.

I want to preserve this original ontological sense of Aristotle's term 'subject' (*hypokeimenon*), and not merely for historical reasons. The true philosophical interest of the subject–predicate analysis of sentences is that it points beyond sentences to their subject in the world. Paraphrasing a formula from Quine, we can say that a subject–predicate sentence is true only if the predicate expression is true of the *object* that the subject expression refers to.[20] Thus the notion of truth | for sentences presupposes the notion of truth for extralinguistic [389] predication, for linguistic expressions being true of objects 'in the world' or in some universe of discourse. In this way the subject–predicate structure of sentences, interpreted in terms of truth, entails the notion of existence for the semantic subject. (This is the backbone of my argument that the three uses—predication, truth, and existence—belong together.)

I use the term 'semantic' here by analogy with the notion of formal semantics in logic, in the sense of giving an interpretation of formal structures in terms of some extralinguistic model, for example in set theory. For sentences about Socrates our model is not set theory but the history of ancient Greece. In the case of the Homeric texts analyzed in my book on *einai*, the domain for semantic interpretation will be the world as described in the Homeric poems, the heroes and events of the Trojan War. For the semantic interpretation it does not matter whether the domain of discourse is provided by history or by epic poetry. Achilles himself is the semantic subject of many sentences in the *Iliad*, just as Socrates himself is the semantic subject of the

---

[20] Quine: 'Predication joins a general term and a singular term to form a sentence that is true or false according as the general term is true or false of the object, if any, to which the singular term refers' (*Word and Object* (Cambridge, MA: MIT Press, 1960), 96).

sentence *He died in 399 BC*. This notion of semantic predication, as a relation between a sentence and an extralinguistic subject that the sentence is about, will be needed for our account of the existential and veridical uses of *einai*.

If we now combine this notion of semantic predication with the earlier notion of basic (first-order) sentences taking concrete nouns as subjects, we see that the grammatical analysis has some definite onto-logical implications. My conception of transformational grammar as a descriptive object-language will properly imply a quasi-Aristotelian or Strawsonian ontology with persons and stable objects as its primary entities, the semantic subjects for first-order sentences. This is not ontology in any very strong sense, since the universe of discourse that represents reality for my sample sentences from the *Iliad* and *Odyssey* is simply the world of the Homeric epic. But the basic sentences describing this world will take persons and individual things as their semantic subjects. In this respect, my use of transformational grammar has the effect of begging the question against two alternative conceptions of basic sentences. The two views I reject are, on the one hand, an empiricist preference for protocol sentences that report something like sense data, Lockean simple ideas or Humean impres-sions, and, on the other hand, a Davidsonian insistence that actions and events be counted as basic entities on the same level as concrete things. I do not claim that the choice of *John runs* or *Socrates is wise* as elementary sentences with individuals as (extralinguistic) subjects is metaphysically justified, only that it is more useful for analyzing the syntax of sentences in a natural language like Greek or English. In such an analysis, an event such as the death of Socrates or the French Revolution will be represented by a predication with individuals (Socrates, people in France) as semantic subject. On this view of first-order sentences, *the death of Socrates* will be analyzed as a nomin-alization of *Socrates died*, and an expression like *the French Revolution* will be construed as a transform from a more elementary *NV* form like *(some) Frenchmen revolted*. This assumption is not intended to solve any | [390]
metaphysical problems, only to serve as a method for the syntactic analysis that follows.

6. We turn now to surveying the various uses of *einai* as the basis for my argument for the unity of the system. With this goal in mind I limit the present survey to copula, existential, and veridical uses.[21]

Since the copula is a strictly syntactic notion, a description of such uses can be relatively straightforward. As we have seen, there are two kinds of copula sentence: the nominal copula, where *einai* is construed with predicate adjectives and nouns, and the locative copula, where it is construed with predicates of place (*in the marketplace, in Athens*). A subclass of the locative copula is the paralocative construction, where the predicate expression is locative in form but metaphorical in meaning: *is in trouble, is in a bad mood*.[22] All of these sentence forms are repeated again in second-order syntax with abstract (nominalized) forms as subject: *Wisdom is a virtue, The outcry was far away, Killing is against the law*. For such second-order sentences we need to reinterpret the principle that a true predication implies the existence of its subject. Instead of speaking of existence for the abstract subject of such sentences, we may say that what is implied by a second-order copula use is truth for some underlying sentence: if the second-order sentence is true, one or more underlying first-order sentences must also be true. To say that wisdom exists means that someone is wise; the occurrence of a revolution means that people revolt; sentences about killing imply that someone may kill.

An analysis of the existential and veridical uses will be more difficult than this account of the copula, since the notions of existence and truth refer primarily not to sentence structure but to the meaning of the verb, or to the meaning of the whole sentence. The problem is how to make this meaning precise enough to serve as a basis for explaining the relations between the linguistic functions of predication, existence, and truth. My strategy has been to use the syntactic analysis as a tool for specifying the logical function of the verb in existential and veridical sentences. I assume that only if we have an accurate description of the

---

[21] This means ignoring the possessive and potential (*esti* plus infinitive) constructions, both of which can be analyzed as special cases of the existential or locative-existential use, if the latter is thought of as meaning something like 'is present, is available' (see *The Verb 'Be'*, pp. 265–71, 272–6).

[22] For examples see *The Verb 'Be'*, pp. 159–64.

syntactic structure of these various uses of *einai* can we give a clear account of their conceptual relations.

7. I take the veridical first, because here the basic syntax is clear and uniform, whereas the existential use of *einai* introduces a baffling diversity of sentence forms. The veridical use (where the verb means 'is true' or 'is the case') is statistically rather rare, and accordingly it has often been treated as a special case of the existential verb. We shall see that, in the end, such a treatment can be justified. If I have chosen instead to give this use its own name and assign to it a separate chapter in the book on *einai*, that is for two reasons. In the first place, this use of *to be* (as in *So be it* or *Tell it like it is*) has venerable credentials. The meaning | of *to be* as 'to be true' must be prehistoric, since the word for   [[391]] truth in languages at opposite ends of the Indo-European world—in India and in Scandinavia—is provided by a derivative of the present participle of **es-* (*san, satya*, etc., direct cognates of *to on* in Greek; so also in archaic English we have the word *sooth*).[23] My second reason for devoting separate attention to the veridical is the fundamental importance of this use of *einai* for philosophy, as one of the preferred expressions for the notion of Being as the object of knowledge. Although for Parmenides, as for Aristotle, Being (*to on*) means many things, it points crucially to the notion of truth as the goal of understanding and the object of knowledge.[24]

˙ By a veridical use generally I mean any occurrence of *einai* that can have the value 'is true' or 'is the case, is a fact'. More strictly speaking, however, the veridical *construction* is a specific sentence form. In the veridical construction a clause containing *einai* is correlated with a clause of comparison containing a verb of saying or thinking: ἔστι ταῦτα οὕτω ὅπως σὺ λέγεις 'Things are as you say (that they are)'.[25] I call the clause with the verb *be* the *essive* clause, and the clause with the propositional attitude of thinking or saying the *intentional* clause. In idiomatic usage the second occurrence of the essive clause is

---

[23] For the evidence from India and Scandinavia see H. Frisk, ' "Wahrheit" und "Lüge" in den indogermanischen Sprachen', *Göteborgs Hogskolas Arsskrift*, 41/3 (1935), 3–6, 28.

[24] In *Metaphysics* 9. 10. 1051ᵇ1 Aristotle says that the meaning of *is* as 'is true' is 'being in the strictest sense' (*to kuriôtata on*). I believe that the veridical sense also fits best with Parmenides' opening claim that 'you cannot know what-is-not' (fr. 2.7), although other values of *einai* are also required for his argument.

[25] Compare sentences 2 and 3 on p. 336 in *The Verb 'Be'*.

normally zeroed; hence we have the simpler form 'Things are as you say'. But this second essive clause will show up after a verb of saying in the more explicit philosophical formulae for truth: 'To say of what is *that it is not*, or of what is not *that it is*, is false; but to say of what is *that it is*, or of what is not *that it is not*, is true' (Aristotle, *Metaphysics* 4. 7. 1011^{b}26). In the idiomatic version where the second essive clause is zeroed we have as the syntactic subject of *einai* a pronoun (*tauta* 'these things') referring to whatever the interlocutor has said, and hence to one or more underlying sentences. Thus the syntax of *einai* in this veridical construction is obviously second-order, since the underlying subject of *einai* is sentential in form. The verb *einai* in the essive clause takes as its subject the content of the underlying sentence; that is, the state of affairs corresponding to the claim expressed in the intentional clause ('what you say'). The logical function of *esti* in the essive clause is to endorse the interlocutor's claim by asserting that precisely this state of affairs obtains or 'exists', that things are 'in reality' the way the interlocutor says that they are. Hence if we think of the obtaining of states of affairs as a particular mode of existence, we can classify the veridical use as a special case of the existential verb.[26] |

[[392]]   The syntax of *esti* in the primary essive clause ('Things *are* this way') can be described as that of a sentence operator, since the verb takes one or more underlying sentences as its source or operand. More precisely, it functions as a *semantical* sentence operator, since it posits the content of the operand sentence in 'reality' (which for Homeric sentences means in the semifictional reality of the epic poems). To explain why it is precisely the verb *einai* that functions as semantical operator, I need to introduce the notion of a sentential truth claim.

For simplicity, I assume that we are dealing here with ordinary declarative sentences; that is to say, with indicative sentences spoken

[26] Matthen has shown how *einai* in the formulae for truth can be interpreted as a kind of existential *is*, taking as its subject what he calls a predicative complex, an Aristotelian unity of thing and predicable roughly comparable to the modern notion of a fact or state-of-affairs ('Greek Ontology and the "Is" of Truth', *Phronesis*, 28, 1983). This will be an attractive solution for anyone who (like De Rijk) thinks it is an advantage to interpret the ancient notion of truth in terms of the modern notion of existence. Thus De Rijk cites Matthen's article as 'epoch making' (*Aristotle*, p. 81). For my own doubts whether it is a philosophical advantage to introduce the modern notion of existence into ancient ontology see my comments in *The Verb 'Be'*, 416–19.

with normal intonation, not with ownerless sentences written on a blackboard. Hence I am abstracting from the distinction between sentence and statement. I claimed earlier that first-order copula uses of *einai* (at least the affirmative uses) normally imply the existence of their semantic subject. We may now add that as asserted sentences they also carry a truth claim, a claim that their sentential content obtains in reality—at least, in the reality of the Homeric world. So copula uses of *einai*, like all declarative sentences, are *implicitly* semantic in two respects: they imply not only the existence of their subject but also the validity of their truth claim. By truth claim I mean whatever it is that the sentence asserts—the content of the sentence understood as candidate for a *positive* truth-value. My notion of truth claim is, I think, just what Wittgenstein meant by his remark in the *Tractatus* (4. 022): 'A proposition *shows* how things stand *if* it is true. And it *says that* they do so stand'. Such a claim is implicit in every declarative sentence. What is distinctive of the veridical construction is to make this claim explicit.

Why is it precisely the verb *to be* that serves as vehicle for an explicit truth claim? I think the answer must lie in the role of copula *einai* as sign of predication. In simpler sentences like *Theaetetus sits* this function is performed by an ordinary verb. But, as Aristotle pointed out, any verb can be replaced by *is* plus participle: *Theaetetus sits* can be replaced by (the Greek equivalent of) *Theaetetus is sitting*. For this and other reasons, the copula verb can be seen as the most general verb, the verb par excellence, and hence as the sign of predication.[27] But every predication in normal declarative form carries a truth claim. Hence the copula verb, as sign of predication, can become the sign of truth claim. (It had already become such a sign in prehistoric times, as the words for 'truth' in India and Scandinavia demonstrate.) That is my explanation of why, in the veridical construction, it is the same verb that serves to make the truth claim explicit. Because *It is F* normally implies *It is truly F*, the verb *is* alone can mean *is true*.

8. A similar explanation can be offered for the use of *einai* as semantic operator in existential sentences. Because the copula verb (like any verb in the indicative) carries an implicit claim of existence

---

[27] For considerations confirming the central position of *einai* in the verbal system of Greek see *The Verb 'Be'*, pp. 388–94.

for its subject, the same verb, when properly emphasized, can serve to make this claim explicit. That is precisely the | function of *einai* in existential sentences. We can see this happening in a variety of ways, corresponding to the diversity of the existential sentence types. I distinguish five existential types in Homer and one post-Homeric type.

[393

Here is a summary of the six existential sentence types:

Type I (*to be* means 'to live', 'to be alive'): *The gods who are forever*;
Type II (locative-existential): *There is a city Ephyre in the corner of Argos*;
Type III (plural of Type II): *There are many paths up and down the camp*;
Type IV (existential proper): *Let there be someone who will speak wiser counsel than this*;
Type V (verb of occurrence): *Around him was a clamor of the dead*;
Type VI (unqualified existence): *Zeus is*; *A centaur is not*.

Of the six existential types listed here, the first and most vivid sentence type is neither explicitly semantic nor syntactically second-order. In this sentence type *einai* functions like an ordinary first-order verb with concrete meaning. This is my existential Type I, where *einai* means 'to be alive', 'to dwell', or 'to be present'. In this type the verb takes persons (humans and gods) as subjects: 'Your parents are still alive'; 'The gods who are forever'.[28] Since the subject is typically a person, and hence a dialogue partner, this is the only case where the verb is declined in the first and second persons; all other existential types appear only in third-person form. Furthermore, *einai* in Type I takes adverbs of time and place, like any normal verb. Why then do we call this Type 'existential'? In such sentences the verb will not be translated by *exists* nor even by *there is*. Nevertheless, this is the first use listed by LSJ among examples of εἰμί as substantive verb, as distinct from the copula; and other authorities treat it similarly. The explanation lies, I suggest, in the universal assumption that *einai* once had a concrete meaning like any ordinary verb. Since Type I sentences present the

---

[28] ἔτ᾽ εἰσί in sentence 1 in *The Verb 'Be'* (p. 241); θεοὶ αἰὲν ἐόντες: sentence 20 (p. 242).

verb with normal syntax, they give us the strongest suggestion of what its original meaning might have been.

More complex from a syntactic point of view are the existential sentences classified in my Types II and III: ἔστι πόλις Ἐφύρη μυχῶι Ἄργεος 'There is a city Ephyre in the corner of Argos'.[29] These are all copula uses of *einai*, usually locative, but with definite existential overtones as reflected in the translation 'there is'. If we ask what corresponds in the Greek to this existential nuance, we can find no answer in the syntax of the verb. Often (but not always) the copula will appear in initial position. Since Greek word order is free, the emphasis given by initial position is of rhetorical rather than grammatical significance. I have suggested that since the copula verb itself implies the reality of its (extralinguistic) subject, it is this implicit existential force of the verb that is brought out by initial position.

A Type II sentence generally serves to introduce either a person as subject for further predication or a topographical item as a point of reference for the subsequent narrative.[30] The existential force of the verb in such sentences seems to be connected with its rhetorical function of *introducing* | *the grammatical subject of the sentence*. The verb   [394] does this by spatially locating the corresponding semantic subject; that is, the person or place that will figure in the narrative that follows. Thus the underlying locative-existential value of the verb ('is present somewhere') is highlighted by this rhetorical act of introducing or 'placing' its subject in the relevant domain of discourse. I suggest that it is these semantic implications, accentuated by rhetorical emphasis on the verb, that we perceive as an assertion of existence for the subject of the verb. But since, although highlighted, this assertion remains implicit in the locative predication (that is, in first-order syntax), we do not have a properly semantic (second-order) use of the verb in existential Type II. What we have is a rhetorically and semantically loaded use of a first-order copula.

The same can be said for sentences in Type III, if we interpret this as the plural form of Type II: πολλαὶ γὰρ ἀνὰ στρατόν εἰσι κέλευθοι 'There are many paths up and down the camp'; ὑμῖν δ' ἐν γὰρ ἔασι ἀριστῆες

---

[29] Sentence 27 in *The Verb 'Be'* (p. 246).
[30] *The Verb 'Be'*, pp. 252–5.

Παναχαιῶν 'Among you are the bravest of all the Achaeans'. In this Type the rhetorical function of the copula verb is reinforced by a locative complement or by a term of quantity (*some, many*). In the negative versions of Types II and III the existential nuance is particularly strong, but locally restricted: οὐδὲ ἔστι ἐν τῆι Σκυθικῆι πάσηι χώρηι τὸ παράπαν οὔτε ὄνος οὔτε ἡμίονος διὰ τὰ ψύχεα 'There is in the whole Scythian land neither any ass at all nor any mule, because of the cold'.[31]

9. In none of the sentence types so far described do we find an explicit assertion or denial of existence, but rather (in Types II–III) a use of the copula verb that is emphatic enough to justify the English translation 'there is'. For a use that is properly existential we turn to Type IV, which is closely parallel in structure to the formula ∃x(Fx) for existential quantification in logic: 'There is an X such that X is F'. In Type IV the verb *einai* serves to posit (or, in the negative, to exclude) an indefinite subject (*someone, something*) for the predication formulated in the relative clause that follows:

νῦν δ' εἴη ὃς τῆσδέ γ' ἀμείνονα μῆτιν ἐνίσποι.

Let there be someone/who will speak wiser counsel than this.

νῦν δ' οὐκ ἔσθ' ὅς τις θάνατον φύγηι . . . / καὶ πάντων Τρώων, πέρι δ' αὖ Πριάμοιό γε παίδων.

Now there is no one/who will escape death at my hands, of all the Trojans and above all of the sons of Priam.[32]

Since the indefinite subject is typically a person ('someone who . . .'), the syntax of the verb might seem to be first-order. But in this sentence type the verb does not stand on its own; it is construed together with the relative clause on which it functions as a sentence operator. Thus the subject of *einai* is not a definite individual but as it were a bound variable, anyone or anything that satisfies the condition specified in the relative clause.[33] The semantic function of *einai* in Type IV | is precisely to make explicit the reference, positive or negative, to a semantic subject, ⟦395

---

[31] Sentences 51, 56, and 75 in *The Verb 'Be'* (pp. 261, 263, 273).

[32] Sentences 86 and 84 in *The Verb 'Be'* (p. 278).

[33] The verb of the subordinate clause is generally not *einai*, since the poet avoids verbal repetition. In *The Verb 'Be'*, pp. 281–2, 316, I described the nonrecurrence of *einai* as characteristic of Type IV; my error was corrected in a review by Seth Bernadete ('The Grammar of Being', *Review of Metaphysics*, 30 (1977)).

to an extralinguistic entity corresponding to the grammatical subject of the underlying open sentence: *X will speak wiser counsel, X will escape death at my hands.* Thus not only the syntax but also the semantic role of the verb in Type IV is like that of the existential quantifier: to affirm (or to deny) the availability of an object satisfying certain conditions, to posit (or exclude) a subject of which certain predicates are true. Here again we recognize the conceptual link between truth for predication and existence for the subject of predication.

Type IV may serve as the paradigm for what we mean by an existential use of *einai*. As semantic sentence operator, the verb here shares a function with the use of *einai* in the veridical construction. As we have seen, in both sentence types *einai* serves to make explicit the extralinguistic reference, either for the subject of a sentence (in Type IV) or for a whole sentence (in the veridical). And in each case the semantic sentence operator has only two values (*esti* and *ouk esti*, positive and negative), endorsing or rejecting the descriptive content of its operand sentence.[34] But the syntactic difference between these sentence forms is decisive for the distinction between existence and truth, between existential and veridical uses of the verb. In Type IV *einai* operates only on the subject of the operand sentence (that is, on the relative pronoun *hos* 'who' introducing the subordinate clause), whereas in the veridical it operates on an entire sentential structure, on whatever it is that the interlocutor has said and that the speaker confirms. What the veridical *einai* 'posits' in reality is the content of this sentential structure, the corresponding state of affairs. What is posited by the *einai* of Type IV is the existence of one or more individuals satisfying the condition specified in the relative clause.

10. Turning to existential Type V, we find a sentence form that is closer in syntax to the veridical construction. In Type V the subject of the verb is an abstract action noun representing the predicate verb in a more elementary sentence. In sentences of Type V *einai* functions as a verb of occurrence, affirming or denying that the action of the underlying sentence takes place:

---

[34] For this notion of a semantic sentence operator and its connection with the locative notion of *being present* (in the world, in the universe of discourse), see *The Verb 'Be'*, pp. 310–14.

ἀμφὶ δέ μιν κλαγγὴ νεκύων ἦν,

Around him was a clamor of the dead.

Here the abstract noun *clamor* (κλαγγή) is a nominalization of the verb κλάζειν in the underlying sentence *The dead clamored around him.*

ἐκ γὰρ ’Ορέσταο τίσις ἔσσεται,

There will be vengeance from Orestes,

with *vengeance* (τίσις) as nominalization from the underlying form *Orestes will take revenge.*

ἀλλ’ οὐ σοί γ’ ’Οδυσεῦ, φόνος ἔσσεται ἔκ γε γυναικός,

For you, Odysseus, there will be no murder at a wife's hand,

with *murder* (φόνος) as nominalization from *Your wife will not murder you.*[35]

With an abstract noun as subject, the syntax of the verb in this sentence Type is | clearly second-order. Here *einai* operates on its [396] target sentence by taking as subject the nominalized form of an underlying predicate verb (*to clamor, to take revenge, to murder*). Thus the syntactic analysis of *einai* is quite distinct in Type V, but its semantic function can be seen as parallel to that of the sentence operator in the veridical and in Type IV. Here also ἐστί (or ἦν in the past) serves to posit its semantic subject—in this case the verbal action—as 'real', that is, as occupying a place in the universe of discourse.

Notice that it is our syntactic analysis of the varying relation between *einai* as sentence operator and its underlying operand sentence that permits us to distinguish the function of the verb in these three cases, and thus explain why we translate *einai* as 'is the case' in the veridical, 'there is' or 'exists' in Type IV, and 'occurs', 'takes place' in Type V. These are distinctions that *we* make, on the basis of our own translation and syntactic analysis. For the Greek speaker these will be simply three uses of the same verb, the very same verb that appears in ordinary copula sentences. Hence the Greek speaker will not be inclined to distinguish veridical from existential uses, or either from the ordinary copula.

One monumental consequence of this lexical equivalence between different syntactic uses of *einai* is that philosophers thinking in Greek will not generally feel the need to distinguish entities from events or states of affairs. When they speak of *ta onta*, 'beings' or 'the things that

---

[35] Sentences 9, 99, and 100 in *The Verb 'Be'* (pp. 283, 284).

are', they may be referring to the existence of individuals and natural kinds, to astronomical events like eclipses and phases of the moon, or more generally to facts and whatever is the case in the world. This makes the logic of some Greek ontological discussions quite baffling to us.[36] Our translations and analyses take for granted the distinction between things, events, and states of affairs. However, these are distinctions not made by the linguistic usage in Greek but waiting for the philosophers to sort out. Insofar as they manage to do so, it is not always in ways that are familiar to us.[37]

11. I have saved for the end a discussion of existential Type VI, the unqualified assertion or denial of existence for individuals and kinds of things, where *einai* is construed 'absolutely', with no locative or nominal complements: οὐδ' ἔστι Ζεύς 'Zeus is not'; εἰσὶ θεοί 'The gods are'; οὐκ ἔστι κένταυρος 'There is no centaur'.[38] The absence of any predicative complement makes this use of *einai* syntactically parallel to the modern verb *to exist*. Hence only in this case is it natural to translate *esti* as 'exists'.

I find no examples of this sentence type in Homer. Type VI appears in Greek | literature only with the rise of theological skepticism in the   [397]
age of the Sophists, in the second half of the fifth century BC. In Greece, at any rate, this use of *einai* to mean something like 'exist' presupposes a climate of theoretical speculation and an attitude of doubt concerning objects of traditional belief (like the doubt expressed in the biblical verse 'The fool hath said in his heart, "There is no God" ').

Type VI provides an ancient precedent for the kind of existential statements that are characteristic of post-Cartesian philosophy. (Recall Heidegger's radical question cited from Leibniz: Why is there anything at all rather than nothing?) Thus Type VI serves to express a more

[36] For example, when Aristotle distinguishes questions of 'if it is' (or 'whether it is or not') from questions of 'what it is' (in *Post. An.* 2. 1–2), we naturally take him to be distinguishing between existence and definition. Some of his examples fit that interpretation, but others do not. Compare the quotation from Melissus in *The Verb 'Be'*, p. 305, where three occurrences of *einai* vary between (in our analysis) existential Type VI, copulative with 'true' as predicate, and veridical-existential. It is clear that Melissus intends to make the same point with all three uses of *einai*. For a similar variation in Plato's use see above, n. 14.

[37] Thus the ontology of Aristotle in the *Categories*, often regarded as a reflection of common sense, can be seen rather as the result of a struggle to provide an alternative to the Platonic construal of predication. See W. Mann, *The Discovery of Things* (Princeton, NJ: Princeton University Press, 2000).

[38] Illustrations in *The Verb 'Be'*, pp. 300–5.

speculative notion of existence, by contrast with the ordinary conversational forms illustrated in Type IV. We have seen that, unlike the implicit existential force of *einai* in Types I–III, sentences of Type IV are explicitly concerned with the existence or nonexistence of a subject, but with existence qualified in two respects: (1) the class of possible subjects is specified by the context (speakers in the council meeting for our first example, sentence 86 cited above in section 9) or by the text itself (Trojans, above all the sons of Priam, in the second example, sentence 84); and (2) what is affirmed or denied is not the existence of a subject generally but the subject for specific predication, spelled out in the relative clause. The second qualification has its parallel in the *Fx* component in existential quantification $\exists x(Fx)$: in both cases, what is posited is not a subject in general but a subject satisfying definite predicates. However, the first qualification marks a difference between normal speech and the formalized discourse of logic. In the idiomatic sentences of Type IV the subject whose existence is affirmed or denied is not any object in the universe but something of a definite sort: a person qualified to speak, a Trojan warrior. These sentences deal not with unqualified existence, being something rather than nothing (as when we discuss whether God exists, or the existence of the external world), but rather with qualified or contextual existence, the existence of a specified kind of thing (a speaker or a warrior) in a definite context (a meeting or a battle) as subject for a specific predication. In the speculative Type VI the sortal specification of the subject is retained (a god or a centaur), but both the contextual restriction and the specific predication have disappeared.

As a result, the syntax of this sentence type is not transparent. The explicit existential force of *einai* recalls the semantic sentence operator of Type IV, but in Type VI we have no operand sentence. Perhaps the most natural construal of Type VI is to see it as affirming or denying a subject for any arbitrary predication, a generalization of Type IV that maintains the sortal restriction on the subject of *einai* (e.g. gods or centaurs) but eliminates any specification of the predicates by zeroing the relative clause. To the 'absolute' syntax of *einai* in Type VI, restricted in this case neither by predicative complements nor by relative clause, corresponds an equally unqualified affirmation or denial of existence for the subject.

How did this speculative sentence type arise? For an intuitive understanding of the force of the verb in Type VI, I suggest that the denial comes first. The affirmation | of existence can then be seen as secondary, as a response to skeptical doubts: 'You say that Zeus does not exist? I say that he does!'. But what exactly did the doubter mean by saying 'Zeus is not'? If we are right to think of Type IV as the paradigm for an existential use of *einai*, the semantic function of *einai* will be to posit a subject for predication. Hence to deny that Zeus *is* is to deny that Zeus can be a subject for any true predication whatsoever. Everything they say about Zeus is false—and not only false but inevitably false, because there is no such subject to talk about! The denial of existence in such a case is a denial of truth for an entire tradition, the tradition of the poets and the priests. This reading of *Zeus is not* explains the zeroing of the relative clause that we would expect to find on the basis of the syntax of Type IV. In Type VI denials of existence there is no reason to specify conditions to be satisfied by the proposed subject, because the not-being of the subject guarantees in advance the nullity of every predication.

[398]

If this is the correct interpretation of Type VI, it is easy to see why the surface syntax of the verb is systematically misleading, as Ryle and others have observed. For in this absolute construction *einai* seems to represent a first-order predicate, like a normal verb. The surface syntax of *einai* seems to be just the same as in Type I, where the verb means 'be alive' or 'be present', or in the quasi-existential uses of the locative copula in Types II–III, such as 'There are no asses in all of Scythia, because of the cold'. It is this misleading syntax that gives rise to the notorious question, Is existence a predicate? It may be a predicate after all, but not a first-order predicate. That *einai* in Type VI, despite appearances, is not a normal, first-order verb is clear from the fact that it does not take complements of time or place, unlike the same verb in Types I–III.

The failure to notice this discrepancy has led some philosophers astray, as it led philologists to combine Types I and VI in what they took to be the primitive (or at least the oldest known) use of *einai* in Greek. My catalogue of archaic sentence types shows that Type VI is not likely to be a primitive use of *einai*, since it does not appear before the late fifth century. And my syntactic analysis indicates that, far from being a normal predicate as in Type I, *einai* in Type VI is best understood by analogy to the existential sentence operator of Type IV, which specifies its operand sentence in a relative clause. It is precisely the absence of this relative clause that makes Type VI so problematic.

Alternatively, of course, we might construe the absolute syntax of *einai* in Type VI as the result of zeroing the predicate in a copula sentence, as was suggested earlier, in section 3: *X is* is short for *X is something or other*. This interpretation of Type VI ties it more closely to the copula construction, but does not account for its strong existential value. The explicitly existential force of Type VI (being something rather than nothing) is much better explained by a derivation from the semantic sentence operator of Type IV.

12. Having surveyed the various uses of *einai*, we can now consider the question how these uses hang together as a system. I have already pointed to an answer on the basis of the syntactic analysis, but before pursuing this line of | thought let us see what can be said on the subject of the lexical meaning of the verb.   [399]

Any attempt to derive the different uses of *einai* from a single *Urbedeutung* or fundamental meaning will plausibly begin either from the vital-locative sense 'live, dwell' attested for persons in sentences of Type I or from the more general locative sense: 'be present, be available, *vorhanden sein*'.[39] To some extent, this quasi-existential meaning is automatically implied by every copula use of *einai* with locative complements: *Socrates is here*, *Socrates is in the agora*. That is why the absolute, 'existential' use of the verb can also be seen as the result of zeroing the adverbial of place in this locative construction: *Socrates is (somewhere)*. Existence is, as it were, location generalized or left indeterminate. Such a locative-existential sense of the verb corresponds to the old Greek notion (attested from Gorgias to Aristotle) that 'whatever is, is somewhere; what is nowhere is nothing'. Hence when Plato wanted for the first time to define a nonspatial notion of reality for the

---

[39] For the latter view see C. J. Ruijgh, 'A Review of Ch. H. Kahn, *The Verb "Be" in Ancient Greek*', *Lingua*, 48 (1979), 43–83.

Forms, he needed to locate them in a *noêtos topos*, an intelligible space (*Republic* 6. 508c1).

It is generally recognized that this local sense must have been one of the oldest meanings of the Indo-European root **es-*. Thus the OED suggests that 'the primary sense' of the English verb *be* was 'to occupy a place (i.e. *to sit*, *stand*, *lie*, etc.) in some specified place', from which was derived the more general sense 'to be somewhere, no matter where, to be in the universe or realm of fact, to have a place among existing things, to exist'.

As we have noted, the literal sense of 'being-there' or 'being-present' is implicit in every use of the locative copula, and reinforced in the sentences classified as locative-existential, which includes most of the sentences in Types II and III, e.g. 'There is a city Ephyre in the corner of Argos' (cited above). On the other hand, in the most common of all uses of *einai*, the copula construction with predicate adjectives and nouns, the literal meaning of 'being in a place' is completely absent: *Socrates is wise*, *Socrates is a philosopher*. Still, what we do have in the case of the nominal copula is a kind of shadow of the local sense in what linguists recognize as the stative aspect of *einai*.[40] This fundamental lexical value of *einai* as verb of state or station, in opposition to the mutative-kinetic aspect of verbs for *become*, is particularly strong in Greek, because it is supported by two unique morphological contrasts. In the first place, unlike other verbs derived from the Indo-European root **es-*, the Greek verb *einai* has kept its durative stem throughout the conjugation, and has admitted no non-durative or aorist forms from other roots (as the English verb *is* has admitted both *be* and *was* from roots other than **es-*, and Latin *esse* has admitted *fui/fuisse*). In addition, the stative-locative value for εἰμί *be* is reinforced by the opposition with its near-homonym, εἶμι 'I go'. This opposition between two archaic -μι verbs gives our verb εἰμί *be* the implicit meaning 'to stay' by contrast with 'to go'. This convergent set of linguistic | peculiarities for *einai* helps us to understand why, in traditional Greek thought, *to be* is *to be somewhere*. [[400]]

---

[40] For the importance of the stative-mutative or static-kinetic contrast between *be* and *become* in Greek as in other languages see *The Verb 'Be'*, pp. 194–8.

In the book I presented this locative interpretation of *einai* as a diachronic myth, the derivation of all uses of the verb from one primitive meaning; and I proceeded to reject it as a mythical account of linguistic prehistory.[41] However, in the form presented here, without diachronic claims, this account gives a plausible lexical description of the intuitive meaning of *einai* in all its uses. The basic meaning of the verb is 'to be present, be available', with a paradigm use for persons 'to live, to dwell (somewhere)'. The local meaning is weakest, of course, in the case of the nominal copula, the most common use of all (as in *Socrates is wise*). But even here, in what is sometimes regarded as the 'mere copula', we find a kind of analogue to the locative sense in the static-durative aspectual value that is particularly strong in the case of the Greek verb *to be*. Thus, in addition to its syntactic role as sign of predication, *einai* as copula retains a lexical suggestion of standing still and remaining as-is. It is this stative-durative value, present in every copula use, that was transformed by Parmenides into the notion of eternal being: 'It never was nor will be, since it *is* all together now' (fr. 8. 5). And this unchanging Being of Parmenides is still conceived in locative terms: 'equal to itself in every direction', 'like the bulk of a rounded sphere, balanced equally from the center in every way' (fr. 8. 43, 49–50). We can say that Parmenides created the metaphysical concept of Being by bringing together all of the aspects and nuances of the Greek verb into a single concept of the immutable Fact or Entity: *to eon*, 'that which is'.[42]

Before leaving this discussion of the locative values of *einai*, we may note how widely such metaphorical extensions of the notion of place or situation can serve to express the ideas of existence and reality, and not only in Greek. Thus I have here systematically employed the metaphors of positing and placing in the domain of discourse in order to explicate the semantic notions of truth and existence. It is no accident that a similarly irreducible use of the imagery of location turns up in the otherwise very different Heideggerian characterization

---

[41] *The Verb 'Be'*, pp. 375–88.

[42] See further on Parmenides' use of the verb in *Presocratic Philosophy: Essays in Honour of Alexander Mourelatos* (Aldershot: Ashgate, 2002; repr. here as Essay 8).

of existence as *Dasein*, literally 'being-there', or as *in-der-Welt-sein*, 'being-in-the-world'.

13. This is, I think, as far as we can go in accounting for the lexical meaning of the Greek verb *to be*. But this lexical account does nothing to establish a conceptual unity for the uses of *einai* that might justify the Greek project of ontology as an inquiry into the concept of Being. For that we must go back to the analysis of sentence structure and semantic function for the existential and veridical uses, and see how these are related to the predicative function of the verb that I propose as the conceptual basis for the entire system.

Let me retrace the earlier steps in my argument. We begin with the notion of predication as illustrated in the simplest sentence structure, in the distinction | between noun and verb as originally proposed by ⟦401⟧ Plato in the *Sophist*.[43] Plato defines noun and verb both syntactically, as combining to produce a sentence, and also as semantic functions: the verb signifies action (*praxis*) and the noun signifies agent (*prattôn*) or thing (*pragma*). This semantic dimension is carefully developed in Plato's brief account. His sample sentences (*Theaetetus sits, Theaetetus flies*) are said to be 'about' (*peri*) their subject in the dialogue, Theaetetus himself, and the true sentence says 'the things that are' (*ta onta*) concerning him (263b). Plato's goal in this discussion was to define true and false statements, and thus he concludes with the veridical use of *einai* just quoted. But in order to articulate the notions of truth and falsehood, Plato was obliged first to provide an analysis of predicative sentence structure in terms of the basic word classes of universal grammar, noun and verb. Formally speaking, nouns and verbs are easy to distinguish in Greek (although as far as we know no one had previously bothered to distinguish them). But the functional distinction that Plato pointed out is not a peculiarity of Greek, or even of Indo-European. As Edward Sapir, the great specialist in exotic languages, remarked, 'there must be something to talk about and something must be said about this subject of discourse once it is selected ... The subject of discourse is a noun ... The form which

---

[43] The distinction is new in the *Sophist*. Before Plato, and even in Plato's earlier writings, *onoma* meant 'name' and *rhêma* simply meant 'phrase' or 'expression'. Cf. *Cratylus* 399b1, where *rhêma* clearly means 'phrase', not 'verb'.

has been set aside for the business of predicating . . . [is] the verb . . . No language wholly fails to distinguish noun and verb.'[44]

Thus Plato's discovery of sentential syntax was at the same time a recognition of the fundamental conditions for any descriptive use of language. The terminology of subject and predicate comes only with Aristotle, but the insight is the same: that the subject–predicate (noun–verb) structure of sentences reflects, within language, the semantic structure of reference and description that connects our use of language to what we are talking about. I have called attention from the beginning to this fundamental ambiguity in the concept of predication: on the one hand, a syntactic relation between linguistic components within a sentence; on the other hand, a semantic relation between a sentence or sentence component and its significatum in the world. For it is just this extralinguistic or semantic function of predication that permits us to understand the central place of copula syntax in the unified system of *to be*.

We return to the simple copula sentence: *Socrates is wise* or *Socrates is in the agora*. When asserted normally as a statement, such a sentence entails three kinds of semantic relation. (1) If the sentence is true, the subject must exist; that is, there must be something the sentence is about. (2) The sentence makes a truth claim; that is, it claims that things are in fact as it says that they are. (3) This claim entails that the attribute in question (being wise, or being in the agora) actually belongs to the subject; that is, that the corresponding property 'occurs' or is | instantiated in this particular case. To these three semantic [402 conditions correspond the three different uses of *einai* as semantic sentence operator: (1) the existential use for subjects in Type IV sentences ('There is someone/no one who does such and such'); (2) the veridical construction for one or more complete sentences ('Things are as you say'); and (3) the verb of occurrence for predicates in Type V ('There will be vengeance from Orestes', i.e. Orestes will be a revenger). It is because the ordinary use of the copula as sign of predication in a first-order sentence normally bears these three semantic implications—existence for a subject, truth claim for the sentence,

---

[44] The full citation from E. Sapir (*Language: An Introduction to the Study of Speech* (New York: Harcourt, Brace, 1921; repr. 1949), 119) is given in *The Verb 'Be'*, p. 51.

and belonging for the predicate—that the same verb can also serve as sentence operator in the three types of second-order sentences whose function it is to make these semantic claims explicit.

Of course in simple noun–verb sentences predication occurs without the verb *to be*. The copula verb is required only when the predicate expression is an adjective or a noun.[45] In such sentences we recognize the minimum role of the copula as (1) verbal form carrying the marks of person, tense, etc., (2) predicator, joining with the adjective or noun to form the predicate expression or verb phrase, and hence (3) sign of sentencehood, completing the subject–predicate form. It is this triple function that is meant when we describe the copula verb as *sign of predication*. In simpler sentences of the form *Socrates walks, Theaetetus sits* this triple function is performed by the verb alone. As copula, *einai* serves as the verbalizer, making a verb phrase out of a verbless predicate. Furthermore, as already pointed out, in the periphrastic construction *einai* can replace any verb in the language. Thus we have *Socrates is walking, Theaetetus is sitting* (or their Greek equivalents) as reshapings of the noun–verb sentence. In traditional theory the copula form became canonical and the copula verb, rather than the verb in general, came to be regarded as the sign of predication. We are not bound by this theory. But we do recognize that *to be* performs the predicative function for a wide variety of sentence forms—more so than any other verb in the language. As the principal predicative verb, *einai* can represent both the form of predication and the specific semantic relations that are entailed by predication.

Thus the network of uses for *einai* serves to articulate a larger conceptual structure that brings together the notions of predication, truth, and existence. The copula use represents predication as such, in both its syntactic and its semantic function. The semantic implications of predication are articulated by existential and veridical sentence types, including Type V sentences that express the occurrence or realization of a predicate concept. None of these notions—predication,

---

[45] According to the theory of the nominal sentence, Greek allows sentencehood without a verb, at least in sentences where the verb would be in the third-person singular. I have argued that the so-called nominal sentence is a feature of surface structure only, and that *einai* is present in the underlying structure even in this case, as is shown by its appearance on the surface in past and future tenses and in oblique modes. See *The Verb 'Be'*, app. B.

truth, existence, instantiation—can be adequately explicated without reference to the other three. Thus it is this twofold structure of predication, both syntactic and semantic, that provides conceptual unity for the system of sentence forms with | *einai* that expresses not [403] only the basic subject–predicate connection in copula sentences, but also the semantic notions of existence for the subject, truth for the sentential content, and occurrence or instantiation for predicates. And it is the conceptual unity of this linguistic system of uses for *einai* that justifies, if anything can, the philosophical interest of the concept of Being in Greek philosophical thought.

14. Let me close by returning to the fundamental contrast between the concept of Being, as articulated in this system of uses for *einai*, and the notion of existence in modern thought since Descartes. Our account of the system has assigned no special role to the speculative use of the verb in sentences of Type VI ('The gods are', 'A centaur is not'). Furthermore, the relatively marginal position of such sentences in the discussion of Being by the Greek philosophers reflects the fact that the notion of existence as such plays no clearly defined role—is not thematized—in ontological speculation from Parmenides to Aristotle.[46] Questions of existence are not of central importance in Greek metaphysics, as they are in the tradition initiated by Descartes, where attention is focussed on such topics as: If I can be certain of my own existence, can I be sure of anything else? Do material objects exist? How can I know that there are other minds? Is the past real?

How are we to account for this radical difference between the two traditions? Part of the explanation must lie in the role played by skepticism. The radical challenge of skepticism—What, if anything, can we know with certainty?—is historically secondary in ancient philosophy. It is true that skeptical concerns were formulated early on, by Xenophanes, but they do not come to play a dominant part in Greek philosophy until the rise of the Second Academy in the third century BC, after the four major systems of classical thought had been

---

[46] This is not to deny that Aristotle discusses particular problems (such as the being of the void or the infinite and the reality of Platonic Forms) that we can identify as questions of existence. See G. E. L. Owen, 'Eleatic Questions', *Classical Quarterly*, 10 (1960), 84–102, repr. in Owen, *Logic, Science, and Dialectic: Collected Papers in Greek Philosophy*, ed. M. Nussbaum (Ithaca, NY: Cornell University Press, 1986) and ch. 3 above.

formulated. By contrast, both the skeptical challenge and the epistemology required to answer it are central from the beginning in modern philosophy, both in Descartes's own thought and in that of his successors such as Hume and Kant.

The modern notion of existence is not a product of skepticism. (I have suggested that this notion originates in a post-biblical metaphysics dominated by a view of the world as created *ex nihilo* by a transcendent God.[47]) Nevertheless, the central position of this notion in modern philosophy is, I submit, closely correlated with skeptical concerns. We have seen that speculative claims of existence, as formulated in Type VI sentences, first appear in the fifth century BC in response to skeptical doubts. This evidence from early Greek literature suggests that such general assertions and denials of existence do not arise spontaneously in ordinary discourse. They are a product of enlightened speculation; they arise as a challenge to traditional belief and originally concern only the gods and mythological creatures. The centrality of more general questions of existence in modern philosophy might well be regarded as a historical deviation, | due to the radical   [404] influence of skepticism (for Descartes and his followers) and hence to the dominant role of epistemology in the post-Cartesian tradition. Some of us may think that it is a substantial advantage on the part of classical Greek thought to be relatively free from both—from the radical influence of skepticism and also from the corresponding predominance of epistemology.

One final provocation is suggested by this contrast between the Greek and the modern perspectives. If we are right to think of existence claims as positing semantic subjects in a universe of discourse, we are justified in asking the following question: What is the relevant domain of interpretation for questions concerning the existence of other minds, or the existence of the external world? That is to say, what is the appropriate semantical framework, the relevant logical space within which such objects could be located, or from which they might be banished?

---

[47] See 'Why Existence Does Not Emerge as a Distinct Concept in Greek Philosophy', *Archiv für Geschichte der Philosophie*, 58 (1976), 323–34 (repr. as Essay 3 above).

If we are talking about existence for other minds or for the external world, we can scarcely be talking about location in spatiotemporal reality. But in what other way should these large questions of existence be construed? Is the logical space of sheer existence well defined? The semantic framework I have been using to analyze the extralinguistic functions of predication provides a new way of formulating the old claim that some of these metaphysical questions are meaningless. Thus I would reverse the charge that John Stuart Mill directed against the ancient notion of Being. It is not so much questions of Being as questions of existence that run the risk of incoherence by uncritical extension to an ill-defined domain. Perhaps a great advantage of the ancient concept of Being over the modern notion of existence lies precisely in the fact that the former is securely anchored in the structure of predication, so that for an ancient existence means the existence of a certain kind of subject for definite attributes, and to assert existence is to locate the subject in a particular universe of discourse. The generalized, metaphysical notion of existence, on the other hand, divorced from predication—as the verb *exists* is divorced from the predicative construction—is in danger of floating free without any fixed semantic frame of reference, and hence without definite meaning.

6

The Thesis of Parmenides[*]

If we except Plato, Aristotle, and Plotinus, Parmenides is perhaps the most important and influential of all the Greek philosophers. And considered as a metaphysician he is perhaps the most original figure in the western tradition. At any rate, if ontology is the study of Being, or what there is, and metaphysics the study of ultimate Reality, or what there is in the most fundamental way, then Parmenides may reasonably be regarded as the founder of ontology and metaphysics at once. For he is the first to have articulated the concept of Being or Reality as a distinct topic for philosophic discussion.

The poem of Parmenides is the earliest philosophic text which is preserved with sufficient completeness and continuity to permit us to follow a sustained line of argument. It is surely one of the most interesting arguments in the history of philosophy, and we are lucky to have this early text, perhaps a whole century older than the first dialogues of Plato. But the price we must pay for our good fortune is to face up to a vipers' nest of problems, concerning details of the text and the archaic language but also concerning major questions of philo-sophic interpretation. These problems are so fundamental that unless we solve them correctly we cannot even be clear as to what Parmeni-des is arguing for, or why. And they are so knotted that we can scarcely unravel a single problem without finding the whole nest on our hands.

I am primarily concerned here to elucidate Parmenides' thesis: to see what he meant by the philosophic claim which is compressed into the one-word sentence ἔστι, 'It is'. I take this to be the premiss (or one of

[*] An earlier version of this paper was delivered at Haverford College and at the University of Toronto in February and April, 1967. I am grateful to Sir Karl Popper and Professor Howard Stein for detailed criticism of the earlier draft.

them) from which he derives his | famous denial of all change and   [701]
plurality. I shall thus consider the nature of this premiss, and why he
thought it plausible or self-evident. I shall also look briefly at the
structure of his argument which concludes that change is impossible,
in order to see a bit more clearly how such a paradoxical conclusion
might also seem plausible to Parmenides, and how it could be taken
seriously by his successors. Finally, I shall say a word about the Parmenidean identification of Thinking and Being.

I. The Problem

For an accurate appreciation of Parmenides' thesis we must first have
some idea of the problem to which it was addressed. What was the
question which Parmenides put to himself, and which he thought of
his thesis as answering? As Karl Reinhardt said in a famous sentence:
'The history of philosophy is the history of its problems; if you wish to
explain Heraclitus, show me first where his problem lay'. We must ask:
What was Parmenides' problem? More generally: What is his poem
about?

The usual interpretation is that Parmenides is a philosopher of
Being, that the poem is a revelation of pure, or absolute, or univocal
Being, of true Existence or Reality. But this account of the matter is
uninformative. In the first place, it tends to be circular, because terms
like 'Being' or 'Reality' merely translate, without explaining, Parmenides' reference to ἔστι, εἶναι, or ἐόν. And the result is hopelessly
vague, since a term like 'Being' in English (or in French, or in German)
does not have a meaning which is precise enough for this answer to be
understood without further explanation.[1] |

---

[1] The situation is particularly bad in English, since the participle and gerund are indistinguishable in form. I have noted at least five distinct uses: (1) the participle as an adjective, in
'for the time being', (2) the participle as a noun (or the gerund taken concretely?), in 'a
human being', 'a being of a higher order', (3) the participle replacing the finite verb: 'things
being what they are', (4) the gerund as the nominalization of a *that*-clause: 'their being so glad
to see me came as a distinct surprise', and (5) the gerund (?) as an abstract noun in philosophy:
'Being is not the same as Essence'. How is the fifth use related to the other four? The
connection can scarcely be traced without referring back to the use of ὄν and εἶναι in Greek
philosophy, and ultimately back to Parmenides.

THE THESIS OF PARMENIDES

⟦702⟧ Furthermore, in a historical perspective it is hard to see why 'Being' should be a *problem* for Parmenides. It is he, after all, who introduced both the concept and the term itself into the vocabulary of philosophical speculation. If Being (or τὸ ὄν, or *ens* or *esse* or *Sein*) has been a problem for many philosophers since Parmenides, it is ultimately because of him that they are aware of this problem. But why was *he* aware of it?

If taken as a question about Parmenides' biography, this question must remain unanswered, except by guesswork. But we may put it in more answerable form if we ask: what problems did Parmenides inherit from his predecessors to which his own doctrine of 'Being' might be a response?

Most historians have followed Plato and Aristotle in seeing Parmenides against the background of earlier Greek cosmology. Thus they interpret his doctrine of the one Being as a response to, and criticism of, the various Ionian monisms which sought to explain the natural universe on the basis of a single cosmic principle: air, water, fire, the unlimited. G. E. L. Owen has recently protested against this assumption that Parmenides inherited his subject matter or his premisses from earlier cosmology. He argues that Parmenides wrote not as a cosmologist but 'as a philosophical pioneer of the first water, and any attempt to put him back into the tradition that he aimed to demolish is a surrender to the diadoche-writers, a failure to take him at his word'.[2]

Perhaps this antithesis is too exclusive: a philosopher who sets out to demolish a tradition may nonetheless continue it in a new form. For my part, I am convinced that there is a very intimate connection between Parmenides' argument and the doctrines of his Ionian predecessors,[3] and I doubt whether we can understand him properly if this historical continuity is lost sight of. But I entirely agree with Owen's contention that we must take Parmenides at his word. We must look at his extant poem, | at the questions he raises himself, in order to define ⟦703⟧

---

[2] 'Eleatic Questions', *Classical Quarterly*, 10 (1960), 101.
[3] There is probably also a close link between Parmenides' views and the doctrines of his Italian predecessors and contemporaries, but we know so little of these that speculation on this point appears rather fruitless. In particular, it seems to me circular to attempt to *reconstruct* early Pythagoreanism from indications in Parmenides' poem, and then to interpret the poem as an attack on these views.

the issues to which he addresses himself and the problem with which he actually begins.

Now he certainly does *not* begin with any discussion of the structure of the heavens, or with the problems of the nature and number of the elements. Parmenides' poem contains a cosmology, but it does not *begin* with cosmological questions. The philosophical exposition opens quite abruptly with the statement: 'Come, mark my words: I shall tell you what are the only ways of search there are for knowing or understanding (νοῆσαι).[4] When posed with philological precision, the question 'What is Parmenides' problem?' becomes the question 'What is Parmenides looking for? Where are his "ways of inquiry" (ὁδοὶ διζήσιος) supposed to lead?'.

If this mention of 'ways of search' came at the very beginning of Parmenides' poem, our only means of determining the goal he is trying to reach would be to read on further to see where his investigation leads. As things stand, however, the aim and object of his inquiry are clearly indicated earlier, in the prologue, where the 'ways of search' are poetically prefigured in the road traveled by Parmenides in his chariot—a road which lies 'far from the | beaten track of mankind' (fr. 1. 27). I suggest that a close reading of the proem alone is sufficient to give us a definite answer to the question 'What is Parmenides' problem?', and that this answer is fully borne out by the course of the argument itself.   [704

---

[4] Fr. 2. 2 αἵπερ ὁδοὶ μοῦναι διζήσιός εἰσι νοῆσαι. I take νοῆσαι as loosely epexegetical, or final, with ὁδοί, 'what ways of search there are *for knowing*'; i.e. I do not construe the infinitive as potential with εἰσί, which gives the usual translation: 'the only ways of search that can be *thought of*'. This usual construction provides us with a gratuitous contradiction, since Parmenides goes on to show that the second way is after all ἀνόητος (8. 17; cf. 2. 7). Furthermore, as von Fritz has shown, the sense of νοεῖν in early Greek is not some vaguely psychological notion of 'thinking,' not even the pseudological concept of conceiving or imagining consistently (as in a speculative 'thought-experiment'), but rather one of *noticing, observing, realizing, gaining insight* into the identity of a person, into the facts of a situation and their true implications; νοεῖν is 'a kind of mental perception . . . a kind of sixth sense which penetrates deeper into the nature of the object' ('*Nóos* and *Noeîn* in the Homeric Poems', *Classical Philology*, 40 (1945), 90; cf. the discussion of early philosophic usage, at pp. 223–42). The proper translation of the verb in Parmenides is a term like 'cognition' or 'knowledge': it is paraphrased by γνῶναι, 'to recognize, be acquainted with', at 2. 7.

For a fuller defense of what I take to be the correct interpretation of 2. 2 see Alexander P. D. Mourelatos, *The Route of Parmenides* (New Haven, Conn.: Yale University Press, [1970]), ch. 2 with n. 29.

The chariot journey which Parmenides describes in the proem is literally a voyage of enlightenment: he travels from darkness into light (εἰς φάος, 1. 10). As perceptive readers have always seen, this narrative of the journey to the goddess is an allegorical representation of Parmenides' enterprise as a quest for knowledge, and as an enterprise which attains its goal, since the voyage leads him to a complete revelation of the Truth.[5] Parmenides has done everything possible to render the allegory transparent. The voyager on the right path is 'a knowing mortal', conveyed by wise horses and cunning pathfinders; he is led to the light by the spirits of illumination, the Heliades or 'daughters of the Sun'. A successful conclusion to the expedition is guaranteed from the very first line of the poem: the horses carry him 'as far as desire can reach'. When he attains his destination, the goddess promises to reveal all things to him, but first of all to instruct him in knowledge of the Truth (1. 28–30).

Thus the proem informs us that Parmenides' search is a search for knowledge, that his road leads to complete cognitive success, despite (or rather, because of) the fact that it lies 'far from the track of men'. I wish to emphasize this epistemological coloring of the proem, for I think it offers us the indispensable clue for a correct interpretation of his thesis. The problem which Parmenides raises *from the beginning of his poem* is not the problem of cosmology but the problem of knowledge; more exactly, the problem of the *search* for knowledge, the choice between alternative ways for thought and cognition to travel on in pursuit of | Truth. There is no doubt that the inquiry which Parmenides has in mind is *suggested* by the attempts of the earlier philosophers to elucidate the true nature of things: his term for 'inquiry' (δίζησις) may be regarded as a poetic equivalent for the Ionian word for scientific investigation (ἱστορίη).[6] In his own way, however, investigation takes a

[705]

---

[5] Cf. H. Fränkel, 'Parmenidesstudien', in *Wege und Formen frühgriechischen Denkens* (Munich: Beck, 1955), 158–62; C. M. Bowra, 'The Proem of Parmenides', *Problems in Greek Poetry* (Oxford: Clarendon, 1953), 39: 'He tells of a chariot journey through gates to a goddess, but what he really describes is the transition from ignorance to knowledge'. This is true even on the new reading of the proem proposed by Mansfeld, who wishes to deny the allegorical interpretation and maintain the reality of the revelation. See J. Mansfeld, *Die Offenbarung des Parmenides und die menschliche Welt* (Assen: Van Gorkum, 1964), ch. 4 (pp. 222 ff., and esp. p. 247), and my criticism of Mansfeld's view in *Gnomon*, 52 [1970], 113–19.

[6] In his own way, Heraclitus had also given the traditional concept of inquiry a radically new twist: ἐδιζησάμην ἐμεωυτόν, 'I went in search of myself' (fr. 101).

new route and leads to fundamentally different results. Yet among these results is an explanation of the natural world.

I shall not attempt to resolve the vexing problem of the *Doxa*, the cosmology offered in the second part of the poem. In fact, I believe that on Parmenides' principles it is not really soluble at all. I only wish to remind you that Parmenides himself presents this as an epistemological problem, in the context of a theory of knowledge and error. In addition to the Truth, the goddess will expound 'the opinions of mortals, in which there is no true conviction', and she will explain why it is that a false and deceptive worldview necessarily prevails among men.[7]

The problem of knowledge, and the question whether human beings can possess it or not, is one of the themes which Parmenides has taken over from his predecessors. Xenophanes had insisted that what passes for knowledge among men is only guesswork or conjecture, and he apparently contrasted this semblance of knowing with the total insight possessed by deity alone.[8] The same radical antithesis between human conjecture and divine cognition | runs as a constant ⟦706⟧ leitmotif through the fragments of Heraclitus. But Parmenides' treatment of this traditional theme is novel in at least two respects. On the one hand, with his characteristic sense of logical order, he puts the question of knowledge *first*, as methodically prior, as the architectonic question which assigns to other questions their proper place. Thus his ontology and his cosmology are presented, respectively, as knowledge of the truth and knowledge of mortal opinion. On the other hand, although in the body of his poem Parmenides makes systematic use of the traditional antithesis between human guesswork and divine insight,

---

[7] ἀλλ' ἔμπης καὶ ταῦτα μαθήσεαι, ὡς τὰ δοκοῦντα/χρῆν δοκίμως εἶναι διὰ παντὸς πάντα περῶντα. I understand this to mean roughly: 'You must also learn how what seems (true to men) *had to be acceptable* (to them)—how its acceptance as valid was fitting and inevitable—since this seeming penetrates all things throughout (the mortal universe)'. The outline of Parmenides' intended explanation is clear, I think, from 6. 8–9, 8. 53–60, and fr. 16; but I doubt whether this explanation can be made ultimately coherent, for the reasons given in my review of Mansfeld (cited in n. 5).

[8] Xenophanes, frs. 34–5. For the contrast with divine knowledge see the paraphrase by Arius Didymus in T. Diels and V. Krantz, *Die Fragmente der Vorsokratiker* (Berlin: Weidmann, 1960), 21A24: ὡς ἄρα θεὸς μὲν οἶδε τὴν ἀλήθειαν, 'δόκος δ' ἐπὶ πᾶσι τέτυκται' (= fr. 34. 4). The same contrast is made explicit in Alcmaeon fr. 1. For the theme of human ignorance and divine insight in archaic Greek poetry see Mansfeld, *Offenbarung*, ch. 1.

he breaks through it in the prologue by putting his *own* teaching in the mouth of a goddess. There is no trace here of the epistemological modesty of Xenophanes or Alcmaeon. Even Heraclitus, who casts himself in the role of a prophet, does not go so far. Heraclitus does broadly hint that he is an authorized spokesman for divine wisdom; but Parmenides simply lets the divinity speak for herself. This is the rhetorical, and perhaps also the philosophic, justification for his elaborate proem: to make use of the form of a divine revelation in order to exploit and at the same time transcend the traditional Greek pieties on the subject of the deficiencies of human knowledge. Parmenides' allegory permits him to denounce human blindness with the utmost rigor and generality, while at the same time being able to claim absolute certainty for the doctrines he will propound himself.

II. The Thesis

I have defined Parmenides' problem in general terms as the problem of knowledge, and described his 'ways of search' as alternative modes of seeking to know, as alternative approaches to the truth, only one of which attains the goal. I would now like to suggest that the problem may be more accurately formulated as a question concerning the object of knowledge, and that the alternative ways are different views of the knowable, of what there is to be known. We must now ask ourselves what is the philosophical *content* of the true way, i.e. what is Parmenides' solution to the problem of what (and perhaps also how) we know? |

[707]   The statement of the first way, the way of Truth and reliable Conviction (πίστις), constitutes what I call Parmenides' thesis. It is formulated as a closely linked pair of propositions.

(fr. 2. 3) ἡ μέν ὅπως ἔστιν τε καὶ ὡς οὐκ ἔστι μὴ εἶναι

The first way is *that it is and that it cannot not be.*

This thesis is immediately confronted with its antithesis:

(fr. 2. 5) ἡ δ' ὡς οὐκ ἔστιν τε καὶ ὡς χρεών ἐστι μὴ εἶναι

The next is *that it is not and that it is necessary that it not be.*

We note that the modal clauses of thesis and antithesis ('it is impossible for it not to be' and 'it is necessary for it not to be') are opposed to
one another as contraries, which cannot be true together but might
conceivably both be false, whereas the assertoric or nonmodal clauses
are opposed as direct contradictories, as *p* to *not-p*. I shall for the
moment restrict myself to this simpler form of thesis and antithesis,
on the assumption that any account of the modal opposition must
presuppose a correct analysis of the primary alternatives; that is, of ἔστι
and its denial.[9]

It is the meaning of ἔστι which we must now explicate. But before
we do so I would like to point out that, in thus confronting us with the
bare choice between ἔστι and its denial, Parmenides is | in a way stating   [708]
the principle of noncontradiction, as many scholars have recognized
since the time of Reinhardt. More precisely, we may say that he is
presenting the law of excluded middle in its strong form, with the
disjunction understood as exclusive (as in Stoic logic), so that the
principle of noncontradiction is immediately entailed: '*p* or *not-p*,
but not both'. Now the law of noncontradiction was not formulated
explicitly (as far as we know) until Plato's *Republic* (4. 436b–437a); and
the excluded middle is first recognized as such by Aristotle (*Met. Γ*. 7).
But these principles are here on the tip of Parmenides' tongue, and it
is not very difficult to imagine that he could have explained them

---

[9] Why does Parmenides add the modal clauses in 2. 3 and 2. 5? I have no definite solution,
but the following possibilities are worth considering: (1) By adding Impossibility to the thesis
and Necessity to the antithesis, he intends to restate each one in its strongest form: 'It is
impossible that *not-p*' is both logically and rhetorically equivalent to 'It is necessary that *p*'. (2)
By opposing 'It must not-be' to 'It cannot not-be', Parmenides may wish to leave (apparent)
room in between for the third way, the path of mortals, as the way of possibility or
contingency: 'Possibly (sometimes, in some respect) it is; possibly (sometimes, in some
respect) it is not'. (3) By giving each thesis this double expression, Parmenides is able to
indicate that it is not the form of negation as such which is objectionable, not even the form
οὐκ ἔστι (since it appears in the modal version of the true thesis), but only the negation of ἔστι
in its elementary or ground-level use. When this primary negation occurs, it must be met by a
corresponding negation at the metalevel, by a *rejection* of the basic negation. So we have
double negations in 2. 3 (οὐκ ἔστι μὴ εἶναι) and 6. 2 (μηδὲν δ᾽ οὐκ ἔστιν), explicit rejections in
7. 1 ('this will never be established, that . . .') and 8. 8 ('it cannot be asserted nor apprehended
that . . .').
  Note that those three explanations are all mutually compatible, but that it is hardest to find
evidence in the text for (2). For a plausible defense of it, however, see G. E. L. Owen, 'Eleatic
Questions', *Classical Quarterly*, 10 (1960), p. 91 with n. 1.

orally to his disciples. For we have the disjunction even more neatly put at 8. 16: ἔστιν ἢ οὐκ ἔστιν, 'it is or it is not'. Since it is precisely this principle of the excluded middle (taken together with non-contradiction) that underlies the technique of indirect proof or *reductio* which is so skillfully employed by Parmenides and his pupil Zeno, I think that we might defend ourselves against the charge of misinterpretation by 'insinuating the future', as Richard Robinson called it, if we claim for Parmenides a conscious use of this principle in his poem. In fact, I am not sure we can understand Parmenides' argument at all if we deny him the use of the laws of excluded middle and noncontradiction as fundamental (though not quite formulated) axioms. But for the moment we must return to the thesis, ἔστι, and attempt to specify its sense.

The first point which calls for notice is that this thesis is even simpler in Greek than in English, since it consists of the single word ἔστι, 'is', with no subject term corresponding to the 'it' which we must provide in translation. Before we can ask what is the subject of Parmenides' thesis, we are obliged to ask: Is there a subject here at all?

The answer to this question may be either yes or no, depending upon what one means by a subject. Certainly Parmenides' thesis has no *grammatical* subject: a Greek sentence (like a Latin, Italian, or Spanish sentence) may quite normally consist only of a single word when, as here, that word is a finite verb. Compare, in Italian, *parlo*, 'I am speaking', *vengo*, 'I am coming', *canto*, 'I sing'. The more serious question is: Must such a one-word sentence nevertheless have a *logical* subject, specified by the context | or by the situation of utterance? For example, the Italian sentences just cited have for their logical subject *I*; namely, the speaker in each case (when such sentences are actually used, and not merely quoted).[10] It would seem that some one-word sentences have no logical subjects; namely, the so-called impersonal verbs, like Greek ὕει, 'it is

[709]

---

[10] By the logical subject here I mean the *person* who speaks, and not the word 'I' (or in Italian, 'io'). What I am calling the logical subject might therefore be more properly described as the real or extralinguistic subject. As traditionally used, the term 'logical subject' is indeed ambiguous: it sometimes serves to designate a linguistic expression, sometimes (as here) an entity or object. In the present context this ambiguity is harmless: the question whether ἔστι has a real (extralinguistic) subject will simply be reformulated as the question whether the dummy subject 'it' can be replaced by a more significant *expression* in our explanatory paraphrase of Parmenides' thesis.

raining', or νίφει, 'it is snowing' (and their equivalents in Latin or Spanish). Even though in English we are obliged to provide 'it' as grammatical subject in such sentences, it makes little or no sense to ask, '*What* is raining?'. (It is true that the Greeks could ask, or at least answer, this question: they sometimes said Ζεὺς ὕει, 'Zeus is raining'. But we may perhaps ignore this fact as an oddity of Greek idiom.) However, in most cases it does make sense to ask what is the logical subject of a sentence which has no grammatical subject. For example, *veni, vidi, vici* provides us with three such sentences. It is perfectly reasonable to ask, 'Who came? Who saw? Who conquered?'. And of course we know the answer, because we think of these sentences as uttered (or written) by Caesar. In other cases the subject is 'provided', as we say, by the preceding context.

It has been maintained that in the case of Parmenides' ἔστι no subject is to be provided.[11] But the verb ἔστι is not normally used in Greek as an impersonal in the sense just described. It generally occurs either with a grammatical subject or with a logical subject easily identified from the context.[12] Hence I think it is | legitimate to ⟦710⟧ suppose that Parmenides' thesis *does* have a logical subject, and we have a right to ask what this is. If the poem is as carefully composed as it seems to be, then the subject should be clear from what precedes. But what precedes the thesis is the proem. What hints does the proem offer concerning the logical subject for ἔστι?

---

[11] This is notably the view of H. Fränkel. For references and discussion, see L. Tarán, *Parmenides* (Princeton, NJ: Princeton University Press, 1965), 36; Tarán also claims that the verb is used impersonally here, with no subject understood.

[12] This point deserves more discussion than would be appropriate here. Let me say briefly that ἐστί is almost never construed impersonally in its primary or first-order occurrences, where it figures as the only verb in the sentence. Most of the constructions which could be plausibly described as impersonal are syntactically of a higher order, where ἐστί functions as a kind of sentence operator governing another verb form or clause: ἔστι ἐλθεῖν, 'it is possible (for someone) to go'; αἱρετέον ἐστί, 'Yes one must choose'; δῆλόν ἐστι ὅτι, 'it is clear that...'. The interesting exceptions to this generalization are certain rare primary uses of the verb where the logical subject is vaguely *the situation* or *things* (as specified by the context); e.g. *Il.* 9. 551: Κουρήτεσσι κακῶς ἦν, 'things went badly for the Kouretes'; εὖ ἔσται, 'it will be all right'. Those who claim that Parmenides' use of the verb is impersonal must have something like the latter construction in mind. But this use of εἶναι is unintelligible without the adverbial 'predicate', just as the former constructions are impossible without a subordinate verb form. Thus neither provides a proper parallel to the bare ἔστι of Parmenides.

The proem tells us that Parmenides' way is a search for knowledge which attains its goal. This suggests that the logical subject of the first way, the way of Truth and Conviction, is precisely the goal of knowledge, the aim or object of that philosophic desire which is expressed in the very first line of the poem and which haunts every verse: the subject of Parmenides' thesis is the object of knowing, what is or can be known.[13] Of course this is a very incomplete specification of the subject. One does not learn much science when one learns that science is about *the knowable*. But this is all that Parmenides needs to take for granted in order for his thesis to be understood. The subject is here specified only in a formal or a very general way. The actual denotation will be clarified by the predicative content of the thesis itself.

We must now specify this predicative content. What does ἔστι mean here? Modern interpreters generally assume that we must choose between the existential and the copulative use of 'is', and since ἔστι occurs here without any additional predicate, | there is a strong [711] tendency to suppose that it means 'exists'. In a recent study, however, I have argued at some length that there is another absolute use of the verb ἔστι in Greek (which I call the veridical), which plays a much more central role than the idea of existence does in Greek speculation about Being.[14] I cannot repeat the evidence here. I shall simply cite the facts that ἔστι ταῦτα in Greek means 'these things are so'; that the participle ὄν (or ἐόν), 'what is', means 'what is so', i.e. the truth or the facts of the case; and that Aristotle lists this use of 'is' (meaning 'is true' or 'is the case that') as one of the fundamental senses of the verb which calls for philosophical attention (*Met. Δ. 7*).

Now if we take ἔστι here in the veridical sense, the appropriateness of precisely this assertion in precisely this context is immediately plain. Parmenides' thesis ὡς ἔστι means 'it is the case', where *it* is the subject (or the object) which we know. Parmenides is making the obvious, but

---

[13] I am arguing this point on the basis of the proem alone, where I think the evidence is unmistakable. The same conclusion would follow even more directly if one accepts my rendering of the immediately preceding line as 'These are the only ways of search there are *for knowing*'. See n. 4 above.

[14] See 'The Greek Verb "to be" and the Concept of Being', in *Foundations of Language*, 2 (1966), esp. pp. 248–53 (repr. here as Essay 1).

not entirely trivial, claim that whatever we know, whatever can be known, is—and must be—determinately so, that it must be actually the case in reality or in the world. If we restate Parmenides' claim in the modern, formal mode, it might run: '*m* knows that *p*' entails '*p*'. This claim would generally be regarded as noncontroversial. It calls for no argument, and in fact Parmenides offers none. He merely asserts that his thesis is true: 'This is the way of Conviction, for Conviction follows Truth' (2. 4).[15]

For better or worse, however, the ancients were not interested in doing philosophy in the formal mode. Parmenides offers a thesis not about the entailment relation between certain propositions but about the necessary connection between knowledge (νοεῖν) and its object, and his claim can be adequately expressed only in ontological terms. In the material mode, then, the thesis may be rendered as: 'It (whatever we can know, or whatever there is to be | known) is a definite fact, an actual state of affairs'. Both the existential and the predicative uses of 'to be' are involved here, as partial aspects of the veridical use of ἔστι or ἐόν for the object of knowledge. In analyzing the ontological implications of this use we must distinguish three aspects or facets: (1) there must be a denotation, an existing subject which we are talking about or cognizing (we might compare Wittgenstein's *object*); (2) there must be a predication or saying-something about this subject (compare Wittgenstein's *sense*: a possible situation presented and affirmed); and (3) the state of affairs which we assert must itself be actual or 'existing', if the cognition is true.[16] Parmenides himself does not distinguish these three

[712

---

[15] For a similar suggestion that '"*m* knows that *p*" entails "*p*"' be regarded as the Law of Parmenides, on the strength of fr. 2. 7, see J. Hintikka, *Knowledge and Belief* (Ithaca, NY: Cornell University Press, 1962), 22 n. 7 (who adds a reference to *Gorgias* 454d for the impossibility of 'false knowledge'). But I do not think it is correct to distinguish νοεῖν as a 'verb of thinking' from γιγνώσκειν as a 'verb of knowing', as Hintikka suggests. See n. 4. above.

[16] A less elaborate but comparable analysis of τὸ ὄν as the object of knowledge is offered by Plato in *Republic* 5 (476e). I take it that he has Parmenides' thesis in mind and is expounding it accurately when he asserts that (1) whoever knows (γιγνώσκει) knows something (τι) rather than nothing, and (2) knows something *which is* (ὄν) rather than *which is not* (οὐκ ὄν); 'for how could something which is not be known?... That which is completely is completely knowable (γνωστόν); that which is not in any way is unknowable in every way'. Plato thus remains faithful to Parmenides' first two paths. From the Eleatic point of view, his ontological heresy is to admit a third way, middle ground between Being and Not-Being, which is 'such that it both is and is not' (477a6).

notions, but I think that *we* must do so if we wish to see clearly what is involved in his ontological-veridical use of ἔστι for the object of νοεῖν, and thus be in a position to criticize his argument for the impossibility of plurality and change.

Before proceeding to the argument, let me point out exactly how I am proposing to revise the standard account of his thesis.

1. Parmenides is concerned with *knowledge* in the sense in which it implies Truth, i.e. with true cognition, not with *thinking* in some vague psychological sense, nor even with *what can be thought* in some pseudological sense of the 'thinkable' as what can be conceived coherently or without contradiction.

2. The 'it' which we must take as subject of ἔστι is tentatively identified as *the knowable*, the object of cognition.

3. The 'is' which Parmenides proclaims is not primarily existential but veridical: it asserts not only the reality but the determinate being-so of the knowable object, as the ontological | 'content' or   [[713]]
correlate of true statement. Thus his thesis involves the concept of existence at two levels:

a. existence for the subject entity, *that which is*;

b. existence or reality for the fact or situation which characterizes this entity in a determinate way (in Wittgenstein's sense of the *Bestehen von Sachverhalten*, 'the existence of states of affairs').

4. Hence the 'it is not' which he rejects would deny *both* assertions, and would claim:

a. that an object for cognition does not exist, that there is no real *entity* for us to know, describe, or refer to; and

b. that there is no determinate *state of affairs*, no *fact* given as object for knowledge and true statement: whatever we might wish to cognize or describe is simply not the case.

I submit that this interpretation of the thesis fits the text of fragment 2 like a glove: it is immediately clear that *it is (so)* is 'the way of Conviction (πίστις)', of reliable belief, since 'Conviction follows Truth' (i.e. Truth lies on this road, or at the end of it); and that *it is not (so)* is 'a way of no information, a way from which no tidings come',[17] in fact not a true way at all (as Parmenides says at 8. 17), 'for you cannot know *what is not*, nor can you point it out'.[18] | [714]

III. The Argument

Such is the thesis of Parmenides, almost a truism, or, as some would say, 'a logical feature of our concept of knowledge': what we know and truly say must be, *in reality*, as we know and say it to be in thought and in language. By his systematic parallel between *knowing*, *saying*, and *Being*, Parmenides suggests a correspondence theory of Truth; and in fact he will go further and identify these three terms. But in the first instance his thesis is much less demanding. As a premiss for his argument, ἔστι claims only that something must be the case in the world for there to be any knowledge or any truth.

Let us now try to see how Parmenides travels from such a plausible premiss to such wildly paradoxical conclusions about the impossibility of plurality and change. And it is worth recalling, with some surprise, that it is precisely these scandalous conclusions which have been so demonstrably creative in western science and philosophy. For it is clear that, however unwilling they were to accept Parmenides'

---

[17] παναπευθής ἀταρπός, literally, perhaps 'a trail which one cannot locate because one can get no information as to its whereabouts'. Mourelatos (*The Route of Parmenides*, ch. 1) emphasizes the Homeric connotations of the journey on which the traveler is 'lost beyond tidings'; but I think the philosophical reference of παναπευθής here is not to the traveler but rather to the *content* of this negative way (i.e. to the way itself) as an impossible object for knowledge.

[18] The usual translations of οὔτε φράσαις in 2. 8 ('nor can you utter it', Burnet, Raven; 'nor could you express it', Tarán) apparently saddle Parmenides with the strange view that it is impossible to tell a lie or to mention a fictitious entity—or the even stranger view that it is impossible to utter the words οὐκ ἔστι! In fact the Homeric usage of φράζειν for *pointing out a course, showing the way* gives an entirely natural sense here. (Cf. Herodotus 7. 213, where Ephialtes 'made known the path' (ἔφρασε τὴν ἀτραπόν) which led the Persians through the mountains behind Thermopylae.) One can no more indicate or point out to another the way of nonentity (the way which is not) than one can be acquainted with it in the first place (οὔτε γνοίης). It is perhaps an intentional irony here that Parmenides introduces this sentence with a second-order *affirmative* use of φράζω: 'This way, I point out to you, is one . . . which one cannot point out'. There is a similar irony in the epithet 'nameless' (ἀνώνυμος) applied to this path in 8. 17: the goddess refuses to give it a name because of its nonexistence, though of course she can (and continually does) refer to it in her discourse.

uncompromising monism, neither Anaxagoras nor Empedocles nor Democritus, neither Plato nor Aristotle, felt they could reject his teaching without serious discussion, and not without incorporating parts of it within their own doctrines. In modern times, Parmenidean conceptions have continued to play an important role in metaphysics and science alike. On the one hand, Bradley's metaphysical monism is almost consciously Eleatic.[19] On the other hand, Meyerson and others have recognized the principle of causality and the conservation laws of classical physics as the remote but legitimate offspring of Parmenides' unchanging Being. More recently, Popper has suggested that 'the field theory of Einstein might even be described as a four-dimensional version of Parmenides' unchanging three-dimensional | universe'.[20]   [[715]]
How are we to understand the permanent relevance of a doctrine which, taken literally, might seem to be either madness or sheer sophistry?

This is a large question. All I can offer here by way of an answer is a brief analysis of the central argument of the poem, in order to suggest the extraordinarily wide scope and concentrated power of his reasoning.

In the first part of fragment 8 Parmenides claims to show that τὸ ἐόν is ungenerated and indestructible; he immediately goes on to assert that it is without a past or future, and that it is uniform or homogeneous (ὁμοῖον). Furthermore, he proceeds to infer that it is immobile and that it is unique without further argument, as if these features followed directly from the denial of generation and destruction. Now, if one looks closely, Parmenides does not even argue against destruction. He argues *only* against the possibility of γένεσις or coming-to-be, and assumes that the symmetrical denial of passing away, as well as the denial of past and future and the assertion of uniformity and unique- ness, all follow *trivially* (as it were) from his argument against coming- to-be. Either Parmenides' reasoning is full of inexplicable holes, or he thinks of his argument against coming-to-be as having a very general

---

[19] 'His [Bradley's] dialectic is the dialectic of Parmenides and Zeno rather than the dialectic of Hegel' (J. Passmore, *A Hundred Years of Philosophy*, 2nd edn. (New York: 1966), 59).
[20] *Conjectures and Refutations*, 2nd edn. (London: Routledge & Kegan Paul, 1965), 80. Popper also describes Parmenides as 'having fathered theoretical physics' (ibid. 79).

applicability.[21] Is it possible that his argument is strong enough to support all the conclusions he seems to derive from it? |

[716]   I suggest that the answer is 'yes': that Parmenides' argument succeeds in proving all of this if it proves anything at all. In other words, insofar as Parmenides' argument is valid as a refutation of coming-to-be, it is also valid as a refutation of perishing, time, motion, and heterogeneity or diversity of any kind. Let me explain.

The argument has the form of an indirect proof with an initial dilemma, or perhaps trilemma. Assuming that what-is has come to be (or *could* come to be), Parmenides asks, 'What birth then will you seek for it? How and whence was it increased?'; that is, what did it develop out of? (8. 6–7). He considers two or, as I think, three possibilities:

(1) what-is came from what-is-not;
(2) what-is has come to be, but not *from* anything;
(3) what-is comes to be from what-is, i.e. from something *else* which is real.

The first two alternatives are logically equivalent for Parmenides, since Not-Being for him is nothing, i.e. not anything at all. But he distinguishes them rhetorically, and cites distinct reasons for rejecting each one.

1. It cannot come from what-is-not, because we have already agreed that what-is-not is unknowable and (in some sense) unsayable: what is nonexistent, with nothing predicated of it, and nothing

---

[21] The argument to which I refer corresponds to the reasoning in fr. 8. 6–21 and includes the establishment of the premises for the subsequent inferences in 8. 22–49, where we have as direct corollaries of the central argument: (a) the principle of immobility or invariance (8. 26–30), (b) the identity of cognition and its object (8. 34–9; cf. frs. 3 and 6. 1), itself derivable from (c) the principle of monism, or the uniqueness of what-is (8. 36–7; cf. οὖλον μουνογενές. . . . ὁμοῦ πᾶν / ἕν in 8. 4–6). Excluded from my analysis are at least two distinct arguments: (1) that since what-is is entirely homogeneous, therefore it is indivisible and continuous (8. 22–5), and (2) that because what-is cannot be incomplete or deficient, therefore it is surrounded by a Limit (8. 30–3). In the last 12 verses of the Discourse on Truth (8. 38–49) it is more difficult to say how far we have additional inferences, how far merely an expanded résumé of what has already been proved.

For a defense of the view that Parmenides' argument involves a denial of time but not necessarily of space see my review of Tarán's *Parmenides* in *Gnomon*, 40 (1968), 127–32.

true of it is just nothing at all. Hence generation from what-is-not means generation *ex nihilo*. (1) collapses into (2).

2. Generation *ex nihilo*—with no antecedents—is totally irrational: 'What need could have stirred it up to grow later rather than sooner, if it began from nothing?'. This is essentially the principle of sufficient reason, invoked here to justify the principle of causality: if something happens now, but did not happen earlier, there must be some χρέος, some requirement or necessity determining *this* to happen rather than that, and *now* rather than some other time. There must be something to make a difference. *Nothing* cannot be the cause, because nothing makes no difference.

717] | So far the structure of the alternatives considered may be represented by a simple schema:

$$0 \rightarrow R$$

where '0' represents Not-Being or nothing, 'R' represents Reality or what-is, and the arrow represents the alleged process of generation. If the positions of '0' and 'R' are reversed, the arrow represents perishing and the same arguments might be used to prove it impossible. (The argument against (1) applies without change; the argument against (2) would have to be reformulated for the case of perishing.) But Parmenides says nothing of this. Instead he merely emphasizes the rigorous nature of the dichotomy between R and 0: 'Thus it must be altogether or not at all' (8. 11).

The argument against alternative (3) is extraordinarily compressed, and I must expand it, for I think it is here that the full generality of his refutation is suggested. What he says is, 'Nor will the strength of conviction ever allow *anything besides itself* to arise (become) out of what-is.[22] For this reason, Δίκη does not relax her fetters and release

---

[22] I accept (with Reinhardt and Tarán) Karsten's emendation ἐκ τοῦ ἐόντος (γίγνεσθαί τι παρ' αὐτό) for ἐκ μὴ ἐόντος in 8. 12. In fact my whole analysis of the argument might be regarded as a reasoned plea for the necessity of reading τοῦ for μή in this passage. Without this correction, the unquestionably Parmenidean argument which I have reconstructed—Parmenidean in the sense that it relies entirely for its cogency upon the initial dichotomy strictly conceived—is not actually to be found in the text of the poem! A recent attempt to defend the traditional text only succeeds in showing how much weaker the argument is according to that text. (See Charlotte L. Stough, 'Parmenides' Way of Truth, B 8. 12–13', *Phronesis*, 13 (1968), 91–107.) In addition to the various holes pointed out above, even Parmenides' refutation of generation now 'seems to beg the question' (ibid. 104), since on this reading there is no shred of a proof to show that *what-is* cannot be generated from *what-is*.

(what-is) for coming-to-be or for perishing, but holds it tight' (8. 12–
15). Note that Parmenides now includes perishing too in his denial,
but no further argument is offered. We are merely reminded of the
initial disjunction: 'The judgment on these matters depends on this:
either it is or it is not. Now it has already been decided, as is necessary,
to abandon the latter as unknowable and nameless, for it is no true way,
but (to judge) that the former *is* and is true'. The next | verses state,   [718
rather than argue, that *it was* and *it is going to be* are both incompatible
with *it is* (8. 19–20). And, as I mentioned earlier, the attributes of
immobility, uniformity, and uniqueness are now assumed, as if they
somehow followed from the argument against coming-to-be.

What is happening here? I suggest that the key to the reasoning lies
in the phrase 'nothing else can come-to-be *besides* being', over and
above what is (8. 12–13). On the third hypothesis, what-is serves as the
starting point or antecedent for the process of becoming. But then the
result of this process must be something else, something which was not
there at the beginning: otherwise, nothing has *become*. The conclusion,
which Parmenides omits but which he indicates by his reminder of the
initial dichotomy, is that if the result is distinct from the starting point,
but the starting point is *what-is* (by hypothesis), then the result would
be *what-is-not*. Consider the following schema:

$$R_1 \rightarrow R_2$$

This is the schema for coming-to-be out of Reality or what-is, but it is
also the schema for *any change whatsoever*. If R_1 is what-is, then R_2 must
be either (1) the same, or (2) different. Now if it is the same, no change
has occurred. But if it is different, then R_2 is *what-is-not*, and that is
impossible, as was decided in the original dichotomy. In other words,
our schema for change now collapses into $R \rightarrow 0$ (which is the
schema for perishing); and, since the second term is inadmissible, it
follows that coming-to-be, perishing, and change in general are impossible. QED.

The argument can easily be applied to temporal distinctions. Assume
that the arrow is the arrow of time. If R_1 is *what-is*, then R_2, to
be different, must be what-is-not. (We get the schema $R \rightarrow 0$ once
more.) Hence the future is nonexistent. But suppose now that R_2 is

what-is. Then R$_1$, to be different, must be what-is-not. The schema is
$0 \rightarrow R$. Hence the past is equally nonexistent and impossible. For the
proofs of diversity and uniqueness, we simply reinterpret the arrow each
time to mean 'is unlike' (in the proof of uniformity) and 'is not identical
with' (in the proof of uniqueness). It is all absurdly simple: the rigor of the
initial dichotomy, with the rejection of *it is not* as unintelligible, excludes
all schemata except 'R = R'. Being is | self-identical, hence unique and   [[719]]
immutable. 'It lies by itself (= alone), remaining (itself) the same in the
same (condition).'[23] The principle of Monism and the principle of
Invariance are, for Parmenides, merely different expressions of the identity of the real with itself.

What is wrong with this argument? Clearly we must be prepared
either to criticize the argument or to accept its radical conclusions. But
the familiar charge that Parmenides confused the existential and predicative senses of 'to be' is too superficial to touch the argument as I have
reconstructed it. Even Aristotle's more astute criticism, that Parmenides
takes *being* as univocal whereas it is in fact a term 'said in many ways'
(*Physics* 1. 3), does not touch the heart of the argument. Perhaps the most
pointed objection to Parmenides is that he fails to distinguish between
being-different-from-what-is (being different from something that exists, or
from something that is the case) and *being-what-is-not*, in the sense of
being nothing at all. By failing to make this distinction, Parmenides in
effect begs the question in favor of Monism and Invariance: there cannot
be two distinct entities or two situations that actually obtain, since if the
second is to be different from the first then *one* of the two must be null
and void. Now to draw the necessary distinction between 'not being X',
in the sense of being different from X, and 'not-being' *tout court*—to
distinguish negation as difference from negation as nonentity—was
precisely the task of Plato in the *Sophist*. It was no easy matter in
Greek, where the involvement of the existential and predicative values
of the verb in the veridical usage of εἶναι (and the absence in classical
Greek of any distinct verb meaning 'to exist') led to easy confusion
between negation, falsehood, and nonentity. Parmenides' argument
seems to turn upon the illicit and unspoken assumption that being-the-
case—the veridical ἔστι understood objectively as an existing object

---

[23] 8. 29 ταὐτόν τ' ἐν ταυτῷ τε μένον καθ' ἑαυτό τε κεῖται.

characterized by an actual state of affairs—specifies a definite *kind* of Being, and even a particular entity, so that whatever is different from what-is-the-case cannot be another fact or another thing, but | must be   [720] *not-the-case*, i.e. must be false and/or nonexistent. Hence there cannot be two facts or two things. Either it is or it is not: that is the whole story.

IV. Conclusion

The critic who refuses Parmenides' radical monism will claim that his argument is valid but unsound, since it relies upon an unacceptable premiss. But this is the general form for criticism of any rigorous and unified metaphysical position. We must recognize the fact that, by his reasoning in the Discourse on Truth, Parmenides brought into being western philosophy in the technical sense, as the sustained argument for a general thesis involving a lucid analysis of the concepts underlying rational thought on topics such as truth, cognition, contradiction, totality, homogeneity, continuity, and symmetry. If philosophy as rational cosmology begins with the Milesians, philosophical argument and conceptual analysis begins with Parmenides. And Parmenides is more than a precursor. By the very starkness and simplicity with which he announced the principles of Monism and Invariance in the archaic hexameters of his poem, he opened up a rational intuition of immense scope and power, within which most of the central principles of Greek science and ontology are contained in concentrated and compressed form, like the Japanese flowers which unfold from tiny capsules dropped into water. The history of western science and metaphysics might be written as the sequence of alternative restrictions and special applications of the principles which Parmenides himself applied universally in unrestricted form. This may be seen in the two most striking ancient examples of a revised Eleatic doctrine, in Plato's ontology of unique and immutable Forms and in the atomistic reduction of the real to solid bodies, internally invariant and forever indestructible, but subject to a change of external relations in empty space. The general form for a pluralist revision of Eleatic ontology, applicable to the major physical theories of the fifth century BC but not only to them, is well expressed in the aphorism of a twentieth-century philosopher: 'Objects

are what is unalterable and subsistent; their configuration | is what is   ⟦721⟧
changing and unstable'.²⁴ Parmenides himself pointed the way to a
physical application of his doctrine along these lines in the section on
Mortal Opinion, where a minimum pluralism of *two* elemental forms
serves to generate the phenomenal world by their mixture and inter-
action.

I would like to close by emphasizing one aspect of Parmenides'
monism which is often overlooked or denied in the standard com-
mentaries but which had an important development in ancient and
medieval philosophy and significant parallels in modern monism since
Spinoza and Hegel. This is the identification of Mind and Being; that
is, of cognition with its object.

τὸ γὰρ αὐτὸ νοεῖν ἐστίν τε καὶ εἶναι

For knowing and being are the same (fr. 3)

ταὐτὸν δ' ἐστὶ νοεῖν τε καὶ οὕνεκεν ἔστι νόημα

Knowing and the goal [or aim or motive] of knowledge are the same

(8. 34)

It would be tedious to defend this obvious rendering of the lines
against other more recherché interpretations which have enjoyed greater
favor in the modern literature on Parmenides. I simply point out that the
identification of cognition (or thought) with its object is reformulated
within the context of the doctrine on Opinion,²⁵ and that, within the
section on Truth, the same identification is repeated, and extended to
include language, in | another enigmatic verse where the usual transla-   ⟦722⟧
tions are almost wholly devoid of grammatical plausibility:

---

²⁴ Wittgenstein, *Tractatus Logico-Philosophicus*, trans. C. K. Ogden (London: Routledge &
Kegan Paul, 1922), 2. 0271. The formula also fits Plato's doctrine of Forms, if for 'configura-
tion' one reads 'sensible reflection or imitation'.
²⁵ Fr. 16. 2–4 τὸ γὰρ αὐτό / ἔστιν ὅπερ φρονέει, μελέων φύσις ἀνθρώποισιν / καὶ πᾶσιν καὶ
παντί. The interpretation of these verses is difficult. I understand them roughly as follows:
'For the thought of men (νόος as antecedent from the preceding clause) is the same as what it
thinks, i.e. as the nature of the members in men, in everyone [or everything] and in all [or in
the All]'. Here cognition, sensation, or thought (νόος, φρονέειν) does *not* entail truth, since
we are in the realm of opinion; but such cognition is still identical with its object: in this case,
with the mixture of the two elemental forms in man and in the universe. (Note that it makes
no difference whether one takes φύσις as subject or object of φρονέει, in apposition to νόος or
to ὅπερ, since what the sentence asserts is precisely the identity of the two terms. The
ambiguous syntax of φύσις is a typically Parmenidean device for *expressing* this identity.)

χρὴ τὸ λέγειν τε νοεῖν τ' ἐὸν ἔμμεναι

Cognition and statement must be what-is (i.e. must be true and real).[26]

Assuming that this is what he meant, why *should* Parmenides identify cognition with its object, true statement with what it states? The answer is, I think, a simple one: either it is or it is not. Either knowledge and true speech are Being or they are nothing at all. The disjunction is exclusive: there is no middle ground and no gradations. Now it seems obvious that Parmenides would not want to identify knowledge and truth with nonentity (which would be the only alternative). The fact that ἐόν in Greek means 'truth' as well as 'Being' makes it all the more natural for him to insist that true statement and cognition cannot be nothing. It is falsehood and error which belong with τὸ μὴ ἐόν, 'what is not (so)'. This connection is particularly plausible in Greek, but certainly not restricted to that language. Consider Descartes, who writes: 'It is clear that everything which is true is *something*' (*patet enim illud omne quod verum est esse aliquid*).[27] As for false ideas, says Descartes, they derive from | nonentity: 'Je les tenais du [723 néant'.[28] The immediate ontological framework of these remarks in Descartes is scholastic and Augustinian, but its foundations are Greek, and ultimately Parmenidean.

I said earlier that Parmenides' parallel between saying, knowing, and being suggests a correspondence theory of truth, but that in fact he

---

[26]   The most natural syntax (reflected in my translation) is to take the articular infinitives τὸ λέγειν τε νοεῖν τε as subject of the infinitival clause with ἔμμεναι, and to take ἐόν as predicate (so Karsten, Heidel, Verdenius, and originally Diels). This involves giving to λέγειν the pregnant sense of '*true* statement' (as in the case of φάσθαι and φατόν in 8. 8). Essentially the same meaning results from taking ἐόν as *object* of the articular infinitives: 'Knowing and asserting what-is must *be* [real]' (so Fränkel). Here the sense is excellent but the syntax more difficult. It is perhaps just barely possible to construe ἐὸν ἔμμεναι as a noun clause, object of the first two infinitives: 'It is necessary to say and to know that what-is *is*' (so roughly Diels and Kranz); but here the syntax is very harsh and the sense weak. I think it is certainly *impossible* to construe the first two infinitives as potential with ἐόν: 'It needs must be that *what can be spoken and thought* is' (with Burnet and many others). As far as I can see, there is no such construction with the participle ἐόν in Greek. Hence I can find no evidence in 6. 1 to support the standard interpretation of Parmenides' thesis as 'whatever can be thought can [or does? or must?] exist'. But this interpretation is in any case incompatible with the normal meaning of νοεῖν in early Greek (see above, n. 4, and further discussion below).

[27]   *Meditations* 5, ed. C. Adam and P. Tannery (Paris: Vrin, 1983), vii. 65.

[28]   *Discourse on Method* IV, ed. C. Adam and P. Tannery (Paris: Vrin, 1983), vi. 34.

identifies these three terms. A real distinction between knowledge and its object, or between language and the world, is excluded by his rigid dichotomy. Such a distinction is all the more alien to his philosophy insofar as the logical laws (excluded middle, noncontradiction, identity) which he has discovered in thought and in language are understood by him as constituting the very structure of the real. For some philosophers this relationship between logic and ontology could be described in terms of isomorphism or homomorphism, as a common structure shared by language and the world, a common form for cognition and its object, whether imposed by the knower on the known, or conversely, or somehow pre-established separately for each. But for Parmenides this isomorphism can only be conceived as identity.

Both the philosophic significance of Parmenides' identification and its historical importance will be clearer if we bear in mind the similar doctrine of Aristotle, who insists that 'knowledge (ἐπιστήμη) in act is identical with the thing known' (*De Anima* 431^{a}1). In its second formulation, this principle is even more explicitly Parmenidean: The faculty of intellect (νοῦς) in act *is* the things which it apprehends.[29] As in the case of Parmenides, this noetic identification has a counterpart at the phenomenal level: the sensory faculty in act is identical with the sensible forms it receives.[30] It seems clear that this Aristotelian doctrine is not a form of idealism as normally understood, but something more like neutral monism. The nature of this identification is certainly obscure, and would call for much further discussion. It is worth noting, however, that both in Parmenides and in Aristotle the identity is characterized by a curious asymmetry: it is always νοῦς or νοεῖν which is identified with—or reduced to—its object, never conversely. Parmenides never says that Being is thinking (or | being-thought); [[724]] Aristotle does not say that the intelligible objects are themselves intelligent (except in the special case of the First Mover, where the identity does seem to be symmetrical). This general asymmetry reflects the extent to which such monism remains 'realistic': knowing is

---

[29] *De Anima* 431^{b}17; cf. 430^{a}3; 417^{b}23–4, 431^{b}21 ff., etc.
[30] *De Anima* 425^{b}26–426^{a}26, 431^{b}23 ff.; cf. 424^{a}17–24.

founded in Being; science and logic rest upon ontology; the mind does not impose its forms but receives them from the object it knows.

It is through its Aristotelian reformulation that the Parmenidean identification of knowing and Being has exerted its historical influence. This identification is firmly established in Neoplatonism, where the Platonic Forms themselves lose their independent status and are ultimately indistinguishable from νοῦς, the noetic principle which guarantees their unity. A curious destiny this, for the Parmenidean identification—to have imposed itself on Aristotle and Plotinus (despite the divergence from Plato's own view), and yet to have remained unrecognized in much of the standard modern scholarship on Parmenides!

7

Being in Parmenides and Plato

Despite the silence of Aristotle, there can be little doubt of the importance of Parmenides as an influence on Plato's thought. If it was the encounter with Socrates that made Plato a philosopher, it was the poem of Parmenides that made him a metaphysician. In the first place it was Parmenides' distinction between Being and Becoming that provided Plato with the ontological basis for his theory of Forms. When he decided to submit this theory to searching criticism, he chose as critic no other than Parmenides himself. And when the time came for Socrates to be replaced as principal speaker in the dialogues, Plato introduced as his new spokesman a visitor from Elea. Even in the *Timaeus*, where the chief speaker is neither Socrates nor the Eleatic Stranger, the exposition takes as its starting point the Parmenidean dichotomy.[1] From the *Symposium* and *Phaedo* to the *Sophist* and *Timaeus*, the language of Platonic metaphysics is largely the language of Parmenides.

One imagines that Plato had studied the poem of Parmenides with considerable care. He had the advantage of a complete text, an immediate knowledge of the language, and perhaps even an Eleatic tradition of oral commentary. So he was in a better position than we are to understand what Parmenides had in mind. Since Plato has given us a much fuller and more explicit statement of his own conception of Being, this conception, if used with care, may help us interpret the more lapidary and puzzling utterances of Parmenides himself. |

Recent attempts to specify with precision the philosophical content [238] of Parmenides' notion of Being can be divided into two groups, one of

---

[1] *Timaeus* 27d5: 'The first distinction to be made is this: what is the Being that is forever and has no becoming, and what is that which is always becoming but never being?'.

which takes the existential and the other the predicative function of *to be* as fundamental. The most powerful advocate for the first view was G. E. L. Owen, and he has been followed by a number of recent authors.[2] On the other side, Alexander Mourelatos has presented a full-scale interpretation of Parmenides along predicative lines;[3] and my own exegesis of ἐστί as veridical belongs in the same camp.[4] My aim here will be to defend a veridical-predicative interpretation, | and to [239] give my own view a more adequate formulation. In the concluding section of the paper I will argue that Plato's use of *to be* in Parmenidean statements of his own ontology generally follows the same veridical-predicative pattern and thus tends to confirm this view as an interpretation of Parmenides.

First, however, a word about what is at stake. It would be naive to assume that we could identify Parmenides' meaning for ἐστί with one

[2] Owen's view was first presented in 'Eleatic Questions', *Classical Quarterly*, 10 (1960), 84–102, further developed in 'Plato and Parmenides on the Timeless Present', *Monist*, 50/3 (1966), 317–40. These are reprinted as the first two essays in G. E. L. Owen, *Logic, Science, and Dialectic: Collected Papers in Greek Philosophy*, ed. Nussbaum (Ithaca, NY: Cornell University Press, 1986). Recent followers include Michael Stokes, *One and Many in Presocratic Philosophy* (Washington, DC: Center for Hellenic Studies/Cambridge, MA: Harvard University Press, 1971), 131–2; Jonathan Barnes, *The Presocratic Philosophers* (London/Boston: Routledge & Kegan Paul, 1979), i. 160–1; David Gallop, ' "Is" or "is not"?', *Monist*, 62, (1979), 61–80, and the same author in *Parmenides of Elea: Fragments* (Toronto: University of Toronto Press, 1984), 7–9; Alfonso Gomez-Lobo, *Parménides* (Buenos Aires: Charcas, 1985), 71. Leonardo Tarán also takes ἐστί as 'exists' (*Parmenides* (Princeton, NJ: Princeton University Press, 1965), 32, 36–8). For a subtle variant on the existential interpretation see E. Tugendhat, 'Das Sein und das Nichts', in *Durchblicke: Martin Heidegger zum 80. Geburtstag*, ed. V. Klostermann (Frankfurt: Klostermann, 1970), 138 ff.

[3] A. P. D. Mourelatos, *The Route of Parmenides* (New Haven, Conn.: Yale University Press, 1970), ch. 2. The most important precedent for the predicative view is the interpretation of ἐστί as the 'being of judgment: the *is* of affirmation', in G. Calogero, *Studi sull'Eleatismo* (Rome: Tipografia del Senato, 1932), 6.

[4] I did not see this clearly when I defended the veridical interpretation in 'The Thesis of Parmenides' (repr. as Ch. 6 above) and 'More on Parmenides', in *Review of Metaphysics*, 22/4, (1969), 700–24, and 23/2, (1969), 333–40. In *The Verb 'Be' in Ancient Greek* (Dordrecht: Reidel, 1973; repr. Indianapolis, Ind.: Hackett, 2003) I tried to uncover the deeper links between the veridical use and the copula functions of ἐστί. (See esp. pp. 407–8; cf. 186–7, 190, 226, 355–60).' In syntactic terms we may see the absolute construction of veridical ἐστί as the limiting case of what Owen called the elliptical copula: the need for an implied predicate has simply dropped out of sight. A veridical interpretation of ἐστί is also given by J. Jantzen, 'Parmenides zum Verhältnis von Sprache und Wirklichkeit', *Zetemata*, 63 (1976), 112–18. And see now P. Aubenque, 'Syntaxe et sémantique de l'être dans le poème de Parménide', in Aubenque (ed.), *Études sur Parménide*, ii (Paris: Vrin, 1987).

or another of the various uses of the verb in ordinary, nonphilosophical Greek. Parmenides developed a philosophical conception of Being for the first time. Before he wrote, there was no such thing as ontology, no theoretical account of *what is*. So this conception must ultimately be understood in its own terms, as a metaphysical innovation; it cannot be reduced to one or more values of the verb *to be* in Homer or Herodotus. At the same time, what Parmenides started from was the pretechnical usage of *to be*; and in order to comprehend his innovation the only tools at our disposal are, on the one hand, the ordinary uses of *to be* in Greek, and, on the other hand, the conceptions of modern grammar and logic by means of which these uses are to be analyzed. The question before us is: Which set (or sets) of ancient uses, described by which set of modern terms, provides the best conceptual net for capturing the thought of Parmenides and the logic of his argument, within the context of his own age? Thus we have to make a double choice and satisfy two kinds of criteria. We must select both the ancient uses and the modern descriptions which are to serve as instruments of clarification. And our goal is not only to make sense of Parmenides as a thinker of the early fifth century BC but also to understand the power of his argument from a more general philosophical point of view.

I shall argue that, although the reading of ἐστί as 'exists' provides Parmenides with an argument that is philosophically interesting | from [240] a contemporary perspective, since it resonates with some influential twentieth-century puzzles about existence,[5] this sense for ἐστί is linguistically implausible for Parmenides' time and unsatisfactory both for the interpretation of the poem and for the understanding of Parmenides' impact on Plato. But I should make clear that my objection holds only against the view that 'exists' provides the best translation or the most adequate analysis of Parmenides' verb. If the existential view is modified to claim only that an assertion of existence for the subject is *included* in the content of Parmenides' ἐστί, this claim becomes compatible with my own interpretation of ἐστί as

---

[5] See e.g. Owen, 'Plato and Parmenides', p. 321: 'denials of existence . . . are either self-refuting if they have a genuine subject or senseless if they have not'. Compare Gallop, *Parmenides of Elea*, p. 9. Barnes (*The Presocratic Philosophers*, i. 170–8) pursues an analogy with Berkeley.

veridical-predicative. For neither does the veridical rendering 'it is so' or 'it is the case' pretend to offer an adequate account of ἐστί in the poem. I maintain only that an interpretation along veridical lines is the best device for locating the initial, pretechnical use of ἐστί that serves as Parmenides' point of departure in the proem and in fragment 2. For a full account of ἐστί,[6] which might figure in a rational reconstruction of the argument as a whole, we must go deeper.

I

Our fuller account begins with a distinction between three levels of analysis. These are (1) the veridical as a lexical value of the Greek verb, rendered by the translations 'it is true', 'it is so', etc.; (2) the surface syntax of the verb in the veridical construction: 'things are (in fact) as you say or think (that they are)' often abbreviated to 'these things are' (ἔστι ταῦτα) or '(they) are so' (ἔστι οὕτω);[7] and (3) the deep structure of the veridical, what is logically implied by this use of the verb. In surface syntax the veridical uses are normally absolute, | as in typical ⟦241 cases of the existential; i.e. the verb is not construed with a predicate word or phrase. But in the deep structure there is naturally, even necessarily, a predicative element. For something to be the case, for there to be a fact of the matter, what we are talking about must be in some definite condition: there must be *something which holds* or something *which is true* of the subject. But of course there must also be a subject of which this holds.[8] So whether a veridical use includes a grammatical subject (as in ἔστι ταῦτα) or none (as in ἔστι οὕτω), it will

---

[6] A word on the accent of ἐστί. Since this verb form is normally enclitic, and orthotone only in initial or quasi-initial position, there is no reason to accent it ἔστι unless it is quoted in a sentence context where the verb occurs in the relevant position. The ancient practice and its modern deformations are discussed in my *The Verb 'Be' in Ancient Greek*, pp. 420–2. The ancient rule is now followed in A. H. Coxon's edition, *The Fragments of Parmenides* (Doven, NH: Van Gorcum, 1986).

[7] See *The Verb 'Be'*, pp. 334–7.

[8] I am assuming that basic sentences in Indo-European (if not in all languages) are logically of subject–predicate form: there is something one is talking about, and something which is said about this subject. Impersonal verbs (such as ὕει, 'It is raining') are an apparent exception, since there is no grammatical subject (though Greek will often provide one: Ζεὺς ὕει, or in

in either case directly imply both an assertion of existence ('*there is something* which is so-and-so') and also a predicative use of the verb ('something *is* so-and-so'). |

242⟧   The central point of controversy can be located in the question whether the very first occurrence of ἐστί in B 2, for the true road of inquiry, is to be construed as existential or as veridical-predicative. And, first of all, what are we talking about? In reference to what is the assertion ἐστί to be understood? G. E. L. Owen proposed as subject 'what can be thought or spoken of', 'what can be talked or thought about; for the proof of its existence is that, if it did not exist, it could not be talked or thought about'.[9] Against this I propose that the subject in question is the object of Parmenides' quest, the goal to which the 'roads of inquiry' are supposed to lead, in other words the Truth conceived as object or content of the knowledge the goddess has promised to reveal (B 1. 29).[10] The initial postulate, the assumption which makes truth and knowledge possible and Parmenides' quest capable of success, is that 'it (something, whatever we are going to find out about) is the case', 'it really is in some definite way', 'it truly is something-or-other'. The claim is simply one of *reality* for an object of knowledge and discourse. What this reality consists in remains to be specified.

I shall not reargue the case here for an initial definition of the subject in terms of the quest for knowledge rather than as Owen's possible subject for thought and speech. I submit that my definition emerges

modern Greek βρέχει ὁ Θεός). Logically speaking, however, what we are talking about in such a sentence is the weather, or, more vaguely, what is going on out there. The predicate element, what is said about this subject, consists of the specific content and truth claim provided by the verb. For the connections between subject–predicate structure in surface syntax and the deeper functional distinction between referring and predicating see *The Verb 'Be'*, ch. 2, esp. pp. 51–3.

[9] 'Eleatic Questions', pp. 94–5. Similarly David Gallop: 'what is there to speak and think of'; 'thought and speech must have an object' ('"Is" or "Is Not"', pp. 68–9).

[10] For detailed argument in support of this view see *The Thesis of Parmenides*, pp. 702–10 (Ch. 6 above). Similarly Barnes, *The Presocratic Philosophers*, i. 163, 'the implicit object of *dizēsios* is the implicit subject of *esti*'. Note that this does not exclude the possibility, even the certainty, that the goal of Parmenides' inquiry is in some sense the nature of things, what his predecessors also sought to investigate: his δίζησις is continuous with their ἱστορία. But the outcome is so different that he prefers to leave the object of his new knowledge unspecified, except by his new formula, namely *what is*, what is really there.

172 CHARLES H. KAHN

naturally from the entire proem and from the context of B 2, whereas Owen's definition, cunning as it is, comes out of nowhere. Or, rather, it comes from nowhere in the immediate or preceding context; it has to be read back into B 2 from the interpretation of later fragments, and from dubious interpretation at best.[11] But rejecting | Owen's definition   [243 of the subject does not entail rejection of the existential reading for ἐστί (as Barnes has shown). Parmenides in B 2. 3 can be read as saying: the object of knowledge exists and it is impossible for it not to exist, 'for you cannot know or point out *what does not exist*' (τό γε μὴ ἐόν B 2. 7).

My objections to this reading are of two kinds, both linguistic-historical and philosophical. To take the philosophical objection first: it is simply false to say that you cannot think or talk about (point out in speech, φράζειν) what does not exist. And the falseness of this would be obvious to any Greek who reflected for a moment on the profusion of monsters and fantastic creatures in traditional poetry and myth, from Pegasus to the children of Gaia with a hundred arms and fifty heads apiece (Hesiod, *Theogony* 150). Neither Parmenides nor his followers would imagine for a moment that Hesiod's description (and some hearers' naive belief) might suffice to usher such items into existence.[12] Even if we prefer to take νοεῖν in its stronger reading as a verb of achievement, 'to know' or 'to understand' and not merely 'to think' or 'conceive of', we can still insist that such nonentities are subjects of knowledge after all: one can know of them that they do not exist, that they are described by Hesiod, etc. It is surprising to see that the charms of the existential reading are so great that recent commentators are willing to saddle Parmenides with a grossly fallacious starting

---

[11] Namely, the modal reading of B 3 ('it is the same thing that can be thought and that can be') and the parallel reading of τὸ λέγειν τε νοεῖν τ' ἐόν in B 6. 1 as 'what can be spoken and thought'. (I ignore here the issue whether νοεῖν should be rendered 'thinking' or 'cognizing'.) For B 3 this is certainly not the most *obvious* reading, even if it has become the most familiar, by force of repetition. For B 6. 1 the reading in question is, from the linguistic point of view, the least plausible of the 5 or 6 construals that have been proposed for this baffling verse. (For discussion of this verse, see the Appendix to this Essay.) As Tugendhat has pointed out in reference to B 3, it is a mistake to base an interpretation on sentences whose construction is seriously disputed (see 'Das Sein und das Nichts', p. 140).

[12] Compare Gorgias' explicit discussion of this point: Scylla and Chimaira are μὴ ὄντα (nonentities) which nevertheless can be, and in fact are, objects of thought (φρονεῖται) in DK 82 B. 3, 80.

point, even when their aim is to give him 'a metaphysical outlook which is intelligible, coherent, and peculiarly plausible'.[13] The existential reading of ἐστί gives him a starting point | that is very difficult [244] (though perhaps not strictly impossible) to defend.[14] The veridical reading, by contrast, guarantees that his initial claim will be both philosophically impeccable and close to common sense. Knowledge implies truth, and truth is 'telling it like it is'. Both truth and knowledge necessarily refer to some reality, some objective fact of the matter, some 'thing that is' (ἐόν).[15]

Aside from these philosophical considerations, there are strong historical grounds for doubting the narrow existential reading of ἐστί. First of all, questions of existence never play the central role in ancient philosophy that they have occupied in modern thought since Descartes. Important studies by Vlastos and Owen have warned us against taking the ontological concerns of Plato and Aristotle to be focussed on questions of existence.[16] Owen in particular has emphasized again and again that εἶναι in Plato's *Sophist* or Aristotle's *Metaphysics* rarely means 'to exist' *simpliciter*; it normally means *to be this or that*, to be something definite; so that an apparently absolute use of the verb should frequently be read as an elliptical copula. It seems ironic that the influence of Owen's earlier 'Eleatic Questions' has

---

[13] Barnes, *Presocratic Philosophers*, i. 161. Barnes acknowledges that (on his reading of *is* as 'exists') Parmenides' metaphysics 'is based upon a falsehood and defended by a specious argument' (i. 172). There are certainly problems with the argument, as we shall see. But I am not convinced that Parmenides needs to worry about the modal fallacy Owen and Barnes ascribe to him. The appearance of fallacy is largely generated by the unnecessary modal reading of B 3 and B 6. 1. In B 2 the modals are best interpreted as *necessitas consequentiae*: if something is to be investigated, cognized, and understood, *it must be the case* or *be real*.

[14] For a partial defense see Montgomery Furth's reading of *is* as existential in 'Elements of Eleatic Ontology', in A. P. D. Mourelatos (ed.), *The Pre-Socratics* (Garden City, NY: Anchor, 1974), 249–58.

[15] This is the objective correlative to the claim in the formal mode that '*M knows that p* entails *p*'. J. Hintikka long ago correctly described this as 'Parmenides' law'. See his *Knowledge and Belief* (Ithaca, NY: Cornell University Press, 1962), 22 n. 7.

[16] G. Vlastos, 'Degrees of Reality in Plato' (1965), repr. in *Platonic Studies* (Princeton, NJ: Princeton University Press, 1973), esp. pp. 65–6; G. E. L. Owen, 'Plato on Not-Being', in G. Vlastos (ed.), *Plato I* (1970), 223–67 (repr. in *Logic, Science, and Dialectic*, pp. 104–36). In 'Aristotle on the Snares of Ontology' (in R. Bambrough (ed.), *New Essay on Plato and Aristotle* (New York: Humanities, 1965)) Owen still spoke in terms of existence but emphasized that, for Aristotle also, 'to be is always to be something or other' (*New Essays*, p. 76 = *Logic, Science, and Dialectic*, p. 264).

[[245]] | served to postpone the application of this insight to the interpretation of Parmenides, where the anachronistic assumption still prevails that existence as such is thematized in Greek thought.

The linguistic record also makes it unlikely that an unadorned ἐστί in a poem of the early fifth century should be read as 'exists'. There are of course existential uses of the verb in all periods of the language, beginning with Homer. But in the older texts these uses fall into certain well-defined groups, which do not include purely existential claims of the form εἰσὶ θεοί, 'There are gods' or οὐκ ἔστι Ζεύς, 'There is no Zeus'. The oldest examples of sentences of this purely existential type come from the middle and late fifth century, and they are specifically concerned with the existence of the gods.[17] The typical existential use in earlier texts serves to introduce (or sometimes to deny) a subject for further predication: ἔστι πόλις Ἐφύρη . . . 'there is a city Ephyre, in a corner of Argos'; νῦν δ' οὐκ ἔσθ' ὅς τις θάνατον φύγῃ, 'now there is no one who will escape death'.[18] In such uses the existential value of the verb is of course clear, and it is only a question of time until it emerges as an independent sentence form. But in the earliest texts that form occurs only when the subject is a person and the sense of the verb is not simply 'exists' but (roughly) 'is alive'.[19] The best-known expression of this type is for the gods: θεοὶ αἰὲν ἐόντες, 'the gods who are forever'. The pure existential sentence can be seen as an extension of this type to nonpersonal subjects.[20] Thus in Heraclitus B 30 we have (κόσμος) ἦν ἀεὶ καὶ ἔστιν καὶ ἔσται πῦρ ἀείζωον, where the syntax of the verb is overdetermined: 'it ever was and is and will be: everliving fire' (construing the verbs first | as existential, then as   [246 copula). By Parmenides' time a pure existential use is certainly possible; there may be at least one case in the extant fragments of

---

[17] See *The Verb 'Be' in Ancient Greek*, ch. 6, and esp. pp. 300–6. The only wholly independent syntax for existential ἐστί/ὤν in the earlier texts is the vital use for persons (existential Type I, ibid. 240–5).

[18] *The Verb 'Be'*, pp. 245 ff. and 277 ff. The two examples illustrate existential Types II and IV, respectively.

[19] See the reference to Type I in n. 17.

[20] Pherecydes B 1 is an intermediate case, hesitating between the vital and the pure existential: Χρόνος ἦσαν ἀεὶ καὶ Χθονίη. In Heraclitus the only other possible instance of a pure existential seems to be εἰ ταῦτα μὴ ἦν in B 23, where however the construal is uncertain and the wording may belong to Clement.

his poem.[21] But this sentence type remains marginal, as we can see from the prose fragments of Parmenides' followers, Zeno and Melissus. A typical example is Zeno B 1, which begins with what seems to be a pure existential: εἰ δέ ἐστιν 'if these things exist (namely, a plurality)'. But when the same thesis is resumed two sentences later, the syntax is more ambiguous: οὕτως εἰ πολλά ἐστιν, which can be read as either 'if many things exist' or copulatively as 'if things are many'. (It is actually the predicate syntax that is favored by what follows: 'necessarily, they must be both small and large'.) A similar ambiguity pervades the usage of the verb in the fragments of Melissus, where in B 1 εἰ τοίνυν μηδὲν ἦν can be construed either as 'if nothing existed' or 'if it was nothing'. (Here again the predicative construal seems more plausible, in view of πρὶν γενέσθαι εἶναι μηδέν in the preceding clause: 'necessarily, before it came to be it was nothing'.) In other fragments, such as Melissus B 8, the use of εἶναι oscillates between existential, copulative, and veridical constructions.[22] The syntax tends to be clearer in Plato, but his usage of the verb is equally variable. Some absolute uses of ἐστί serve as pure existential, others as veridical.[23] Many assertions of existence take existential-locative form.[24] When Plato wants emphatically and unmistakably to assert the existence of an item, he resorts not to an existential but to a copula use of to be and says that the thing in question is something (τι εἶναι) rather than nothing (μηδὲν εἶναι).[25]

Thus the linguistic evidence indicates that the use of ἐστί as syntactically independent verb with the sense 'exists' (*simpliciter*) is a | rather [[247]] late and unstable development in Greek, one that is fully established only in connection with the existence of the gods and the creatures of myth. By contrast, the absolute use of the verb with veridical force is already standard in Homer, as in the Ionic prose of Herodotus.[26] It is,

---

[21] Parmenides B 6. 2, μηδὲν δ' οὐκ ἔστιν, 'There is no such thing as nothing' on my reading; but many will interpret this as a potential ἐστίν (with understood εἶναι). For other possible cases of the pure existential see the Appendix to this essay.

[22] See my discussion of Melissus B 2 in *The Verb 'Be'*, p. 305.

[23] There are examples of pure existential uses at *Phaedo* 76d7, e3, e4, 77a3, cited in my Essay 4 above, n. 14. For veridicals see below.

[24] e.g. *Phaedo* 72a7, τὰς τῶν τεθνεώτων ψυχὰς εἶναί που; 73a1, εἰ μὴ ἦν που ἡμῖν ἡ ψυχὴ πρὶν ἐν τῷδε τῷ ἀνθρωπίνῳ εἴδει γενέσθαι. Cf. Vlastos, *Platonic Studies*, p. 65 n. 31.

[25] *Prot.* 330c1; *Gorgias* 495c3–5, 500d7; *Phaedo* 74a9–10, etc.

[26] *The Verb 'Be'*, pp. 335–55.

I submit, by far the most natural reading for an emphatic, syntactically independent ἐστί in an archaic text.

But of course if Parmenides begins with a veridical ἐστί he does not end there. My earlier exegesis failed to make clear how the veridical value serves Parmenides only as an entering wedge, to guarantee an initial acceptance of his ontological thesis by establishing a necessary connection between the pursuit of knowledge and the assertion of ἐστί. Once the reader's assent to ἐστί has been secured in B 2, Parmenides proceeds beyond the veridical notion to develop other aspects of the ontological claim entailed by this assertion. And one of the first aspects to be elaborated is the existential idea: *what is* must be something rather than nothing. This existential value plays a central part in the rejection of coming-to-be and perishing in B 8. 6–18. The intuitive connection is expressed in English when we speak of coming-to-be as 'coming into existence' and of perishing as 'ceasing to exist'. So it is clear why a denial of nonexistence makes perishing impossible (ceasing to exist would mean starting to nonexist) and coming-to-be unintelligible (coming into existence would mean coming out of nonexistence). In order to express this thought unambiguously, Greek will make use of the terms 'something' (τι) and 'nothing' (μηδέν). Coming into existence will be *coming from nothing*; ceasing to exist will be *going into nothing*. So we find μηδέν as an explication of οὐκ ἔστι in B 6. 2 and B 8. 10: *being nothing* turns out to be the false way that has already been rejected in B 2. As Parmenides says, μηδὲν οὐκ ἔστιν 'there is no such thing as nothing' (B 6. 2). And in Greek that seems even more tautologous than in English.

Intuitively speaking, then, we can say that the verb takes on an existential value in the argument against coming to be and perishing. Formally speaking, however, that argument does not depend upon assigning any particular value to ἐστί. We need only assume that the original dichotomy is exhaustive as well as exclusive. Then if anything | comes into being, it must come either (1) from not-being, or (2) from nothing at all, or (3) from being.[27] But (1) has been ruled out in B 2,

[248]

---

[27] I accept Reinhardt's emendation ἐκ τοῦ ἐόντος for ἐκ μὴ ἐόντος at B 8. 12, which makes the argument much stronger and more symmetrical. But my claim in the text does not depend on this correction.

since *what is not* is no object for assertion (φάσθαι) or cognition (νοεῖν): *what is not* is nothing at all. But (2) if *what is* comes from nothing, i.e. not *from* anything, then there is no reason for it to come to be 'later rather than sooner'—the argument from sufficient reason.[28] Finally, (3) it cannot come from *being* because then it would become something *besides* being (παρ' αὐτό), i.e. something different from being; but that (by the initial disjunction of B. 2, repeated at B 8. 15–16) could only be not-being. So if coming-to-be from being involves any change, it can only mean ceasing-to-be, i.e. perishing, going into not-being. But not-being has been ruled out: 'for nothing is or will be / other, outside of what is' (B 8.36–7 f). Since the initial dichotomy applies to everything, anything distinct from *what is* must be *what is not*. This premiss, taken together with the rejection of *what is not*, gives Parmenides a formally valid argument against all change, diversity, and plurality of any kind, including temporal differences such as *was* and *will be*. If *what was* is different from *what is*, it must be *what is not*. More generally, for any *X*, if *X* is different from what is, *X* is not.

This devastatingly simple argument is, I believe, the secret of Parmenides' extraordinary success with the next generation of Greek cosmologists. Anaxagoras, Empedocles, and the atomists all accepted the conclusion that nothing real (ἐόν) comes to be or perishes, even though their faith in Parmenides' logic was not sufficient to bring them to deny plurality and diversity. What is wrong with the argument lies buried so deep in the linguistic functions of *to be* and the logical functions of negation that no real clarity could emerge until Plato, after long wrestling with the puzzles of not-being, allowed his Eleatic Stranger to commit the act of patricide by showing how *what is not* must also be acknowledged *to be*, just as much as *what is*. But Plato's *Sophist* comes more than a century after Parmenides' poem. In | [249] the meantime the implications of Parmenides' argument might be ignored, but they could not be refuted. Furthermore, the power of Parmenides' ontological vision does not depend solely on the logic of his proof. He relies also on the strong intuitive values of ἐστί and ὄν in Greek, which represent in concentrated form certain basic functions of

---

[28] See Owen's comments in *Monist*, 50/3 (1966), 325–6 (= *Logic, Science and Dialectic*, pp. 33–4).

the verb *to be* in Indo-European. Two of these functions have already been noticed here: (1) the veridical use of verb and participle for truth and reality, and (2) the lexical value 'exists' or 'there is'. The most common occurrence of the verb in the language, however, is (3) the copula, of which Parmenides makes abundant use. The signposts along the way of *what is* (B 8. 2) point to so many true predications: 'it *is* ungenerated and imperishable' (ἐστίν in B 8. 3), 'it *is* all alike' (ἐστίν in B 8. 22), 'it *is* all full' (B 8. 24), 'continuous' (8. 25), 'immobile, unbegun, unceasing' (8. 26–7, 39), 'perfected in every direction' (8. 42), 'inviolate or intact' (8. 48).[29] These copula uses of *to be* spell out the content which was implicit in Parmenides' initial assertion of ἐστί. And this content is in turn conditioned and supported by two other fundamental values of *to be*: (4) the stative-durative value of *is* in contrast to *becomes*, and (5) the locative use (*is here, there*, or *somewhere*), which is often connected with assertions of existence (*there is . . .*).[30] In Greek, as in other languages, one of the most common suppletive verbs for *to be* is *to stand*, where locative and stative nuances are combined. Thus εἶναι in Greek, like *es-* in Indo-European, can be described as *a verb of station* as opposed to a verb of motion.[31] But in Greek the nuance of stability and permanence is strongly reinforced by the purely durative aspect of the verb. In this case morphology adds additional support to the stative-mutative (or static-kinetic) contrast between *being* and *becoming*, since the Greek verb *to be* is almost unique among its Indo-European cognates in admitting no aorist morpheme and incorporating no forms from the contrasting copula *bhu-* into its conjugation (as Latin incorporated *fui* and English *be*).[32] If the existential value of the verb underlies the first argument | against coming-to-be at B 8. 6–18, it is the present-durative aspect of ἐστί and ἐόν that supports the rejection of past (ἔγεντο) and future (πέλοιτο, μέλλει ἔσεσθαι) at B 8. 19–20; and it is the static nuance of stability or 'standing still' that reinforces the argument against motion and change.

⟦250⟧

---

[29] I count some 30 ordinary uses of copula *to be* (with predicate nouns and adjectives) in the fragments. See the Appendix to this Essay.

[30] For locative-existential uses see *The Verb 'Be'*, pp. 164–7, 261–4, 271–7. For examples in Parmenides see the Appendix to this Essay.

[31] *The Verb 'Be'*, p. 198.

[32] *The Verb 'Be'*, p. 219; cf. pp. 195–8.

Furthermore, the locative or locative-existential associations of the verb are presupposed in the argument for continuity and density of ἐόν at 8. 22–5: 'there is not more here (τῇ μᾶλλον) that would bar it from holding together, nor any less; but all is full of *what is*'.[33] In the conclusion of the argument against motion at B 8. 29–30 the locative, durative, and stative values converge: 'remaining the same in the same (place), it lies by itself / and so will it remain fixed hereafter'. The emphasis here on *being the same* permits us to recognize one more function of *to be*: (6) for the assertion of identity. Being is the same with itself; what is other than being *is not*.

In summary we can say that Parmenides has constructed his new ontological conception of Being by drawing together in a unified whole the rich diversity of values, meanings, and functions associated with the most fundamental verb in the language. If I have argued for the primacy of the veridical idea as a key to understanding this complex vision, my reasons have been three: (1) the veridical is the best-attested use for syntactically independent occurrences of the verb in archaic texts; (2) the veridical ἐστί gives the best philosophical sense to the claim that 'you cannot know *what is not*'; and (3) the logical structure | of the veridical involves both existence and predication, and [251] thus serves to introduce *all* values for the verb *to be*. Hence the predications which spell out the import of this initial ἐστί will develop not only the existential but also the present-durative, locative-spatial, and static-permanent implications of this basic assertion. The predicative function is the vehicle which conveys *all* values of the verb. And this rich diversity of aspects for Being is brought together into a single

---

[33] Some commentators have doubted that τῇ at B 8. 23 has its normal local value ('here'), but that seems to me guaranteed by the context (the argument for continuity) and by the expanded repetition of the same argument at 8. 44–8 (cf. τῇ ἢ τῇ in 8. 45). The spatial imagery is unmistakable in συνέχεσθαι at 8. 23, repeated as ἱκνεῖσθαι εἰς ὁμόν at 8. 46. Hence πελάζει in 8. 25: 'Being is adjacent to Being' (Coxon). For the spatial intuition underlying Parmenides' description of τὸ ἐόν as a homogeneous plenum, a symmetrical, isotropic continuum, 'like the mass of a well-rounded sphere', see G. De Santillana, *Prologue to Parmenides* (Cincinnati, Ohio: University of Cincinnati Press, 1964), esp. pp. 18–25. In Plato this geometric conception gets separated off from the notion of Being proper and is elaborated as the Receptacle of the *Timaeus*. The two conceptions are reunited in the seventeenth-century Platonism of Henry More (cited by De Santillana, *Prologue* p. 24). For the cosmological implications of Parmenides' notion of spatial symmetry see David Furley, *The Greek Cosmologists*, i (Cambridge: Cambridge University Press, 1987), 54–5.

whole by means of the logically connected notions of unity, uniformity, symmetry, continuity, and identity.

Parmenides' positive conception of *what is* thus attains a high degree of conceptual coherence and unity. Unfortunately, the same cannot be said for the corresponding negative notion of *what is not*. For Not-being (τὸ μὴ ἐόν) is a fatally confused notion, combining in a specious unity a number of quite diverse, logically unconnected ideas. Depending upon which function of *is* is negated, not-being can represent either falsehood, negative predication, nonidentity, nonexistence, or nonentity, i.e. nothing at all. The combination of all these forms of negation in a single notion is a conceptual monster, as Plato was finally to point out.[34] It is here, in the negative branch of his initial dichotomy, that the charge of fallacious equivocation brought against Parmenides by Aristotle and Eudemus is ultimately justified.

II

My earlier formulation of the veridical view has been carefully criticized by David Gallop, who argues in favor of the existential reading. It will be worth looking at Gallop's remarks to see what force they have against the present interpretation. Gallop offers three objections to the veridical reading of ἐστί in B 2.

[1] It would be extremely feeble for [the goddess] to reason merely that some truth must needs obtain, on the ground that one logically could not | know what is false. For it is perfectly conceivable, as a skeptic might well respond, that no one knows anything, precisely because there is no truth to be known. To insist in face of this that there must be truth, in order for there to be knowledge, would simply be to beg the question.[35]   [252]

---

[34] Perhaps Parmenides had some inkling of this, since he describes the way of *is not* as 'unheard of' (παναπευθής), 'incomprehensible' or 'unthinkable' (ἀνόητος), and as no true way. For a different analysis of the fallacy, in terms of the confusion between νοεῖν conceived on the analogy of perception (where one either sees something or nothing) and the structure of λέγειν as saying something about something (so that making a negative assertion does *not* mean saying nothing), see E. Tugendhat, *Das Sein und das Nichts*, pp. 139–40.

[35] Gallop, ' "Is" or "Is Not"?', p. 66.

This objection seems to me misconceived. There is no reason to suppose that Parmenides is arguing against a skeptic who is prepared to deny the possibility of knowledge or truth. In this respect, Owen's original comparison of Parmenides' argument to Descartes's *cogito* is misleading. The argument presupposes a commitment not only to Inquiry (δίζησις) but to pursuit of Truth (ἀλήθεια in B 1. 29 and 2. 4) as a subject worthy of trust and conviction (πίστις B 1. 30, πειθώ 2. 4). The initial question is: What assumption must we start from, what way must be traveled, if we are to have any hope of reaching this goal?

[2] The status of Kahn's knowable object is unsatisfactory . . . 'A definite fact, an actual state of affairs' . . . seems to be of the wrong logical type to serve as the bearer of such attributes as 'ungenerable', 'imperishable', 'whole', and 'immovable' (B 8. 3–5). Such properties . . . could characterize only what has the status of an entity, an individual *thing*. What the goddess seems to be talking about throughout B8 is not a fact or a state of affairs, but a thing with certain attributes which she is proving to belong to it.[36]

This would be an objection to my view only if we had reason to believe that Parmenides was careful to respect the distinction of logical type between things or substances and facts or propositional structures. But, alas, the Greek philosophers are notoriously lax in this regard. Plato's description of the Forms regularly combines propositional and thing-like characteristics. Even Aristotle, whose doctrine of categories is in part designed to capture just this distinction, does not always respect it in developing his theories of substance, essence, and form. Standing at the beginning of the Greek ontological tradition, Parmenides is not likely to be more scrupulous. On my reading, the veridical ἐστί of B 2 directly entails both existential assertion and predicative construction. If the logical subject of ἐστί shifts from the complex 'fact of the matter' in B 2 to the subject component of this fact in B 8, that is no more than a harmless synecdoche, a natural and nonfallacious movement from whole to part. | [253]

[3] Thirdly, if we take the rejection of 'what is not' as the denial that 'what is not the case' can be an object of knowledge, we do not obtain a sense of 'is not' strong enough, or in any way suitable, to yield the conclusions of

---

[36] Ibid.

B 8 ... In order to disprove generation and perishing (B 8. 6–21), it is not a
false proposition whose thought or utterance must be prohibited, but a
negative existential statement.[37]

I have insisted throughout that the assertion of veridical ἐστί in B 2.
3 will include an assertion of existence for a subject. Hence the denial
of this ἐστί in B 2. 5 will include a denial of existence. And that is
where fallacy enters. For if we think of the veridical ἐστί as asserting
'There is a subject X which has attributes A, B, C', the denial οὐκ ἔστι
can mean either (1) the sentence as a whole is false, or (2) X does not
exist, or (3) one or more of the attributes fails to hold. Parmenides'
argument depends upon ignoring this ambiguity and passing directly
from (1) to (2), from *is not* to μηδέν, nothing at all. The Owen–Gallop
reading, taking ἐστί unequivocally as 'exists' in B 2, aims to give
Parmenides a valid argument against coming-to-be and perishing.[38]
But (in addition to the philosophical and linguistic objections
rehearsed above) it does so at the price of cutting the logical link
between the existential ἐστί of B 2 and the copula uses of the verb in
B 8. (It is just this understanding of B 2 that provokes the old complaint
that Parmenides confused existential and copula uses.) Such a narrowly
existential reading of ἐστί also cuts the historical link between the
Parmenidean and Platonic conceptions of Being.

III

The *Symposium, Phaedo,* and *Republic* expound a theory of Forms that
takes its ontological basis from the Parmenidean distinction between
Being and Becoming, reinforced by the parallel oppositions between
reality and appearance, between what is intelligible and what is sensible. It is the introduction of this Eleatic metaphysics (somewhat
misleadingly referred to as the 'separation' of the Forms) that distinguishes the doctrine of the middle dialogues from the conception of

---

[37] Gallop, ' "Is" or "Is Not"?', p. 67.

[38] As construed by them, however, the argument is not valid after all, since it contains a
glaring modal fallacy. See Gallop, *Parmenides of Elea,* p. 24, with references to Owen and
Barnes in n. 71 (on p. 38).

eidos and *idea* in the *Euthyphro* and the *Meno*, where the | distinction   [[254]]
between a single form and its many instances is clearly drawn but not
elaborated in ontological terms. The *Symposium* gives a brief summary
of the new theory, delivered in apocalyptic style without sustained
argument and limited to a single Form, the Beautiful. The *Phaedo*,
by contrast, formulates the theory for a whole range of Forms and
develops this doctrine systematically throughout the dialogue. It is
from the *Phaedo*, then, and from the introductory discussion of
Forms in *Republic* 5, that we can best see how Plato's presentation of
his own ontology follows faithfully in Parmenides' footsteps.

The *Phaedo* first presents the Forms as constituents of the truth, the
object of the philosopher's quest. Plato's word for 'inquiry' in this
context, ζήτησις at 65b10, is the prose equivalent of Parmenides'
poetic δίζησις in B 2. 2. When the ontological vocabulary of τὸ ὄν
and τὰ ὄντα is introduced as target of this inquiry (65c3 and 9), the
connotations are unmistakably veridical: the participles of *to be* alter-
nate throughout this section with words for truth.[39] Hence these
participles clearly bear the idiomatic sense that we know from the
use of τὸ ἐόν and τὰ ὄντα in Herodotus, Thucydides, and other fifth-
century authors. But just as an initial veridical ἐστί in Parmenides will
unfold in a richer ontological structure as the poem proceeds, so Plato
in the *Phaedo* will pass from this common-sense notion of τὰ ὄντα, as
the reality reported by true statements or grasped by reliable cognition,
to more technical uses of *to be*.

The first definite reference to a Form comes at *Phaedo* 65d4: 'Do we
say that the just itself is something or nothing' (τι εἶναι . . . ἢ οὐδέν).
The existence of the Form is asserted by a copula construction for
εἶναι. Other Forms are then mentioned (beautiful, good, magnitude,
health, strength) and the doctrine is generalized: 'And, to sum up, I am
speaking of the reality of all the rest, i.e. of what each of them really is'
(τῆς οὐσίας ὃ τυγχάνει ἕκαστον ὄν, Burnet's rendering on 65d13). In
this, the first general reference to the Forms in any Platonic text, the
nominalization οὐσία which expresses the reality of the Forms simply
brings together the veridical and predicative values of the verb in
what proceeds (with an implicit existential value as well, though no

---

[39] *Phaedo* 65b–66d, with Burnet's comment on 65c3.

existential use has occurred in this context); but | these values are now   ⟦255
focussed on the semitechnical, specifically Platonic formula ὅ ἐστι:
What F (really) is or *What is (truly) F*, where veridical nuance and
predicative syntax are combined. This formula later appears as the
systematic designation for the Forms: αὐτὸ ὅ ἐστιν at 74b2, 74d7,
etc.[40] The formula is of course derived from the τί ἐστιν question of
the earlier dialogues. Together with the complementary notion
of participation, it represents perhaps the only essential component
of Plato's conception of Being for which there is no precedent in
Parmenides.

   If we turn to Plato's more definitive statement of his doctrine in
the *Republic*, we find exactly the same pattern. Plato introduces the
terminology of 'being' with an informal, quasi-idiomatic use of the
participle ὄν for the object of knowledge, what is real or true; he then
proceeds to predicative uses of *to be* which culminate in his own
technical phrase ὅ ἐστιν as a designation for the Forms. The Forms
are first invoked in book 5 in order to specify the sense in which
philosophers may be defined as 'lovers of the spectacle of truth
(ἀλήθεια)' at 475e. The general theory is briefly summarized by way
of three ordinary predicative uses of *to be* (ἐστίν, εἶναι at 475e9, εἶναι at
476a6), whose veridical overtones are emphasized by the contrast with
to seem (φαίνεσθαι at 476a7). But the first emphatic or 'ontological' use
of the verb occurs a bit later, at 476e, in characterizing the object of
knowledge: 'Does the one who knows know something or nothing
(τι ἢ οὐδέν)?'. Glaucon answers: 'He knows something'. 'Something
which is (ὄν) or which is not (οὐκ ὄν)?' 'Which is; for how could
something which is not (μὴ ὄν γέ τι) be known?' The echo of
Parmenides B 2. 7 is unmistakable; the verb for knowing (γιγνώσκειν)
is the same in both texts. But being (ὄν) cannot mean existence here,
since the assertion of existence has already been made by the contrast
of something (τι) with nothing (οὐδέν).[41]

   Plato immediately proceeds to delineate more sharply the
Parmenidean dichotomy as he understands it. 'So what is completely

---

[40] For further discussion of the ontological vocabulary of the *Phaedo*, see Essay 4 above.

[41] For fuller argumentation against the existential reading of ὄν in this context, see Essay 4 above, pp. 112–13. For the veridical reading compare Aristotle, *Post. An.* 1. 2. 71ᵇ25: the premises of a scientific syllogism must be true (ἀληθῆ), ὅτι οὐκ ἔστι τὸ μὴ ὂν ἐπίστασθαι.

(τὸ μὲν παντελῶς ὄν) is completely knowable, what is not in any way
256] (μὴ ὂν δὲ | μηδαμῇ) is in no way knowable' (477a3). Plato is concerned
to find an object for *doxa* in between: 'if something is in such a
condition as both to be and not to be' (εἰ δὲ δή τι οὕτως ἔχει ὡς
εἶναί τε καὶ μὴ εἶναι). So far the syntax of the verb in this context is
apparently absolute, with no hint of a predicate expression. The
possibility of a predicative construction begins to emerge with the
characterization of knowledge as 'naturally set upon *what is* (as its
object), to know of *what is* that (or how) it is' (ἐπιστήμη μὲν ἐπὶ τῷ
ὄντι πέφυκε, γνῶναι ὡς ἔστι τὸ ὄν, 477b10). There can be no question
here of reading *is* as 'exists'. Of course the object of knowledge is
assumed to exist; but that claim, as we have seen, was expressed
without any use of the verb. In the passage just quoted the verb asserts
more: that this object *is in some definite way*. That the absolute use of *to
be* is pregnant here with the predicate construction will be made clear
in the sequel, by a string of copula sentences at 479a–b. But in the
meantime the existential value of the verb will also be exploited, in the
exegesis of the negative form μὴ ὄν, 'what is not', in terms of μηδέν
'nothing': 'But will it not be correct to call *what is not* not even one
thing but nothing?' (478b12). Finally, the predicative construction
becomes explicit when Plato explains how the many things which
lie 'in between being and not-being' both are and are not: 'Is there[42]
any one of the many beautiful (things) which will not appear ugly?'
Glaucon responds: 'Necessarily, they will somehow appear both beautiful and ugly' (479b1). 'And for each of the many, *is* it rather than *is*
not that thing which one says it to be?' (πότερον οὖν ἐστὶ μᾶλλον ἢ οὐκ
ἔστι ἕκαστον τῶν πολλῶν τοῦτο ὃ ἄν τις φῇ αὐτὸ εἶναι, 479b9).

What we have here is the essential 'ambiguity' of predication
(ἐπαμφοτερίζειν, 479b11) which is for Plato characteristic of partici-
pants in the Form, and which distinguishes them from the unequivocal
being-what-it-is of the Form.[43] When the Forms are reintroduced in
Republic 6, it is by the implicit contrast with such ambiguity for the

---

[42] Note the existential use of ἐστὶ here (my Type IV, 'is there anyone who . . .') at 479a6,
and an ambiguous but possibly existential εἶναι at 479a4.

[43] Compare the sticks and stones of *Phaedo* 74b8, which 'sometimes appear equal,
sometimes not' (according to one MS reading) and the denial of such ambiguity for the
Form of Beautiful at *Symposium* 211a.

many good and beautiful things that the Beautiful itself and the Good itself are said to be just *what is* (ὅ ἐστιν, 507b7). The Form is just 'what truly *is* beautiful' or perhaps 'what (being) beautiful truly *is*'[44]. With this formula for the *is* of essential predication and definitional identity Plato has gone beyond Parmenides' conception of Being. But the Parmenidean overtones are still audible, and they are reinforced in what follows in books 6 and 7 by the systematic stative-mutative opposition between Being and Becoming, tending now to coincide with the original veridical opposition between Being and Seeming (beginning at 508d). Here for the first time Plato brings together the full orchestration of his neo-Eleatic ontology in order to provide an appropriate metaphysical background for his attempt to depict the Form of the Good.

My aim here has not been to analyze Plato's use of *to be* in the formulation of his own ontology, but only to demonstrate how faithfully Parmenidean he is in his progression from an initial, quasi-idiomatic use of ἐστί for truth and reality to more philosophically loaded, 'ontological' uses of the verb in which existential and predicative functions are combined with connotations of truth, stability, and permanence. With certain obvious modifications, Plato has revived the Eleatic notion of Being as a powerful and coherent metaphysical concept. Parmenides' negative conception of τὸ μὴ ὄν, on the other hand, turns out to be far less satisfactory. In *Republic* 5 Plato had apparently taken over this notion of τὸ μηδαμῇ ὄν ('what is not in any way') without misgivings, and perhaps also without fallacy, since he construed it only as the blank object of ignorance. But in later works he is persistently concerned with teasing out the puzzles of falsehood conceived as saying or thinking *what is not*: fleetingly in the *Euthydemus* (248b–c; cf. 283d and 286c7) and the *Theaetetus* (188d–189c), then more systematically in the *Sophist*. Here it is a visitor from Elea, 'companion of the circle of Parmenides and Zeno' (216a), who will successfully distinguish the unintelligible concept of 'what is not in any way' (237b7, 239c4, 258e6–259a1) from the coherent use of μὴ ὄν for nonidentity and negative predication. In the *Sophist* veridical being

---

[44] The second interpretation of ὅ ἐστι reflects Alexander Nehamas's reading of self-predication for the Form ('the F is F') as meaning 'The F is *what it is to be* F'.

is carefully analyzed as 'saying of what is *that it is* concerning | a subject' [258]
(236b), whereas the problematic concept of not-being is dissolved into
distinct negations for falsehood, identity, and predication. A long and
laborious effort of analysis was required to bring to light the confusions
hidden in Parmenides' argument. But these confusions infect only the
negative concept of *what is not*. The positive conception of Being
emerges unscathed, to dominate the metaphysical tradition of the
West for many centuries to come.

Appendix: Parmenides' use of εἶναι

I count 88 occurrences of εἶναι in the fragments, plus 5 occurrences of
πελέναι used synonymously, giving a total of 93 forms. (There would
be one more if we read ἔστι γὰρ οὐλομελές in B 8. 4 with DK.) The
examples fall into two groups: (1) the strong or ontological use of the
verb, which is what we are trying to interpret, and (2) ordinary uses of
εἶναι, comparable to what can be found in nonphilosophical texts.
I count 33 instances of the ontological use, which I exclude from this
grammatical survey. (This number can be slightly larger or smaller,
depending upon how certain dubious cases are decided.) The ontological use occurs, for example, in ὅπως ἐστίν and μὴ εἶναι in B 2. 3, in
οὐκ ἔστιν and μὴ εἶναι in B 2. 5, τὸ μὴ ἐόν in B 2. 7, εἶναι in B 3, τὸ ἐόν
and τοῦ ἐόντος in B 4. 2, and frequently throughout B 8. More
interesting from the strictly grammatical point of view are the ordinary
uses. I count 31 cases of the nominal copula (with predicate nouns and
adjectives), 4 cases with locative predicates, 6 or more instances of the
existential verb broadly conceived (including locative-existential and
existential-potential), leaving about a dozen cases too controversial to
classify. Examples follow.

1. The copula with predicate nouns and adjectives, by far the most
   frequent among ordinary uses (31 instances). Examples include:
   πειθοῦς ἐστι κέλευθος in 2. 4, ξυνὸν δέ μοί ἐστιν in 5. 1,
   ἀνώλεθρόν ἐστιν in 8. 3 etc. So also βαιότερον πελέναι at 8. 45.

2. The locative verb, or the copula with locative predicates (4
   occurrences): ἐκτὸς πάτου ἐστίν in 1. 27, ἀπεόντα παρεόντα in
   4. 1, and a stronger, figurative use of the locative in 8. 15: ἐν τῷδ᾽
   ἐστιν.

3. Ordinary existential uses include:

(a) three examples of locative-existential: ἔνθα … εἰσι in 1. 11, ταύτῃ δ᾽ ἐπὶ σήματ᾽ ἔασι in 8. 2, and (on my reading) ὅπως εἴη … τῇ μᾶλλον τῇ δ᾽ ἧσσον at 8. 47–8: 'so that there would be more of it here, | less of it there' (the locative sense of εἴη here   [259] seems clear to me, though others may disagree);

(b) at least one existential-potential: ὁδοὶ … εἰσι νοῆσαι in B 2; 'there are these ways for cognition' (pure potentials are discussed below under (d));

(c) two cases of my type IV ('There is no one who …') at 8. 46–7: οὔτε γάρ … ἐστι τό κεν παύοι … οὔτε … ἐστιν ὅπως … 'There is nothing to keep it apart, nor is there anything such as to be more or less …' (omitting here two ontological uses of ἐόν and the locative-existential εἴη listed above under (a));

(d) Are there any pure existential uses outside of the thirty-odd debatable ontological cases? As noted above, I count μηδὲν δ᾽ οὐκ ἔστιν in 6. 2 as existential ('There is no nothing'); but most commentators construe it as potential under the influence of ἔστι γὰρ εἶναι in the preceding verse (6. 1), where the potential reading 'it is possible (for it) to be' is widely accepted. The potential construction is also generally admitted for ὡς οὐκ ἔστι μὴ εἶναι in 2. 3 ('that it is not possible for it not to be'), since the contrasting clause in 2. 5 (ὡς χρεών ἐστι μὴ εἶναι, 'that it is necessary for it not to be') supports a modal reading of οὐκ ἔστι. However, an existential reading could be (and actually has been) defended both for ἔστι γὰρ εἶναι in 6. 1 and for οὐκ ἔστι μὴ εἶναι in 2. 3 ('there is being' 'there is no not-being'). If the existential reading were accepted here, we might have *no* example of the pure potential (impersonal ἐστί plus infinitive) in all the fragments.

There are also five cases of past and future tense for εἶναι and one for πελέναι which might be construed as existential ('there was', 'there will be'). That reading is defensible for οὐδέ ποτ᾽ ἦν οὐδ᾽ ἔσται at 8. 5 ('It never existed in the past, nor will it exist in the future'); but the present tense ἐστίν in the same verse points rather to the strong ontological reading '*What is* was not, nor will it be'. The same ambiguity holds for πέλοιτο (or πέλοι) in 8. 19, and for μέλλει ἔσεσθαι in 8. 20. I am more inclined to find a pure existential in 8. 36, οὐδὲν γὰρ <ἢ> ἔστιν ἢ ἔσται | ἄλλο πάρεξ τοῦ ἐόντος, 'There neither is nor will be anything else besides *what is*'. But since ἐστίν and ἔσται are also to be taken as copulative here, with ἄλλο as predicate, the syntax is overdetermined, as in Heraclitus B 30: see above.

In sum, I count 3 cases of the pure existential in Parmenides (6. 2, and 8. 36 twice), but none is beyond dispute.

4. Other dubious cases:

1. 32 χρῆν δοκίμως εἶναι. Too notorious to require discussion here.

3. 1 νοεῖν ἐστίν τε καὶ εἶναι. I take ἐστίν as an ordinary copula, but most would read it as potential. (Similarly for ἐστὶ νοεῖν at 8. 34.)

8. 34 οὕνεκέν ἐστι νόημα. I have no idea what is the correct construal for ἐστί here.

19. 1 οὕτω...καὶ νῦν ἔασι, 'exist'? 'have their being by opinion' (κατὰ δόξαν)? |

[260]

6. 8 πέλειν τε καὶ οὐκ εἶναι: here and in 8. 40 (εἶναί τε καὶ οὐχί) the verb expresses mortal error, but by reference to Parmenides' own strong conception of *what is*. We might regard these as quasi-ontological uses.

We are left with over 30 syntactically absolute occurrences of εἶναι and πελέναι that bear the full ontological weight of Parmenides' new vision. Grammatical analysis is of limited use in dealing with these cases.

I have left for the last the most disputed case of all, B 6. 1: χρὴ τὸ λέγειν τε νοεῖν τ᾿ ἐὸν ἔμμεναι. I list, in order of decreasing linguistic merit, the various construals that have been proposed.

1. 'It is necessary (χρή) that speaking and cognizing (τὸ λέγειν τε νοεῖν τε) be real-and-true', ἐὸν ἔμμεναι', with the participle taken as ontological predicate, the infinitive as copula. This is the only unforced construal of the clause, and it also fits best with the natural reading of B 2 as an identification of νοεῖν with εἶναι.

2. 'This (τό) is what one must say and think: being *is*' (ἐόν as subject of the infinitive). This is grammatically possible but clumsy, and it involves a difficult demonstrative force for τό.[45] Logically it is

---

[45] For objections see Tarán, *Parmenides*, p. 55.

vacuous, since participle and infinitive will have the same strong, ontological value.

3. 'It is necessary to say and think that this (τό) is Being' (ἐόν as ontological predicate with copula syntax of ἔμμεναι as in 1). This proposal of Coxon is apparently new but otherwise plausible, and it avoids the vacuity of 2.

4. 'It is necessary that speaking and thinking *what-is* be real' (both ἐόν and ἔμμεναι having ontological force, but taking ἐόν as object of the double articular infinitives). This suggestion of Fränkel is more ingenious than most, but it gives roughly the same sense as 1 by a more circuitous route.

4A. There is an alleged alternative to 4 with the same syntax but a weaker sense for ἔμμεναι: 'It is necessary to say and to think *what is*' (Tarán). But the construction of ἔμμεναι now becomes obscure, and it is hard to believe that this verb in Parmenides could be so superfluous.

5. Hardest of all is the currently most popular reading: 'What can be spoken and thought must *be*', taking τὸ ἐόν in the potential construction with two embedded infinitives, after Burnet. As Verdenius has observed, 'It is doubtful whether τὸ λέγειν ἐόν, "that which can be said", would be correct Greek'.[46] (Verdenius prefers 1 as 'the most obvious translation', which he traces back to Karsten, Diels, and Heidel.[47]) I am on record as declaring construal 5 | to be 'certainly *impossible*', since I had found no   [261 instance of potential ἐστί in participial form, much less with the articular participle.[48] David Furley and others have disagreed;[49] Furley cites[50] an example of the potential construction in participial form after all, from Demosthenes 50.22: καὶ ἐκβῆναι οὐκ ὂν οὐδὲ δειπνοποιήσασθαι (where, however, the participial

---

[46] W. J. Verdenius, *Parmenides: Some Comments on his Poem* (Groningen: Batavia, 1942), 36 n. 2.

[47] Ibid. 37 and n. 1.

[48] 'The Thesis of Parmenides', p. 722 n. 26; repr. in Essay 6 above.

[49] 'Notes on Parmenides', in E. N. Lee et al. (eds.), *Exegesis and Argument: Studies in Greek Philosophy Presented to Gregory Vlastos* (Assen: Von Gorcum, 1973), 11 n. 37.

[50] After H. Hölscher, *Anfängliches Fragen: Studies zur Frühen Griechischen Philosophie* (Göttingen: Vandenhoeck & Ruprecht, 1968), 98–9.

construction poses no difficulty in its context, surrounded as it is by other participles in the genitive absolute). The embedded position for an infinitive can be paralleled by Simonides' τὸ μὴ γενέσθαι δυνατόν. In the face of these parallels I should perhaps reduce my verdict of impossibility to 'extremely harsh and contorted'. I continue to believe that no one would construe the verse this way except under pressure from a previously established view of what Parmenides should be saying. N.-L. Cordero reports that the MSS of Simplicius all read χρὴ τὸ λέγειν τὸ (and not τε) νοεῖν τ' ἐὸν ἔμμεναι.[51] But this is surely an error of dittography, and the correction τε (which goes back to Karsten and Brandis) must be right.

---

[51] *Les deux chemins de Parménide* (Paris: Vrin, 1984), 110 n. 1, citing Tarán's and his own consultation of the MSS.

8

Parmenides and Plato Once More

FOR ALEX MOURELATOS

This seems a happy occasion to return to Parmenides, in order both to clarify my own interpretation of Parmenidean Being and also to emphasize the affinity between what I have called the veridical reading and the account in terms of predication that Alex Mourelatos gave in his monumental *The Route of Parmenides*.[1] It is good to have this opportunity to acknowledge how much our views have in common, even if they do not coincide. And perhaps I may indulge here in a moment of nostalgia, since Alex and I are both old Parmenideans. My article 'The Thesis of Parmenides' was published in 1969, just a year before Alex's book appeared. That was nearly thirty years ago, and it was not the beginning of the story for either of us. My own Eleatic obsession had taken hold even earlier, with an unpublished master's dissertation on Parmenides, just as Alex had begun with a doctoral dissertation on the same subject. So, for both of us, returning to Parmenides will have some of the charm of returning to the days of our youth.

I want to begin, however, not with Parmenides himself but with his impact on Plato, and with the curious fact that Aristotle gives an entirely different account of the background of Plato's theory of Forms. Aristotle never mentions Parmenides in this connection; instead it is Socrates, the Pythagoreans, and the Heraclitean Cratylus whose combined influence is said to have led Plato to posit metaphysical

---

[1] Mourelatos, *The Route of Parmenides* (New Haven, Conn.: Yale University Press, 1970). This is affinity with a difference, as Alex has pointed out. See n. 9 below.

Forms (*Metaph. A.* 6). It is striking how much emphasis Aristotle places here on Pythagorean influence (much more than in the corresponding passage of *M.* 4): 'The Pythagoreans say things exist by imitating the numbers, Plato says by participating <in them>, changing only the word' (*Metaph. A.* 6. 987^{b}10–13). This Pythagorean origin for Plato's doctrine has sometimes been taken seriously by historians. But from the context we can see that in *A.* 6 (unlike *M.* 4) what Aristotle has in view is not so much the teaching of the *Phaedo* and *Republic*—what *we* call the Theory of Forms—but rather the later theory that he associates with the 'unwritten doctrines'. For Aristotle goes on to specify that the One and the Dyad of Great and Small are treated as 'elements' (*stoicheia*) of the Forms by Plato (987^{b}19–27). In the same context he mentions 'the mathematicals' as situated between Forms and sensibles (987^{b}15), and he reports that the Forms as numbers were derived from the Great and Small 'by participation in the One' (987^{b}21). Thus it is clear that Aristotle's report in *A.* 6 reflects the atmosphere and teaching of the Academy in Plato's last years, or even in the time of Speusippus, when it became fashionable to see Platonism as a continuation of Pythagorean philosophy.

Considered as a claim about the historical origin of the Theory of Forms Aristotle's statement about the Pythagorean origin of the theory is highly implausible—even more implausible than his claim that Plato became a Heraclitean under the influence of Cratylus. Aristotle's emphasis on the importance of flux for Plato is probably also based on his experience in the Academy in Plato's later years, when attention was focussed on works like the *Theaetetus* and *Timaeus*, where the analysis of flux plays an essential role in the argument. | (And this, says [[82]] Aristotle—namely, that all sensibles are always in flux—is something Plato believed 'also later', 987^{b}1.)

I do not wish to engage in Aristotle-bashing. But as historians of philosophy we must be on our guard when dealing with Aristotle's comments on his predecessors. Despite their philosophical interest, these comments are not, as a rule, historically reliable. For example, Aristotle seems not only inattentive to the Parmenidean influence on Plato, but equally insensitive to what we see as the fundamental importance of Parmenides' argument for the cosmologies of Anaxagoras and Empedocles. (He does recognize Eleatic influence on the atomists, but strangely identifies it not with the attack on coming-to-be but with a denial of the void.)

If to test Aristotle's claim concerning Pythagorean influence on Plato's metaphysics we look to the dialogues for traces of this influence, the best evidence comes from the role of *peras* and *apeiria* in the *Philebus*. For this is an unmistakable echo of the two cosmic principles that we know from the fragments of Philolaus.[2] But of course the *Philebus* is one of Plato's later dialogues, and does not represent the 'classical' theory of Forms. Similarly, Plato's mathematical interpretation of nature in the *Timaeus* is unmistakably Pythagorean in inspiration. But again this belongs to Plato's latest period.

When we look for Pythagorean influence in the works generally assigned to Plato's 'middle period', the evidence is very different. There are certainly traces of Pythagorean ideas in Plato's cosmological myths, in his views on immortality and reincarnation, and in his concern with mathematics.[3] But I can find no evidence whatsoever to support Aristotle's claim for Pythagorean influence on the doctrine of metaphysical Forms as presented in the *Phaedo* and *Republic*. Pythagoras himself is mentioned once, in *Republic* 10 (600b), as founder of an educational community. Otherwise the only explicit reference to Pythagoreans in the entire Platonic corpus is the statement in *Republic* 7 where they describe astronomy and acoustics as 'sister sciences' (530d). This looks like a quotation from Archytas fr. 1, where the same phrase applies to the quadrivium of arithmetic, geometry, astronomy, and music. Plato's Pythagorean friend Archytas was a great mathematician, and we may reasonably believe that he had a considerable influence on Plato's conception of mathematics. But of course not all the mathematics in Plato is derived from Archytas; there is no suggestion that either Theodorus or Theaetetus was a Pythagorean. And there is no evidence that Archytas had a metaphysical theory of the Platonic type.[4] It may have been a personal contact with the

---

[2] *Philebus* 16c–e. Compare DK 44 B 1–2; C. Huffman, *Philolaus of Croton* (Cambridge: Cambridge University Press, 1993), 37–53.

[3] See in particular the evidence for the Pythagorean origin of much of the *Phaedo* myth, assembled by P. Kingsley, *Ancient Philosophy, Mystery and Magic* (Oxford: Clarendon, 1995), chs. 7–9.

[4] On Geoffrey Lloyd's reading, the *Seventh Epistle* suggests that Archytas was not much good at metaphysics ('Plato and Archytas in the *Seventh Letter*', *Phronesis*, 35 (1990), 159–74).

Pythagorean milieu around Archytas in his second and third Sicilian voyages that persuaded Plato to pay more serious attention to the Pythagorean duality of *peras–apeiria*. But, as we have noticed, this concern with 'limit' and 'unlimited' is conspicuous only in Plato's later work. (It appears in the *Parmenides* (158d) as well as in the *Philebus*; and compare 'the unlimited sea of Unlikeness' in the *Statesman* myth, 273d6.) There is no trace of this cosmological principle in Plato's earlier reference to Philolaus in the *Phaedo* (61d), where only the destiny of the soul is under discussion.

It seems clear, then, that Aristotle, who was personally familiar with the Pythagorean preoccupations of Plato's later years, has misleadingly projected this influence back into the earlier period before his own arrival in Athens. Despite Aristotle's testimony, every modern historian knows that the metaphysical background for Plato's theory of Forms is provided not by the Pythagoreans but by Parmenides. Of all Presocratic philosophers it was Parmenides who exerted the deepest influence on Plato's thought.[5] And in the dialogues Parmenides is the one and only interlocutor who is allowed to defeat Socrates in argument. It is as a follower of Parmenides | that the Stranger from Elea is [[83]] given the role of continuing the work that the Platonic Parmenides had begun, in the critical examination of Plato's own theory in the *Sophist*, where Parmenides' doctrine is subjected to similar treatment. It is worthwhile reflecting here on Plato's designation of Parmenides as his peer, or even as his master, capable of administering a lesson in dialectic to Socrates, who is on this occasion seen as a novice in philosophy.

The choice of Parmenides as spokesman for Plato's own radical critique of the Theory of Forms, in the first section of the *Parmenides*, can be seen from many points of view. However, the following consideration seems to me of primary importance. Parmenides is the only philosopher whose criticism of Plato's doctrine would not call into question the fundamental metaphysical conception that underlies this doctrine. For that conception is directly derived from Parmenides'

---

[5] Cf. Guthrie: 'The greatest single influence on Plato after Socrates was Parmenides' (*A History of Greek Philosophy*, iv (Cambridge: Cambridge University Press, 1975), 34). [See J. A. Palmer, *Plato's Reception of Parmenides* (Oxford: Oxford University Press, 1999).]

own theory of Being, as a mode of reality beyond coming-to-be and perishing, free from the phenomenal diversity and variability of the world of human experience. Hence when Parmenides warns Socrates that if he gives up positing the Forms 'he will have nowhere to direct his thought, and he will utterly destroy the power of dialectic' (135b–c), we know that neither Parmenides in the dialogue nor Plato as its author is at all tempted to give up this conception. And so we are not surprised when, a few moments later, Parmenides compliments Socrates for focussing our philosophical attention not on visible things 'but on those things that one can best grasp in rational discourse (*logos*) and consider to be Forms (*eidē*)' (135e). Even in the act of formulating objections to Plato's theory, Parmenides can play the role of the true Platonic philosopher, because he and Plato share the same fundamental conception of metaphysical reality.[6] And that is why, in the same dialogue, when Parmenides' own thesis is put up for critical analysis, it is not his conception of Being that is subjected to scrutiny but only his monism: the thesis that what-is *is one*.[7]

Of course we know that, besides giving up monism, Plato has emended Parmenides' ontology in a number of crucial respects. Between immutable Being and unknowable Not-Being he has admitted the mixed realm of Becoming, which both is and is-not (*R.* 5. 476 ff.). Plato has thus accepted the derivative, inferior reality of the phenomenal realm—the realm that Parmenides' goddess seems to regard solely as a region of error and falsehood. And Plato will end, in the *Sophist*, by denying the coherence of the Parmenidean thesis that what-is-not cannot be anything at all, and that it is therefore unknowable.

There is an important story to be told of Plato as a revisionist Eleatic, the heir and corrector of Parmenidean metaphysics. But that is not my topic here. I want to come to Parmenides by way of his impact on Plato. I will take for granted that we are all familiar with the distinctly Parmenidean features in Plato's account of the immutable Being of the

---

[6] So Parmenides can comfortably say 'as we say' or 'as we assume' in referring to the doctrine of Forms (133b6, 134c1).

[7] Plato's emphasis on Parmenides' monism is somewhat puzzling, since in the poem of the historical Parmenides unity (*hen*) is only one among many attributes of *to eon* (B 8. 2). Perhaps monism became more prominent in Eleatic tradition after Zeno. Or perhaps Plato emphasizes monism as the aspect of the Eleatic teaching that he rejects.

Forms, as presented in the *Symposium*, *Phaedo*, and *Republic*. I would only call attention here to two less conspicuous passages that point to Plato's early interest in Parmenides. We find Parmenides' name mentioned, probably for the first time in the Platonic corpus, in Phaedrus' speech in the *Symposium*, where Phaedrus quotes the verse that we know as B 13: 'first of all the gods she contrived Eros' (178b). And of course the Parmenidean elements in Diotima's revelation later in the same dialogue are well known.[8]

Can we find Parmenides lurking in any dialogue earlier than the *Symposium*? I suggest that we may recognize a discreet echo of Parmenidean dialectic in the mischievous speech in the *Protagoras* where Socrates misinterprets Simonides' poem. In this shockingly sophistical | ⟦84⟧ performance Socrates focusses on the contrast between being and becoming: Pittacus was wrong to say 'Hard it is to be good' (χαλεπὸν ἐσθλὸν ἔμμεναι). Instead he should have said 'It is hard enough for a man to *become* good' (γενέσθαι ἄνδρα ἀγαθόν). 'For a man to become good and remain in this condition is impossible and not human; a god alone can have this privilege' (*Prt.* 344b–c). So in this somewhat forced interpretation Socrates exploits the contrast between permanent, divine Being and mutable human Becoming. If we are right to detect here a playful anticipation of the metaphysical dualism that will be proclaimed by Diotima in the *Symposium*, it may be no accident that the *Protagoras* also presents, in a more dialectical context, the earliest allusion to self-predication (in the assumption that justice is just and piety pious, 330c–d). As many scholars have noticed, the *Protagoras* and the *Symposium* are artistically linked to one another by an overlap of participants: except for Aristophanes, every speaker in the *Symposium* also appears in the *Protagoras*. And if we bear in mind these passages from the *Protagoras* and *Symposium*, we will be less surprised by the sudden appearance of Parmenides himself in the dialogue named after him.

I come now to the interpretation of Parmenides and to the connections between my veridical *esti* and the predicative exegesis that Alex Mourelatos has given, in terms of the sentence frame

— is —.

---

[8] See e.g. my discussion in *Plato and the Socratic Dialogue* (Cambridge: Cambridge University Press, 1996), 343.

As Alexander Nehamas once pointed out to me, the fundamental division between interpretations of Greek ontology—whether in Parmenides, Plato, or Aristotle—depends upon whether one takes existence or predication as the primary basis for understanding *einai*. And it is precisely on this question that Alex and I are in agreement, against those like Owen, Barnes, and Gallop who take *esti* in Parmenides as existential. My veridical reading of *esti* and Alex's predicative function are both aspects of the propositional structure of language and thought.[9] What I call the 'veridical' value of the verb is an isolated focus on the truth claim implicit in any predication. More precisely, the veridical verb may refer either to the intentional content of such a predicative claim—the fact as asserted in judgment or discourse—or to its objective correlate, the actual fact or state of the world that makes the claim true. Conceptually, the former presupposes the latter, as the notion of truth claim presupposes the notion of truth. Hence, both for idiomatic usage and for Parmenides, the primary veridical notion is that of fact or state of affairs, what obtains 'out there', independently of what we say or think, and what makes what we say or think true or false.[10] |

[9] It was only in Alex's response at the Austin conference that I finally understood the essential disagreement between his interpretation and mine. For Alex it is important that the 'is' of Parmenides remain an open predicational form, '— is —' without quantification and without specification for subject and predicate. In my interpretation the focus on truth and reality is essential, and hence the predicational form must be understood as logically 'closed', in a generalized truth claim. Alex had in fact pointed out long ago that in his view Parmenides' *hôs estin* was to be construed not as the assertion of a thesis but as a route of inquiry proposed for consideration. See *Review of Metaphysics*, 22 (1969), 740–1.

[10] For documentation on the veridical see Kahn, *The Verb 'Be' in Ancient Greece* (Dordrecht: Reidel, 1973; repr. Indianapolis, Ind.: Hackett, 2003), 331–54. In earlier discussions I did not make sufficiently clear the logical and linguistic priority of the 'objective' *einai* for the fact as such (for example, ἔστι ταῦτα ὥσπερ σὺ λέγεις, 'these things are as you say'), over its 'intentional' use to characterize the true statement or truth claim (λόγος ἐών, 'a true account'). Some phrases are intermediate between the two: λέγειν τὸ ἐόν, λέγειν τὰ ὄντα, 'give a true account', 'say what is so'. For an important passage which relies upon this subtle ambiguity, see *Tht.* 186c–e with my discussion in Kahn, 'Some Philosophical uses of "To Be" in Plato', *Phronesis*, 26 (1981), 119–26 (repr. as Ch. 4 above).

That veridical *einai* refers primarily to fact rather than to truth claim is clear from the occurrences in past and future tense (Kahn, *The Verb 'Be'*, pp. 345–51). (This point was suggested by a comment Sarah Broadie made at the Austin conference.)

⟦85⟧ It may be misleading, or at least anachronistic, for us to debate the relative merits of the predicative, veridical, and existential interpretations. For one thing, these are notions introduced from modern grammar and logic for the sake of analytical clarity, but they may not accurately map the functions of the Greek verb. And, furthermore, even if we succeed in identifying distinct uses of *einai* in ordinary or poetic Greek, we must recognize that what Parmenides has created in his poem is an entirely new philosophical notion of Being, for the expression of which the diverse functions of *einai* are assembled and integrated into a complex unity.

If in previous publications I emphasized the veridical notion, that was, first of all, because it had been too often overlooked in the interpretation of Parmenides. But there are also good historical and philosophical reasons for preferring 'it is so' or 'it is the case' to 'it exists' as a prima facie, 'first try' reading of the syntactically isolated, unadorned *esti* of fr. 2. Let me briefly remind you of these reasons.

1. Linguistically speaking, the syntactically absolute (or 'complete') use of *esti* and its participle in the sense of truth (as in λέγειν τὸ ἐόν in Herodotus, λέγειν τὰ ὄντα in Thucydides, ἔστι ταῦτα as a response in Plato) is idiomatic and familiar in early Greek (and apparently continues a prehistoric Indo-European idiom), whereas an absolute use of *esti* for 'exists' is practically unattested before the late fifth century (except for the special use with persons as subjects, where *esti* means 'is alive').[11] | ⟦86⟧

2. Philosophically, the justification in B 2 for accepting *esti* and rejecting *ouk esti*, because 'you cannot know what-is-not (*to mê eon*)', makes much better sense if we read it as 'you cannot know (*gnoiês*) what is not the case' than if we read it as 'you cannot know what does not exist'. Knowledge requires as its object truth, or what obtains. As Hintikka once pointed out, the epistemic principle ' "M knows that *p*" entails *p*' might be called Parmenides' law. It is clearly in this sense that Plato understands the inference, as we can see from his echo of this argument in *Republic* 5: the object known must be an *on*, 'for how could something that-is-not (*mê on ti*) be known (*gnôstheiê*)?' (476e7–477a1).

---

[11] The earliest evidence for the use of absolute *esti* with the meaning 'exists' is probably Protagoras B 4: 'Concerning the gods, I cannot know either that they are or that they are not (οὔθ᾽ ὡς εἰσὶν οὔθ᾽ ὡς οὐκ εἰσίν)'.

3. Finally, there is the evidence from the context of the poem: the notion of truth is directly relevant in fr. 2, where the thesis *that it is* (*hopôs esti*) is called 'the path of Persuasion (*Peithous esti keleuthos*), for she accompanies Truth (*Alêtheiêi gar opêdei*)'. The reference here to truth and persuasion or belief (*peithô*) echoes the goddess's promise in B 1 that 'you will learn all things' (*puthesthai*, *mathêseai*), including 'the unshakable heart of persuasive Truth'.[12] As this larger context makes clear, the route of *esti* is the only correct road for thought (*noêsai*) to travel on, precisely because it is the route of inquiry (*zêtêsis*) that leads to knowledge of the truth.

I want to call attention to this strong epistemic context provided by the proem with its emphasis on Truth, and also on persuasion or conviction (*pistis* in B 1. 30) as the appropriate response to a true account. For this context tells against the weaker 'intentional' reading of *eisi noêsai* in B 2. 2, as the only two ways 'that can be thought of'. This Burnet–Owen reading of the argument (which is reinforced by the tendentious translation of τὸ λέγειν τε νοεῖν τ᾽ ἐόν in B 6. 1 as 'what can be spoken and thought') introduces a modal-intentional concern with the thinkable and sayable which may be philosophically attractive to modern ears, but which obscures Parmenides' fundamental preoccupation with knowledge and truth.[13] I submit that Parmenides' urgent pursuit of knowledge in the proem, together with the goddess's promise of a fully reliable revelation, provides decisive evidence in favor of the epistemic reading of B 2. 7 ('for you cannot know what-is-not') and against the merely intentional reading of this verse as 'you cannot conceive what does not exist'.[14]

---

[12] Reading ἀληθείης εὐπειθέος ἦτορ, not εὐκυκλέος in B 1. 29.

[13] For my argument against this modal reading of B 6. 1 χρὴ τὸ λέγειν τε νοεῖν τ᾽ ἐὸν ἔμμεναι as 'it is necessary that what can be spoken and thought of exist' see Kahn, 'Being in Parmenides and Plato', *La Parole del Passato*, 43 (1988), 260–1 (repr. as Ch. 7 above). This is the most problematic verse in the poem, and the modal reading is the *least* plausible of the five or six possible construals. The only natural reading of B 6. 1 is grammatically straightforward and philosophically sound: 'It is necessary that *legein* and *noein* be *eon*' (with ἐόν as predicate and ἔμμεναι as copula). Since there is nothing at all besides *to eon*, if *legein* and *noein* are anything at all, they can only be *eon*.

In any case, as Tugendhat and others have pointed out, it is bad method to base any interpretation on a heavily disputed passage like B 6. 1.

[14] This was the reading proposed by Victor Caston at the Austin conference. Something of this sort is required by the modal-intentional interpretation of the argument made popular by Owen: 'the proof of its existence is that, if it did not exist, it could not be talked or thought about' (Owen, 'Eleatic Questions', *Classical Quarterly*, 10 (1960), 60, citing B2).

I continue to believe, therefore, that the veridical notion is the right place for a reading of Parmenides' argument to begin.[15] But of course it cannot end there. We cannot offer 'it is so' as an adequate interpretation of Parmenides' *esti*. As I have suggested, Parmenides' new conception of Being must be seen as a complex assemblage and unification of a half dozen different functions of the verb *einai* in Greek. These include: | [87]

1. the veridical use of the verb to express the objective fact or reality corresponding to a true statement;

2. the claim of existence for the subject;

3. the copula use, for asserting predicates of the subject;

4. the stative-durative value of 'is' in contrast to the kinetic-mutative value of 'becomes';

5. the locative use with complements of place, which is often connected with an existential nuance (as in our expression 'there is ...'; so in Greek *to be* is *to be somewhere*); and

6. 'is' as asserting identity, which can be regarded as a special case of predication (that is, identity construed as convertible predication, with subject and predicate reversed): thus Parmenides' Being is 'the same, remaining in itself and by itself' (B 8. 29).

The inherent stative-durative value of the verb reinforces Parmenides' claim that Being is unchanging, that it neither was nor will be but 'is all together now' (B 8. 5). The locative function of *esti* as a verb of place or station underlies Parmenides' conception of Being as spatially extended and continuous. The notions of location and identity converge in the conception of Being as symmetrical: 'like the bulk of a well-rounded sphere, equally balanced from the center in every direction' (B 8. 43–4).

From the linguistic point of view, then, Parmenides can be seen as forging his new, metaphysical concept of Being by exploiting and

---

[15] An essentially equivalent view is presented in the recent interpretation of Parmenides by Edward Hussey: '*alêtheiê*, in the sense of "reality", is the intended subject' of *esti*; 'If *alêtheiê* is thought of as a "summed state of affairs," then to say that there actually exists such a thing is just the same as to say that it is the case' ('Pythagoreans and Eleatics', in C. C. W. Taylor (ed.), *Routledge History of Philosophy*, i (London/NY: Routledge, 1997), 134.

fusing together the whole range of uses and meanings for the verb.[16] Hence I would object to an existential reading of *esti* only to the extent that it is presented as self-sufficient, and as excluding the copula construction. In claiming that *einai* is essentially a predicative verb I mean to suggest that *every* philosophical use of *esti*—and not only in Parmenides—is potentially predicative. That is why the notion of existence can be so misleading as a basis for interpretation. In English (and in most modern languages) existence and predication are thought of as mutually exclusive, since an expression like 'it exists' does not admit the copula construction. If we think of an existential use in this sense, as *excluding* a predicative complement, such uses of *einai* are probably not to be found in Greek.

My view of *einai* as always potentially predicative gets strong support from an important study by Lesley Brown.[17] In a critical review of the notion of an 'incomplete use' of the verb introduced by G. E. L. Owen, Brown points out that verbs do not divide into one-place and two-place predicates, as relations do. As she puts it (following Anthony Kenny), verbs can exhibit 'variable polyadicity' (p. 54). Brown argues that it is therefore a mistake to think of a 'complete use' of *einai* as one that excludes a predicative complement. Her model for a complete use is

Jane teaches.

which allows (but does not require) a syntactic complement such as 'Jane teaches French' or 'Jane teaches mathematics'. Similarly, Brown suggests, in Plato's Greek 'X is' always allows a complement 'X is Y', without change of meaning for the verb. And hence (I add) it is misleading to translate a complete or absolute use of *esti* by English 'exists', precisely because the latter excludes the predicative construction which the former allows. (There is an additional discrepancy between *esti* and 'exists', to be specified below.) By contrast, our locution 'there is', which implies or suggests existence, easily admits a complement: 'There is an X (which is) Y'. So in Greek, every

[16] For a fuller statement of this view see Kahn, 'Being in Parmenides and Plato', pp. 249–51 (repr. as Ch. 7 above).
[17] 'Being in the Sophist: A Syntactical Enquiry', *Oxford Studies in Ancient Philosophy*, 4 (1986), 49–70.

absolute or quasi-existential use of *einai* can be thought of as awaiting further specification; that is, as pregnant with the copula construction. Corresponding to this syntactic difference between 'exists' and a 'complete' use of *esti* is a semantic discrepancy that is more difficult to specify. The flavor of this distinction is suggested | by Vlastos's obser- [[88]] vation that existence does not admit of degrees, it is all or nothing;[18] whereas 'being' in Greek allows of more and less, as in Plato's notion of *ontôs on* and in his distinction between *to mê on* and *to mêdamôs on*. The gap between 'exists' and the strong use of *esti* also shows up in Plato's lack of interest in what Brown calls 'the Pegasus point': the possibility of true predications for nonexistent subjects. She suggests that Plato's failure to make this point is due to the fact that 'he cannot distinguish non-existence from not being anything at all'.[19]

I would put it more charitably. In Plato's Greek '*X* is *Y*' entails '*X* is', whereas in English 'Pegasus is a mythic creature' does not entail 'Pegasus exists'. Hence Plato's 'complete' use of *esti* (with no comple-ment supplied or presupposed) is not correctly rendered by 'exists'.[20] For Plato, any subject under discussion is a being: any *ti* is an *on*.[21] We might say that, for better or worse, Plato simply lacks our notion of existence—the notion illustrated in a denial of existence for Pegasus or Santa Claus. Aristotle does show more interest in nonexistent subjects like centaurs and goat-stags, but it is not clear that anything in his distinction between *einai haplôs* and *einai kata ti* corresponds to our notion of existence.[22]

The compatibility and union between existential force and copula construction, which I claim is typical of the Greek verb, can be illustrated by some familiar philosophical examples. The background

---

[18] 'Degrees of Reality in Plato', in R. Bambrough (ed.), *New Essays on Plato and Aristotle* (London: Routledge & Kegan Paul, 1965), repr. in *Platonic Studies* (Princeton, NJ: Princeton University Press, 1973), 65.

[19] 'Being in the Sophist', 61 n. 16.

[20] See also J. Malcolm, 'Plato's Analysis of *to on* and *to mê on*', *Phronesis*, 12 (1967), 130–46.

[21] *Sophist* 237c–d; *Parmenides* 132b7–c1. A. A. Long and D. N. Sedley suggest that the Stoic distinction between *ti* (something) and *on* (being) makes the latter equivalent to 'exists' (*The Hellenistic Philosophers* (Cambridge: Cambridge University Press, 1987), i. 163–4). I believe there will still be a difference, but the Stoic distinction is clearly incompatible with Plato's usage.

[22] See Lesley Brown's discussion of the Aristotle passages in 'The Verb "To Be" in Greek Philosophy: Some Remarks', in Steven Everson (ed.), *Companions to Ancient Thought*, iii (Cambridge: Cambridge University Press, 1994), 233–6.

is provided by Homer's reference to the gods as *theoi aien eontes*, 'the gods who are (or live) forever'. (I would count this as a quasi-existential use of the verb.) It is this Homeric formula that Heraclitus is echoing when he speaks in B 30 of the *kosmos* which 'always was and is and will be—everliving fire': *ên aei kai estin kai estai pur aeizôon*. Here the three occurrences of the verb (*ên kai estin kai estai*) must be construed twice, first as complete or quasi-existential with *aei* (the *kosmos* is forever, like the gods), and then as copula with *pur aeizôon*. The grammar of the verb is the same in the *Symposium*, when Plato's Diotima introduces the Beautiful itself. The description begins with the Homeric formula for a being 'which is forever (*aei on*), neither coming-to-be nor perishing... not beautiful in one respect, ugly in another... not being somewhere (*pou on*)... but itself by itself being forever uniform (*monoeides aei on*)' (211a–b).[23] Here the existential, locative, and ordinary copula uses of the verb practically coincide.

Plato is of course following not Heraclitus but Parmenides, in the grammar of *einai* as in the metaphysics of Being. Thus in Parmenides B 8, which introduces the signposts marking the way *that it is*, the verb occurs four times in the first three lines.

μόνος δ' ἔτι μῦθος ὁδοῖο
λείπεται ὡς ἔστιν· ταύτηι δ' ἐπὶ σήματ' ἔασι
πολλὰ μάλ', ὡς ἀγένητον ἐὸν καὶ ἀνώλεθρόν ἐστιν.

In these verses a modern commentator may classify the first occurrence as existential or veridical (ὡς ἔστιν), the second as locative-existential (ταύτηι δ' ἐπὶ σήματ' ἔασι), the third and fourth as copulative (ἀγένητον ἐὸν καὶ ἀνώλεθρόν ἐστιν). But an ancient reader would probably recognize only more or less emphatic uses of a single verb with a single (unanalyzed) meaning. |

[[89]]   The same failure to respect the distinctions that modern grammar and logic would impose on uses of *einai* is also characteristic of the passage in which Plato introduces his most systematic discussion of the problems of Being and Not-Being. In *Sophist* 237c–238c *to mê on* and *ta onta* are at first presented in what seem to be complete or 'existential'

---

[23] ἀεὶ ὂν καὶ οὔτε γιγνόμενον οὔτε ἀπολλύμενον... οὐ τῆι μὲν καλόν, τῆι δ' αἰσχρόν... οὐδέ που ὂν ἐν ἑτέρωι τινι, οἷον ἐν ζώωι ἢ ἐν οὐρανῶι ἢ ἔν τωι ἄλλωι, ἀλλ' αὐτὸ καθ' αὑτὸ μεθ' αὑτοῦ μονοειδὲς ἀεὶ ὄν (*Smp.* 211a1–b2).

uses. It is in this syntactically complete form that the Parmenidean principle is enunciated, that *to mê on*, 'what-is-not', cannot be applied to or combined with *to on*, 'what-is' (237c). Apparent violations of this rule are then introduced where the construction of the verb is first unmistakably copulative ('it *is* unthinkable and unsayable' at 238c10, 238e6) and, second, veridical (at 241a1, a false statement is described as 'saying *mê einai* of *ta onta* and saying *einai* of *ta mê onta*'). In order to avoid incoherence and contradiction, the Eleatic Stranger insists that they must refute Parmenides and force the conclusion 'that Not-Being *is* in some respect (*hôs esti kata tî*) and that Being in turn in some way *is not* (*hôs ouk esti pêi*)' (241d6). No doubt the long discussion that follows will illustrate or imply some important distinctions, and these may or may not correspond to distinctions we want to draw between different uses of *einai*. But the problem—as Plato defines it—is not to distinguish uses of *einai*, but to make clear how one can correctly combine the negative and positive constructions of the verb so as to give a coherent account of true and false statement. It is not at all obvious that Plato found it either necessary or desirable to make our distinctions between existence and predication, between predication and identity, or between any of these and the veridical use of *einai* for being-so or being-the-case. (Aristotle does, of course, make some of the relevant distinctions. His scheme of categories analyzes various predicative functions of *einai*, and in *Metaph. Δ.* 7 he distinguishes this from the veridical use. But Aristotle nowhere recognizes an existential use as such. Does he ever distinguish an *is* of identity?)

I want to defend Parmenides' positive account of Being as a coherent, unified vision.[24] And I think his refutation of coming-to-be is [90] formally impeccable, once one accepts the | premise (which Plato will

<hr>

[24] At the Austin conference Victor Caston objected that the veridical (even when construed objectively, as fact rather than truth claim) was incompatible with the other uses of *einai*, since its subject must be something with propositional structure, whereas the other uses normally take individual entities or things as subject. This parallels David Gallop's objection: a fact or state of affairs 'seems to be of the wrong logical type to serve as the bearer of such attributes as "ungenerable," "imperishable," "whole," and "immovable" . . . What the goddess seems to be talking about is not a fact or state of affairs but a thing with certain attributes' ('"Is" or "Is Not"?', *Monist*, 62 (1979), 66).

I think the best answer is to refer to Wolfgang Mann's recent book, *The Discovery of Things* (Princeton, NJ: Princeton University Press, 2000), which shows how great an innovation it was for Aristotle to introduce the 'common sense' ontology of things with attributes. And

deny) that *esti* and *ouk esti* are mutually exclusive, like *p* and not-*p*. And it is precisely this assimilation of the '*is* or *is not*' dichotomy to a law of logic—to '*p* or *not-p*'—that accounts for the extraordinary effectiveness of Parmenides' argument, its acceptance by the fifth-century cosmologists, and the difficulty that Plato encountered in answering it. However, if the rich, positive account of Being that results from Parmenides' amalgamation of the entire range of uses and meanings of *einai* turns out to be a long-term success (as the fruitful ancestor of ancient atomism, Platonic Forms, and the metaphysics of eternal Being in western theology), the corresponding negation in Not-Being is a conceptual nightmare. Depending on which function of *einai* is being denied, *to mê on* can represent either negative predication, falsehood, nonidentity, nonexistence, or nonentity—that is to say, nothing at all. The fallacy in Parmenides' argument lies not in the cumulation of positive attributes for Being but in the confused union of these various modes of negation in the single conception of 'what-is-not'. That is why Plato saw fit to criticize his great predecessor with respect to the notion of Not-Being, while making positive use of the Parmenidean notion of Being.

even Aristotle, who does in principle distinguish predicative from veridical uses, does not always respect that distinction in technical contexts (notably in the discussion of *ei estin* questions in *APo.* II). In general, Greek philosophers are not sensitive to the distinction between propositional and nonpropositional subjects of *einai*.

Postscript on Parmenides

Parmenides was my first love in philosophy. I had once thought to write a book on Parmenides, but there always seemed to be too many unsolved problems. I conclude these essays by returning to three problems that do seem soluble, and that do not involve the concept of Being: Parmenides' relation to natural philosophy, the direction of the chariot ride in his proem, and the epistemic preference for Fire.

1. Parmenides and physics

Parmenides belongs, with Heraclitus, to the second wave of Greek philosophers, those whose work (at the end of the sixth or beginning of the fifth century) can take for granted the existence of a new naturalistic cosmology. The investigation of nature (*peri phuseôs historia*) that had begun in Miletus was then spreading throughout the Greek world. Heraclitus and Parmenides have in common some version of the new natural philosophy, by reference to which they can define their own philosophical views. But neither Heraclitus nor Parmenides is primarily a practitioner of this new enterprise of explaining the world in quasi-scientific terms. Both can best be seen as spectators and commentators on the new worldview. Heraclitus has thought about physics, but also about life and death. He has investigated the nature of things, but he has also investigated himself. Thus he has integrated the new conception of nature into a much larger view of the meaning of life and death, the human and the divine.

Parmenides' relationship to the new natural philosophy is more complex. On the one hand, he introduces a view of Being that stands

outside of the cosmological tradition; but in the second part of
the poem he presents a detailed cosmology of the Milesian type.
Parmenides' cosmology is not strictly Ionian; it has certain distinctive
features (such as transmigration) that mark it as belonging to the
western or Pythagorean branch of the tradition. But Parmenides'
metaphysical innovation is designed to undermine both the western
and Ionian versions of cosmology: the whole enterprise has now been
demoted to the rank of untrustworthy 'opinions of mortals'.

It is Parmenides' account of Being, in part 1 of the poem, that
serves as point of departure for the metaphysics of Plato and
Aristotle. But initially, in the fifth century, it is Parmenides' physical
theory, the doctrine of elements outlined in part 2 of the poem, that
provides the pattern for Anaxagoras, Empedocles, and the atomists. It
is Parmenides who introduces the new concept of element, as a basis
for explaining the world of change by the mixing and unmixing
of fundamental constituents, themselves immune to change. The
argument against coming-to-be and perishing in part 1 has as its
response the development of an element theory in part 2: a theory of
what survives change. Parmenides' metaphysics thus provides the basis
for his physics.

Parmenides presents this theory of two elements, Fire and Night, in
the context of a detailed cosmology. Because of our almost total
ignorance of the western tradition before Parmenides, it is impossible
for us to evaluate the degree of originality in Parmenides' own cosmology. I assume that the old Cornford–Raven attempt to reconstruct
an earlier Pythagorean view from Parmenides' text (a view that
Parmenides would be reacting against) no longer has any supporters.
The method of reconstruction was circular; and the illusion of an early
Pythagorean doctrine, constructed by inference from Parmenides'
text, has been effectively destroyed by the critical work of Walter
Burkert. We must simply accept the fact that Parmenides' cosmology
is the earliest known example of the Italian tradition.

We can only guess how much of his own life Parmenides had
devoted to the study of nature, how much of his cosmology he has
taken over from his unknown predecessors. A striking fact is that his
poem is the first Greek text to report two important scientific discoveries. One is to identify the Morning Star with the Evening Star;

in other words, to recognize the planet Venus (Diels-Kranz A 1. 23; A 40a.). This identity had been known in Babylon for many centuries, but it is unknown to Hesiod, and it is not mentioned in any Greek text before Parmenides. Parmenides' other innovation is more momentous: he realizes that the moon's light is dependent on light from the sun (B 14–15). This is practically equivalent to recognizing that lunar eclipse is due to the shadow of the earth—a discovery usually attributed to Anaxagoras. Was Parmenides himself practicing observational astronomy? Is he personally responsible for either of these two scientific breakthroughs? We simply do not know. But we may reasonably conclude that if Parmenides himself was not doing original work in astronomy, he was at least acquainted with the best knowledge of his time. To that extent, part 2 of his poem represents a genuine contribution to early Greek natural philosophy or protoscience. Nietzsche once suggested that Parmenides in his early years was a student of astronomy and physics and had worked out his own cosmology, before undergoing something like a metaphysical conversion to the higher knowledge of Being (*Philosophy in the Tragic Age of the Greeks*, sec. 9). This is an attractive story, since it accounts for the full development of a physical theory in the second part of the poem.

Nevertheless, Parmenides denies the attribute of truth to this elaborate cosmology. He continues to pursue natural philosophy, but only as the way of *doxa*, defined by contrast with the way of Truth which is the way of Being. This Truth-versus-Doxa dichotomy provides Parmenides with an epistemic framework within which the Ionian cosmology can be reinterpreted. Seen within this framework, what we call science or protoscience is no more than deceptive appearance, 'the opinions of mortals, in which there is no true trust' (B 1. 31). Parmenides' cosmology is intended to be the best of its kind, 'so that no view of mortals will ever surpass' it (B 8. 61), a claim twice echoed by Plato in the *Timaeus* (29c7, 48d3). But despite its powerful structure as the first element theory and despite its rich empirical detail, this cosmology is offered only as unreliable 'opinions of mortals', presented in a 'deceptive ordering (*kosmos*) of verses' (frag. 8. 52), with a punning reference to the deceptive notion of a physical *kosmos*. Nevertheless, the inclusion in the poem of such a full-scale exercise in *peri physeôs historia* establishes Parmenides' unmistakable continuity with the

Ionian tradition. His radically new view is designed not to replace but to reevaluate the naturalist enterprise by subordinating it to his more profound vision of Truth and Reality (alêtheia, 1. 29). At the same time, by giving to physics an explanatory foundation in permanent elements, Parmenides transforms the Ionian study of nature into something approaching the form of a modern scientific theory, the model for later reductive theories such as atomism. Once again, Parmenides' gift to physics is a direct result of his metaphysics.

It remains to be seen if Parmenides, or anyone else, could give a coherent account of the nature of the physical world according to the radical dualism of his dichotomy between Truth and Opinion. If the physical opposition of Fire and Night is the result of a mistake made by mortals, who are thus responsible for producing the world of *doxa,* why or how could mortals exist in the first place? The ontological status of the world of appearance must remain problematic, unless it is supported by a derivation from Being. That is why Plato chose to revise Parmenides' doctrine by recognizing an intermediate realm of Becoming, which participates in Being and hence both is and is not.

2. The direction of the chariot ride in the proem

Until recently the cognitive preference for light over night in the cosmology has led most commentators to assume that the emphatic phrase ἐς φάος in line 10 of the proem was intended to present the allegorical voyage of the *kouros* as a voyage from darkness into light. Furthermore, this view of a pervasive light–night symbolism seemed confirmed by the fact that the *kouros* is escorted by Sun Maidens who have just left behind them the halls of Night (l. 9). But this long-standing interpretation of the proem was challenged by J. S. Morrison in a 1955 article[1] claiming that Parmenides' voyage was better understood as a *katabasis*, an initiation into the mysteries of the underworld.

---

[1] 'Parmenides and Er', *Journal of Hellenic Studies*, 75 (1955), 59–68.

Since then articles by Walter Burkert[2] and David Furley[3] have supported Morrison's suggestion, and established a new trend against the reading of the proem as a voyage from darkness to light. (Burkert argues that the direction of the chariot ride is neither up nor down but horizontal: 'the Beyond lies neither above nor below but simply very, very far away', p. 15.) A recent discussion of this question by Mitchell Miller[4] argues for a deliberate ambiguity. Against the view of Alexander Mourelatos and others that Parmenides leaves the topography of the journey 'blurred beyond recognition', Miller finds 'a clear, and clearly contradictory, double sense' for the direction of the chariot ride (p. 23 n. 39). Parmenides, he thinks, wants to have it both ways.

There is some basis for Miller's claim of ambiguity. If Parmenides had wanted to make the path of the chariot ride unmistakably clear, there would be no room for disagreement on this matter between good scholars. In fact Parmenides has created his own mythical landscape, with mixed topography, and some features are suggestive of the underworld. But as an indication of *direction*, the notion of a *katabasis* cannot be correct. I will endeavor to show that this interpretation misconstrues both the imagery and the symbolism of the proem.

There are a dozen references to motion in the proem but only one specification of where all this movement is going. That is the phrase ἐς φάος, 'to the light' in verse 10. There is no counterbalancing indication of a movement downwards or into darkness. It is true that, in its immediate context, the phrase ἐς φάος refers directly to the movement of the Heliades leaving the halls of Night (as Morrison and others have insisted). But the function of the daughters of the Sun, and their motive in leaving the house of Night, is to lead the *kouros* somewhere. Where are they leading him? There is no other direction indicated, either for the Heliades or for the chariot or for the horses that draw it. In the first five verses of the proem the verb φέρειν occurs 4 times, the

---

[2] 'Das Proömium des Parmenides und die Katabasis des Pythagoras', *Phronesis*, 14 (1969), 1–30.

[3] 'Notes on Parmenides', in E. N. Lee et al. (eds.), *Exegesis and Argument* (Assen: Van Gorcum, 1973), 1–15.

[4] 'Ambiguity and Transport: Reflections on the Proem to Parmenides' Poem', *Oxford Studies in Ancient Philosophy*, 30 (2006), 1–47.

verbs ἱκάνειν, πέμπειν, ἄγειν, and ἡγεμονεύειν each once. That makes
8 verbs of motion in 5 verses. An alert reader must ask: Where is all this
motion going? Where does the 'way of the goddess' lead? A hint
comes with the participle αἰθόμενος for the axle blazing in the wheel
(v. 7), to be echoed a few lines later by αἰθέριαι for the gates themselves
(v. 13). A second, stronger hint is given by the identity of the Heliades
(in verse 9), the daughters of the Sun who will know how to guide the
chariot on the sun's path. The significant parallel to Phaethon was
pointed out long ago by Bowra; according to that story, the Heliades
helped Phaethon set off on his ill-fated journey with the chariot of the
Sun.[5] The parallel would suggest that Parmenides' *kouros* is also traveling through the sky, on a path like that of the sun. And the one and
only definite answer to the question 'Where is all this going?' comes in
the words ἐς φάος in the emphatic initial position at the beginning of
verse 10. This specifies, first of all, the movement of the Heliades out
of the halls of Night. But where are the Heliades going? If they
immediately drop their veils, that is presumably a signal that they are
now at home, having left their overnight visit in the halls of Night.[6]
Their home is of course the realm of the sun, the realm of light. And it
is precisely there (ἔνθα, v. 11) that the gates are to be found, the gates
that are αἰθέριαι—aloft, in the sky. There is no hint so far of any
movement except upwards, into the sky (αἰθήρ) and into the light. If,
narrowly construed, the phrase ἐς φάος modifies only the movement
of the Heliades out of the halls of Night, in rhetorical terms, coming as
it does in the strong initial position of verse 10, this phrase specifies all
the movement of the first 10 lines. That is why, until recently, all
commentators have understood Parmenides' journey as a voyage into
the light.

Why then do some readers now look for a *katabasis*, a voyage down
into the underworld? There is no basis for this, as far as I can see, in the
first ten verses of the proem. (The halls of Night have been mentioned

---

[5] C. M. Bowra, 'The Proem of Parmenides', in *Problems in Greek Poetry* (Oxford:
Clarendon, 1953), 38–53 (1st pub. in *Classical Philology*, 32 (1937), 97–112). This is still the
best discussion of the proem.

[6] So rightly A. H. Coxon: 'The Heliades "push back their mantillas from their heads" and
increase their speed because they have reached the light which is their natural habitation'
(*The Fragments of Parmenides* (Dover, NH: Van Gorcum, 1986), 161).

in verse 9, but only as a place that the Heliades have left behind.) It is only in verse 11 that supporters of the *katabasis* reading can begin to find references to the underworld, first in the Hesiodic associations of the introductory ἔνθα in verse 11, together with the designation of the gates through which the *kouros* must pass as 'the gates of the paths of Day and Night'. Thus Morrison claims: 'The mention of the house of Night, and of "the gates of the paths of Day and Night" with their threshold, enables us to identify the place as the familiar region of poetic tradition about the underworld'.[7] But this is special pleading. The house of Night is mentioned here only as left behind.[8] The emphatic ἔνθα, 'There!', introducing the gates at the beginning of verse 11 is to be located not by its occurrence in the *Theogony* but by its context in Parmenides' proem. Furthermore, according to *Odyssey* 10. 86, the 'paths of Day and Night' are not found in the underworld but simply very far away, in the land of the Laistrygonians. The gates themselves are here said to be αἰθέριαι, 'celestial' or in the sky (αἰθήρ). Nothing in the proem points to a subterranean location. Some of Parmenides' mysterious language is reminiscent of Hesiod's account of the underworld, but with a difference. Thus Hesiod's underworld threshold is made of bronze, Parmenides' threshold is of stone (λάινος οὐδός, v. 12). Dikê as gatekeeper is not to be found in Hesiod's underworld; on the contrary, Hesiod in the *Erga* has Dikê seated next to Zeus in Olympus. Clearly Parmenides is creating his own mythical landscape for his own mythical chariot ride, using as raw material whatever in the poetic tradition suits his purpose. But that Parmenides' chariot is not traveling underground or into any cave but aloft, through the sky, is first suggested by the parallel to Phaethon with the company of the Heliades, and then guaranteed by the description of the gates through which he must pass as αἰθέριαι (v. 13).[9]

---

[7] J. S. Morrish, 'Parmenides and Er', *Journal of Historical Studies*, 75 (1955), 59.

[8] The text does not support Furley's suggestion that the Sun Maidens 'come to meet Parmenides and take him back home with them—back into the House of Night' (*Exegesis and Argument*, p. 2). I can find no evidence for this return trip. On the contrary, if the Heliades were heading right back into the House of Night, why would they remove their veils on leaving it?

[9] Miller and others have seen Hesiodic associations in the χάσμα that appears when the gates fly open in v. 18, recalling the deep pit of Tartarus in *Theogony* 740. But 'chasms' are not necessarily in the underworld. Morrison himself draws the parallel with the double set of

The mythology of the proem comes to an end when the goddess greets the *kouros* and assures him that his celestial chariot ride is approved by Themis and Dikê—he was not, like Phaethon, sent on his way by a μοῖρα κακή (1. 26)! What follows the meeting is no longer myth but a revelation of Truth. Of course the mythical language of the epic persists throughout the poem, borne by the hexameter form. But the *kouros* and his chariot have no role to play after the proem.

From the literary point of view, the proem focusses on two points: the driving effort and passion of the journey, and the formidable solidity of the gates that must be opened and entered. It is natural to see these two points as allegory for the intellectual passion (θυμός) of Parmenides' inquiry into truth, and for the difficulty of his intellectual breakthrough into the conception of Being as presented in the body of the poem. Should we (with many commentators) see in the journey of the *kouros* a reflection of some personal occasion of enlightenment on Parmenides' part, a genuine experience of being transported into a higher cognitive realm? Of course the text itself cannot guarantee what lies behind it in the author's own life. Still, the radical nature of his claims, in both ontology and epistemology, and the acute sense of distance from the views of ordinary mortals strongly suggest that Parmenides himself had had the powerful experience of a revolutionary insight, which he has chosen to present to us in this imaginative form.

As far as I can see, there is no real parallel to this proem in the literature of archaic Greece. The notion of poetry as divine revelation is of course common from Homer on, and Hesiod has described his own meeting with the Muses on Helicon. But Hesiod's description is given as a naturalistic report, not as a mystic chariot ride. Empedocles claims to be divine, but he does not report supernatural experiences. The chariot of song is familiar as a poetic device, but not as a personal narrative. There may well have been closer parallels in the lost revelation literature of the sixth or early fifth century. But my guess is that Parmenides was as daring and unprecedented in his construction of the proem as he was in the doctrine of the poem itself.

χάσματα in the myth of Er, one pair going into the heavens, one pair into the earth (*Rep.* 10. 614c–d). And the paradoxical phrase χάσμ' ἀχανές may have the effect of neutralizing any Hesiodic associations.

Without the natural poetic gift of Xenophanes or Empedocles, Parmenides has nevertheless chosen to use the medium of epic poetry rather than the new prose of Ionian philosophy, presumably because he has something to say of more general importance than could be expressed in a purely technical treatise. Furthermore, he has enhanced the traditional authority of the epic genre by this elaborate narrative of a special revelation. Whether or not the proem reflects a definite personal experience, it certainly articulates a claim to special knowledge. At the same time, the mystical or magical character of the opening narrative is designed to prepare the way for an entirely rational message. It is in this sense that the proem is allegorical. The physical details are worked out with great care, but we are not asked to believe that Parmenides (or anyone else) was physically transported in a chariot escorted by the daughters of the Sun.

It is because the proem is so carefully crafted that it seems important to get an accurate view of the direction of Parmenides' journey. The recent interpretation of his trip as a *katabasis* fails to do justice to the unified light imagery of the poem as a whole, and also to the essential rationality of its message. It is not the shadowy region of the underworld and the darkness of νὺξ ἀδαής, 'unknowing Night', but the bright light of the αἰθήρ, the sunlit sky, that symbolizes Parmenides' passion for the Truth and the goal of his chariot ride. (Why would he need a chariot to go underground?) That is why his guides are daughters of the Sun, his axle is blazing (αἰθόμενος), the gates are celestial (αἰθέριαι), and he is being led towards the light (ἐς φάος). It is probably no accident that the poem describes the traveler as an εἰδὼς φώς, a 'knowing mortal' (verse 3); that is, as a person qualified for revelation, with a play on the meaning of φάος as light. (The pun is paralleled in fragment 14, where the Homeric verse-ending ἀλλότριον φῶς for an alien mortal alludes to the borrowed light of the moon.) Thus the light imagery of the proem is, from the beginning, associated with the positive notion of knowledge, just as the negative figure of night is later associated with silence and ignorance. All of this is turned upside down if we construe Parmenides' chariot ride as a *katabasis*.

This conclusion will be confirmed in the following discussion of a notorious crux in a later fragment.

3. The epistemic preference for Fire

μορφὰς γὰρ κατέθεντο δύο γνώμας ὀνομάζειν
τῶν μίαν οὐ χρεών ἐστιν, ἐν ὧι πεπλανημένοι εἰσίν

B. 8. 53–4

Mortals have made up their mind to name two forms, one of which it is not right (to name), in which they have gone astray.

Much ingenuity has been expended in the attempt to make τῶν μίαν here mean something other than what it says; namely, that mortals were wrong to name *one of these two forms*. The statement is of course paradoxical, since the two forms of Fire (or Light) and Night are defined as opposites and apparently as logically dependent on one another. It would seem that either both forms are right or both are wrong. This poses a serious problem of interpretation. But the rule of good method for a difficult text is the same here as for fragments 3 and 6. 1 (discussed above, pp. 163, 189–91): first let the text say what it does seem to say, and then try to make sense of it. Once one begins to play with alternative construals of the syntax (as commentators have tended to do with these difficult passages), the enterprise of interpretation is in danger of becoming arbitrary. Instead of extracting a meaning from the text, we impose one upon it.

Given what the verse says, we must ask what reason Parmenides could have had for identifying mortal error with *one* of the forms rather than with both. There is a clue in the properties attributed to the two forms in the following verses: 'to one form they assigned a blazing fire of flame, being mild, immensely light, the same with itself in every way, but not the same as the other; but the other in itself opposed, unknowing night, a dense and heavy body' (trans. after Coxon). The negative associations of night are emphasized here by identifying night with ignorance (ἀδαής); light, on the other hand, is favored as a gentle *being* (ἤπιον ὄν, 8. 57) and characterized by one of the properties of Being itself ('the same with itself in every way', echoing the symmetry of *what-is* in 8. 42–9). Furthermore, one of the epithets of fire repeats the term αἰθέριον that appeared twice in the proem. We have seen the importance of this epithet.

Following these hints, we can recognize Night as the form it was not right to name. The epithet ἀδαής applied here to Night reflects the ignorance of mortals in introducing this form. That does not mean that the other form, Light or Fire, is identical with true Being. The introduction of Night transforms Being into the less pure form of Fire. (Although Fire is the positive representative of Being, it is not true Being once it is relativized by opposition to Night, and thus becomes an object of the senses rather than of *nous*.) But the two verses quoted do imply that the positive form points in the right direction. In the second part of the poem we are of course within the deceptive cosmology of mortal error. But we can say that, within this cosmology, Light reflects the principle of truth and knowledge. Thus Light serves as both the symbolical and the physical representative of Being *within* the world of mortal opinion and perception. (So correctly Aristotle *Met.* 987ª1: 'Parmenides ranks the hot with Being, the other principle with Not-Being'.) Theophrastus reports that this asymmetry between the two forms was developed systematically in a lost passage on cognition: 'thought becomes better and purer because of the hot.... He says the corpse does not perceive light and heat and sound because of the loss of fire, but it perceives cold and silence and the opposites' (A 46 in Diels-Kranz). And the surviving fragment on cognition (B 16) confirms, for the world of physics and sensation, the identity between thought and its object expressed in fragments 3 and 8. 34: 'Thus mind (νόος) for humans is the same as what it thinks (φρονέει), the nature of human limbs'. As the corpse thinks only darkness, so the εἰδὼς φῶς, the knowing mortal, will think mostly light.[10]

---

[10] See Vlastos's paper, 'Parmenides' Theory of Knowledge', *TAPA*, 77 (1946), 66–77 (repr. in his *Studies in Greek Philosophy*, vol. 1) for a full discussion of the epistemological implications of the light symbolism.

9

Questions and Categories

*Aristotle's doctrine of categories in the
light of modern research*

The topic 'questions and categories' is suggested by the fact that, in the
original list of categories given by Aristotle, the names of six out of ten
categories are interrogative in form: *What is it?* (τί ἐστι), *How much?*
(ποσόν), *Of what sort?* (ποιόν, qualis), *Towards what?* or *Relative to what?*
(πρός τι), *Where?* (ποῦ) and *When?* (ποτέ).[1] And in the case of the four
categories whose names are not interrogative in form, it is easy to
represent them as answers to questions: *What did he do?* for action
(ποιεῖν); *What did he suffer?* for passion or being-acted-upon (πάσχειν);
What is he wearing? or *How is he disposed?* for the category of having or
habitus (ἔχειν); and *What is his position?* or *How is he situated?* for posture
or situs (κεῖσθαι). Hence it is an old observation, made by William of
Ockham and probably not for the first time, that Aristotle's classification of the categories is derived from a list of interrogative forms or
questions asked in reference to a given subject—in reference to a man,
for example, or some other individual substance. As Ockham says,
every uncombined term (i.e. every uncombined word or concept) 'by

H. Hiż (ed.), *Questions*, 227–8. All Rights Reserved.
Copyright © 1978 by D. Reidel Publishing Company, Dordrecht, Holland.

[1] Strictly speaking five of the category names are the indefinite forms which differ from
the interrogative only in intonation, as reflected in the post-Aristotelian written accents: πού,
'somewhere' instead of ποῦ, 'where?', etc. (The name of the first category, when given in this
form rather than as οὐσία, 'substance', is always interrogative: τί ἐστί, 'what is it?' even when
abbreviated as τὸ τί 'what?'.) Literally, then, the five names in question are 'so much' or 'of
some quantity', 'of some sort', 'relative to something', 'somewhere', and 'at some time (or
other)'. The logical relation between the interrogative and indefinite forms is precisely that
between 'where?' and 'somewhere' in English. The latter is a kind of variable or place-holder
for a whole range of possible or appropriate answers to the question 'where?', 'when?', etc.

which one can answer a question posed concerning a substance is in some category. . . . But other uncombined terms are not in any category'.[2] The categories of Aristotle do not represent a complete logical inventory, a classification of all terms or concepts represented in language. They do attempt to classify all the terms of a basic object language, where these terms are specified by the questions that can be asked or answered concerning an individual subject. Hence the number of categories will be determined by the number of fundamentally distinct questions that can be raised concerning such a subject. As has often been pointed out, the full list of ten given in the *Categories* and in *Topics* 1.9 suggests that Aristotle must have taken a human being as his specimen subject, for only in this case would the two minor categories, Posture and Having (or Clothing) be natural topics of inquiry.[3]   [[4]]

There is, then, a factual connection between Aristotle's list of categories and the linguistic forms of question or inquiry. But what is the philosophical significance of this connection? Reflection on this matter may proceed along two quite distinct lines of thought, each of which could provide material for a study devoted to questions and categories. On the one hand, we might consider Aristotle's doctrine simply as an early example of the genre, and widen the concept of category to include modern theories of logical, conceptual, and grammatical categories. Our topic would then become: the connection between interrogative forms and categorial distinctions in general. On the other hand, we may keep our attention fixed on Aristotle's doctrine but generalize the remark about interrogative forms to

---

[2] William Ockham, *Summae Logicae Pars Prima*, ed. P. Boehner (St Bonaventure, NY: Franciscan Institute Publishing, 1951), p. 108. Ockham implies that this observation was suggested by Averroes: 'Sumitur autem distinctio istorum praedicamentorum, sicut innuit Commentator 7° Metaphysicae, ex distinctione interrogativorum de substantia sive de individuo substantiae' (ibid. p. 107).

[3] See Gillespie (1925: 80 ff.) and the quotations from Gomperz and Grote cited by H. P. Cooke (1938) in his introduction to the Loeb edition of the *Categories*. So also J. L. Ackrill (1963: 79): 'The actual examples strongly suggest that he [sc. Aristotle] thinks about answers to questions about a *man.*'

In *Post. An.* 2.1 Aristotle lists four quite different questions or subjects of inquiry (τὰ ζητούμενα) that classify four types of knowledge: (1) *Is p the case or not?* (2) *Why is p so?* (3) *Does x exist?* or *Is there an x?* and (4) *What is x?* Except for the last (τί ἐστι) these questions have no relation to the categorial scheme, and hence their role in Aristotle's theory of science will not be discussed here.

include other grammatical or linguistic considerations. Our topic will then be: the significance of the connections between Aristotle's scheme of categories and certain facts of grammar, including the grammar of questions in Greek. It is this second topic that I propose to study here: I will discuss Aristotle's theory, not category theories in general. But we must first look briefly at the more general topic, not only because of its intrinsic interest but also in order to detect the unconscious and almost inevitable influence which more recent doctrines of categories tend to exert upon our understanding of Aristotle.

Modern theories of categories are all formulated in the shadow of Kant. Kant was the first to break with the Aristotelian tradition in this matter and to introduce a fundamentally new theory of categories as 'pure concepts of the understanding', as functions of judgment which provide the a priori and necessary conditions for any rational experience of the world. A 'conceptual' view of categories, with their a priori, necessary status relativized to 'our conceptual scheme', is still influential, particularly in Oxford. But most contemporary theories of logical and grammatical categories owe less to Kant than to Husserl, and to the doctrine of *Bedeutungskategorien* or semantic categories development in the second volume of *Logische Untersuchungen* (originally published in 1901; second edition in 1913). In a study entitled 'The distinction of independent and dependent meanings (*Bedeutungen*) and the idea of pure grammar', Husserl proposed the notion of a 'purely logical grammar' (*reinlogische Grammatik*) in which the theory of semantic categories occupies a central place. According to Husserl, these formal categories of meaning, together with the laws of their combination, constitute the a priori foundations for logic and language in general. In his insistence upon attaching a priori and apodictic certainty to our recognition of these laws, Husserl remains faithful to Kant. But by explicitly recasting the categories in terms of grammar and linguistic meaning, he opens up the road to the future. (Kant himself had pointed to a connection between the study of categories as a priori concepts and the investigation of rules of grammar, but he had done nothing to explore this connection. See his remark in the second paragraph of the Appendix 'Of the System of the Categories', *Prolegomena to any Future Metaphysics*, § 39.

The basic contrast which Husserl lays down as a criterion for the discovery and definition of categories is the distinction between the *meaningful* and the *meaningless*. Husserl is of course not the only thinker to introduce this distinction into the philosophical bloodstream of the twentieth century: one need only mention Russell's theory of types, which was first published in 1903. But Husserl's action is decisive in founding the doctrine of categories upon the criterion of meaningfulness. In his view, the laws of pure grammar will determine which combinations of meaning-units or of their corresponding linguistic expressions will form a meaningful whole (*Sinneseinheit*) rather than a meaningless jumble (*Unsinn, das Sinnlos*). Meaningfulness in this sense (like the 'cognitive meaning' of later positivism) is the minimal condition for scientific thought and discourse; logical consistency or possible truth is for Husserl a further, additional condition. (A logical contradiction, he points out, is not a case of meaninglessness but a special case of the meaningful: namely, the necessarily false.) This minimal condition of semantic unity, insofar as it is not due to accidental peculiarities of particular languages, can be spelled out in 'a priori laws' of meaning-combination and meaning-transformation.[4] The semantic categories in terms of which these laws must be formulated are defined as classes of meanings (or classes of the corresponding expressions) that are substitutable for one another in the same formal environment without loss of meaningfulness for the semantic whole within which they are substituted (Husserl, 1913, vol. II, part 1: 319). Husserl is thus probably the first thinker to give a systematic formulation to the notion of substitution-classes that is taken for granted in all modern logic (as the range of values for a variable) as well as in linguistics (as distributionally equivalent word-classes).

The typical formal environment representing a semantic whole within which partial substitution may occur is of course a sentence or a sentence frame. Hence, if we reinterpret the intuitively apprehended 'meanings' of Husserl's theory in terms of 'expressions' or

---

[4] Edmund Husserl (1913: vol. II, Part I, 317): 'Die Bedeutungen unter apriorischen Gesetzen stehen, welche ihre Verknüpfung zu neuen Bedeutungen regeln'. For the concept of semantic kernel (*Kernform, Kerninhalt*) and transformation, see ibid. pp. 324–6. For some comparisons between Carnap and Husserl, see Bar-Hillel's article, 'Husserl's conception of a Purely Logical Grammar', *Philosophy and Phenomenological Research*, 17 (1956–57), pp. 362–9.

linguistic symbols, we see that his criterion of meaningfulness directly prefigures the notions of well-formedness and grammaticality (in other words, sentencehood) in contemporary logic and linguistics. For his notion of an intra-categorial substitution as one that occurs without loss of meaningfulness becomes the modern notion of inter-substitutability without loss of sentencehood or 'salva grammaticality'. And Husserl's concept of a *Bedeutungskategorie* thus reappears as Carnap's notion of a kind of symbol or a 'genus of expressions', the notion which serves as a basis for the 'formation' and 'transformation rules' of logical syntax (Carnap, 1937: 167–70).

I cannot undertake to trace the historical continuity between Husserl and Carnap in any detail. A major link was certainly provided by the Polish school of logicians. And in this connection the great creative figure was Leśniewski. It was Leśniewski who, under the direct inspiration of Husserl's *Logische Untersuchungen*, worked out the first systematic theory of 'semantic categories' for a formalized language. Leśniewski's system is particularly well designed to map the grammatical categories of natural languages, since its resources for the construction of formal categories are much richer and more flexible than the limited number of expression-types in Frege–Russell logic. Leśniewski's work remained largely unpublished, however, and his most explanatory manuscript was destroyed in the Warsaw uprising of 1944.[5] Hence the influence of Leśniewski's theory of semantic categories was exercised to a large extent by way of the application of similar ideas to natural language by Adjukiewicz, for example in his work on syntactical connexity (Adjukiewicz, 1935). It was through Adjukiewicz and the other Polish logicians, including Tarski, that these ideas reached Carnap. (For this connection, see Carnap, 1937: 167.) And today, as a result of the work of Carnap, Tarski, Bar-Hillel, Zellig Harris, Noam Chomsky, Richard Montague and others, we have a rich development of formal syntax and formal semantics, within which a number of alternative systems of grammatical categories are defined with great precision.[6]

---

[5] I am indebted to Henry Hiż for this and other information about Leśniewski.

[6] On different kinds of grammatical categories see H. Hiż (1960). For categorial grammars see John Lyons (1968), 227–31. For categories in Montague grammars, see R. Montague (1974).

We also have a more informal notion of semantic category made popular by Gilbert Ryle's concept of a category mistake. Ryle's article 'Categories' is of special interest to us, since it deals directly with the interpretation of Aristotle's doctrine and also establishes a link between categories and questions.

Ryle was one of the few British philosophers to make a serious study of Husserl's work. (He has been known to say that he learned German by reading the *Logische Untersuchungen*.) But the philosophical motivation of his views on categories owes more to Wittgenstein and Carnap than to Husserl. Wittgenstein in the *Tractatus* had no explicit doctrine of logical categories, though like everyone else he made implicit use of the notion of a substitution class of symbols or expressions.[7] But it was Wittgenstein who introduced the twentieth century to the idea that 'most of the propositions and questions to be found in philosophic works are not false but nonsensical' and 'arise from our failure to understand the logic of our language' (*Tractatus* 4.003). 'In order to avoid such errors we must make use of a sign-language . . . that is governed by *logical* grammar—by logical syntax' (3.325). Carnap notoriously rejected Wittgenstein's view that the rules of this logical syntax cannot be coherently formulated, but he followed Wittgenstein with a vengeance in holding that 'the sentences of metaphysics are pseudo-sentences which on logical analysis are proved to be either empty phrases or phrases which violate the rules of syntax' (Carnap, 1937: 8).

Ryle's article 'Categories' appeared in 1938, one year after the English edition of *The Logical Syntax of Language*. His debt to Carnap (or, perhaps, the direct convergence of their thinking on these matters) is acknowledged by a reference on precisely the point which concerns us here: the philosophical significance of Aristotle's method of classifying predicates or terms by reference to the kind of question they answer. Ryle explains and justifies this procedure by observing that a question may be analyzed as a sentence frame, where the interrogative word serves as a gap-sign to indicate the type of expression or

---

[7] Wittgenstein (1921: 33, 3.344): 'What signifies in a symbol is what is common to all the symbols that the rules of logical syntax allow us to substitute for it'.

sentence-factor that can fill the gap. And in this connection Ryle refers to Carnap's discussion of 'w ... questions'.[8]

What concerns us is not so much Ryle's agreement with Carnap as the notion of logical category which he defines and which he attributes in principle to Aristotle: 'To say that a given proposition-factor is of a certain category or type, is to say that its expression could complete certain sentence-frames without absurdity. ... And by distinguishing varieties of sorts of questions, Aristotle is using a general method for exhibiting varieties of type of the factors which would be answers to those questions or complements to those gap-signs' (Ryle, 1938: 174 f.). And a category-mistake occurs, of course, when an expression or sentence-factor of the wrong type is combined with an inappropriate sentence frame. The result is an absurdity.

Ryle's term *absurdity* echoes Husserl's notion of *Unsinn* or meaninglessness. But the philosophical motivation of his view is much more in the spirit of Carnap's doctrine of pseudo-sentences. As Ryle himself says (1938: 174), an example like *Saturday is in bed* violates no rule of grammar. And furthermore, as his later work shows, what Ryle has in view is not so much the patent absurdity of such sentences as the hidden absurdity of philosophical sentences that apparently make surface sense but which, upon analysis, turn out to be nonsensical in the way Wittgenstein had suggested. But Wittgenstein's charge that philosophical confusion arises from the failure to understand 'the logic of our language' is now specified as the claim that such errors consist in a confusion of categories.

This would not be the appropriate occasion for a systematic critique of the notion of a category mistake. But it seems clear to me that the notion tends to blur the distinction between (1) obvious non-sentences which violate the rules of grammar in some straightforward way, like *A man and is*, to take one of Husserl's examples (1913: vol. II,

---

[8] Ryle's article contains two references to Carnap (Ryle, 1938: 173 n. and 184). Compare Carnap (1937: 296): 'A w ... question demands in reference to a certain sentential function the assertion of a closed full sentence (or sentential framework)'. In such a question 'the genus of the arguments requested' may be indicated by 'a specific w ... interrogative (such as "who", "where", "when")'. Ryle's sensitivity to the role of questions as an instrument of logical analysis may also reflect a native Oxford tradition. Thus Cook Wilson had taught that the logical subject–predicate structure of a statement could be determined only by reference to the question it was answering. See Passmore (1966: 246).

part 1: 326), (2) problematic cases of odd, silly or perplexing sentences which seem to be grammatical but do not make obvious sense, such as *Saturday is in bed* or *Colorless green ideas sleep furiously*, or *A kidney has an ant*, and (3) philosophical doctrines expressed in sentences which have no surface oddity about them but which, it is claimed, rest upon illegitimate analogies or upon the conceptual confusion of treating radically unlike things as if they were somehow comparable. Like Husserl, modern syntax is concerned to discover the rules that explain why examples of type (1) are unacceptable as sentences. Some grammarians would also attempt to deal with examples like (2). It seems rather doubtful that any theory of grammar can adequately account for the oddity of most examples of this second type, but at least the problem is one which a linguist may reasonably regard as falling within his domain.[9] Not so, however, for the analogies which Ryle discovers underlying traditional dualism, and whose illegitimacy he denounces as the 'category mistake' of the Ghost in the Machine. The history of the notion of a category violation from Husserl to Ryle's 'Categories' (1938), and from 'Categories' to *The Concept of Mind* (1949), is a step-by-step shift from (1) to (2) to (3): from problems that obviously belong to grammar, to problems that dubiously belong to grammar, to problems that clearly do not belong to linguistics at all. This extension of the notion of 'category-mistake' has above all the result of providing philosophers with a new, more elegant, and more flexible version of the neo-positivistic technique for denouncing one's opponent's doctrines as 'meaningless', 'senseless', or 'lacking in cognitive content'.

We may here take our leave of Ryle and other modern theories of categories, pausing only to notice the effect that familiarity with such theories must tend to have on contemporary interpretations of Aristotle's doctrine. One effect lies in the expectation that Aristotle's scheme was designed to classify linguistic expressions or, as Ryle puts it, sentence-factors. This view has been carefully refuted by Ackrill,

---

[9] For an ambitious sketch of a theory of 'subcategorization' and 'selection rules' that might cover this ground, see Noam Chomsky (1965), 148–61. We recognize, I think, some echo of Husserl and Ryle in Chomsky's claim that a sentence like *The kidney has an ant* 'is not false or impossible but senseless' (p. 161).

and it need not be further considered here.[10] A more subtle and pervasive effect of the modern view of categories, however, is the tendency to think of Aristotle's doctrine as 'setting limits of cognitive meaning', as concerned with the conditions of sense and absurdity like the semantic theories of Husserl, Carnap, or Ryle. Thus a recent survey of the general topic of categories begins with the following characterization, which is directly followed by an account of Aristotle's theory:

Philosophical categories are classes, genera, or types supposed to mark necessary divisions within our conceptual scheme, divisions that we must recognize if we are to make literal sense in our discourse about the world. (Thompson, 1967: 46)

This view of categories leads the author to ask 'what, according to Aristotle's theory, would be the sort of thing often called today a "category-mistake"?', adding the specification that 'with a genuine category mistake there is no literal meaning to restore' (Thompson, 1967: 47–8). It turns out, however, that there seems to be at most one passage in Aristotle which may plausibly be interpreted as using the scheme of the categories to expose a mistake that results in literal nonsense.[11]

---

[10] 'The categories classify things, not words.' 'It is not linguistic items but the things they signify which are "said of a subject"' (Ackrill, 1963: 73, 75 and *passim*). This view is certainly correct, if 'things' translates ὄντα. But of course it remains to be specified just what ontological status can be assigned to 'things' like qualities, relations, and the species and genus of a substance. It turns out, I think, that the linguistic dimension will be essential in any full explication of what Aristotle means by κατηγορεῖσθαι. What is certain is that Aristotle's theory of categories is not formulated as a theory of linguistic meaning or linguistic structure, and hence not properly as a doctrine in linguistics at all, though there is perhaps a natural linguistic 'translation' of the doctrine as a theory of elementary sentences or deep structure. See in this connection the interesting suggestion of Gillespie (1925: 80 f.) that in canonical form the sentences analyzed by the categories take the proper name of a person as grammatical subject.

For a reasoned rejection of the view that Aristotle's categories are designed to detect or diagnose semantic anomalies, see also J. M. E. Moravscik (1967), 138 f.

[11] Thompson's example of Aristotle exposing 'a genuine category mistake' is *Posterior Analytics* I.22, 83ᵃ33, where the Platonic Forms are dismissed as 'mere noise' (τερετίσματα, 'chirpings') after an analysis of predication based on the categorial scheme. Even this example, when examined in context, does not fit the conception of categories as a device for drawing the line between sense and nonsense. Aristotle's point against Plato is that a property like 'white' cannot be a self-subsistent entity but can exist only as the attribute of

Our brief survey of modern theories from Husserl to Ryle makes clear how natural it is to approach Aristotle's doctrine of categories with the assumption that it is designed to establish conditions of meaningful discourse and to draw the line between literal sense and nonsense. But there is in fact no evidence to support this assumption. It is true that, as we shall see, Aristotle's scheme of categories does serve to analyze the logical structure of what is said, and to distinguish this from the surface structure of the words in which it is said. But the scheme is not designed, nor is it used, to distinguish sentences from pseudo-sentences or sense from nonsense. It is distinctively modern to conceive of 'categories' as part of a theory of meaning in this sense, and it is a pure illusion to project such a conception onto Aristotle's doctrine. The illusion is of course enhanced by the fact that Aristotle, in his concern to draw distinctions that are not reflected in the forms of language, does naturally speak of language, of sentences, of 'meaning' or 'signifying'; and does indeed take linguistic or gram- matical facts into consideration. All the more reason, then, to bring into clear focus— and clearly reject—the illusion that his theory of cat- egories is a theory of meaning in the modern sense, that his divisions represent grammatical or semantic categories based upon some criter- ion of meaningfulness, or that his doctrine of predication can be equated with the modern logico-linguistic notion of 'predicates'.

But if Aristotle's system of categories is neither a grammatical nor a linguistic theory, we must nevertheless face the question: why are his most important categories designated by the ordinary interrogative forms of colloquial Greek? One plausible answer to this question was proposed by Émile Benveniste in an influential article entitled 'Catégories de pensée et catégories de langue' (1958), which directly connects Aristotle's distinctions with linguistic peculiarities of Greek. Benveniste assumes that Aristotle's intention was to draw up a list of conceptual categories (*catégories de pensée*); he regards the scheme 'as the

---

some substance. To treat 'white' as an independent entity is, indeed a category mistake, in that it means putting 'white' in the wrong category. But this is literally a mistake, not a piece of nonsense. Aristotle's characterization of the Forms here as 'mere noise' is deliberately abusive, but it does not involve the explicit use of any criterion of meaningfulness. So much is clear from the following words: 'and if they exist, they are irrelevant to our discussion'. For more on this passage see above, p. 250.

inventory of properties which a Greek thinker judged to be predicable of an object, and consequently as the list of a priori concepts which, according to him, organize our experience' (Benveniste, 1958: 65). We are not concerned here with the Kantian turn that Benveniste gives to this notion of 'concept', but rather with his thesis as to the true source of the categorial distinctions. Benveniste claims that 'these distinctions are originally linguistic categories (*catégories de langue*)' and that Aristotle, while attempting to discover universal and a priori concepts, 'in fact simply turns up with some of the fundamental categories of the language in which he thinks.' The grouping of predicates corresponds 'not to attributes discovered in things but to a classification emanating from the language itself' (1958: 66). Thus the first six categories all refer to nominal forms: 'substance' or 'whatness' (οὐσία, τί ἐστι) indicates the class of nouns; the paired terms 'quantity' (ποσόν) and 'quality' (ποιόν) represent two types of adjectives closely associated in Greek from the earliest texts (with their correlative forms ὅσος-οἷος and τόσος-τοῖος: cf., ἀλλοῖος, μοῖος). These two categories 'are thus clearly grounded in the system of forms of the language'. Behind 'relation' (πρός τι) we find 'another fundamental property of Greek adjectives, that of furnishing a comparative', as indicated in the form μεῖζον, 'greater', which Aristotle himself cites as an example of this category. Again, 'place' (πού) and 'time' (ποτέ) are coupled by their formal symmetry (which reappears in οὗ-ὅτε, τοῦ-τότε) and represent a class of adverbs and locative case-forms. Thus the first six categories reflect nominal forms; by contrast, the last four represent verbal forms. 'Action' (ποιεῖν) and 'being-acted-on' (πάσχειν) obviously correspond to the active and the passive voice, as Aristotle's examples show: τέμνειν 'to cut', καίειν 'to burn', as opposed to τέμνεσθαι 'to be cut', καίεσθαι 'to be burnt'. What about the remaining two categories, ἔχειν, 'having', or *habitus*, and κεῖσθαι, 'posture', or *situs*? Benveniste points out that the two examples of κεῖσθαι are both verbs that have *middle* forms only (ἀν ἄκειται, 'he is lying down', κάθηται, 'he is sitting'), and that the middle voice 'is equally irreducible to the active and to the passive', and denoted for a Greek thinker 'a manner of being as characteristic as the two other voices', (Benveniste, 1958: 69). Finally, for ἔχειν, 'to have', Benveniste proposes the sense of 'being in a certain state', as represented by the *perfect* forms of the verbs which Aristotle lists as examples: ὑποδέδεται, 'he is shod', 'he has sandals on', ὥπλισται, 'he is armed', 'he has armor on'.

Ingenious as is Benveniste's explanation, and reflecting as it does the special insight of a professional linguist, it is quite striking to discover that his hypothesis was anticipated in detail by F. A. Trendelenburg over a century ago. Trendelenburg's own aim was to defend Aristotle's scheme against Kant's and Hegel's charge that it was an unmethodical and random assortment of concepts by showing that it was in fact derived from a systematic grammatical analysis.[12] The grammatical derivation of the ten categories in Trendelenburg's view coincides almost exactly with that proposed by Benveniste: 'substance' from nouns or 'substantives'; 'quantity' from numerical adjectives; 'quality' from descriptive adjectives; 'relation' from comparative adjectives. The fifth and sixth categories are assigned to adverbial forms: adverbs of place ('where') and of time ('when'). The last four categories are derived from verbal forms just as in Benveniste's view, using Aristotle's illustrative examples as a guide. The only difference is that Trendelenburg connects 'posture' (κεῖσθαι) with intransitive verbs rather than with the middle voice; but this is roughly the same account given in terms of syntax rather than morphology.

When we ask what philosophical significance is to be assigned to these correlations, however, the views of Benveniste and Trendelenburg diverge sharply. The modern linguist believes that Aristotle was unconscious of the grammatical basis for his categories and that, although he intended to classify the attributes of objects, he was involuntarily led to recognize 'the distinctions which his language exhibits between its principal classes of forms' (Benveniste, 1958: 70). The nineteenth-century philosopher and historian, on the other hand, sees Aristotle as deliberately utilizing these grammatical distinctions as the clue for a systematic choice and arrangement of the categories. But

---

[12] See especially Trendelenburg, 1846: 23 f. and 1852: 54 f. with note to p. 55. Trendelenburg had first published his views in a Programmschrift *de Aristotelis categoriis*, Berlin, 1833. Benveniste's presentation of his parallel view as a novelty strongly suggests that he was unaware of Trendelenburg's theory, although much of the nineteenth-century German literature on the categories was devoted to refuting it. It was Vuillemin (1967: 75 n.) who pointed out the parallel.

230 CHARLES H. KAHN

according to Trendelenburg such grammatical considerations served Aristotle only for the initial discovery of the scheme. Once discovered, he developed the categories in such a way as to neglect their origin and consider only the intrinsic nature of the objects and concepts classified.[13]

Benveniste's suggestion that Aristotle was as it were forced by the structure of Greek to choose just these categories is really indefensible, as Vuillemin has pointed out.[14] In this and many similar cases, linguistic relativism draws a fallacious inference from a trivially true premiss. It is of course true that no one is free to think outside the structure of any language, if by 'thinking' one means thinking thoughts expressible in language. (And unless we specify this sense for 'thinking', the claim may not be true at all. Musicians, artists, even scientists would deny that all their thinking is linguistic in form. Einstein is said to have perceived some of his major theoretical insights at first in a kind of musical or pre-linguistic intuition, before spelling them out in statements and formulae.) But if to express one's thoughts one must inevitably use the forms of the language, it does not follow that one cannot use these forms to draw distinctions which the language itself initially ignores, or use these same forms to deny the importance of other distinctions which the language imposes. As we shall see, Aristotle makes use of the categories in both ways, but primarily in the former: to show, for example, that a term like *good* or like *belongs to* (ὑπ ἄρχειν) represents different logical structures corresponding to different categories. In such matters the form of a thinker's conceptual freedom is defined by, and thus dependent upon, his relation to a given language (or to several, if he knows more than one); but his use of that freedom is not determined by the structure of the language in question.

---

[13] 'Aber die grammatischen Beziehungen leiten nur und entscheiden nicht' (Trendelenburg, 1846: 209). 'Ita Aristoteles categoriarum genera ex grammaticis fere orationis rationibus invenisse videtur, inventas autem ita pertractavit, ut, relicta origine, ipsam notionum et rerum naturam spectaret' (1852: 55).

[14] See Vuillemin (1967), pp. 76 f., 110. Vuillemin's long study of the *Categories* (pp. 44–125) contains a subtle attempt to show that Aristotle's table of categories is characterized by an elaborate formal organization, based in a systematic way upon his theory of predication and preparing (via the Postpredicamenta, *Cat.* 10–15) for the metaphysical development.

But if Benveniste's larger claim can be set aside without hesitation, that is not the case for Trendelenburg's more cautious statement of the hypothesis of the grammatical origin of Aristotle's scheme. It is true that Trendelenburg's view has also been generally rejected by students of the categories, but their reasons are not always cogent.[15] Most of the opposition fails to distinguish between the question of origin and the question of philosophic intent or motivation. Because Aristotle's intention in constructing the scheme, as judged from the use he makes of it, is clearly not linguistic or grammatical, it is inferred that the scheme itself cannot (or should not) have been based on grammatical distinctions. But there are two quite distinct questions: (1) why construct a scheme of categories? and (2) why choose this particular set of categories? In answer to (1), the evidence (above all from the *Topics*) suggests that Aristotle's aim was to set up distinctions of logical importance that were often overlooked because of superficial uniformity in their linguistic expression. But in order to draw these distinctions it was of course legitimate (and, in some sense, inevitable) that he should rely after all upon contrasting terms and phrases from the language itself. Why this particular list of ten? The grammatical considerations alleged by Benveniste and Trendelenburg represent a plausible conjecture, as long as we add the qualification that Aristotle chose just those linguistic contrasts (as between *where* and *when, acting* and *being acted upon*) which seemed to him of genuine philosophical importance.

We know after all that such grammatical clues could have guided Aristotle, because we see that they did in fact guide a modern logician. Bertrand Russell once wrote:

Although a grammatical distinction cannot be uncritically assumed to correspond to a genuine philosophical difference, yet the one is *prima facie* evidence of the other, and may often be most usefully employed as a source of discovery. . . . In what follows, grammar, though not our master, will yet be taken our guide (Russell, 1903: 42).

---

[15] Trendelenburg (1846: 194 f.) mentions the immediate opposition of Ritter, Zeller, and Spengel. To these we may add the monograph of Bonitz (1853), which is a direct attack on Trendelenburg's view. See more recently the sympathetic remarks of E. Kapp (1920: 223 n. 12 and 236) who nevertheless rejects Trendelenburg's grammatical thesis. Gillespie (1925: 80) has a more positive appreciation.

In principle Russell's procedure corresponds exactly to Trendelenburg's hypothesis for Aristotle. Of course there are significant differences which limit the force of this parallel. Unlike Aristotle, Russell can refer to an established grammatical theory, fixed since antiquity and essentially unchallenged down to his own time. Furthermore, Russell explicitly depicts his own inquiry as one of 'philosophic grammar', involving a logical analysis of 'the proposition'. Aristotle and Plato, on the other hand, were pioneering innovators at the very beginning of our grammatical tradition. They could not take for granted any grammatical theory as a guide. Furthermore, they carefully distinguished their own grammatical terminology in the analysis of sentence structure from their logical or ontological terminology in the theory of predication—the theory of which Aristotle's categories form a central part.[16] Thus the *Categories* introduce their topic as 'things signified by what is said without combination', where the phrase 'without combination' (κατὰ μηδεμίαν συμπλοκήν) shows precisely that Aristotle is here not concerned with sentence structure or propositional form.

The fact remains that the grammatical correlations noticed independently by Trendelenburg and Benveniste do exist, and the suggestion that they may have served as a clue to Aristotle's choice of just these ten categories is a historical conjecture that we can neither confirm nor refute. Despite the absence of any adequate grammatical theory in his time, Aristotle's powers of insight were probably equal to the linguistic discoveries that Trendelenburg ascribes to him. But unfortunately we have no direct evidence as to the origin of the scheme, since nowhere do we find it *in statu nascendi*. Both in the *Topics* and in the *Categories*, which are pretty much certainly the two oldest among the extant works in which the categories appear, the doctrine is introduced as a finished whole, with the same ten categories named in the same order (*Topics* 1.9: *Cat.* 4). If we compare Trendelenburg's conjecture with the suggestion made by Gomperz (1912: 39), that Aristotle 'imagines a man standing before him, say in

---

[16] For the systematic distinction between the grammatical terminology (ὄνομα, ῥῆμα) and the corresponding terms for subject (ὑποκε ίμενον) and predicate (κατηγορούμενον), see Kahn (1973: 46–8).

the Lyceum, and passes in successive review the questions which may be put and answered about him', we see that the two conjectures are not only equally plausible, but fully compatible. Aristotle may indeed have begun by analyzing and classifying the kinds of questions that can be asked about a given man. And he may well have been guided in this analysis at first by the more common interrogative forms of the language, and then by other linguistic distinctions that reflect concepts of philosophic importance, like the distinction between the active and the passive voice. But of course his classification was not dictated by the forms of the language. There are, for example, many Greek interrogative forms of which he took no account (including πότερος 'which of two?', πόθεν 'whence', ποῖ 'whither?', πῶ ς 'how?', as well as the declined forms of τὶ ς: τοῦ, τινός 'whose?' 'from whom?', τίνι 'for whom?').

There is more to be said on the conjectural origins of Aristotle's scheme, but this can best be said below, in connection with what I call Stage Zero of the theory. For convenience and clarity of exposition, I shall divide my discussion of the categories in Aristotle's extant works into three stages, corresponding to three treatises or groups of treatises. Stage One is represented by the theory of categories in the *Topics*. Stage Two corresponds to the doctrine of the *Categories* and the *Analytics*. Stage Three is the doctrine of *Metaphysics* Δ.7 and, more generally, the doctrine of the *Metaphysics*, the *Physics*, and other systematic treatises such as the *De Anima* and the *Nicomachean Ethics*. In Stage One the table of ten categories is presented as a classification of predicates and types of predication; there is no corresponding analysis of subjects and consequently no theory of primary substances as the basic subjects of predication. Stage Two provides us with the doctrine of primary substance and with Aristotle's classical analysis of predication; but there is still no theory of Being structured by the categories. In Stage Three we get the full 'ontological' application of the categorial scheme, as an answer to the question ποσαχῶς λέγεται τὸ ὄν; 'In how may ways is Being said?' or 'How many ways are there for a thing to *be*?' (less accurately: 'How many senses are there for the word *being*?'). It is, I think, indisputable that the exposition of the doctrine falls into these three stages, and it is natural to think of these stages as chronologically distinct. But the chronological sequence can scarcely be urged as a matter of historical fact, since there is no external

234 CHARLES H. KAHN

evidence for the relative dating of the treatises. I myself see no reason to doubt that the *Metaphysics* is later than the *Categories*, and that the *Analytics* are later than the *Topics*. But the relative date of the *Topics* and the *Categories*[17] is not easy to establish, and in every case there is the possibility that later additions have been made by Aristotle himself to an 'early' treatise.[18] In the case of Aristotle's extant treatises almost all chronological conclusions are based upon internal evidence only, and hence they have no justification beyond the light they shed on internal discrepancies of doctrine or formulation. For our purposes, the division into three stages could just as well be understood as a convenience of exposition rather than as an historical claim. In this case—and, I believe, in most other cases of 'development' within the extant treatises—the sequence of stages represents moments in the progressive development and exposition of a single, complex doctrine, rather than shifts from one view to another view incompatible with the first. When Aristotle wrote the *Topics* he did not have (or if he had, he preferred not to mention) the doctrines of primary substance and the multivocity of Being. But once he had formulated these doctrines, there is little or nothing in the use made of the categories in the *Topics* that he would be required to give up. (The same probably holds *mutatis mutandis* for the relationship between his account of argument in the *Topics* and his theory of the syllogism in *Prior Analytics* I; though in the discovery of the syllogism there is a much greater element of novelty, and hence of discontinuity, than in the development of the theory of categories.)

The three stages represented in the extant works must have been preceded by an initial phase of reflection and discovery, a stage in which the list of categories as we find it fixed in *Topics* I.9 and *Categories* 4 gradually took shape. We may label this Stage Zero, since it is

---

[17] I agree with Ackrill (1963) in assuming without argument that the *Categories* is an authentic work of Aristotle. This has rarely been questioned by Aristotelian scholars writing in English, but one may note that a recent study in French refers to 'the author of the *Categories*' in a way that suggests he is not Aristotle (Mansion, 1968: 197 note).

[18] Thus the first chapter of *Topics* I, which contrasts dialectic with scientific demonstration and offers the same definition of 'syllogism' as in the *Prior Analytics*, was probably added or rewritten after the *Analytics*. Contrast the last chapter of the *Topics*, i.e. *Sophistici Elenechi* 34, which looks back on a completed task with obvious satisfaction, but with no similar hint of greater things to come.

unattested by any document and must be reconstructed from circumstantial evidence only. As we have seen, part of this evidence is
provided by (1) the names and ordering of the ten categories and (2)
the nature of the examples given. To this we may add (3) the name
category (κατηγορία) itself, and (4) the most likely starting point in
Plato's late work (namely, *Sophist* 251A–B). There are finally (5) some
indirect clues in the way the categories are referred to in the *Topics*,
which we take as the 'earliest' work in which the doctrine appears.

STAGE ZERO. To begin with the characteristic name, κατηγορία is the
abstract action noun from the verb κατηγορεῖν, which Aristotle adapts
from its old juridical sense 'to accuse (*X* of doing *Y*)', 'to speak against
(*X* and charge him with *Y*)' in order to create the new technical term
'to predicate (*Y* of *X*)', that is: 'to say of (*X* that it is *Y*)'. Aristotle needs
a new technical term for he is the first one to work out an explicit
theory of 'predication' or 'saying *Y* of *X*'. But of course an awareness of
the problem of predication is something that Aristotle inherits from
Plato. Plato's own concern with this problem is most dramatically
expressed in the *Sophist*, where Plato, while struggling with the difficult task of defining Being and Not-Being, suddenly shifts to what
seems a more tractable difficulty: 'let us say in what way we address the
same thing by many names.'[19] The interlocutor asks for an example,
which is provided as follows:

We speak of a man, for example, and name him many things [or 'we apply
many names to him'], attributing colors to him and figures and magnitudes and
vices and virtues, and in all these cases and thousands of others we say not only
that he is a man, but also that he is good and an infinity of other things; and in
other instances too on the same principle we thus posit [as subject][20] each thing
as one and again call it many things and by many names (*Sophist* 251 A8–B3).

---

[19] *Sophist* 251A5: λέγωμεν δὴ καθ' ὅντινά ποτε τρόπον πολλοῖς νόμασι ταὐτὸν τοῦτο
ἑκάστοτε προσαγορεύομεν. Note that the verb προσαγορεύειν here prefigures Aristotle's use
of κατηγορεῖν. It occurs frequently in this way in Plato, but never becomes a technical term.
Cf. *Soph.* 223D6, 232A6, 236C4, etc. The disadvantage of προσαγορεύειν (and προσειπεῖν,
etc.) from Aristotle's point of view is that it tends to suggest 'semantic' predication of word for
thing, rather than the thing-thing attribution that Aristotle has primarily in view.

[20] As has been noted by others (e.g. Kapp, 1920: 245 n. 31), ὑποθέμενοι here ('positing as
subject') directly prefigures Aristotle's term ὑποκείμενον, 'subject', literally 'what is posited
[as a basis for predication]'.

Here Plato confronts the problem of predication in terms of the One and the Many: beneath the semantic contrast of one thing, many names, lies the more strictly logical (or ontological) problem of one subject (e.g. one man), many attributes. Plato moves on quickly to the Communion of Forms as providing the conditions for true and false discourse, and to the analysis of discourse itself in terms of the simplest proposition, consisting of one noun (or name) and one verb: *Theaetetus flies, Theaetetus sits.* Aristotle follows the same path but more slowly, pausing to deal at length with each topic as it arises. The noun–verb analysis of the proposition is pursued in the *De Interpretatione*, but the corresponding logical-ontological relation of subject to attribute is dealt with in the *Categories* and, more generally, in the theory of predication. It is essential to recall that in this theory the terms for 'subject' (ὑποκείμενον) and 'predicate' (κατηγορούμενον) do not refer to linguistic items or sentence-constituents but to the extralinguistic things which are 'said' or signified in sentences. (For Aristotle as for Plato, the terms for the corresponding sentence-constituents are ὄνομα 'noun' or 'name', and ῥῆμα 'verb'.) Just as in the pre-philosophical use of κατηγορεῖν for 'accusation' a crime is asserted of a man, so in κατηγορεῖν as 'predication' an attribute is asserted of a subject entity, and typically of a man.

Whereas Plato is concerned here only with the fact that many attributes are asserted of a single subject, Aristotle pauses to consider how many different ways there are of asserting attributes, or of 'saying something of something'. (λέγειν τι κατά τινος: we must not translate this as 'saying one thing of *another* thing', since one of the key results of Aristotle's categorial analysis is to distinguish accidental predication, in which one thing is asserted of another, from essential predication, in which the predicate is not other than the subject.) He thus distinguishes the ten forms or 'figures of predication' (τὰ σχήματα τῆ ςκατηγοριῶν) or the ten kinds or 'genera of predications' (τὰ γένη τῶν κατηγοριῶν). The latter designation may have been the earliest one, since it appears in *Topics* 1.9. Aristotle seems to have followed Plato in taking a human being as specimen subject. As we have seen, in distinguishing the kinds of things that can be said of such a subject he may well have been guided by grammatical hints, though not in any slavish way. The result is a kind of rough sketch of the analysis of an object-language for basic subjects (concrete individuals) and simple or elementary predicates. But to describe Aristotle's scheme in this way calls for several qualifications. In the first place, Aristotle is out to classify not words but things, not predicate-expressions but attributes or properties. Secondly, as a classification of predications or predicates, the scheme does not initially apply to the subjects of discourse as such. A concrete subject is taken as given; predication in the first category simply specifies *what it is*. (Thus τί ἐστι rather than οὐσία is the intitial designation of this category in *Topics* 1.9.) Furthermore, as a classification of basic attributes the scheme is possibly incomplete (for instance, psychological predicates like *thinking* or *feeling pain* do not have any obvious place), probably redundant (*habitus* or Having and *situs* or Posture may be included under Quality as ἕξις and διάθεσις, as Aristotle perhaps recognized in later lists, where these two minor categories are no longer mentioned), and certainly incoherent in one respect. This concerns the category Time or 'when', which cannot provide simple predicates for individual subjects. *Socrates is today* and *Socrates was yesterday* are not proper sentences either in English or in Greek. Here I suspect Benveniste's accusation may be partially justified. Aristotle was genuinely misled by the surface parallelism between ποῦ 'where' and πότε 'when', since both represent fundamental classes of adverbs with standard verbs: *Socrates runs in the Lyceum, Socrates runs today*. But in this use the adverb is of course not predicated of the subject: like many adverbs, it modifies the verb.[21] The first-order use of adverbials of place, as in *Socrates is in the Lyceum*, has no equivalent for adverbials of time. I can see no principle to justify the category 'when' that would not require us also to introduce other second-order adverbial concepts such as *easy, difficult, fast, slow*, for which the scheme provides no place.[22] And the anomaly shows up in Aristotle's

---

[21] Such adverbs are thus naturally regarded as second-order predicates, or functions of functions. Compare Harris's (1968: 183) treatment of adverbs like *slow (slowly)* and *easy (easily)* as f^2 (functions of functions) rather than f^1 (functions of basic arguments) in his 'abstract system'.

[22] Perhaps we might justify Aristotle's inclusion of this category by pointing out that while other adverbial modifiers are optional, some indication of time is obligatory (in Greek, and indeed in Indo-European), since it is expressed in the tense of the verb. Kurt von Fritz suggests to me (in a letter) that the inclusion of time or 'when', although grammatically anomalous, 'just goes to show that Aristotle's viewpoint from the very beginning was not a

philosophical applications of the scheme: there is no derivative concept of 'change of time' corresponding to change of place, change of
quality, of quantity and of substance.

For the philosophical motivation of the scheme in Stage Zero our
safest guess would be: to pursue in detail the analysis of predication
which Plato had recognized as a problem, and to show how many
different kinds of predication can be distinguished under the apparently unitary form of basic statements, i.e. under the elementary
sentence forms of Noun–Verb or Noun + Copula + Predicate.[23]
Beyond this one might add: and to prepare the ground for a rejection
of Plato's doctrine of Forms. But for this guess there would not be any
clear circumstantial evidence. In choosing a human being as his specimen subject, he is, as we have seen, following a good Platonic precedent. We could imagine Stage Zero as belonging to Aristotle's first
work as a docile disciple, if we supposed that he ever was such.

To specify the relationship between linguistic and philosophic
considerations at this stage, perhaps the best formula is the one we
have quoted from Russell. In exploring the diversity of predication
(that is, of the relationship *Y is said of X*), Aristotle attends to linguistic
distinctions not as his master but as his guide, at least for surveying the

---

purely grammatical or linguistical one', but that he appreciated the ontological importance of
the parallelism of space and time, explicitly recognized later by Kant (and then translated into
terms of epistemology, as generally with Kant). I would like to emphasize my agreement with
the view that Aristotle's interest in the question of categories was *never* a purely grammatical
or linguistic one. His recognition of the category 'when' prepares for the analysis of the
concept of time in the *Physics* (IV.10–14), just as the category 'where' prepares for the analysis
of place (*Physics* IV.1–5). I mean only to suggest that the original choice of just these ten
categories can be understood only in terms of a grammatical analysis of the various ways of
saying *Y* of *X*, where *X* is a concrete individual such as a man; and that when it is so
understood the inclusion of 'when' is seen to rest upon a linguistic mistake—a mistake which
Aristotle is obliged to correct in certain philosophical contexts, as when he silently omits
'when' in his analysis of change by reference to the categories.

[23] So Kapp (1920: 245 n. 32): 'Was bei der Kategorienlehre ursprünglich behauptet wird,
ist die *Verschiedenheit* der Glieder der Einteilung gegenüber dem Schein der Einerleiheit'. We
have some fragmentary suggestions that other fourth-century thinkers regarded predication,
particularly in the copula form *A is B*, as problematical, apparently on the assumption that *is*
must have some one meaning (whether 'exists' or 'is identical with'). For attempts to avoid
the copula in predication, see *Physics* 185^b 27–32. For the view of Antisthenes that of any one
thing only one λόγος can be asserted, see *Metaphysics* 1024^{b}32 and Gillespie (1913). For the
importance of these discussions for understanding Aristotle's theory of categories, see Apelt
(1891), 201–11.

terrain. The different interrogative forms, together with the various grammatical distinctions noted by Benveniste and Trendelenburg, are utilized by him in order to make clear that a sentence of the type *X is Y* (or *XY's*, where *Y* stands for a verb) may express a number of quite distinct kinds of judgmental or conceptual ties, corresponding to a number of different kinds of factual configurations and, ultimately, to a number of different kinds of entities: substances, qualities, quantities, and the like. Thus the categorial scheme takes a linguistic analysis only as its point of departure: the intended movement is in a different direction. On the one hand, a grammatical distinction may be, in Russell's words, *prima facie* evidence of a philosophical difference. On the other hand, many crucial differences will ordinarily be masked by similar linguistic expression. Hence the theory moves *from* grammatical considerations to an analysis of the underlying logical or conceptual structures, with the aim of revealing ontological differences. In this sense the theory of predication was intended, from the beginning, to become what it is explicitly in the *Metaphysics*: a contribution to the analysis of being, to the theory of the structure of reality. Aristotle's conception of the strict parallelism between language, thought, and reality (as sketched in *De Interpretatione* 1) guarantees that the only philosophically interesting analysis in linguistic terms will be one that seeks to avoid or expose logical fallacies by revealing and reflecting in discourse the real connections between things. In this perspective philosophical grammar, conceptual analysis, and ontology are not properly distinct enterprises, though different aspects may predominate at different stages of the investigation. And in an analysis of *how Y is said of X*, linguistic considerations will naturally predominate at the beginning.

STAGE ONE. The *Topics* is the 'earliest' work in which we can see the scheme of categories being used, and the only work outside the *Categories* in which the full list of ten categories is given (in 1.9). But although the scheme is occasionally employed throughout the nine books of *Topics* and *Sophistici Elenchi* (= *Topics* IX), it was clearly not designed specifically for this purpose. The *Topics*, Aristotle's first work in logic (see *Soph. El.* 34), was conceived as a systematic handbook for that curious philosophical game which Aristotle calls 'dialectic', and which consists in trying to win an argument according to stylized rules modeled on the procedure of a Socratic ἔλεγχος or cross-examin-ation.[24] In its external relation to the *Topics* the categorial scheme contrasts sharply with the fourfold division of 'predicables' (definition, genus, property, accident) on which the whole structure of the work rests.[25] The discrepancy between the categorial scheme as such and its use in the *Topics* shows up, for example, in the choice of a subject of predication. The dialectical game is normally played with theses of a general nature that take universal terms as subject, such as *whether all pleasure is good* or *whether any pleasure is good*. 'Pleasure' is of course not an individual substance, and in fact not a substance term at all. It will rarely happen that a dialectical debate focusses on a thesis with a given man or individual substance as subject, and there will be no particular preference for subjects in the first category. (In this respect the dialect-ical thesis of the *Topics* prefigures the syllogistic premiss of the *Analytics*, which consists almost exclusively of general terms, with no limitations on the category of the subject.) Hence although *Topics* 1.9 lists the two anthropocentric categories of Posture and Having, the treatise scarcely makes any use of them. Instead it introduces an entirely new perspec-tive, of which we assumed no trace in Stage Zero. According to this enlarged perspective of *Topics* 1.9, in place of a fixed individual subject such as a man, the choice of subject ranges from category to category, whereas the question 'what is it?' (τί ἐστι), which originally designated the first category, now specifies essential—that is, transitive—predica-tion within each category. In Stage Zero we assumed a fixed subject (or at least a fixed type of subject) and distinguished the various questions that could be asked concerning it; each question determined a range of possible answers that constituted a particular class or 'genus of predications' (γένος τῶν κατηγοριῶν). Thus in the initial analysis a

---

[24] For this 'dialectical' background of the *Topics* and of Aristotle's approach to reasoning, see Kapp (1942), chapter I: 'The Origin of Logic as a Science'; also Gillespie (1925: 79–84).

[25] For this contrast and for the role of the categories in the *Topics* see Kapp (1920), to whom I am much indebted here. It is unfortunate that Kapp's important article on the *Topics*, first presented as his Habilitationsschrift in 1920, was not published until 1968. As a result it was unavailable to the scholars participating in the Oxford Symposium Aristotelicum on the *Topics* in 1963, whose papers are published in *Aristotle on Dialectic* (1968), ed. G. E. L. Owen. In particular, S. Mansion's article 'Notes sur la doctrine des categories dans les *Topiques*' would presumably have looked rather different if the author had been familiar with Kapp's study.

See also the important remarks on the development of the category doctrine in Kapp (1942: 23, 37–42).

predicate figures as one answer to a given question, and a genus of predication includes all possible or 'appropriate' answers to the same question (whether true or false). On this view, the question *what is it?* specifies the first category. In the new perspective of Stage One as represented by *Topics* 1.9, the category of the subject varies while the question *what is it?* applies within every category.[26] It is obvious that the former perspective must be the original one, since not only does it explain the interrogative form of categories like ποσόν, ποιόν, etc., but it alone permits us to distinguish the various categories, whereas the second perspective must simply take this distinction for granted. We need both perspectives, however—that is, we need the more flexible scheme of Stage One, in which the question *what is it?* belongs primarily to the first category, but secondarily to any category—in order to reach the first major philosophical achievement of the theory: the generalized distinction between essential and accidental predication, between predication within one category and predication across categorial boundaries.[27] The philosophical consequences of this distinction are left for the *Analytics* to draw; but the possibility of drawing them is given by the wider standpoint of *Topics* I, which also provides the needed terminology in the phrase ἐν τῶτί ἐστι κατηγορεῖσθαι 'predicated in answer to the question *what is it?*'[28] The notion of

---

[26] 103^{b}27–39: 'It is clear from these [categorial distinctions] that someone who indicates the *what-is-it* (ὸτὸ τί ἐστι σημαίνων) sometimes indicates substance (οὐσίαν σημαίνει), sometimes quantity, sometimes quality, sometimes another of the [kinds of] predications. For when a man is displayed (ἐκκε ίμενον) and he says the thing displayed is a man or is an animal, he says *what it is* and indicates (σημαίνει) its substance (οὐσίαν, literally 'being' or 'is-ness'); when a white color is displayed and he says the thing displayed is white or is a color, he says *what it is* and indicates quality; similarly, when a cubit length is displayed and he says that the thing displayed is a cubit or is a length (μέγεθος), he says *what it is* and indicates quantity; and similarly for the rest. For each of these, if it is said itself of itself [the species, e.g. *man* or *white*, of the concrete object] or if the genus [e.g. *animal* or *color*] is said of it, indicates *what it is*. But when [each] is said of another, it does not indicate *what it is* but how much or what quality or one of the other [kinds of] predications.'

[27] See the last two sentences quoted in the preceding note. Compare *Topics* 120^{b}21–6, where ἐν τῷ τί ἐστι κατηγορεῖσθαι is contrasted with ὡς συμβεβηκὸς (κατηγορεῖσθαι), and the former is indicated by the expression ὅπερ λευκόν 'what white [is]' and ὅπερ κινούμενον 'what being-moved [is]' as the essence of something, in contrast to συμβέβηκε κινεῖσθαι, *being moved* as a supervenient accident that may or may not apply to the subject. For the importance of this distinction in connection with the Third Man argument, see below; and compare Owen (1965: 135 f.).

[28] First occurrence in *Topics* 1.5, 102^{a}32, and frequently thereafter.

essential as opposed to accidental (cross-categorial) predication thus arises at the point of convergence between, on the one hand, the rudimentary categorial analysis of predication (with an initially limited use of *what is it?* for subjects in the first category only), and, on the other hand, the wider concern for definition and genus-classification of all kinds of subjects that is characteristic of dialectic. This wider, definitional function of the *what-is-it?* question continues the older use of the τί ἐστι question by Plato, and presumably by Socrates before him, in the search for definitions; the narrower application of the phrase to the first category is specifically Aristotelian.

The combination of both perspectives seems to be a new departure in the *Topics*. In another respect the *Topics* continues what we have assumed as the viewpoint of Stage Zero. Since the categories are 'kinds of predications (or predicates)', the subject of predication itself is in principle not classified by them. Insofar as primary substances like an individual man are not properly predicates at all, they do not have an obvious place in the first category, understood literally as a 'kind of predication'. But of course Aristotle does in fact want to include them in this category. This inclusion, or this readjustment of the notion of a category, dominates the scheme as presented in the *Categories*. It rarely occurs explicitly in the *Topics*, which in this respect remains more faithful to the etymological sense of κατηγορία.[29]

The philosophical motivation for the scheme of categories in the *Topics* is to a large extent clear and uniform throughout: it serves to analyze diversity of meaning—that is, to reveal differences of logical structure, differences that affect the truth value of the sentence—within the uses of a single linguistic form, and thus to expose fallacy in argument. More specifically, its primary functions in the *Topics* are (1) to distinguish the various uses of a term that is homonymous or 'said in many ways', and (2) to resolve fallacies based on the form of linguistic expression (σχῆμα λέξεως). (In the present context,

---

[29] The inclusion of individual substances in the first category is most clearly suggested in the *Topics* by the use of the term τόδε τι to designate this category. Cf. *Topics* 144ᵃ20, *Soph. El.* 169ᵃ34–6, 178ᵇ37–179ᵃ10. At 179ᵃ1–2 Aristotle seems to say that the individual Coriscus (or his name?) signifies the first category, designated as τόδε τι. But the *Topics* show no trace of a distinction between primary and secondary substance (except for the analysis of the Third Man in *Soph. El.* 22).

'homonymy' and 'said in many ways' are used interchangeably for what we may call multivocity. For the later distinction, see note 47 below.) The scheme is so convenient that its applications are not limited to these two functions. For example, it can also serve as a test of definitions: the genus must belong to the same category as the species defined (IV.I.120^b36–121^a9). But the two uses mentioned are the most characteristic. Thus the first application of the scheme in *Topics* 1.15 is to analyze the multivocity of the term *good* (107^a3–12). And the most intensive use of it is in the *Sophistici Elenchi*, in connection with the fallacy of expression (λέξις). Chapter 22 of this book begins: 'And it is clear how we are to confront the fallacies which are due to the fact that things not the same are said in the same way, since we possess the genera of predications (ἐπε ἱπερ ἔχομεν τά γένη τῶν κατηγοριῶν, 178^a5)'. The categorial distinctions are specifically designed to point out differences in things which are not really 'said in the same way, but seem to be so because of the expression' (διὰ τήν λέξιν, 178^a24), to point out, for example, that a verb such as *to see* (ῥᾶν), which is active in form like *to cut*, in fact indicates passivity or being-acted-upon like the passive form *to be cut*. And in the very next sentence Aristotle himself draws the parallel between this kind of linguistic deception and homonymy (178^a24–8).

It is in this connection that the categories are used for the first time in the discussion of a major philosophical issue, not in the *Topics* as such but in the ninth book on Fallacies (*Sophistici Elenchi*). The scheme does not appear in the five or six topical devices (τόποι) specifically aimed for arguing against 'those who posit Ideas'.[30] But the categorial analysis is used, curiously enough, to show how the Third Man argument against the Forms can be refuted, by denying that the universal *man* 'which is predicated in common of all [particular men]' is a substance or τόδε τι, a definite individual subject, but by insisting instead that it must be 'a quality or relation or quantity or something of this sort' (178^b36–179^a10). This breaks the regress by refusing to allow the universal predicate *man* to function in turn as the subject of transitive or essential predication. Unlike 'Socrates is a man', '*Man* is

---

[30] See Solmsen (1968: 59 f.), who gives a list of the passages (footnote 2 to p. 59). Many of them are discussed in detail by Owen (1968).

244 CHARLES H. KAHN

(a) man' is not a τί ἐστι predication in the first category, and it is not even true, if *Man* itself is not a concrete individual (τόδε τι). This means avoiding the regress by giving up the Platonic conception of the Forms as independent entities (οὐσίαι), but Aristotle is polite enough not to point this out. Whether for reasons of personal discretion or because of the limited and almost pre-philosophical role he assigns to dialectic as studied in the *Topics*, Aristotle is not prepared to present the scheme of the categories here as a machine of demolition for use against the ontology of Forms. The categories figure merely as an instrument of logical analysis, a contribution to the theory of meaning in the specifically Aristotelian sense of revealing logical differences under surface similarities of language. And 'primary substances' or sensible individuals are not yet terminologically distinguished from 'secondary substances' (their species and genera).

Of course we need not believe that the author of the *Topics* (including the book of *Elenchi*) could not see where this logical analysis was heading. He is certainly no orthodox Platonist: there is something almost provocative about this long, systematic account of 'dialectic without the Forms', as Solmsen (1968) has called it. And Aristotle's treatment here of the Third Man argument clearly implies the anti-Platonic consequence which he does not state. He may have composed the *Categories* practically at the same time, and in this treatise the ontological implications of the categorial scheme are quite unmistakable. Does it follow that the scheme was designed from the beginning with the problem of Forms in view, as Aristotle's own way of dealing with the Third Man argument? The suggestion has been made by G. E. L. Owen, and presented with great learning and acuteness, that 'Aristotle's criticism of Plato led him to draw some distinctions in his account of predication', in fact that such criticism 'lay at the root of his theory of predication and the categories' (Owen, 1965: 137). It had been noted independently by Kapp (1920: 238 f.) and Wilpert (1949: 89, n. 132) that the treatment of the Third Man in *Soph. Elenchi* 22 is closely paralleled by a statement of the argument quoted by Alexander from Aristotle's lost treatise *De Ideis* (fr. 4 Ross = fr. 188 Rose). Now the *De Ideis* is concerned at length with arguments for and against the existence of Forms, reflecting lively controversy over this theory in the early Academy. It is natural to suppose, then, that Aristotle actually began his study of predication with these controversies in mind, and that he came to the scheme of categories, and to the doctrine of substance which completes it, as his solution to a problem which Plato himself had raised in the Third Man argument (in *Parmenides* 132A–B)—a solution which is at the same time a rejection of the theory of Forms as such. This is the account of the origin of the categories that Owen (1965) develops in some detail.

The view presented here is not strictly incompatible with this account, though it differs considerably from it in emphasis. If I have assumed (with Kapp and Gillespie) that Aristotle's reflections on predication took their starting point from the *Sophist* rather than from the Third Man of the *Parmenides*, that is not because I claim to know where Aristotle in fact began. (Nor is there any reason to suppose that he could not have had both aspects of the problem of predication in view from the beginning.)[31] The starting point in the *Sophist*, with its relatively modest logical problem of how one man can be said to be many things, has the advantages of simplicity and economy. It permits a straightforward linear account of a step-by-step development (or at least a step-by-step exposition) of the doctrine, beginning with attention to ordinary questions about a particular man, and gradually rising to the metaphysical confrontation with the Forms. It also offers a natural explanation of the initial list of ten categories, including Having and Posture, a list that is not so easy to explain if one begins immediately with problems in the theory of Forms. Hence I would accept Owen's account of the roots of the theory only as applying to Stage Two—and I would agree that that stage is pretty clearly in view when we get to *Sophistici Elenchi* 22. But there is a certain methodological advantage to presenting Stage Zero and Stage One as 'earlier'.

On the other hand, I think there can hardly be any doubt of the correctness of Owen's principal point (against Jaeger), that Aristotle's

---

[31] In this connection one may compare the attempt of von Fritz (1931) to derive the theory of categories from a double root: (1) from the dialectical analysis of equivocations on the verb *to be*, and (2) from certain ontological difficulties in the theory of Forms, including the Third Man. In principle, then, von Fritz's theory corresponds to a conjunction of Kapp's account of the *Topics* (which I follow) and a kind of anticipation of Owen's connection between the categories and the controversy about Platonic Forms. In detail, however, it differs considerably from both.

logical and metaphysical interests were closely interconnected from the beginning. But it is very much in Aristotle's manner to develop the logical interest in predication separately with primary attention to equivocation and fallacy in argument, until the analysis was fully worked out, and then to apply it to larger philosophical issues when the time was ripe. We may compare the way in which the formal theory of the syllogism was completed in the *Prior Analytics*, before being incorporated within a general account of scientific knowledge in the *Posterior Analytics*. With some qualifications, we may also compare the gradual emergence of the notion of 'focal meaning' in the terminological studies collected in *Metaphysics* Delta, before the crucial application of this notion to the definition of ontology in *Metaphysics* Gamma (to be discussed below, under Stage Three). This pattern of 'gradualism' reflects in part Aristotle's characteristic feeling for the autonomy of a special science or inquiry; but it also reflects a natural reluctance 'to practice pottery on a large jar', as Plato puts it in the *Gorgias* (514E).

STAGE TWO. The ontological implications of the categorial analysis are clearly stated in the *Categories*, probably for the first time.[32] Although Plato's doctrine of Forms is not mentioned in the treatise (which to this extent observes the principle of discretion exemplified in Aristotle's discussion of the Third Man in *Soph. El.* 22), no reader can fail to recognize the consequences of Aristotle's claim that the only true

---

[32] Arguments against the Forms are marshaled in the *De Ideis*, but it is not clear that any of them depend on Aristotle's own categorial scheme. The treatment of the Third Man argument in terms of predication (κατηγορεῖσθαι) in Ft. 4 Ross, seems to prepare the way for the categorial treatment in *Soph. El.* 22. My suggestion is that predication was at first dealt with separately in terms of the categories (Stage Zero and Stage One = *Topics* I–VIII) and in terms of the Third Man (*De Ideis*). *Soph. El.* 22 represents the point where the two treatments of predication converge. At *Soph. El.* 34 (184ᵇ2) Aristotle says he has been engaged in the study of reasoning 'for a long time'. Some of this time may have been spent on the *De Ideis*, as well as on the *Topics*. And the *Categories* probably belong in about the same period. All three—*Categories*, *Soph. El.* 22, and *De Ideis*—seem to be presupposed by the abrupt dismissal of the Forms in *Post. An.* 1.22. In this connection Professor E. Berti calls my attention to the use of πρός τι and ποσόν in *De Ideis* fr. 4 Ross (pp. 126 f.), as showing that the categorial scheme is in fact presupposed by these arguments. Now the distinction between καθ' αὐτό and πρός τι is Platonic (for the passages in the dialogues see Julia Annas, 1974: 266 n. 30); and it served as the basis for a kind of proto-theory of categories in the Academy. But the reference to ποσόν does presuppose Aristotle's own scheme, and if this reference came from the *De Ideis* it would indeed establish the priority of that scheme. However, Julia Annas has more plausibly suggested (1974: 268) that the comment in question was added by Alexander.

οὐσίαι—the only true entities or realities—are primary substances, sensible particulars like an individual man or horse. This anti-Platonic bias of the *Categories* is, as has often been noted, even more extreme than that of later works such as the *Metaphysics*, where, after his open and decisive break with Platonic doctrine, Aristotle is willing to reapply the term πρώτη οὐσία 'primary entity' to forms or essences (*Met.* Z. 1032^{b}2, 1037^{a}5, ^{a}29, ^{b}3, etc.). It is perhaps a mark of its 'early' date, reflecting a period when the break with Platonism was of central concern, that the terminology of the *Categories* so emphasizes Aristotle's commitment to an ontology that is just the reverse of Plato's. (And it is not merely a question of terminology: by recognizing the principle that 'knowledge is of the universal', the ontology of Aristotle's *Metaphysics* becomes in fact more 'Platonic' than that of the *Categories*. This is of course no reason for doubting the authenticity of the *Categories*. Whether the two doctrines of οὐσία are compatible is too large a question to discuss here, but in any case both conceptions are deeply imbedded within the *Metaphysics* itself.) Since concrete individuals are the basic subjects, of which everything else is predicated, 'if there were no primary substances it would be impossible for there to be anything else' (*Cat.* 2^{b}5). In the case of secondary substances like man or animal, the form of designation (τὸ σχῆμα τῆ ς προσηγορίας) seems to signify a concrete entity (τόδε τι), but in fact it rather signifies a quality (ποιόν τι). 'For the subject is not one, as in the case of primary substance, but man and animal are said of many [subjects]' (3^{b}16). The logical point made against the Third Man argument in *Soph. El.* 22 is thus reformulated in the context of a theory of substance or entity (οὐσία) where the ontological claim is unmistakable: no universal is a substance. The message for Platonism is clear, if still implicit. It is made explicit later, for example in *Metaphysics* Z.13 where Aristotle argues at length that no universal is a substance, for 'if we do not grant this there are many [undesirable] consequences, including the Third Man' (1039^{a}2); and there the immediate connection with the rejection of Forms is established in the following chapter (*Met.* Z.14).

Chapters 2–5 of the *Categories* offer a systematic exposition of Aristotle's theory of predication. In this theory, the subject–predicate relation is primarily ontological: the subjects (ὑποκε ίμενα) are *entities*; what is predicated of them are *properties* or *attributes*. In a secondary sense, the relation 'being predicated of' is also seen as semantic, in the technical sense of 'semantic' in modern logic: the *name* of an attribute or the *word* (ὄνομα) that designates it may be predicated of the *thing* that is subject (e.g. at 2ᵃ20–32). The subject–predicate relation is thus primarily a relation of thing to thing and secondarily a relation of thing to word. Aristotle never regards predication as a grammatical or linguistic relation of word to word, nor does he ever speak of subject and predicate as *concepts* united in judgment (though he does occasionally speak of judgment itself as the 'combination' or synthesis of concepts: σύνθεσις νοημάτων in *De Int.* 1, 16ᵇ12–14; ch. 3, 16ᵇ20–5; *De Anima* 430ᵃ28, συμκλοκὴνοημάτων at 432ᵃ11).³³ The application of the subject–predicate analysis, and with it the categories, to the theory of judgment and to the analysis of the proposition as expressed in words are both post-Aristotelian, although they are natural continuations of Aristotle's own line of thinking about these questions. As a matter of historical fact, the notion of categories as 'concepts' (νοήματα) is one that is simply unattested for Aristotle—just as unattested as the much later notion of grammatical 'categories' as word-classes. Aristotle does of course recognize Noun and Verb as what we would call word-classes. But he never calls them 'categories' nor does he connect them with the categorial scheme in any way. (On one occasion, however, he does allude to a connection between the grammatical noun–verb analysis of the sentence and his own theory of predication. At *De Int.* 3, 16ᵇ7–12 he remarks that the verb or ῥ ῆμα is always 'the sign of things said of something else', i.e. the sign of an attribute belonging to a subject. And in the same context he says of *is*—as copula verb—that it is not the sign of a thing or a fact, πρ ᾶγμα, but of a σύνθεσις: 'the sign of a composition which cannot be understood without the components', i. e. without the presence of subject and predicate term.³⁴)

---

³³ For these four distinct senses of 'predication' (syntactic, semantic, judgmental, and ontological), see Kahn (1973: 40–5). According to Passmore (1966: 247), three of these four senses were distinguished long ago by Cook Wilson.

³⁴ *De Int.* 16ᵇ22–5. For the development of this remark into the modern theory of the copula, above all by Abelard, see Kahn (1972). Note that in the context of *De Int.* 3 the exact status of the copulative σύνθεσις is not determined, but it is most naturally understood as the composition of the subject and predicate concepts in judgment, which 'indicates' (σημαίνει) or posits a combination of subject and predicate 'things' (ὄντα) in nature (i.e. in a fact or an entity), and is in turn 'indicated' or signified by the verb *is* in a sentence of the form *A is B*. Compare the words–thoughts–things relations articulated in *De Int.* 1.

In this fully developed theory of predication the categories are presented in a new way, to include subjects as well as predicates. Hence the term κατηγορία (with its suggestion that the scheme classifies only predicates or modes of predication) is avoided in the initial exposition, where the ten classes are introduced as collecting whatever is signified by 'things said without combination', i.e. by uncombined terms without the form of propositional unity. The result is to define the range of the categories as the domain of basic entities and properties, the *significata* of simple terms or basic words. This elimination of the reference to predicate position means that, in effect, the contents of the ten categories are now identified with the terms of Aristotle's syllogistic. (It is essential for the syllogism that its terms admit subject and predicate position indifferently, since at least one term in every syllogism must figure in both positions.) Another move in the direction of the 'scientific' applications of the scheme may perhaps be seen in the fact that only the four major categories are discussed in any detail, and their discussion seems to prepare the way for the analysis of different kinds of change and other topics (such as discrete and continuous quantity) that will be pursued in the *Physics*.

In one respect the doctrine of the *Categories* appears narrower than that of the *Topics*. We have seen that *Topics* 1.9 introduced a double construal of the scheme, which is presented first by keeping the subject constant and varying the question asked, and then by letting the subject range from category while the question remains a constant *what is it?* (τί ἐστι). Now the *Categories* makes almost exclusive use of the first construal. The *what-is-it?* question and the corresponding notion of essential predication (ἐν τῷ τί ἐστι κατηγορεῖσθαι) do not range over the categories but seem restricted to the category of substance. Hence the temptation might arise to regard the *Categories* as 'earlier' than the generalization of essential predication in *Topics* 1.9, and even to regard it as representing the primitive Stage Zero of the doctrine which we found missing from the extant works. But this view would certainly be mistaken. There are many indications that the *Categories* cannot provide the 'original' formulation of the theory that is presupposed in the *Topics*. For one thing, the characteristic title τὰ γένη τῶν κατηγοριῶν 'kinds of predications' is never used in this treatise and, as we have observed, the term κατηγορία itself does not appear when the categories are introduced in chapter 4. Yet the *Categories* cannot belong to a period *before* this terminology came into use; the treatise shows familiarity with the derivative use of κατηγορία in which it does not designate 'predication' or 'predicate' as such but serves to replace the fuller construction 'kind of predication' (γένος τῶν κατηγοριῶν), i.e. as an abbreviated designation for what we call a 'category'. (Compare *Cat.* 8, 10^{b}19–23 with *Topics* 103^{b}25, 27, 29, 39. The term κατηγορία also occurs in its primary sense of 'predication' in *Cat.* 5, 3^{a}35–7.) This initial avoidance of the standard terminology is of course no accident in the *Categories*: it hangs together with the explicit inclusion of primary substances in the first category, which is therefore no longer a genus of *predicates*. (The same innovation explains why the question *what is it?* is not used here as a designation for the first category. The designation of a primary substance as such, by pointing or even by pronouncing a proper name, would not normally count as an answer to that question.) Because the theory of the *Categories* emphasizes the role of individual substances as the fundamental subjects which underlie all predication, it neglects the pursuit of essence or definition (τί ἐστι) for categories other than substance as a merely distracting consideration. But although the *Categories* does not focus on this wider notion of essential predication, it does recognize the existence of such predication outside the first category. 'Being predicated in the essence' (ἐν τῷ τί ἐστι κατηγορεῖσθαι) does not appear under this title in the *Categories*, which speaks instead of 'being said of a subject' (καθ' ὑποκειμένου λέγεσθαι) in a special narrow sense. But this concept is illustrated in *Categories* 2 by an example from the genus of quality: 'knowledge is said of grammar as of a subject' (1^{b}2), that is, it is predicated in answer to the question *What is grammar?* Hence the curious deviations of the *Categories* cannot be explained by assuming that it is more 'primitive' than the theory of the *Topics*. If accidental or cross-categorial predication is presented here under the rather unusual title of 'being present in a subject' (ἐν ὑποκ ειμένῳ εἶναι), this choice of terminology is presumably motivated by a desire to underline the ontological dependence of all other categories upon substance, and ultimately upon primary substance. (Outside of the *Categories*, the phrase 'being present in a subject' seems to occur in this sense only in the *Topics* 127^{b}1–4 and

132^{b}20 ff.) For what is present in a subject is 'incapable of being apart (χωρίς) from that in which it is present' (1^{a}25). Thus the χωρισμός or separate existence of Forms like Justice, Whiteness, Equality or Magnitude is ruled out by definition.

It is in the *Posterior Analytics* that these deeper philosophical consequences of the categorial analysis are for the first time openly and explicitly drawn. (For present purposes I ignore the possibility that some parts of the *Metaphysics* may be 'older' than the *Analytics*.) Demonstrative science is said not to require that there be Forms or 'some unity besides the many [particulars]': it requires only that we be able to predicate 'one thing truly of many' (77^{a}5). It is above all in chapter 22 of *Posterior Analytics* I that Aristotle pushes the theory of the *Categories* to its logical conclusion: 'Whatever does not indicate (σημαίνει) substance must be predicated of some subject, and there is nothing white that is not something else [essentially, substantially] which is white [as an attribute]. For we bid farewell to the Forms. They are mere twirpings; and even if they exist, they do not contribute to this discussion [of predication and scientific knowledge]. For demonstrations are concerned with terms like these [viz. substances and their attributes]' (83^{a}30–5). Plato's theory of Forms was required to account for the objects of knowledge and the ontological conditions of true and false discourse. (See, e.g. *Parmenides* 135 B5–C2.) Now that Aristotle has provided his own theory of scientific knowledge based on the syllogism and his own account of predication according to the categories, he can finally say goodbye to the Forms. The theory is not only incoherent (according to his own reading of the Third Man argument, quoted above); it is also superfluous.

The *Analytics* seem to develop another aspect of the categorial scheme which was not conspicuous in the *Topics* and the *Categories* but which is of great importance for the later history of the doctrine. This is the conception of the categories as the ultimate univocal predicates, the widest genera, each one the highest branch in a Porphyry tree (or in a converging cluster of Porphyry trees) of species-genus terms of increasing generality. The notion that predication is transitive within such a chain is familiar from the *Topics*. ('All the higher genera are predicated of the lower ones', *Topics* VI.5, 143^{a}21; cf. 122^{a}3–7.) Also familiar is the idea that terms like *being* (ὄν) and *one*, because they apply to every item in every category, do not form a genus in the logical sense required for definition (121^b4-8, 127^a26-34; cf. 130^b17). But 'a genus is predicated synonymously of all the species' (127^b6). From all this it might be natural to conclude that the categories themselves, the 'genera of predications', would be the widest genera of definition, the last term of essential transitive predication. But Aristotle himself does not say so in the *Topics*, and perhaps he never says this explicitly anywhere in the *Organon*. The most likely explanation of this fact is that the definitional notion of 'genus', derived from Plato and enshrined in the fourfold scheme of predicables, was originally quite distinct from Aristotle's new notion of 'genus of predication' according to the tenfold scheme of categories.[35] A 'genus of predication' is not, as such, a genus for classifying anything but predicates or attributes. But as the categorial scheme was recast in Stage Two to embrace all the 'things' (ὄντα) signified by simple words, the two notions of 'genus' naturally began to fuse into one. This fusion is probably never complete; perhaps the closest Aristotle himself ever comes to identifying the two is a statement in *Met. Δ*. 28, where difference 'according to the form of predication of being' (καθ' ἕτερον σχῆμα κατηγορίας τοῦ ὄντος) is mentioned as one way of *differing in kind* or *in genus* (ἕτερα τῷ γένει λέγεσθαι, 1024^b10-16). But some fusion of categorial and classificatory genus seems to be implicit by the time we get to *Prior Analytics* I.27. Here Aristotle divides all 'things' (ὄντα) into (1) sensible particulars, that cannot be properly predicated of anything else but are natural subjects for predication, (2) universals, that can be predicated of other subjects and serve as subjects of predication in turn, and (3) the uppermost terms or 'things' that can serve only as predicates for demonstration (43^a25-43). It is difficult to see how these ultimate universals, the upper bounds of strict predication, can be anything other than the categorial genera, the final answer to the *What-is-it?* question for an item within each category. But Aristotle does not make this clear; he reserves an explanation for later (43^a37).

The promised explanation comes in *Posterior Analytics* I.19–22 and most directly in I.22, in the passage immediately following the outspoken rejection of the Forms which we have quoted (from 83^a30-5).

---

[35] See Kapp (1920), 226–8.

Aristotle is here considering whether chains of predication can go on to infinity or whether they must be limited at both ends. The categories are mentioned in connection with the argument that the chain of predicates will not be infinite in the 'upward' direction of increasing universality. 'For of each subject will be predicated what indicates[36] some quality or some quantity or something of this sort or its essential attributes (τὰ ἐν τῇ οὐσίᾳ). But the latter are limited, and the kinds (γένη) of predications are limited. For [these are] either quality or quantity or relation or acting or being-acted-on or where or when' (83^{b}13–17). The first striking feature of this passage is that Aristotle lists only eight categories, with a clear suggestion that the list is complete. The 'anthropocentric' categories of Having and Posture have dropped out of sight, never to reappear. But the second point, which concerns us directly, is that the fact that the number of categories is limited will not prove Aristotle's conclusion, unless the chain of transitive predication is limited within each category. And this can only be so, it would seem, if the category itself is the most universal predicate, the final member of each chain.[37] It is remarkable, however, that Aristotle himself does not say this, neither here nor elsewhere as far as I can see. One is led to suspect that, in some sense, the categories as such were not conceived as proper predicates at all, and certainly not as true genera for definition. At least one passage in the *Metaphysics* seems expressly to deny that 'substance' (οὐσία) is a genus, just as 'being' and 'one' are not.[38] The later notion of the categories as 'primary genera' (πρῶτα γένη) or 'most generic terms' (τὰ γενικ ώτατα) is certainly not

---

[36] σημαίνει. For difficulties in interpreting the term see above, pp. 255 ff.

[37] This is the interpretation of Ross (1949: 384 and 578 f.): 'Aristotle's main purpose is to maintain the limitation of the chain of predication at both ends, beginning with an individual substance and ending with the name of a category' (p. 578). Ross' reference to the *name* of a category is a mistake, a mistake for which Aristotle must bear partial responsibility because of his inconsistent use of the term σημαίνειν. For the view of the categories as highest predicates see Brentano (1862: 102 ff.), with references to Philoponus and others in n. 118, p. 107.

[38] *Met.* 1.2, 1053^{b}22–4, οὔτε τὸ ἐν γένος ἐνδέχεται εἶναι ... οὐδὲ τὸ ὂν οὐδὲ τὴν οὐσίαν. Note that in *Met.* B. 3,998^{b}15–18 the expressions τὰ πρῶτα τῶν γενῶν and τὰ ἀνωτάτω τῶν γενῶν form part of a Platonic doctrine that is being refuted. Occasionally, however, the term γένος alone (where it is not necessarily an abbreviation for γένος τῶν κατηγοριῶν) is certainly used to refer to Aristotle's own categories: *De Anima* 402^{a}23, 412^{a}6; perhaps *Post. An.* 96^{b}19. And compare Brentano (1862: 101), who cites parallel texts in n. 93.

in accord with the letter of Aristotle's treatment, and probably not faithful to its spirit either.

Before passing to the third and final stage of Aristotle's doctrine, we must note another, even more fateful innovation of the *Analytics*. This is the use of the categorial scheme to indicate the diversity of the predicative link itself. 'That X belongs to Y and that X is true of Y must be taken in as many ways as the categories are distinguished.... And similarly for *not belonging*' (*Prior An.* 1.37, 49ᵃ6–8). Since the preceding chapter of the *Prior Analytics* has specified that *belonging* is to be understood 'in as many ways as *being* is said and as *it is true to say that X is Y*', we stand here on the threshold of the multivocity of being: the doctrine that there are as many kinds of 'things' (ὄντα) as there are categories. This final, fully ontological application of the scheme is not formulated until Stage Three, as represented in *Metaphysics* Δ.7. Yet in a sense the ontological application is latent throughout the more purely 'logical' use of the categories in the *Organon*. It is suggested by the doctrine of the *Topics* that 'being' (τὸ ὄν) is not a genus.[39] It is perhaps even more clearly hinted at in the *Categories*, insofar as the categorial classification is understood there as a division of ὄντα or 'things' (cf. *Cat.* 2, 1ᵃ20). The passages just quoted from the *Prior Analytics* go one step farther, but they stop short of the fully ontological formulation. What is stated in these passages is not that there are as many kinds of 'things' as there are categories, but simply that when in formulating a syllogistic premiss we say *X is Y* or *Y belongs to X*, the uniformity of propositional form may conceal a diversity of logical relations between the terms, and the categories can serve to articulate this diversity. *X is Y* does not always mean that Y is a direct or essential predicate of X; it may be a quality or a relation, and these categorial distinctions may be taken 'conditionally or absolutely, either alone or in combination' (48ᵃ8). As an example Aristotle cites the case where one syllogistic term is *there is one science* and the other term is *contraries of one another*. To say that the former belongs to the latter is not simply to say that contraries are one science but rather

---

[39] The doctrines of the *Topics* that τὸ ὄν is not a genus, and that a genus is predicated synonymously of its species (127ᵇ6), do not together entail that τὸ ὄν is predicated homonymously. But the suggestion is a natural one; and it seems to have been made by others before Aristotle: see below, n. 41.

'that it is true to say *of them* (κατ' αὐτῶν) that there is one science of them' (48ᵃ5–9). The point is not that science and contraries are 'things' belonging to different categories (for contraries as such are not classified within any one category), but rather that beneath the single syllogistic scheme *Y belongs to X* there is a complex predicative relation that can be analyzed by means of the categories. Here as elsewhere in the logical works, the categorial scheme serves to reveal the diversity of logical structures beneath a surface similarity of formulation. (By diversity of logical structure I mean a difference that affects either the truth value of a given proposition or the valid inferences that may be drawn from it.)

In two respects, however, these passages from *Prior Analytics* I. 36–7 point to the metaphysical application which characterizes the next stage of the doctrine. In the first place the scheme is explicitly connected with the analysis of ποσαχῶς λέγεται 'in how many ways [a given item] is said'.[40] And in the second place, the verb *to be* (εἶναι) is introduced to indicate an item whose diversity can be analyzed by means of the scheme. No 'earlier' statement that being is 'said in many ways' establishes this direct connection with the categorial analysis.[41]

STAGE THREE. The final conception of the categories as 'genera of beings' or, more typically as 'categories [literally 'predications'] of being'[42] is found throughout the scientific treatises of Aristotle, in

---

[40] This continues, but goes beyond, the use of the categories in *Topics* 1.15 to show that *good* is homonymous (107ᵃ11). The novelty in *Pr. An.* 1.37 is that the categories are invoked not only to show that a term is used in different ways (πλεοναχῶ s at *Topics* 106ᵇ30, etc.) but also to specify in just how many ways (ποσαχῶ s). There is at most a hint of this at *Topics* 106ᵃ2–8. (For the distinction between homonymy and 'being said in many ways', see note 47 below.)

[41] Perhaps the closest 'earlier' anticipation of the multivocity of *being* is in *Soph. El.* 33: οἱ δὲ τὸν Ζήνωνος λόγον καὶ Παρμενίδου λύουσι διὰ τὸ πολλαχῶς φ άναι τὸὲν λέγεσθαι καὶ τὸ ὄν (182ᵇ26) 'Some [i.e. other than Aristotle himself?] refute the argument of Zeno and Parmenides by claiming that *one* and *being* are said in many ways.' On this see Kapp (1920: p. 252 n. 42), who also cites the *Soph. El.* passages where ἁπλῶς εἶναι is distinguished from εἶναι τι: 166ᵇ22, 166ᵇ37–167ᵃ20, 168ᵇ11–16, 169ᵇ10–12, 180ᵃ23–ᵇ39. Cf. *De Int.* 21ᵃ25–33. None of these passages applies the categorial scheme to the multivocity of εἶναι.

[42] The expression γένη τῶν ὄντων never appears as such, in the plural, but at *De Anima* II.1, 412ᵃ6 substance is described as γένος ἔν τι τῶν ὄντων (cf. 402ᵃ23). The more common phrase is κατηγορίαι τοῦ ὄντος: see *Physics* III.1, 200ᵇ28; *Gen. Corr.* 1.3, 317ᵇ6; *Met. Θ.* 1, 1045ᵇ28. Also note σχῆμα κατηγορίας τοῦ ὄντος (*Met. Δ.* 28, 1024ᵇ13). All of these formulae depend upon the fuller expression τὸ ὄν λέγεται κατ ἀτὰ σχήματα τῶν κατηγοριῶν (*Met.* 1051ᵃ34; cf. 1017ᵃ23, 1026ᵃ36).

contrast to the logical works grouped together in the *Organon* where this view of the categories is not fully articulated. This ontological conception coincides with the use of the categorial scheme to distinguish how '*being* is said in may ways': the classification of 'beings' is carried out by distinguishing the ways in which *being* is said. Thus in the first book of the *Physics* this conception of the categories serves to refute Eleatic monism: for '*being* is said in many ways' (185^a21), but Parmenides and others have made the false assumption that '*being* is said in one way' or 'said simply' (185^b31, 186^a24). In *Physics* III.1 the same principle is used to classify the kinds of motion or change, 'for there are as many species ($\check{\epsilon}$ ἴδη) of change as there are of being' (201^a9, after the statement that there is nothing outside the scheme of categories; cf. 225^b5–16, 226^a23 ff., 227^b6, etc.). The categorical division thus serves to distinguish coming-to-be and passing-away, as substantial change, from more superficial changes of place, size, or quality (*De Generatione et Corruptione* 319^a3–18; cf. 317^b5–11). In the *De Anima* the scheme is presupposed as a device for preparing the definition of the psyche by locating it within the 'genus of beings' identified as substance (412^a6; cf. 402^a23–5). In the *Eudemian Ethics* the doctrine is invoked in an argument against the Platonic Form of Good: *good* does not constitute a single thing, since 'it is said in many ways and in just as many ways as *being*' (1217^b25 ff.); and this argument is repeated almost verbatim in the *Nicomachean Ethics* (1096^a17–29). But it is above all in the *Metaphysics* that Aristotle makes systematic use of the categories of being, not so much to refute Plato's doctrine as to establish his own conception of First Philosophy as the study of 'being qua being' (τὸ ὄν ᾗ ὄν).

The most fundamental (and for our purposes the 'earliest') statement of this fully ontological view of the categories is found in *Metaphysics* Delta, the book which is specifically devoted to τὰ πολλαχῶ s λεγόμενα 'things said in many ways'. Chapter 7 deals with the multivocity of 'being' or 'what is':

Being is said, first, per accidens and, next, per se. . . . Things said *to be* per se are as many as things indicated by the figures of predication (τὰ σχήματα τῆς κατηγορίας). For in as many ways as these are said, in so many ways does *to be* (εἶναι) indicate. Now since of things predicated some indicate *what it is* (τί ἐστι), some indicate *of what quality* (ποιόν), some indicate *how much* (ποσόν), some *in relation to what*, some *to act* or *to be acted upon*, some *where*, some *when*, *to be* indicates the same as each of these. For there is no difference between *A man is healthy* and *A man enjoys health* [viz. with the predicate *is healthy* expressed by a single verb form ὑγιαίνει, in contrast to the preceding expression by copula and participle ὑγιαίνων ἐστίν], nor between *A man is walking* or *is cutting* and *A man walks* or *cuts*; and similarly in the other cases. (1017ᵃ22–30)

With one exception, I have rendered this passage as literally as possible, to avoid imposing upon it our own more abstract terminology and our practice of distinguishing between the use and mention of expressions. The exception is the verb σημαίνειν which I have translated throughout as *to indicate*, whereas the more literal rendering might be *to signify*. I have avoided the latter precisely because it could convey the misleading impression that Aristotle is here distinguishing—or attempting to distinguish—between linguistic signs and their 'meanings' or 'denotations'.[43] Quotation marks are not in order here, insofar as these would imply that Aristotle is mentioning the verb *to be* and asserting that it has so many different 'senses' or 'uses'. In fact he is not so much talking about the verb *to be* as, about being or beings, things that are said to be, things as described in different ways. And he expressly claims that the relevant distinctions do not depend in any way upon whether or not the verb *to be* occurs in the description.

Of course Aristotle is concerned here as elsewhere with linguistic formulations, both as masking ontological (or logical) distinctions and as exhibiting distinctions that are not logically significant. But the point of his denying that there is any difference between the noun-verb formulation *A man walks* and the noun-copula-participle form *A man is walking* is precisely to insist that neither *is* nor any form of *to be* need appear in an illustration of 'the many ways in which being is said'. It would be ridiculous to suppose that a sentence like *A man walks* or *A man cuts* illustrates a sense of the verb *to be*! But these sentences do illustrate a figure or form of the predication of being, namely a predication in the category of Action (ποιεῖν). Aristotle relies here on the fact that in Greek the linguistic force of the noun-copula-participle sentence does not stand in sharp grammatical contrast with

---

[43] See the discussion of σημαίνει above, pp. 255 ff.

the simple noun–verb sentence, as do the corresponding forms in English, where the two represent, in effect, distinct tenses. This use of the present periphrastic construction in Greek, which is idiomatic though not very common, provides a convenient device for introducing the verb *is* where it would otherwise not occur, and it thus furnishes Aristotle with a kind of canonical notation to make clear how 'being' or 'what is' is present in, and diversified among, the whole range of categories, regardless of the idiomatic form of the linguistic expression.[44] We may note, incidentally, that the eight categories mentioned here in *Δ*.7 are the same as those listed in *Posterior Analytics* I.22, 83[b]15–17, where, as we saw, the reference to a limited number (πεπέρανται) suggests that the list is complete.

A recent commentator on this passage asks whether Aristotle here means 'to distinguish and classify (1) different ways of understanding propositions of the form "*X* is *F*" or (2) different senses of the word "exist"' (Kirwan, 1971: 141). Neither of these alternatives seems faithful to Aristotle's primary intention, though each gives us a partial insight into the consequences of his analysis. The first suggestion comes closer to Aristotle's aim, if we take '*X* is *F*' as the general form for propositions or assertions. The verb *to be* in Greek, and notably its participle ὄν, can express any form of reality and any type of sentential truth-claim. The strategy of Aristotle's categorial analysis is to reveal the subject–predicate structure of reality underlying every true propositional claim of the elementary or first-order language canvassed by the categories. His aim is to distinguish the 'things' or 'beings' which constitute this structure into 'entities' (οὐσίαι) and 'attributes' (ὑπάρχοντα) and to classify the 'attributes' according to the eight

---

[44] For this 'canonical rewriting' of all sentences in copula form, see Kahn (1973: 212–17). For the idiomatic use of the present periphrastic in Greek, ibid. 134–41. In Greek the simple present tense βαδίζει corresponds in use to the English progressive *is walking*, as well as to the simple present *walks*. The Greek periphrastic form generally exploits some stylistic nuance associated with the copula: asseverative, existential, or stative-locative. For an example of the latter compare Plato, *Meno* 84A3, οὗ ἐστι ἤδη βαδίζων ὅδε (τοῦ ἀναμιμν ἤσκεσθαι), literally 'where he is now in his walking', i.e. how far he has got (in his process of recollection). Aristotle simply ignores the stylistic nuance and treats the two forms as logically equivalent. Indeed, the two expressions represent a single logical structure. That is to say, it makes no difference either to the truth value or to the logical consequences of the assertion whether one says (in Greek) *Socrates walks* or *Socrates is walking*: the latter (ἔστι βαδίζων) can be read simply as an emphatic version of the former.

modes of predication. All 'entities' belong of course in the first category; their initial characterization was given by the doctrine of
'primary substance' in the *Categories*, and the central books of the
Metaphysics will be devoted to a deeper analysis. Among their attributes, some are also 'substantial': these belong to an entity or substance
in virtue of what it is and hence they specify just *what it is*, ὅπερ ἐστίν.
(As the *Topics* put it, they are 'predicated in the essence ἐν τῷ τί ἐστι' of
the subject.) The other attributes are divided according to the seven
remaining categories. If we think of '*X* is *F*' as the general predicative
form for *X* as a substance, we can say that the classification of per se
being in *Δ*.7 is a classification of eight types of attribution (or eight kinds
of attributes) corresponding to eight different substitution classes of
values for the complex variable 'is *F*'.[45] On the other hand if we
translate ὄντα as 'existents', then we can say that by distinguishing a
class of entities and eight kinds of attributes Aristotle has distinguished
eight kinds of existents. (There are only eight, not nine distinct kinds;
the being of the substantial attributes, the species and genus of a
substance, is not different from the being of the substance itself.) If
we insist on the formal mode, we can even rephrase this as a distinction
between eight senses of *exist*. But the artificial nature of this rewriting
of Aristotle's text should be clear from the examples he gives (where *is*
occurs as copula verb), and from his statement that 'it makes no
difference' whether or not the various types of being are expressed
by the verb *to be*.

By calling attention to the logical equivalence of the two sentence
forms *X* is *Y* and *XY's* (where *Y's* is a finite verb form), Aristotle makes
clear that his classification of beings or kinds of being according to the
categories will apply to all sentences of both forms, i.e. to all simple
sentences in the language. And this naturally follows from the way the
scheme was introduced in the *Categories*, as classifying 'things signified'

---

[45] More exactly, the *F*'s are divided by the categorial scheme into eight classes, each of
which determines a distinct value for *is*. This assumes that the subject *X* is a particular
substance. If we let *X* range over the categories and choose *F* each time from the same
category, we of course get the same eight classes of *F* but the value of *is* apparently remains
constant. So this is not the most illuminating point of view from which to understand
Aristotle's claim that *being* (or *what is*) is said in all these different ways.

(or 'things indicated') by all uncombined words, by all subject and predicate terms.

In the *Categories*, the verb σημαίνειν ('signify' or 'indicate') expresses a relation between the various categories and the λεγόμενα or 'things said'.[46] In the context of *Categories* 2 and 4, it is natural to take the 'things said' as the expressions which Aristotle offers as examples: *man, horse, white*, etc. Thus it would be the word *man* which signifies a substance, the word *white* signifies a quality, and so on. But although this is the natural reading for us, it is not the only possible one. The λεγόμενα or 'things said' can also be the concept *man* or the entity *human being* (as described by the word or as intended by the concept). Aristotle's semantic vocabulary is so impoverished, and he shows so little interest in using it carefully, that any commentator is obliged to rewrite the doctrine to some extent in order to give a clear and coherent exposition. Now if we take σημαίνειν in *Categories* 2 and 4 to express a word–thing relation, we will of course expect the verb to represent the same relation in Met. *Δ*. 7. But that makes Aristotle say that the word *to be* (εἶαι) signifies in as many ways as the categories (1017[a]24 and 27). So it is not only the twentieth-century prevalence of the linguistic turn or the philosophical attraction of 'semantic ascent' that tempts a modern reader to understand the doctrine of πολλαχῶςλεγόμενα as an account of different senses for the word *being* or *to be*.

Nevertheless, as I have argued, this reading of *Δ*.7 cannot be entirely correct. Here as often, σημαίνει serves in different occurrences to express different aspects of a complex semantic relationship that includes among its terms not only the word *being* and the ten categories but also the items predicated in each category (τὰ κατηγορούμενα at 1017[a]25), and these 'things predicated' include the actions of walking and cutting, but not the words *walk* and *cut*. Neither the categories themselves nor the 'things' they classify can be properly identified as linguistic expressions. And, as we have seen, even the 'being' that signifies or indicates in all these ways need not be expressed by an occurrence of the verb *to be*, although thanks to a normalizing participial periphrasis it may be so expressed in each case.

---

[46] *Cat.* 4, 1[b]25, τῶν κατὰ μηδεμίαν συμπλοκὴν λεγομένων ἕκαστον ἤτοι οὐσίαν σημαίνει ἤποσὸν ἤποιὸν κτλ.

In order to clarify this obscurely semantic use of the verb σημαίνειν in Δ.7 we may consider a related passage where Aristotle proves that he can be clear and precise in such matters when he chooses. In *Categories* I he tells us exactly what he means by ὁμώνυμα or 'things said in several ways'.[47] When things have only a name in common but the definition [literally 'the account of what the thing is', ὁ λόγος τῆς οὐσίας] which corresponds to the name is different, they are called *homonymous*.[48] Thus it is things, not expressions, that are homonymous. And to some extent it is also things, not expressions, that are said in many ways. The homonymy of *being* would consist in the fact that many things were said to 'be', or called *beings*, that had only the name in common. As Aristotle will point out in *Met. Γ*. 2, since the diverse beings of the categories have more than a name in common, they are not strictly homonymous. But they are nonetheless 'said in many ways', for they certainly satisfy the second clause in the definition of homonymy. The diverse kinds of beings, or the various ways in which they are said to 'be', do not have any single definition or any single account (λόγος) of what it is for them to 'be'. The account will differ for each category: for 'walking' or 'cutting' to be is to be an action; for 'white' to be is to be a color, and hence a quality; for Socrates or Coriscus to be is to be a man, and hence a primary entity or substance.

---

[47] I assume that in the contexts so far discussed Aristotle uses the terms ὁμώνυμα and πολλαχῶς λεγόμενα more or less interchangeably, as for example in *Topics* 1.15. (Compare ποσαχῶς at 106ᵃ2, πολλαχῶς at 106ᵃ9, 11, 14 and 19, but ὁμώνυμον at ᵃ21–2. Similarly we have πλεοναχῶς at 106ᵇ1, ὁμώνυμον at ᵇ4 and ᵇ8, πλεοναχῶς again at ᵇ14, and so throughout.) When we come to *Met. Γ*. 2, it is obvious that (λέγεται) πολλαχῶς is distinguished from ὁμωνύμως, since the former is asserted and the latter denied for τὸ ὄν. But this is a terminological innovation, implying a special, narrow sense for ὁμωνύμως. It is true that the narrow sense was in fact implied by the word μόνον in the definition of *Categories* 1, but Aristotle seems rarely to have taken account of this implication in uses 'earlier' than *Γ*.2.

Once the distinction between multivocity in general (πολλαχῶς λεγόμενα) and the special case of merely verbal homonymy (ὁμώνυμα in the strictest sense) has been clearly drawn, Aristotle of course applies it systematically in the discussion of focal meaning. Hintikka (1973: 6–7) lists three passages from the *Metaphysics* where the terminology of Gamma 2 is presupposed (Z.4, 1030ᵃ29 ff.; Θ.1, 1046ᵃ4–7; K.3, 1060ᵇ3 1 ff.), and one passage elsewhere (*De Ger., et Corr*. 1.6, 322ᵇ29 ff.) where the same distinction might either be presupposed or just coming into view. The same is true for *Physics* VII.4, 249ᵃ21–5 (cited by Hintikka, 1973: 17f.). In the mature usage represented by *Met. Γ*. 2, it seems clear that every case of homonymy is also a case of πολλαχῶς λεγόμενα, but not conversely.

[48] This is Ackrill's translation of the first sentence of the *Categories*, slightly adapted. It seems to me redundant to render λόγος τῆς οὐσίας as 'definition of being'.

But since 'being' itself is no genus, there is no common character that can be cited in the λόγος τῆς οὐσίας, the account that answers the question 'what is it for this to *be*?' for all the categories at once, or even for any two.[49]

Like homonymy, 'being said in many ways' (πολλαχῶς λέγεσθαι) is a threefold relation between (1) a single word or phrase or (in this case) a family of 'paronymous' verbal forms, like *being* *is*, and *to be*,[50] (2) a plurality of diverse things to which the word is applied, and (3) a different account of what the thing is corresponding to for each application, that is, corresponding to each kind of thing to which the word applies. This third item is what we might call a distinct 'sense' of the term, or a distinct 'concept' that it expresses; but Aristotle calls it simply the λόγος τῆς οὐσίας, the account or statement of what it is for something to be *X* (where *X* is the term under discussion). This triple relation structures Aristotle's account of τὰ πολλαχῶς λεγόμενα in *Metaphysics* Delta. Each chapter of the book is unified by (1) its concern with a single term *X* (in our case τὸ ὄν or εἶναι). It is diversified by (2) the variety of kinds or classes of things to which *X* applies. And Aristotle endeavors to clarify this diversity by (3) giving an account or definition of *X* for each application, an acccount which specifies

---

[49] One might object that for every category except substance the common answer might be: for them to 'be' is to be an attribute (ὑπάρχον) or accident (συμβεβηκός) of substance. But although this answer would be true, it apparently does not count as a proper answer to the τί ἐστι question, since no term that applies in more than one category can be predicated univocally across categorial boundaries. The term *accident* thus has the same special, extra-categorial status as *cause, form, matter, potency* and *act*. And of course the term *category* or *predication of being* has this same status, as does the term *being* itself.

[50] For the notion of paronymy, see *Categories* 1. Paronymy is a four-term relation between two things *A* and *B* and the two corresponding words 'A' and 'B' (the 'names' of these things), such that 'A' differs from 'B' by a minor morphological deviation, for example by the change of a suffix, and *B* is in some sense prior to *A* (with reference to these names). In that case *A* is a paronym of (is named from, or has its name taken from) *B*. Thus the grammarian is a paronym of grammar (or, in the formal mode, 'grammarian' is a paronym of 'grammar'), and the brave man is a paronym of bravery. In this sense, all beings (ὄντα) are paronyms of entity or substance (οὐσίαι). But this linguistic relationship of paronymy is not at all the same thing as focal meaning: πρὸς ἓν λέγεσ θ αι as some earlier commentators assumed. For the linguistic relation between ὄντα and οὐσία, or between both and εἶναι, would be exactly the same even if all beings so designated had only the name (i.e. cognate names) in common. In other words, paronymy is compatible with sheer homonymy, since it does not require that *A* and *B* share anything beyond a cognate name. Compare Ackrill (1963: 72 f.).

what it means in this particular case for the thing to be called X. In analyzing the diversity of τ ὄν καθ' αὐτό 'what is per se' or 'being proper'[51] in *Met. Δ*. 7 he offers not a definition but a reference to the scheme of categories. If we are to give a full exegesis of Aristotle's procedure, we must bear in mind that (2) and (3) are not identical. On the one hand (3), the account of the different applications, is given by the list of eight categories (completed by some characterization of each, such as the detailed account given for four of them in *Categories* 5–8). But (2), the things to which *being* applies, are not the eight categories as such but the entities and attributes they classify—not substance but Socrates, Coriscus, man, and animal; not quality but white, black, round, square, knowledge, justice, etc.; not action but walking, running, cutting, and so forth. Thus the three factors in the full relationship are (1) the term *being*, (2) the full range of entities and attributes, and (3) the division into eight categories, with some account of each one.

It is this complexity that is masked or (to put it less kindly) muddled by Aristotle's free and easy use of the term σημαίνειν. And the complexity is increased by the fact that he is concerned not only with the actual use of *to be*, for example in normal copula sentences, but also

---

[51] The interpretation of the contrast between 'being per accidens' and 'being per se' in *Met. Δ*. 7, 1017ᵃ–22 is extremely difficult, and it is rare to find two commentators who agree here. As Kapp (1920: 224 n) says, the terms κατὰ συμβεβηκός and καθ' αὐτό notoriously belong to those whose meaning in Aristotle can only be established by the context; but in this case the context is not very helpful. I persist in the view (shared by Kapp and in effect by Gillespie too) that the clue is to be found in *Post. An.* 1.22, where κατὰ συμβεβηκς κατηγορεῖν is opposed to κατηγορεῖνἁπλῶς as random predication (without regard to the logical status of subject and predicate) to predication in canonical form, according to the scheme of the categories, with substance as the subject of discourse. For a recent discussion of the problem see J. W. Thorp (1974) who believes the solution just proposed is untenable in view of the fact that two of Aristotle's examples of being per accidens are in the proper form: *a man is musical* (1017ᵃ9, 14). In both cases, however, this proper form is treated as equivalent to its converse: *the musical (one) is a man*, that is to say, the essential distinction is disregarded. From the point of view of extension, and hence of example, predication in good form is of course a special case of random predication.

   If, as I suggest, καθ' αὐτά εἶναι here is to be understood by reference to κατηγορεῖσθ αι ἁπλῶς in *Post. An.* 1.22, then the meaning is: things are said to be per se in as many ways as attributes are predicated of subjects, that is, in the various ways distinguished by the scheme of categories (with a substance as subject of predication). Seven of these eight ways will of course be εἶναι κατὰ συμβεβηκός in terms of another contrast, in which only substance is ὄν καθ' αὐτό; see e.g. *Met. Z*. 1, 1028ᵃ20–31.

with potential uses (we might say, with 'zero uses') of the verb in sentences that can be rewritten in copula form. He is concerned, in short, with predication or attribution in general (for that is what *being* means here), and not with the verb as such. He is also concerned with what we would call the *existence* of subjects and attributes, but the notion of existence is conceived in such a way as to be fully absorbed into the analysis of attribution, as we shall see. With all this in mind we may try to give a more accurate account of what is intended by σημαίνειν in our passage from Δ.7 as follows. I give an interpretive paraphrase after each section of the translation (using 'indicate' for σημαίνειν throughout).

'Things said to be per se ('said to be in their own right') are as many as are indicated by the figures of predication.' The 'things' in question correspond to (2), the full set of entities and attributes. These are numbered (ὅσα) in eight classes, as 'indicated' or 'signified' by (3) the eight categories or forms of predication. To all of the items in (2) is (or may be) applied (1) the term *being*, but in the eight distinct ways specified by (3). Aristotle is here developing, by means of his own categories, a lesson taught by Plato in the *Sophist*: to be is always to be something-or-other. (Compare Owen, 1965, 2: 76 f.) There is no intelligible concept of being or existence in general, which is not the being of something definite. Hence to be is always to be something definite. With regard to the beings envisaged here, to be (or to exist) is always to be a substance, to be a quality, or to be a member of some other category. (This leaves many questions open: for example, in what way can essences or matter and form be said to be? But to answer such questions the doctrine of categories is not enough. We need other concepts of being, such as potency and act.)

'For in as many ways as [these] are said, in so many ways does *to be* indicate.' The term *being* applies to all items in (2), but in the eight distinct ways (τοσαυταχῶς) marked by (3).[52] The subject of 'these are

---

[52] In the second clause, (beginning ὁσαχῶς at 1017ᵃ23) the subject of λέγεται is the categories or the categorial items, whereas the subject of σημαίνει is the term εἶναι. The verb σημαίνει thus covers both the denotation of all categorial items by the verb *to be* and the eight connotations or 'ways' of denoting which are here distinguished (τοσαυταχῶς). The same is true for σημαίνει in the preceding clause (1017ᵃ23), where (*pace* Kirwan) the subject of the verb is the categories (τὰ σχήματα τῆς κατηγορίας).

said' (λέγεται) should properly be all the entities and attributes in (2), but of course as diversely said according to (3) the categorial scheme (ὁσαχῶς).

'Now since of things predicated (τῶν κατηγορουμένων) some indicate *what it is*, some indicate *of what quality*, some indicate *how much*, some *in relation to what*, some *to act* or *to be acted upon*, some *where*, some *when*, *to be* indicates the same as each of these.'

Here it is the categorial items of (2), such as Socrates, man, white, walking, and the rest, that are said to indicate or signify the eight members of (3). (So σημαίνειν here is a thing–thing, not a word–thing relation.) The term *being*, correspondingly, indicates (3) the particular category of the item to which it is applied (Socrates, man, white, etc.). In modern terminology we might say that the connotation of *being* (as substance, quality, etc.) is determined by its denotation in each particular case (as applied to Socrates, white, etc.). The next sentence of the text, beginning 'For there is no difference between *A man is healthy* (ἄνθρωπος ὑγιαίνων ἐστίν) and *A man enjoys health* (ἄνθρωπος ὑγιαίνει)', makes clear that the term *being* is thought of here as expressed by the copula *is*, whether occurring in a copula sentence or virtually present (in 'zero' form) in the noun–verb sentence. Being here is thought of primarily in terms of predication. In a sentence like *A man is healthy*, the term *is* expresses (or 'connotes') primarily the being of the quality health, and only secondarily and indirectly the being of the substance man, insofar as the former depends for its existence upon the latter. In a sentence like *Socrates is a man* or *A man is an animal*, the term *is* expresses the being of the first category alone. Note that in the last clause quoted '*to be* indicates (σημαίνει) the same as each of these', σημαίνει seems to represent a word–thing (or word–concept) relation like 'connotes', a relation between the verb *is* and the corresponding category. But the phrase 'indicates the same as each of these' refers back to the earlier clauses of the sentence ('of things predicated some indicate *what it is*', etc.) where, as we have seen, the subject of σημαίνει is not a word at all but a categorial item like a man, health, or walking; and the semantic relation is that between a particular item and its category, or between a particular denotation of *being* and the corresponding connotation. So there is clearly no hope of assigning any single or uniform interpretation to the term σημαίνειν. Aristotle uses the term freely for all three sides of the triangular relation we have specified: (i) for the word–thing relation between an expression and a particular item in a category (roughly, our 'denotes'), (ii) for the word–thing or word–concept relation between the expression and a corresponding category (roughly, our 'connotes'), and (iii) for the thing–thing or thing–concept relation between a particular item (or denotation) and its category (the corresponding connotation of *being*).

If our analysis has done justice to the semantic complexity of this passage, it is easy to see how misleading it would be to describe Aristotle's procedure here as distinguishing various senses of the term *being*. This description is correct only if by 'senses' of *being* one understands (2) the whole range of entities and attributes to which *being* applies, as classified by (3) the eight 'ways in which *being* is said',[53] i.e. by the categorial divisions. Initially, Aristotle may be seen as distinguishing uses of the word *being*. But ultimately he is concerned to classify beings according to the categorial distinction between kinds of being.

We must note again that, in this conception of being, and as a consequence of Plato's principle that to be is always to be something definite, the concept of existence is in effect absorbed into, and articulated by, the categorial analysis of predication. For Socrates to be or to exist is *to be a man*. For white to exist is *to be a color*, that is *a quality* (belonging to some substance). For walking to exist is *to be an action* (performed by some human being, or by some animal). For three yards to exist is *to be a length*, that is, a *quantity* (possessed by some body). We need to add these phrases in parenthesis in order to specify fully what it is to be a color, an action, or a length—what it is for these attributes to exist. Only in the case of an attribution of substance, as when *man* is predicated of Socrates, is there no need for any such

---

[53] There can be, no more than for σημαίνει, no single adequate translation for τὸ ὄν λέγεται πολλαχῶς 'being is said in many ways'. This means (a) that the term *being* applies to many diverse things, where the diversity can be spelled out by a distinct λόγος for each class of applications. But it also means (b) that things are said to be in various ways, i.e. are said to have various modes of being according to the same diversity. We can combine these formal and material modes in a mixed rendering like 'What is, i.e. the things that are, are said to have being and are called *beings*...'. Nothing less than the mixed rendering can do justice to the complex view that Aristotle is expressing.

specification (since *to be a man* just is *to be a substance* of a definite kind). And this need, which reflects the ontological dependence of the other categories upon substance, will justify Aristotle's claim at Zeta 1, 1028^{a}35 that the account (λόγος) of substance must figure in the account or definition given of the other categories. A definition is a λόγος οὐσίας, an account of what a thing is, or what it is for that thing to be, in other words, for it to exist as that definite thing. Any full account of what a quality is must say that it is *an attribute of a substance*. In this respect, the ontological dependence upon substances entails that the definition of a quality must contain a reference to substance. (It is perhaps a mere looseness of formulation that Aristotle says at 1028a35 that it must contain the λόγος of substance. But perhaps he had in mind the fact that in order to understand what a quality is, one must understand what a substance is.)

We have now reached the fully ontological application of the categorial scheme. Before concluding with a brief mention of the development of this doctrine in the central books of the *Metaphysics*, we may pause to assess the significance here of the linguistic facts with which this study began. We see that in *Met. Δ*. 7 Aristotle begins to delimit and classify a wide range of 'things' or 'beings' (ὄντα) by means of the system of categories worked out in his analysis of the logical structure of predication. The philosophical legitimacy of his procedure here depends in large part upon the fact that the categories of predication have themselves already been delimited. It would be difficult to justify the list of eight categories if they were introduced here for the first time simply as a classification of modes of being or types of 'things'. But, as we have seen, the list of categories has in fact been in use at least since the *Topics*, and in use precisely as a device for analyzing phenomena of ambiguity or multivocity, as part of the larger enterprise of distinguishing the logical structure of what is said from the surface structure of the way in which it is said. As Aristotle claimed in the *Sophistici Elenchi*, we know how to deal with fallacies based upon superficial uniformities of language 'since we have the genera of predications' as our device for logical analysis (*Soph. El.* 22, 178a5). In the *Metaphysics*, where it is no longer a question of resolving fallacious arguments but still one of revealing logical structures under the surface diversities or uniformities of language, it is natural to make use of the device that has proved its mettle in humbler tasks of the same sort. (Here as elsewhere I mean by logical structure whatever makes a difference for the truth value or the logical consequences of what is said.)

Now the naturalness of the categorial scheme was from the beginning recommended to Aristotle's readers and auditors by the fact that it relied upon familiar distinctions of meaning or function between the common interrogative words, and between other obvious linguistic contrasts such as the opposition of active and passive verbal forms, from which the deeper conceptual distinction between acting and being-acted-upon could be distilled. Those commentators who regard the categorial scheme as originally created or discovered for the analysis of 'what is', as a classification of the various kinds of beings 'by simple inspection of reality' as Ross put it,[54] would deprive Aristotle's procedure in Δ.7 of its naturalness, and of its legitimacy also. They would, in effect, make his procedure arbitrary and circular. For if the categorial scheme had originally been formulated as an ontological classification, it would hardly be a step forward to proceed to use the scheme for this purpose in Δ.7, and it would scarcely be an interesting insight to discover that '*being* indicates in as many ways as the categories'. Furthermore, if the scheme is specifically designed for this ontological assignment, the adequacy of the scheme for this purpose must somehow be established, and it is not easy to see how one could justify this particular list of categories as a direct account of reality. The whole point of Aristotle's application of the categories to the analysis of being is that the scheme had originally been introduced as a natural and obvious device for making some distinctions in what is said about a given subject, and that its value had already been established by its use in analyzing predication, in revealing multivocity, and in clarifying the logical structure of what is asserted. It is, I think, of crucial importance

---

[54] See Ross (1924) I, LXXXV, who quotes with approval the view of Bonitz that the categories are 'essentially a classification of realities'. Bonitz (1853: 10) himself said: 'Das gesammte Bereich des Gedachten oder des Seienden ... wird in zehn oberste Classen eingeteilt, deren einer ein jeder Gegenstand unserer Vorstellung oder erfahrungs-mässigen Auffassung anheimfallen muss'. Similarly Zeller (1879: 258 ff.). More recently De Rijk (1952: 76) has claimed that the doctrine of the categories 'was, in its first stage (i.e. in the *Categories*), a rough division of beings'.

not only for tracing the development of the doctrine of categories but also for understanding what kind of an enterprise Aristotle takes ontology to be, to realize that the road to an analysis of Being passes not by way of a direct inspection of reality, nor by an inventory of the objects of experience or the concepts which structure our knowledge of the world (for in that case how could one explain the absence of the concept 'cause' from the categories?), but by way of the analysis of λόγος 'rational discourse' and the theory of predication, conceived of as the assignment of attributes or properties to entities in the world. If we so construe the scheme of categories as to forget that κατηγορίαι τοῦ ὄντος means literally *'predications* of being', we lose the key to understanding Aristotle's metaphysics as a theory of being qua being.

We do not need to deny that, from the beginning, Aristotle had the ontological application of the categories in mind. But what a reading of the *Topics* and the other logical works clearly shows is that the scheme is developed there without any direct anticipation of the ontological doctrine, primarily as a useful instrument for distinguishing predications and analyzing arguments, a scheme organized on the basis of some very modest linguistic and logical observations, and specifically upon the kinds of questions that can be asked about a man in the marketplace.

Having now reached the stage represented in the *Metaphysics*, where the scheme of categories provides an account of the 'many ways in which *being* is said', we cannot follow the doctrine of categories further without embarking on a general discussion of Aristotle's ontology. Some mention must be made, however, of the primary use of this doctrine in the *Metaphysics*, the use for which the survey of ποσαχῶ ς λέγεται τὸ ὄν in Δ.7 is the direct preparation. This is the doctrine of 'focal meaning', the doctrine that although being is said in many ways it is not strictly homonymous, but that these various ways are all related to a single central case and thus form a systematic unity (πρὸς ἕν λέγεσθαι 'said in relation to one [thing]').[55] Aristotle's stellar use of

---

[55] For the term 'focal meaning' and for the importance of this concept in permitting Aristotle to recognize the possibility of a general metaphysics, see Owen (1960). He points out (p. 166) that the assertion in *Eudemian Ethics* I.8, 1217[b]34–5 that there is no one science of being (τὸ ὄν) represents an extreme consequence of the homonymy of *being*, against which Aristotle himself is reacting in *Met. Γ*. 2 and Z.1 with his doctrine of focal meaning.

this doctrine in the *Metaphysics*, in chapter 2 of Book Gamma and chapters 1 and 4–5 of Book Zeta, is the application of 'focal meaning' to the multivocity of *being* as articulated by the categories. Before considering this central case, however, we must observe that the doctrine itself is a general one: it applies not only to *being* but to many other terms that are 'said in several ways'. Even in its application to *being*, the doctrine is not strictly limited to the scheme of the categories; thus among the things said 'to be' in a derivative or secondary way are not only the items in the seven non-substantial categories but also the becomings and destructions, the privations and negations, of substance and its attributes (*Γ*.2, 1003^{b}7–10). If we first consider terms other than *being* in the lexical survey of *Metaphysics* Delta, we can see the notion of focal meaning taking shape in a number of chapters where Aristotle is concerned not simply to distinguish and define the different ways in which a given term is said, but where he also seeks to identify a 'strict' and 'primary' use from which the others are in some sense derived or on which they logically depend.[56] It looks as though in working out this systematic study of 'things said in many ways' Aristotle came to see the importance of a fact to which he had at first paid little or no attention: namely, that the diverse applications of any single term that he had been in the habit of describing as homonymous rarely if ever had 'only a name in common'.[57] Even his specimen of homonymy in *Categories* 1, the use of the term ζῷον 'living thing' for pictures or images as well as for animals, is not a merely verbal coincidence, since Greek art is largely devoted to renderings of men and animals, and a good likeness seems to be 'alive'. But the philosophical terms studied in *Metaphysics* Delta often show

---

[56] Thus the analysis of *necessary* in *Δ*.5 ends with the characterization of absolute or unqualified necessity as τὸ πρῶτον καί κυρίως ἀναγκαῖον 'what is primary necessity and strictly so called' (1015^{b}11). Even more revealing for the emergence of focal meaning is the remark on φύσις 'nature' in *Δ*.4, 1015^{a}13–19, where the other notions of nature are shown to be derived from, or dependent on, ἡπρώτη φύσις καί κυρίως λεγομένη 'the primary and strictest case of nature', which is the form or essence (οὐσία) of 'things possessing a principle of motion in themselves, per se [or in virtue of what they are]'. Compare the 'primary and strictest' case of πρότερον 'prior' at *Cat.* 12, 14^{a}26. In general, the Postpredicamenta (*Categories* 10–15) represent an early study in πολλαχῶς λεγόμενα, a kind of incipient version of *Metaphysics* Delta.

[57] Compare Hintikka (1973: 14 f.) and Aubenque (1962: 190–8).

much deeper and closer logical connections between their various uses.

Once this general insight took shape in Aristotle's thinking, the special application of the notion of primary and secondary uses to the multivocity of *being* was, in effect, given in advance. The primary case of being had already been identified in the claim of the *Categories* that without the being of primary substances there could not be anything else at all (2^{b}5). In the metaphysical doctrine of focal meaning this claim is simply rephrased, with the omission of any special reference to 'primary' substances: the primary being (τὸ πρώτως ὄν) is substance; 'the others are called beings in virtue of the fact that some are quantities of "what is" in this way [sc. in the primary way, as substance], others are qualities of it, others are affects (πάθη) or something else of the sort' (Z.1, 1028^{a}18; cf. Γ.2, 1003^{b}7–19). Thus the doctrine of focal meaning here is precisely the doctrine of the ontological dependence of the other categories on substance. (Hence, despite its great convenience, the term *focal meaning* may be misleading, insofar as it suggests that Aristotle is relating senses of the verb *be* to some primary sense, rather than relating different kinds of being to one primary case of being.) And it is, furthermore, the claim that items in the first category have a peculiar right to the title of ὄν 'what is', because only substances are ὄν ἁπλῶς 'being simply, without qualification': there is some doubt whether things like walking and enjoying health and sitting are being or not being, 'for none of them either is naturally in its own right, nor is it capable of being separated from substance.⁵⁸ . . . It is because of the latter [viz. substance] that each of them is, so that substance will be the primary being and not being-qualified (ὄν τι) but being simply and without qualification (ὄν ἁπλῶς)' (Z1, 1028^{a}20–31). Finally, the ontological dependence of the other categories on substance will be reflected in the logical fact that the definitional account (λόγος) of what substance is will be present in, or presupposed by, the account of the other categories (Θ.1, 1045^{b}29–32, referring back to Z.1, 1028^{a}35 and Z.4–5).

---

⁵⁸ Reading οὐδὲν γὰρ αὐτῶν ἐστιν οὔτε καθ᾽ αὑτὸ πεφυκὸς οὔτε χωρίζεσθαι δυνατὸν τῆς οὐσίας at 1028^{a}22–4, with Ross and other editors. Jaeger (in the Oxford Classical Text) brackets πεφυκός.

Thus the multivocity of the term *being*, like the categorial account (λόγος) which structures this manifold, forms a unified system by its reference to, and its dependence upon, a single nature and principle (πρὸς ἕν καὶ μίαν τινὰ φύσιν, *Γ*.2, 1003ᵃ33; πρὸς μίαν ἀρχήν, 1003ᵇ6), which is the being of substance, 'because of which the others are beings too' (Z.1, 1028ᵃ29–30). The philosophical importance of this doctrine is, first, that by uniting the diverse range of beings into a single structure it explains and justifies the possibility of First Philosophy as the study of being as such (τὸ ὂν ᾗ ὄν). Although being does not constitute a single genus, it may nevertheless provide the object for a single science in virtue of the systematic unity constituted by these relations of dependence upon the primary being of substance. The scheme of categories, reinterpreted in the context of focal meaning, thus serves to redefine ontology—the ancient study of Being inherited from Parmenides and Plato—as primarily the study of Substance or entity (Z.1, 1028ᵇ2–7). And this involves, of course, more than a shift in terminology. It means moving the philosophical concept of Being or reality away from the 'otherworldly' implications of Eleatic and Platonic doctrine, which relies heavily on the 'veridical' connotations of τὸ ὄν as *true* reality, the ultimate or underlying object of true knowledge, standing in some kind of ontological contrast with the world of falsehood and appearance.[59] Instead, Aristotle's doctrine of οὐσία proposes a 'thisworldly' concept of being, a descriptive rather than a revisionary metaphysics (to use Strawson's terms) oriented towards a commitment to the commonsense ontology implied in everyday talk about ordinary subjects, about 'entities' such as men and mammals, cabbages and kings. Of course the Platonic strain in Aristotle's thinking remains vital, and it exerts ontological pressure in a different direction through the claim that knowledge and definition take as their object the essence and the universal (*Met*. Z, 1031ᵇ6, 1035ᵇ34, 1036ᵇ8, ᵃ28, etc.). Being is still, for Aristotle as for Plato, the object of knowledge and the correlate of true discourse. But even in his theory of definition, which remains relatively Platonic in its concern with 'essence without matter' (1032ᵇ14), Aristotle's new

---

[59] For the 'veridical' nuance of τὸ ὄν in Greek, see Kahn (1973: 331–70): for the importance of this for understanding the Greek view of Being, see Kahn (1966).

QUESTIONS AND CATEGORIES 273

ontological orientation introduces a crucial distinction. Just as *being* (εἶναι) and *what is* (τὸ ὄν) belongs primarily to substance but derivatively to the other categories, so the essence (τὸ τί ἐστι 'the what-is-it?' and τὸ τί ἦν εἶναι 'the being-what-it-is'[60]) and the definition which formulates the essence belong primarily to substance and derivatively to beings in the other categories. Of course it is possible to define a quality or a quantity; if it were not so, geometry could not be a science.

---

[60] I take τὸ τί ἦν εἶναι to be an ordinary articular infinitive, construed on the pattern of τὸ ἀνθρώπῳ εἶναι 'the being for a man', 'the being which belongs to man', with the dative noun replaced by the τί ἐστι question cast in the philosophical imperfect (to suggest that it has already been answered): 'the being [for *x*] as determined by its definition, by what we have formulated in answer to the question *what is it?* The original or literal sense of the expression is 'its being what-it-is', or more fully: 'the being or existence of the thing (which may be specified in the dative) as determined by its specific form or essence, the latter being identified in the definition, in answer to the question *'what is it?'*. Thus there is or could be a clear difference in principle between the more existential formula τὸ τί ἦν εἶναι which refers (or at least might refer) to the complete being of the thing in question, its existence as determined by its essence, and the more strictly essential τὸ τί ἐστι, which refers to the form alone, as specified in the definition. In practice, however, Aristotle rarely if ever attends to this difference, and, for a variety of reasons (including the subordinate place of existential nuances in his conception of εἶναι, and also because of other uses for τὸ τί ἐστι, as a designation for the first category and for essential predication in general) he regularly employs τὸ τί ἦν εἶναι simply as a frozen formula for definitional form or essence (e.g. *Met.* Z. 4, 1030ᵃ6; and even in an 'early' text like *Topics* I.5). Thus he can conclude that it is 'essence without matter' οὐσία ἄνευ ὕλης (Z.7, 1032ᵇ14); and the psyche can be defined as the τὸ τί ἦν εἶναι of the body (*De Anima* II.1, 412ᵇ11). The fuller, existential connotations of τὸ τινι εἶναι have simply disappeared, and one may doubt that they were ever of any real importance for Aristotle. (On the other hand, he is not completely oblivious to the existential implications or presuppositions of the verb even in the purely definitional formula τὸ τί ἐστι, as his remarks at *Post. An.* II.7, 92ᵇ4–11 make clear. Note that the expression there for 'the existence of man' is τὸ εἶναι ἄνθρωπον, not τὸ εἶναι ἀνθρώπῳ. And see further Owen (1965: 2).

The same conclusions follow from the more common reading of this formula (following Bonitz) as a kind of abbreviation for τὸ τί ἦν (τὸ) ἐκείνῳ εἶναι 'what it was for that thing to be'. On philosophical grounds, this reading may be slightly more illuminating. (But it too must confront the fact that the *psyche* is scarcely 'what we have defined as the being of a living body', if 'being' is understood in a natural way to include the material existence of an extended body. On any reading, this fuller sense of εἶναι has been lost sight of in the technical usage of τὸ εἶναι.) But this common reading seems to be grammatically dubious and historically implausible. No explanation is forthcoming for the systematic omission of the second τό, which this view presupposes. (See Bassenge, 1960, esp. pp. 19–25.) And since on this view τί ἦν ceases to be a natural transformation of the τὸ τί ἐστι formula (where the subject of the question is normally represented by a noun or nominalized adjective, not by an infinitival construction), the frequent equivalence of the two expressions for essence becomes difficult to understand. Bassenge's study (1960) seems to come to the correct conclusion, though by a rather circuitous route. See Hick's commentary on *De Anima* 412ᵇ11 for a briefer statement of the grammatically correct interpretation.

But these definitions are, in the ontological perspective, derivative and dependent in a way that the definition of substances is not (Z.4, 1030ª17–b7; Z.5, 1031ª1–14; see our discussion above, p. 264). This is the final development of the double perspective on the categories proposed in *Topics* I.9: the question τί ἐστι *what is it?* belongs primarily to the first category, but it has a secondary use in each of the others.

This is as far as we can or need go in following the use of the categorial scheme in the *Metaphysics*. The doctrine of categories is not, after all, the central thesis in Aristotle's ontology. It provides a kind of introduction to metaphysics and to theoretical philosophy in general, by sorting and circumscribing the domain of things that are beings per se, 'in their own right'. When the categorial scheme is applied in connection with the focal meaning of *being*, it effects a preliminary unification and ordering of this domain in its ontological dependence on substance or 'entity'. But in the final analysis the scheme does not tell us what is to count as an entity or how the structure of a substance is to be understood. The deeper analysis of substance itself and its relation to the dependent beings must be carried out by the use of different concepts, φυσικῶς not λογικῶς as Aristotle will sometimes say, concepts derived not from the theory of predication but designed specifically for the analysis of natural motion and change: concepts like mover and goal (τέλος), matter and form, potency and act. Both physics and metaphysics culminate in the theory of the Unmoved Mover, the entity (or entities) whose being is actuality, the final cause of all motion and change, the 'primary substance' on which all other substances depend (Λ.7, 1072b14; cf. Γ.2, 1003b16–17, E.1, 1026ª27–31). In this ultimate perspective for ontology, which Aristotle himself never worked out in full detail, the preliminary contribution of the categories in distinguishing substance from the various kinds of dependent beings must seem quite modest and elementary. All the more reason, however, why the categorial scheme itself should be firmly rooted in humble, everyday questions like *What is it? How big? Of what sort or quality? In relation to what? Where?* and *When?*[61]

University of Pennsylvania

---

[61] I want to express my appreciation to John Ackrill, Enrico Berti, Kurt von Fritz, Henry Hiż and G. Verbeke for helpful criticism of this study.

Bibliography

ABELARD, P., *Dialectica*, 2nd edn., ed. L. M. De Rijk (Assen: Van Gorcum, 1970).

—— *Logica 'Ingredientibus'*, ed. Bernhard Geyer in *Beiträge zur Geschichte der Philosophie und Theologie des Mittelalters*, xxi (Aschendorff: Munster, 1919–27).

ACKRILL, J. L.: 1963, *Aristotle's 'Categories' and 'De Interpretatione'* (Oxford: Clarendon).

ADJUKIEWICZ, KAZIMIERZ: 1935, 'Syntactic Connexion', in *Polish Logic, 1920–1939*, ed. Storrs McCall (Oxford: Clarendon, 1967), 207–31.

ANNAS, JULIA: 1974, 'Forms and first principles', *Phronesis* 19, 257–83.

APELT, OTTO: 1891, 'Die Kategorienlehre des Aristoteles', in *Beiträge zur Geschichte der griechischen Philosophie* (Leipzig: Teubner), 101–216.

ARISTOTLE, *Aristotle's Categories and De Interpretatione*, trans. J. L. Ackrill (Oxford: Oxford University Press, 1963).

—— *Aristotle's Prior and Posterior Analytics*, ed. W. D. Ross (New York: Oxford University Press, 2003).

—— AUBENQUE, P., 'Syntaxe et sémantique de l'être dans le poème de Parménide', in P. Aubenque (ed.), *Études sur Parménides* (Paris: Vrin, 1987).

AUBENQUE, PIERRE: 1962, *Le problème de l'etre chez Aristote* (Paris: Presses Universitaires de France).

BÄCK, A., *Aristotle's Theory of Predication* (Leiden/Boston/Koln: Brill, 2000).

BARNES, J., *The Presocratic Philosophers* (London/Boston: Routledge & Kegan Paul, 1979).

BARNES, J., SCHOFIELD, M., and SORABJI, R. (eds.), *Articles on Aristotle* iv (London: Duckworth, 1979).

BASSENGE, FRIEDRICH: 1960, 'Das τὸ ἐνὶ εἶναι und das τὸ τί ἦν εἶναι bei Aristoteles', *Philologus*, 104, 14–47 and 201–22.

BENVENISTE ÉMILE: 1958, 'Catégories de pensée et catégories de langue', in *Problèmes de linguistique générale* (Paris: Gallimard, 1966), 63–74.

BERNADETE, S., 'The Grammar of Being', *Review of Metaphysics*, 30 (1977), 486–96.

BONITZ, HERMANN: 1853, *Über dle Kategorien des Aristoteles* (Vienna: Staatsdruckerei).

BOWRA, C. M., 'The Proem of Parmenides', in *Problems in Greek Poetry* (Oxford: Clarendon, 1953), 38–53.

BRENTANO, FRANZ: 1862, *Von der mannigfachen Bedeutung des Seienden nach Aristoteles* (Freiburg: Herder).

BROWN, L., 'Being in the Sophist: A Syntactical Enquiry', *Oxford Studies in Ancient Philosophy*, 4 (1986), 49–70.

—— 'The Verb "To Be" in Greek Philosophy: Some Remarks', in Steven Everson (ed.), *Companions to Ancient Thought*, iii (Cambridge: Cambridge University Press, 1994), 212–36.

BRUGMANN, K., and DELBRÜCK, B., *Grundriss der vergleichenden Grammatik der indogermanischen Sprachen* (Strasbourg: Trübner, 1886–1900).

BRUNNSCHWIG, J., 'La théorie stroïcienne du genre suprême et l'ontologie platonicienne', in J. Barnes and M. Mignucci (eds.), *Matter and Metaphysics* (Naples: Bibliopolis, 1988).

BURKERT, W., 'Das Proömium des Parmenides und die Katabasis des Pythagoras', *Phronesis*, 14 (1969), 1–30.

BURNET, J., *Phaedo* (Oxford: Clarendon, 1911).

BURNYEAT, M., 'Plato on the Grammar of Perceiving', *Classical Quarterly*, 26 (1976), 29–51.

CALOGERO, G., *Studi sull'Eleatismo* (Rome: Tipografia del Senato, 1932).

CARNAP, RUDOLF: 1937, *The Logical Syntax of Language*, trans. A. Smeaton (London: Routledge and Kegan Paul).

CHANTRAINE, P., *Morphologie historique du grec*, 2nd edn. (Paris: Klincksieck, 1947).

CHOMSKY, NOAM: 1965, *Aspects of the Theory of Syntax* (Cambridge, MA: M.I.T.).

COOKE, HAROLD P.: 1938, *Aristotle, The Organon I: The Categories*, The Loeb Classical Library (London: Heinemann).

COOPER, J., 'Plato on Sense-Perception and Knowledge: *Theaetetus* 184–186', *Phronesis*, 15 (1970), 123–46.

CORDERO, N-L., *Les deux chemins de Parménide: édition critique, traduction, études et bibliographie* (Paris: Vrin, 1984).

COXON, A. H., *The Fragments of Parmenides: A Critical Text with Introduction, Translation, Ancient Testimonia and Commentary* (Assen/Maastricht: Van Gorcum, 1986).

DAVIDSON, D., 'On the Very Idea of a Conceptual Scheme', *Proceedings and Addresses of the American Philosophical Association*, 47 (1973–74).

DE RIJK, LAMBERTUS M.: 1952, *The Place of the Categories of Being in Aristotle's Philosophy* (Assen: Van Gorcum).

DESCARTES, R., *Oeuvres de Descartes*, vi–vii, ed. C. Adam and P. Tannery (Paris: Vrin, repr. 1983).

DIELS, H., and KRANZ, W., *Die Fragmente der Vorsokratiker*, 3 vols. (Berlin: Weidmann, 1960). [= D.-K.]

DÖRRIE, H., 'Hypostasis: Wort and Bedeutungsgeschichte', *Nachrichten der Akademie der Wissenschaft zu Göttingen*, Phil.-Hist. Klasse 3 (1955), 35–92.

EBBESEN, S., 'The Chimera's Diary', in S. Knuuttila and J. Hintikka (eds.), *The Logic of Being: Historical Studies* (Dordrecht: Reidel, 1986).

ERNOUT, A., '*Exsto* et les composés latins en *ex-*', *Bulletin de la société linguistique de Paris*, 50 (1954).

ERNOUT, A., and MEILLET, A., *Dictionnaire étymologique de la langue latine: histoire de mots* (Paris: Klincksieck, 1985).

FESTUGIÈRE, A. J., *La révélation d'Hermès Trismégiste, iv: le Dieu inconnu et la gnose* (Paris: D. Gabalda, 1945–54).

FINE, G., 'Knowledge and Belief in *Republic* V', *Archiv für Geschichte der Philosophie*, 60 (1978), 121–39.

FRÄNKEL, H., *Wege und Formen frühgriechischen Denkens: Literarische und philosophiegeschichtliche Studien* (Munich: Beck, 1955).

FRISK, H., '"Wahrheit" and "Lüge" in den indogermanischen Sprachen', *Göteborgs Hogskolas Arsskrift*, 41/3 (1935), 1–39.

FRITZ, K. VON, '*Nóos* and *Noeîn* in the Homeric Poems', *Classical Philology*, 40 (1945), 223–42.

FURLEY, D., 'Notes on Parmenides', in E. N. Lee et al. (eds.), *Exegesis and Argument: Studies in Greek Philosophy Presented to Gregory Vlastos* (Assen: Van Gorcum, 1973).

—— *The Greek Cosmologists*, i (Cambridge: Cambridge University Press, 1987).

FURTH, MONTGOMERY, 'Elements of Eleatic Ontology', in A. P. D. Mourelatos (ed.), *The Pre-Socratics: A Collection of Critical Essays* (Garden City, NY: Anchor, 1974).

GALLOP, D., *Plato: Phaedo* (Oxford: Clarendon, 1975).

—— '"Is" or "Is Not"?', *Monist*, 62 (1979), 61–80.

—— *Parmenides of Elea: Fragments* (Toronto: University of Toronto Press, 1984).

GILLESPIE, C. M.: 1913, 'The Logic of Antisthenes', *Archiv für Geschichte der Philosophie*, 26, 479–500.

——1925, 'The Aristotelian Categories', *Classical Quarterly*, 19, 75–84.

GILSON, E., *L'être et l'essence* (Paris: Vrin, 1948).

GOICHON, A.-M., *Lexique de la langue philosophique d'Ibn Sina* (Paris: de Brouwer, 1938).

GOMEZ-LOBO, A., *Parmenides: Texto griego, Traducción y Comentario* (Buenos Aires: Charcas, 1985).

278   CHARLES H. KAHN

GOMPERZ, THEODOR: 1912, *Greek Thinkers*, vol. 4, transl. by G. G. Berry (London: Murray).

GRAHAM, A. C., '"Being" in Linguistics and Philosophy', *Foundations of Language*, 1 (1965).

GROTE, G., *Aristotle*, 3rd edn. (London: 1883).

GUIRAUD, C., *La phrase nominale en grec de Homère à Euripide* (Paris, Klincksieck, 1962).

GUTHRIE, W. K. C., *A History of Greek Philosophy*, iv (Cambridge: Cambridge University Press, 1975).

HADOT, P., 'La distinction de l'être et de l'étant dans le *De Hebdomadibus* de Boèce', *Miscillenea Medievalia*, 2 (1963), 143–53.

—— *Porphyre et Victorinus* (Paris: Études Augustiniennes, 1968).

HARRIS, Zellig: 1968, *Mathematical Structures of Language* (= *Interscience Tracts in Pure and Applied Mathematics* 21) (New York: John Wiley).

HERMANN, G., *De Emendanda Ratione Graecae Grammaticae* (Leipzig: Gerhard Fleischer, 1801).

HINTIKKA, J., *Knowledge and Belief: An Introduction to the Logic of the Two Notions* (Ithaca, NY: Cornell University Press, 1962).

—— 'Aristotle and the Ambiguity of Ambiguity', *Time and Necessity* (Oxford: Clarendon, 1973), 1–26.

—— 'The Varieties of Being in Aristotle', in S. Knuuttila and J. Hintikka (eds.), *The Logic of Being: Historical Studies* (Dordrecht: Reidel, 1986), 81–114.

HIŻ, HENRY: 1960, 'The Intuitions of Grammatical Categories', *Methodos*, 12, 1–9.

HÖLSCHER, U., *Anfängliches Fragen: Studien zur Frühen griechischen Philosophie* (Göttingen: Vandenhoeck & Ruprecht, 1968).

HUFFMAN, C., *Philolaus of Croton* (Cambridge: Cambridge University Press, 1993).

HUSIK, ISAAC: 1904, 'On the Categories of Aristotle', *Philosophical Review*, 13, 514–528 (reprinted in *Philosophical Essays*, Oxford: Blackwell, 1952).

HUSSERL, EDMUND: 1913, *Logische Untersuchungen*, 2 vols. in three parts, 2nd edn. (Tübingen: Niemeyer).

HUSSEY, E., 'Pythagoreans and Eleatics', in C. C. W. Taylor (ed.), *Routledge History of Philosophy*, i (London/New York: Routledge, 1997), 128–74.

JACOBI, K., 'Peter Abelard's Investigations into the Meaning and Functions of the Speech Sign "Est"', in S. Knuuttila and J. Hintikka (eds.), *The Logic of Being: Historical Studies* (Dordrecht: Reidel, 1986), 81–114.

JANTZEN, J., 'Parmenides zum Verhältnis von Sprache und Wirklichkeit', *Zetemata*, 63 (1976), 112–18.

—— 'Sensation and Consciousness in Aristotle's Psychology', *Archiv für Geschichte der Philosophie*, 48 (1966), 43–81.

KAHN, CHARLES H.: 1966, 'The Greek Verb "to be" and the Concept of Being', *Foundations of Language*, 2, 245–65.

——1972, 'On the Terminology for *Copula* and *Existence*', *Islamic Philosophy and the Classical Tradition: Essays presented to Richard Walzer* (Oxford: Cassirer).

——1973, *The Verb 'Be' in Ancient Greek* (= *The Verb 'Be' and its Synonyms*, Part 6) (Dordrecht: Reidel).

KAHN, C. H., Review of L. Tarán, *Parmenides, Gnomon*, 40 (1968), 127–32.

—— Review of Mansfeld, *Die Offenbarung des Parmenides, Gnomon*, 52 (1970), 113–19.

—— 'More on Parmenides', *Review of Metaphysics*, 23 (1969), 333–40.

—— *The Verb 'Be' in Ancient Greek* (Dordrecht: Reidel, 1973; repr. Indianapolis, Ind.: Hackett, 2003).

—— 'On the Theory of the Verb "To Be"', in M. Munitz (ed.), *Logic and Ontology* (New York: New York University Press, 1973), 1–20.

—— 'Linguistic Relativism and the Greek Project of Ontology', in G. M. C. Sprung (ed.), *The Question of Being: East–West Perspectives* (University Park, Pa.: Pennsylvania State University Press, 1977).

—— 'Questions and Categories: Aristotle's Categories in the Light of Modern Research', in H. Hiz (ed.), *Questions* (Dordrecht: Reidel, 1978), 227–78.

—— 'Some Philosophical Uses of "To Be" in Plato', *Phronesis*, 26 (1981), 105–84.

—— *Plato and the Socratic Dialogue* (Cambridge: Cambridge University Press, 1996).

KANT, I., *Critik der reinen Vernunft* (Riga: Hartknoch, 1781).

KAPP, ERNST: 1920, 'Die Kategorienlehre in der aristotelischen Topik' (Habilitations-schrift), in *Ausgewählte Schriften* (Berlin: de Gruyter, 1968).

——1942, *Greek Foundations of Traditional Logic* (New York: Columbia).

KAPP, E., *Ausgewählte Schriften* (Berlin: de Gruyter, 1968).

KINGSLEY, P., *Ancient Philosophy, Mystery, and Magic* (Oxford: Clarendon, 1995).

KIRK, G. S., and RAVEN, J. E., *The Presocratic Philosophers* (Cambridge: Cambridge University Press, 1957).

KIRK, G. S., RAVEN, J. E., and SCHOFIELD, M., *The Presocratic Philosophers*, 2nd edn. (Cambridge: Cambridge University Press, 1983).

KIRWAN, CHRISTOPHER: 1971, *Aristotle's 'Metaphysics', Books Γ, Δ, and E* (Oxford: Clarendon).

KNEALE, W., and KNEALE, M., *The Development of Logic* (Oxford: Clarendon, 1962).

KNUUTTILA, S., and HINTIKKA, J. (eds.), *The Logic of Being: Historical Studies*, (Dordrecht: Reidel, 1986).

KÜHNER, R., and GERTH, B., *Ausführliche Grammatik* (Hanover/Leipzig: Hahn, 1904).

LACEY, A. R., 'Plato's *Sophist* and the Forms', *Classical Quarterly*, NS, 9 (1959), 43–52.

LIDDELL, H. G., SCOTT, R., and JONES, H. S., *A Greek–English Lexicon* (1843). [= Liddell–Scott–Jones]

LLOYD, G. E. R., 'Plato and Archytas in the *Seventh Letter*', *Phronesis*, 35 (1990), 159–74.

LONG, A. A., 'Parmenides on Thinking Being', in G. Rechenauer (ed.), *Frühgriechisches Denken* (Göttingen: Vandenhoeck & Ruprecht, 2005).

LONG, A. A., and SEDLEY, D. N., *The Hellenistic Philosophers*, 2 vols. (Cambridge: Cambridge University Press, 1987).

LORIAUX, R., *Le Phédon de Platon, Commentaire et Traduction* (Namur: Secrétariat des publications, facultés universitaires, 1969).

LYONS, JOHN: 1968, *Introduction to Theoretical Linguistics* (Cambridge: Cambridge University Press).

MCDOWELL, J., *Theaetetus* (Oxford: Clarendon, 1973).

MALCOLM, J., 'Plato's Analysis of *to on* and *to mê on*', *Phronesis*, 12 (1967), 130–46.

MANN, W., *The Discovery of Things* (Princeton, NJ: Princeton University Press, 2000).

MANSFELD, J., *Die Offenbarung des Parmenides und die menschliche Welt* (Assen: Van Gorcum, 1964).

MANSION, SUZANNE: 1968, 'Notes sur la doctrine des catégories dans les *Topiques*', *Aristotle on Dialectic: the Topics*, ed. G. E. L. Owen (Oxford: Clarendon), 189–201.

MANSION, S., *Le jugement d'existence chez Aristote* (Louvain: Éditions de l'Institut Supérieur de Philosophie, 1946).

MATTHEN, M., 'Greek Ontology and the "Is" of Truth', *Phronesis*, 28 (1983), 113–35.

MEILLET, A., *Introduction à l'étude comparative des langues indo-européennes*, 8th edn. (Paris: Hachette, 1937).

MEILLET, A., and VENDRYÈS, J., *Traité de grammaire comparée des langues classiques*, 1st edn. (Paris: Champion, 1924).

MILL, J., *Analysis of the Phenomena of the Human Mind* (London: Baldwin & Cradock, 1829; 2nd edn. 1869).

MILL, J. S., *A System of Logic, Ratiocinative and Inductive* (London: Parker, 1843).

MILLER, M. 'Ambiguity and Transport: Reflections on the Proem to Parmenides' Poem', *Oxford Studies in Ancient Philosophy*, 30 (2006), 1–47.

MONTAGUE, RICHARD: 1974, *Formal Philosophy. Selected Papers of Richard Montague.* Edited and with an introduction by Richmond H. Thomason (New Haven and London: Yale).

MORAVCSIK, J. M. E.: 1967, 'Aristotle's Theory of Categories', in *Aristotle. A Collection of Critical Essays*, ed. J. M. E. Moravcsik (Garden City, New York: Doubleday, 1967).

MORRISON, J. S., 'Parmenides and Er', *Journal of Hellenic Studies*, 76 (1955), 59–68.

MOURELATOS, A., *The Route of Parmenides* (New Haven, Conn.: Yale University Press, 1970).

—— (ed.), *The Pre-Socratics: A Collection of Critical Essays* (Garden City, NY: Anchor, 1974).

MULLALLY, J., *The 'Summulae Logicales' of Peter of Spain* (Notre Dame, Ind.: University of Notre Dame Press, 1945).

MUNITZ, M. K. (ed.), *Logic and Ontology* (New York: New York University Press, 1973).

OWEN, G. E. L.: 1960, 'Logic and Metaphysics in some earlier Works of Aristotle', *Aristotle and Plato in the Mid-Fourth Century* (Goteborg: Studia Graeca), 169–90.

——1965 (1), 'The Platonism of Aristotle', *Proceedings of the British Academy*, 51, 125–50.

——1965 (2), 'Aristotle on the Snares of Ontology', in *New Essays on Plato and Aristotle*, ed. R. Bambrough (London: Routledge & Kegan Paul), 69–95.

——1968, 'Dialectic and Eristic in the Treatment of Forms', *Aristotle on Dialectic* (Oxford: Clarendon), 103–25.

—— 'Eleatic Questions', *Classical Quarterly*, 10 (1960), 84–102, repr. in Owen, *Logic, Science, and Dialectic: Collected Papers in Greek Philosophy*, ed. M. Nussbaum (Ithaca, NY: Cornell University Press, 1986).

—— 'Aristotle on the Snares of Ontology', in R. Bambrough (ed.), *New Essays on Plato and Aristotle* (New York: Humanities, 1965).

—— 'Plato and Parmenides on the Timeless Present', *The Monist*, 50/3 (1966), 317–40; repr. in G. E. L. Owen, *Logic, Science, and Dialectic: Collected Papers in Greek Philosophy*, ed. M. Nussbaum (Ithaca, NY: Cornell University Press, 1986).

—— *Logic, Science, and Dialectic: Collected Papers in Greek Philosophy*, ed. M. Nussbaum (Ithaca, NY: Cornell University Press, 1986).

OWEN, G. E. L., 'Plato on Not-Being', in G. Vlastos (ed.), *Plato I: Metaphysics and Epistemology* (Garden City, NY: Doubleday, 1986).

PALMER, J. A., *Plato's Reception of Parmenides* (Oxford: Oxford University Press, 1999).

PASSMORE, JOHN: 1966, *A Hundred Years of Philosophy*, 2nd edn. (London: Duckworth).

PASSMORE, J., *A Hundred Years of Philosophy* (New York: Basic, 1966).

PLATO, *Phaedo*, trans. with notes D. Gallop (Oxford: Clarendon, 1975).

POPPER, K., *Conjectures and Refutations: The Growth of Scientific Knowledge*, 2nd edn. (London: Routledge & Kegan Paul, 1965).

PRANTL, C., *Geschichte der Logik im Abendlande*, 2nd edn. (Graz: Druck, 1885; repr. 1955).

PROCLUS, *The Elements of Theology*, ed. E. R. Dodds (Oxford: Clarendon, 1963; repr. 2004).

QUINE, W. V. O., *Word and Object* (Cambridge, MA: MIT Press, 1960).

ROMANO, F., and TAORMINA, D. P. (eds.), *HYPARXIS e HYPOSTASIS nel Neoplatonism* (Florence: 1994).

ROSS, W. D.: 1924, *Aristotle's Metaphysics*, 2 vols. (Oxford: Clarendon).

——1949, *Aristotle's Prior and Posterior Analytics* (Oxford: Clarendon).

RIJK, L. M. DE, *Aristotle: Semantics and Ontology*, i (Leiden: Brill, 2002).

RUIJGH, C. J., 'A Review of Ch. H. Kahn, *The Verb "Be" in Ancient Greek*', *Lingua*, 48 (1979), 43–83.

RUSSELL, BERTRAND: 1903, *The Principles of Mathematics* (London: Allen and Unwin).

RYLE, GILBERT: 1938, 'Categories', in *Collected Papers* II (New York: Barnes and Noble, 1971), 170–84.

SANTILLANA, G. DE, *Prologue to Parmenides* (Cincinnati, Ohio: University of Cincinnati Press, 1964).

SAPIR, E., *Language: An Introduction to the Study of Speech* (New York: Harcourt, Brace, 1921; repr. 1949).

SARTRE, J.-P., *La Nausée* (Paris: Gallimard, 1938).

SMYTH, H. W., *Greek Grammar*, rev. G. Messing (Cambridge, MA: Harvard University Press, 1956).

SOLMSEN, FRIEDRICH: 1968, 'Dialectic without the Forms', *Aristotle on Dialectic*, ed. Owen (Oxford: Clarendon), 49–68.

SOMMERS, F., 'On Concepts of Truth in Natural Languages', *Review of Metaphysics*, 23 (1969), 259–86.

STEINTHAL, H.: 1890, *Geschichte der Sprachwissenschaft bei den Griechen und Römern* (Berlin: Dümmlers), 1, 206–34.

STOKES, MICHAEL, *One and Many in Presocratic Philosophy* (Washington, DC: Center for Hellenic Studies/Cambridge, MA: Harvard University Press, 1971).

STOUGH, C., 'Parmenides' Way of Truth, B 8. 12–13', *Phronesis*, 13 (1968), 91–107.

TARÁN, L., *Parmenides: A Text with Translation, Commentary, and Critical Essays* (Princeton, NJ: Princeton University Press, 1965).

THOMPSON, MANLEY: 1967, 'Categories', *Encyclopedia of Philosophy*, ed. Paul Edwards, vol. 2 (New York: Macmillan), 46–55.

THORP, J. W.: 1974, 'Aristotle's use of Categories', *Phronesis*, 19, 238–56.

TRENDELENBURG, ADOLF: 1846, *Geschichte der Kategorienlehre* (= *Historische Beiträge zur Philosophie* I) (Berlin: Bethge).

——1852, *Elementa logices aristoteleae*, 4th edn. (Berlin: Bethge).

TUGENDHAT, E., 'Das Sein und das Nichts', in V. Klostermann (ed.), *Durchblicke: Martin Heidegger zum 80. Geburtstag* (Frankfurt: Klostermann, 1970).

VERDENIUS, W. J., *Parmenides: Some Comments on his Poem* (Groningen: Batavia, 1942).

VLASTOS, G., 'Parmenides' Theory of Knowledge', *Transactions and Proceedings of the American Philological Association*, 77 (1946), repr. in D. Graham (ed.), *Studies in Greek Philosophy*, i, (Princeton, NJ: Princeton University Press, 1995).

—— 'Degrees of Reality in Plato', in R. Bambrough (ed.), *New Essays on Plato and Aristotle* (London: Routledge & Kegan Paul, 1965), repr. in *Platonic Studies* (Princeton, NJ: Princeton University Press, 1973).

—— *Platonic Studies* (Princeton, NJ: Princeton University Press, 1973).

VON FRITZ, KURT: 1931, 'Der Ursprung der aristotelischen Kategorienlehre', *Archiv für Geschichte der Philosophie*, 40, 449–96.

VUILLEMIN, JULES: 1967, *De la Logique à la Théologie: Cinque Études sur Aristote* (Paris: Flammarion).

WILPERT, PAUL: 1949, *Zwei aristotelische Frühschriften über die Ideenlehre* (Regensburg: Habbel).

WITTGENSTEIN, LUDWIG: 1921, *Tractatus Logico-Philosophicus*, trans. D. F. Pears and B. F. McGuinness (London: Routledge and Kegan Paul, 1961).

—— *Tractatus Logico-Philosophicus*, trans. C. K. Ogden (London: Routledge & Kegan Paul, 1922).

ZELLER, EDUARD: 1879, *Die Philosophie der Griechen*, Zweiter Teil, Zweite Abteilung, 3rd edn. (Leipzig: Fues).

Index of Names

N.B. Plato and Parmenides are not indexed because large sections of the collected essays deal with them exclusively

Ancient & Medieval Authors

Abelard 42, 49–52
Aeschylus 76
Ammonius 45, 52
Anaxagoras 32, 157
Anselm 64
Aquinas 60, 64
Archytas 194
Aristotle 21, 37–8, 44–7, 56, 65–7,
    72, 77–8, 97, 192–4
Avicenna 43–4
Boethius 43, 60
Democritus 33, 157
Dun Scotus 60
Empedocles 32, 157
Epicurus 58
Galen 58
Heraclitus 148, 174, 189
Herodotus 24, 54–5, 86, 175
Homer 31–2, 86, 175
Melissus 175
Moerbeke, W. 60–1
Philolaus 194
Plotinus 116–17
Priscian 57, 60
Proclus 60–1
Protagoras 22
Pythagoras 193–5
Sextus Empiricus 59
Thucydides 56
Xenophanes 148
Zeno 175

Modern & Contemporary Authors

Bäck, A. 114
Barnes, J. 173
Burkert, W. 211

Burnet, J. 81, 83
Brown, L. 111–12, 202
Davidson, D. 74
Descartes, R. 63–4, 140–1, 164
Furley, D. 190, 211
Gallop, D. 81, 180–2
Harris, Z. 117–18
Heidegger, M. 18, 30, 131, 136
Hermann, G. 41
Jaeger, W. 23
Kant, E. 42
Kirk, G. S. 111
Leibniz, G. W. 131
Martin, G. 18
McDowell, J. 93, 103
Mill, J. S. 18–20, 26, 33, 37–8, 41,
    111, 142
Miller, M. 211
Morisson, J. S. 210
Mourelatos, A. 168, 197
Nehamas, A. 198
Nietzsche, F. 209
Owen, G. L. 40, 66, 80, 111, 145,
    168, 171–3
Popper, K. 157
Quine, W. V. 35, 64, 120
Raven, J. E. 111
Reinhardt, K. 144, 150
Rijk, L. M. de 117
Ross, W. D. 23, 66
Russell, B. 64
Robinson, R. 151
Sapir, E. 137–8
Schofield, M. 111
Verdenius, W. J. 190
Vlastos, G. 106, 108, 173
Wittgenstein, L. 71, 125, 154–5

The manufacturer's authorised representative in the EU for product safety is Oxford University Press España S.A. of el Parque Empresarial San Fernando de Henares, Avenida de Castilla, 2 – 28830 Madrid (www.oup.es/en or product. safety@oup.com). OUP España S.A. also acts as importer into Spain of products made by the manufacturer.